changing the way the world learns[SM]

To get extra value from this book for no additional cost, go to:

http://www.thomson.com/wadsworth.html

thomson.com is the World Wide Web site for Wadsworth/ITP and is your direct source to dozens of on-line resources. *thomson.com* helps you find out about supplements, experiment with demonstration software, search for a job, and send e-mail to many of our authors. You can even preview new publications and exciting new technologies.

thomson.com: *It's where you'll find us in the future.*

Signposts
on
the Way of Torah

Jacob Neusner
University of South Florida
and Bard College

Wadsworth Publishing Company
I(T)P® *An International Thomson Publishing Company*

Belmont, CA • Albany, NY • Bonn • Boston • Cincinnati • Detroit • Johannesburg • London • Madrid
Melbourne • Mexico City • New York • Paris • Singapore • Tokyo • Toronto • Washington

Religion Editor: Peter Adams
Assistant Editor: Kerri Abdinoor
Editorial Assistant: Kelly Bush
Production: Matrix Productions, Inc.
Composition: R&S Book Composition
Copy Editor: Vicki Nelson
Print Buyer: Karen Hunt
Cover Design: Carole Lawson
Printer: R. R. Donnelley, Crawfordsville

Printed in the United States of America
1 2 3 4 5 6 7 8 9 10

For more information, contact Wadsworth Publishing Company, 10 Davis Drive,
Belmont, CA 94002, or electronically at http://www.thomson.com/wadsworth.html

International Thomson Publishing Europe
Berkshire House 168-173
High Holborn
London, WC1V 7AA, England

International Thomson Editores
Campos Eliseos 385, Piso 7
Col. Palanco
11560 México D.F. México

Thomas Nelson Australia
102 Dodds Street
South Melbourne 3205
Victoria, Australia

International Thomson Publishing Asia
221 Henderson Road
#05-10 Henderson Building
Singapore 0315

Nelson Canada
1120 Birchmount Road
Scarborough, Ontario
Canada M1K 5G4

International Thomson Publishing Japan
Hirakawacho Kyowa Building, 3F
2-2-1-Hirakawacho
Chiyoda-ku, Tokyo 102, Japan

International Thomson Publishing GmbH
Königswinterer Strasse 418
53227 Bonn, Germany

International Thomson Publishing
Southern Africa
Building 18, Constantia Park
240 Old Pretoria Road
Halfway House, 1685 South Africa

Library of Congress Cataloging-in-Publication Data
Signposts on the way of Torah/[edited by] Jacob Neusner.
    p. cm.—(Religious life in history series)
   Includes index.
   ISBN 0-534-55769-4 (pbk.)
   1. Judaism. 2. Judaism—History—Modern period, 1750– 3. Judaism—United
States. 4. Judaism—Israel. 5. Holocaust, Jewish (1939–1945)—Influence.
   I. Neusner, Jacob, 1932–   II. Series.
BM40.S44   1998
296—dc21   97-38794

Contents

Preface

The Way of Torah talks about Judaism in the setting of the study of religion. This companion anthology presents writings that speak the language of Judaism. At the same time it augments the description of Judaism, its texts and main traits, set forth in *The Way of Torah*, sixth edition. *Signposts on the Way of Torah* points to the inner life of those who practice a Judaism, with special reference to Classical or Rabbinic Judaism on one side and with extensive attention to the life of Judaism today on the other.

To study religion is to do two things: generalize and compare. If you only know about one religion, you really know nothing about religion at all. Studying religion requires you to generalize from the facts of various religions to the character of religion in general. If I know this religion, what do I know about religion? That is a key question. Studying religion also means to compare and contrast one religion with another. If this anthology proves illuminating, you can use it to try to generalize, to make up your own theses on the character of the religion Judaism and perhaps even religion in general. And you will want to take up the comparison of religions as well. This is best done in class discussion, as you draw on what you learn in these pages and also on what you already know when you come to class, which may involve some other religion altogether. At every point you face the task of translating the writing before you into a starting point for class discussion of questions of broad interest and general intelligibility: the study of religion is a *generalizing* science.

Although this anthology may be read on its own, it engages in a dialogue with its companion text at every point. The book uses the same organization as *The Way of Torah*, with two new units at the end as well—the practice of Judaism in the state of Israel and an account of contemporary Judaic thinking about the future. I have also expanded the treatment of many topics set forth in *The Way of Torah*. The presentation of Reform, Orthodox, and Conservative Judaisms is greatly expanded because the principal Judaisms of the United States and Canada deserve most attention; I have further introduced important contemporary issues because theologians are now debating important problems facing Reform, Orthodox, and Conservative Jews. Writings that convey the piety and faith of the unconventional Judaisms also are featured, with extensive attention to the innovative developments even now emerging from the tradition of Judaism. All of Part III is devoted to the acutely contemporary Judaisms in the United States.

Here, in concrete terms, is how the two books relate:

The Way of Torah, 6th ed.	*Signposts on the Way of Torah*
I. Defining Judaism the Religion	Prologue
II. Classical Judaism	Part I, Chapter 2
The Oral Torah	Chapters 3, 4, 5
Three Important Doctrines	Chapter 11
The Torah's Worldview	Chapter 6
The Torah's Way of Life	Chapters 7, 8, 9
Four Types of Piety	Chapter 10
	Chapter 12
III. Classical Judaism in Modern Times	Part II, Chapter 13
	Chapter 14
Reform, Orthodox, and	Chapters 15, 16, 17, 18, 19, 20,
Conservative Judaisms	21, 22
The Practice of Judaism	Part III, Chapters 23, 24, 25,
in Contemporary North	26, 27, 28, 29, 30, 31
America	
	Part IV, Chapters 32, 33, 34, 35
	Part V, Chapters 36, 37, 38

The presentation of topics treated in *The Way of Torah* is greatly expanded in *Signposts*, especially because at each point a contemporary voice speaking within and on behalf of a particular Judaism is focusing upon issues that people debate even now. Not only do you learn more about Judaism but you hear how people talk about current issues within the faith. In this way I mean to complement the descriptive presentations in *Way* with issues of human interest in *Signposts*, not only to enrich that description but also point toward the inner life of the faithful.

From these pages, you can turn to your friends and neighbors who practice the religion Judaism and bring to conversations with them a better understanding of the religious way of life and worldview that guides their life with God. Perhaps the single most important goal accomplished in *The Way of Torah* and *Signposts on the Way of Torah* is to argue that Judaism is a religion too, not just an ethnicity or a politics or a culture or a cuisine or any of the many other things that Jews make of "being Jewish," both in public and in private, as a community and as individuals.

As in *The Way of Torah*, here the description is meant to serve two kinds of readers. First are the many who know little or nothing about Judaism, to whom Judaism is an unknown religion. From them *The Way of Torah* means to elicit sympathetic understanding of a religion that they are likely to have observed but found different from their own. The engaged writing I have assembled here aims at provoking empathetic engagement with the human situation of that religion. Second are the fewer who know and in some cases practice Judaism. For them *The Way of Torah* and this anthology together mean to inform and clarify, illuminate the darker corners of an already-familiar religion.

Each of the units has its own brief introduction. There I systematically answer three questions: (1) Why is this reading important? (2) What should you notice as you proceed? (3) How should you frame a question for class discussion in response to what you have read?

This book not only complements *The Way of Torah*, 6th ed., but also replaces a prior anthology that has had its own afterlife. In 1974, I edited an anthology to supplement *The Way of Torah*, a now out-of-print work called *Life of Torah: Readings in the Jewish Religious Experience*.[1] As *The Way of Torah* evolved over time, so my interest in merely revising the prior anthology waned, and ideas for a completely fresh approach to the problem of supplementing that textbook with further writings took shape.

Alas, my initial theory of what was needed did not work. I produced an anthology that did not accomplish my goals, so I discarded it and back to the drawing board I went. But I was not alone, for just at that moment there appeared on the scene the editor from heaven, Charles Hallisey. Responding to his cordial and stimulating ideas and challenged by the new editor at Wadsworth, Peter Adams, I determined to try again. Here is the result. If teachers and students find that the writings I have assembled make the study of Judaism still more interesting in its own terms and relevant to the study of religion in general, I assign the credit to my team of editors. I am very lucky to have them as coworkers and I also value their friendship.

In the recent past, after many years of teaching for other purposes altogether, I have returned to giving my Introduction to Judaism course because I have found intelligent student response at the University of South Florida. It was in my classroom at that university that I began to redesign the project and expand its range and scope. I have often described my position there as the best job in the academic world, and my colleagues and students are no small part of the reason. My thanks go to my colleagues for their ongoing interest in my work. Further, I have begun to learn how to teach via television, with two-way audio and one-way video, and now am able to offer my courses on other campuses at the University of South Florida (and in the state university system) besides the main one. Distance learning imposes its own disciplines, presents its own teaching challenges. How *The Way of Torah* and *Signposts* will work as teaching tools in the new setting remains to be seen.

I enjoy the unusual good fortune of a second academic appointment as well, at Bard College, which provides yet another set of cordial and interesting colleagues, both in the Department of Religion and in other departments at the college. Indeed, I treasure the time I spend at Bard, especially with colleagues whom I find so interesting that lunchtime grows longer and more stimulating as the years pass. One of these colleagues is so engaging and genteel as to warrant and accept my instruction, when I leave for a cup of tea: "Don't say anything interesting until I get back." My chair, Professor Bruce D. Chilton, with whom I have now written nearly a dozen books, has made my first three years on the Bard faculty both joyful and exceptionally educational. With the availability of *The Way of Torah* and *Signposts*, I plan to resume the Introduction to Judaism course at Bard.

It goes without saying that I should greatly value getting letters from those who teach or study from both *The Way of Torah* and this anthology, especially

---

[1]Encino: Dickenson Publishing Co., 1974. Third printing, Belmont: Wadsworth, 1980. Sixth printing, 1984; seventh printing, 1987.

letters bearing advice on how to improve both. That advice will be taken very much to heart. Over the past thirty years of the life of *The Way of Torah*, from the first printing of the first edition in 1969, many people have helped me to make the successive editions clearer, more accurate, and more illuminating than, without their counsel, I should have been able to make them.

Jacob Neusner
University of South Florida and Bard College

Prologue:
Defining Judaism

JACOB NEUSNER

Let us begin with a systematic account of what we mean by *Judaism* or *a Judaism*. By *Judaism* people mean many things, depending on the context. Focusing as we do on the interplay between the world in which people live and the ideas they hold to explain that world, I offer a succinct statement of the definition and history of Judaism.

A Judaism is a religion that privileges Scripture's account of Israel *as holy people whose life encompasses the experience of exile and return.*

The original reading of Israel's existence as exile and return derives from the Pentateuch, or the Five Books of Moses, which were composed as we now have them (out of earlier materials, to be sure) in the aftermath of the destruction of the Temple in 586 B.C.E. In response to the exile in Babylonia, the experience selected and addressed by the author of the document is that of exile and restoration. But that framing of events into the text before us represents an act of powerful imagination and interpretation.

A Judaism offers an invented experience. Diverse experiences have been sorted out, various figures have been chosen, and the whole has been worked into a system by those who selected history out of happenings and models out of masses of persons. I say "selected," because no Jews after 586 B.C.E. actually experienced what the aggregate Scripture says happened. None went into exile *and* came back to Jerusalem. So, to begin with, Scripture does not record a particular person's experience. More to the point, if it is not autobiographical, not writing for society at large the personal insight of a singular figure, neither is it an account of a whole nation's story, for the following reason: the original exile encompassed mainly the political classes of Jerusalem and some useful populations alongside. Many Jews in the Judea of 586 B.C.E. never left. And, as is well known, a great many of those who ended up in Babylonia stayed there; only a minority went back to Jerusalem. Consequently, the story of exile and return to Zion encompasses what happened to only a few families, who identified themselves as the family of Abraham, Isaac, and Jacob, and their genealogy became the normative history of Israel. Those families that stayed and those that never came back, had they written the Torah, would have told a different tale altogether.

The experience of that small group is taught in terms of normative lessons of alienation. Here are the lessons people claimed to learn out of the events they had chosen for their history: *The life of the group is uncertain, subject to conditions and stipulations. Nothing is set and given, all things a gift: land and life itself. But what actually did happen in that uncertain world—exile but then restoration—marked the group as special, different, select.*

There were other ways of seeing things, and this Pentateuchal picture is no more compelling than any other. Those Jews who did not go into exile and those who did not "come home" had no reason to take the view of matters that characterizes Scripture. The life of the group need not have appeared more uncertain, more subject to contingency and stipulation, than the life of any other group. The land did not require the vision that imparted to it the enchantment, the personality, that it received in Scripture, namely: "The land will vomit you out as it did those who were here before you." And the circumstance of Iranian imperial policy did not have to be recast into return. So nothing in the system of Scripture—exile for reason, return as redemption—followed necessarily and logically. Everything was invented, interpreted.

That group experience of uncertainty in the century or so from the destruction of the First Temple of Jerusalem by the Babylonians in 586 B.C.E. to the building of the Second Temple of Jerusalem by the Jews formed the model. In that minority genealogy, that story of exile and return, alienation and remission, imposed on the received stories of pre-exilic Israel, expounded time and again in the Five Books of Moses, we find that paradigmatic statement from which every Judaism, from then to now, derives its structure and deep syntax of social existence, the grammar of its intelligible message.

These rules govern the history of Judaism:

1. No Judaism recapitulates any other, and none stands in a linear and incremental relationship with any prior one.
2. But all Judaisms recapitulate the single paradigmatic experience of the Torah of "Moses," the authorship that selected, interpreted, and reflected on the meaning of the events of 586–450 B.C.E.

That experience (in theological terms) rehearsed the conditional moral existence of sin and punishment; suffering, atonement, and reconciliation; and (in social terms) the uncertain and always conditional national destiny of disintegration and renewal of the group. That moment captured within the Five Books of Moses— that is, the judgment of the generation who returned to Zion, led by Ezra, about its extraordinary experience of exile and return—would inform the attitude and viewpoint of all the Israels beyond.

This approach to the definition of Judaism is based on the theory that Judaism as a religion imparted *its* pattern upon the social world and polity, not the other way around. I maintain that the social world recapitulates religion, not that religion recapitulates the givens of society, economy, or politics. Because of the power of a single generative experience (the starting point for all theories of religion), religion shapes the world, not the world religion. This is true of other religions besides Judaism. Specifically, however, it is the Jews' religion, Judaism, that has formed their world and framed their realities.

This definition is meant to account for the character of every Judaism that has emerged through time as well as those yet to come. A particular selection and interpretation of events imposed a singular shape upon all Judaisms that followed it, then to now: These events are understood to stand for exile (identified with everything people find wrong with their life) and return (marking what people hope will happen to set matters right). Each Judaism identifies what is wrong with the present and promises to make things tolerable now and perfect in the indeterminate future. A Judaism therefore stands for a situation to escape, overcome, survive. The repeated pattern of finding the world out of kilter (exile) but then making it possible to live for the interim (return) perpetuates profound resentment: Why here? Why us? Why now? And, to the contrary (and this is the deep resentment): Why not always, everywhere, and forever?

A Judaic religious system, then, recapitulates a specific resentment. Each Judaism, in its own way, addresses and readdresses that same pattern. Even though each goes over the same paradigmatic experience, however, no Judaism recapitulates any other.

Before proceeding to the next stage in the argument, I owe the reader the recognition that the usage *a Judaism,* or *Judaisms,* violates accepted language rules. When people use the word *Judaism,* they use it only in the singular, and they assume that it refers to a single religion, or religious tradition, extending (if not from creation) from Sinai to the present. Instead I refer not only to *a* Judaism but, more commonly, to a Judaic *system.* That is, I define the genus of which I speak, a religion, as well as the species of that genus, a Judaism. Specifically, by a religious system I mean three things that are one:

1. A worldview, which accounts for how things are and puts them together into a cogent and harmonious picture by reference to the intersection of the supernatural and the natural worlds.

2. A way of life, which expresses the worldview in concrete actions and which is explained by that worldview.

3. A social group for which the worldview accounts, which is defined in concrete terms by their way of life and therefore gives expression to the worldview in everyday life and is defined as an entity by that way of life.

A Judaic system, then, comprises not merely a theory—a book—distinct from social reality but an explanation for the group (again: "Israel") that gives social form to the system and an account of that group's distinctive way of life. A Judaism is not a book, and no social group took shape because people read a book and agreed that God had revealed what the book said they should do. Therefore: *A Judaic system derives from and focuses upon a social entity, a group of Jews who (in their minds at least) constitute not* an *Israel but* Israel.

A Judaic system could treat as not essential a variety of rules for everyday life. (In modern times that indifference to rule making for this morning's breakfast proves characteristic of Judaisms.) Or it may fail to articulate elements of a worldview to answer a range of questions others deem fundamental. Contemporary Judaisms do not treat what earlier system builders found absorbing as urgent philosophical questions. But no Judaic system can omit a clear picture of the meaning and sense of the category *Israel.* Without an *Israel,* a social entity in fact and not only in doctrine, we have not a system but a book. And—to repeat—a book is not a Judaism, it is only a book. A Judaism is not about books that theologians, philosophers, or visionaries wrote; these works recapitulate the Judaism but do not define it. When we study a Judaism, we study a theory of the social order, way of life, and worldview that Jews have created and that have sustained their lives. In this book, therefore, my choices of what to treat and what to bypass rest upon this definition of a religious system: *A book is not a Judaism, and a Judaism is not a book*—except after the fact.

We ask how we may know one Judaism from some other. When we identify Judaisms in one period after another, we begin by trying to locate, in the larger group of Jews, those social entities that see themselves and are seen by others as distinct and bounded, and that further present to themselves a clear account of who they are and what they do and why they do what they do: the rules and their explanations, their Judaism. Religion is always social, and therefore also political, a matter of what people do together, not just what they believe in the privacy of their hearts. And a Judaism for its part addresses a social group, an Israel, with the claim that this group is not merely an Israel but Israel; Israel *in nuce*, in its ideal form; Israel's saving remnant; the state of Israel, the natural next step in the linear, continuous history ("progress") of Israel; everything, anything—but always Israel. So a Judaism, or a Judaic system, constitutes a clear and precise account of a social group, the way of life and worldview of a group of Jews, however defined.

This theory denies there is now, or ever was, a single Judaism. It posits no linear and incremental history of one continuous Judaism with a beginning, middle, and end, because there has never been Judaism, only Judaisms. But there was, as we have seen, a single paradigmatic and definitive human experience that each Judaism reworks in its own circumstance and context. In a broader sense, therefore, the present field theory of the history of a given religious tradition that comprises a variety of expressions may be generalized from the case of Judaisms to the following propositions:

1. No religious system (within a given set of related religions) recapitulates any other.

2. But all religious systems (within a given set) recapitulate resentment.
   A single persistent experience for generation after generation captures what, for a particular group, stands for the whole of the human condition: everything all at once, all together, the misery and the magnificence of life.

All Judaisms identify the Torah or the Five Books of Moses as the written-down statement of God's will for Israel, the Jewish people (which, as a matter of fact, every Judaism also identifies as its own social group). On the surface, then, it seems we should specify that formative and definitive moment, recapitulated by all Judaisms, with the story of Creation down to Abraham and the beginning of his family, the children of Abraham, Isaac, and Jacob. Or perhaps we are advised to make our way to the revelation at Sinai and hold that this original point of definition descends from heaven. But allowing ourselves merely to retell the story deprives us of the required insight. Recapitulating the story of the religion does not help us understand the religion. Identifying the story's point of origin, in contrast, does. For the story tells not what actually did happen (the creation of the world, for instance) but how (long afterward and for their own reasons) people want to portray it as happening. The tale recapitulates the resentment about that obsessive and troubling point of origin that the group wishes to explain, transcend, transform.

From then to now, to be an Israel—the social component of a Judaism—has meant to be constantly asking what it means to be Israel. The original pattern meant that an Israel would be a social group whose existence had been called into question and affirmed—and therefore always would be called into question and remain perpetually to be affirmed. Every Judaism would then find as its task the recapitulation of the original Judaism. Each makes its own distinctive statement of the generative and critical resentment contained within that questioning of the given—that deep understanding of the uncertain character of the group's existence in its normal location and under circumstances of permanence that (so far as the Judaic group understood things) characterized the life of every other group but Israel. What was a given for everyone else (so it seemed to the Judaisms addressed to the Israels through time) was a gift for Israel. What all other nations knew as *how things must be* Israel understood as *how things might not be:* renewal, restoration, reconciliation, and (in theological language) redemption instead of annihilation. So that paradigmatic experience, the one beginning in 586 B.C.E. and ending c. 450 B.C.E., made its mark. That pattern, permanently inscribed in the Torah of God to Moses at Sinai, would define for all Israels over all time the nature of resentment demanding recapitulation: leaving home, coming home.

Jews make up Judaisms, each for its occasion, and then those to whom *a* Judaism is Judaism uncover that continuity and connection between their own Judaism and Judaism. Words, not dance; words, not woodworking—these form the signs and signals of the story. And the words, read in context, form sentences, paragraphs—messages, Judaisms, each with its full and complete account of the world and what it means, the way of life and how one lives it, in *an* Israel—a Jewish people.

What is that one systemic trait that marks all Judaisms and sets them apart from all the dances of the dancers and all the carvings of the carvers? It is that perpetual asking of the question that other social groups (in Jews' eyes) seem to have answered for themselves for all time: Who are we? That trait of self-consciousness, that incapacity to accept the group as a given and its data—way of life, worldview constituting the world of an Israel, a Jewish people, in the here and now—is the one thing draws together Judaisms from beginning to end. Another is Jews' certainty that Scripture refers to them in particular, that they form the Israel started by Abraham, Isaac, and Jacob. Jews' persistent passion for self-definition characterizes all the Judaisms they have made for themselves. The jump rhythms of all the jumpers in other cultures, the swirls of all the swirling lines, the incisions of the wood carvers and the tattoos on all the faces—these for the Jews find their counterpart in Jews' obsessive self-consciousness about their group. What others take as the given, the Jews perceive as the received, the special, the extraordinary. And that perception of the remarkable character of what other groups regard as unremarkable requires explanation.

That ongoing wonder about who "we" are and what "we" mean together is something of a puzzle, since why Jews should not yet have found their final answer after so long a trek through history is hardly clear. True, for many the answer lies in the distant past, and their explanation derives from the ancient paradigm. But that is a self-evident evasion, for history answers no questions that we do not identify as questions answered by history—that is, by sequences of events: first this, then that, therefore.... The connectedness of events does not rest on temporal sequence; causation is more complicated than that. The fact that one thing happened in sequence after another does not mean that the first thing caused the event.

As an explanation, therefore, a mere narrative of history is an evasion on one side and a deep misunderstanding of the character of Judaisms on the other. Evasion is the easier way to perceive; people find it easier to recite than to explain. That is why they play out the conventions of show-and-tell and let the answers come from they know not where: self-evidence, mostly. The incomprehension of Judaisms derives from accepting as fact the claim of a single Judaism to constitute Judaism: as it was in the beginning, as it is, and on through time. The linear and incremental story of Judaism that serves today—beginning from Abraham and ending with this morning's events in Jerusalem or Jewish New York or London or Paris—constitutes a profound theological judgment. It does not record how things really were. For no Judaism stands in a linear and incremental relationship with any other. Indeed, none relates to any other at all, except in making selections from a common treasury of historical detritus. But the selections from the rubbish heap of history—the holy books, the customs and ceremonies (so to speak)—always follow the inner logic of a system, which, after the fact, makes its choices, pronounces its canon.

Still, every Judaic system has a set of questions it deems ineluctable and demanding of answers. And, in one way or another, those questions have persisted as the center of system after system. They turn on the identity of the group, they rest on the premise that the group's existence represents choice and not a given of nature or necessity. That obsessive self-awareness, a characteristic trait, masks a deeper experience that evidently defines for one generation after another and for one group of Jews after another the question of self-identification that, collectively, the group must answer. Why, among the settled peoples of time, the Jews—who form along with the Chinese and the Armenians among the oldest peoples of continuous historical existence on the face of the earth—should not have determined for themselves the answers to this question remains for us to find out. To begin with, we recognize only that the question is not a given for all of humankind, that other groups satisfactorily account for themselves and go on to other questions and that the critical tension in the life of Jews presents a surprise and a puzzle.

Ever since the formative pattern imposed that perpetual, self-conscious uncertainty, treating the life of the group as conditional and discontinuous, Jews have asked themselves who they are and invented Judaisms to answer that question. Accordingly, because the definitive paradigm affected their group life in various contexts, no circumstances have permitted Jews to take for granted their existence as a group. Why the paradigm renewed itself is clear: this view of matters generated expectations that could not be met, hence created resentment—and then provided comfort and hope that made coping with that resentment possible. *Promising what could not be delivered, then providing solace for the consequent disappointment, the system precipitated in age after age the very conditions necessary for its own replication.*

PART ONE

Classical Judaism

2   Introduction

What kind of writing do people do within the Judaic religion?[1] We examine two classical texts—tractate Abot, the sayings of the Founders, a collection of wise statements by authorities prominent in the Mishnah, and Genesis Rabbah, a commentary to the book of Genesis produced at a time of acute crisis in the history of Rabbinical Judaism. There we see how the sages read Scripture as if it were a letter from God that arrived this morning and dealt with today's headlines. From the two classical texts, we move to a matter of doctrine that is critical but seldom examined: What has religion to say to the heart? In the case of Judaism, which emotions does the Torah inculcate, and which ones does it discourage? What, in everyday life, does it mean to aspire to do God's will this morning? How do people who keep the commandments explain to themselves what reasonable meanings inhere in them? What does it mean to die in accord with the Torah, and how does the law of the Torah guide a person over the frontier that separates the living from the dead? Finally, how does the Torah's *halakhah*, or body of normative rules of behavior, affect women? These and similar topics from within the framework of the lived religion amplify the description of Judaism from without.

The Way of Torah describes Classical Judaism through its texts and doctrines. But what do people feel, how do they frame an emotional life, in confronting so deeply an intellectual account of their relationship with God? So that the somewhat dry and intellectual presentation taken in *The Way of Torah* may find its balance in a more human and personal account, various, different dimensions of the inner life are explored here.

The power of Rabbinic, or Classical, Judaism lay in its remarkable capacity to define and create the world of Israel, the Jewish people. Israel understood that the nation that had ceased to be a nation on its own land and once more regained that condition could and would once more reenact the paradigm of exile and return. Again, in the Judaism of the dual Torah the social world recapitulates religion, not the other way around. The study of Judaism provides a source of interesting cases for the proposition that religion shapes the world, not the world

---

[1]*Judaic* is the adjective based on the religion Judaism, and it refers only to that religion. *Jewish* (or *the Jewish people*) is the adjective based on the noun *Jew* and refers to the ethnic group. When we refer to opinions various Jews hold in common, we speak of "Jewish opinion." When we refer to positions taken by the classical sources, such as the Torah, and authoritative, learned expositors of those sources, we speak of *Judaic*, as in "Judaic writings," writings that belong to the Torah, as distinct from "Jewish writings," writings produced by ethnic Jews, whether of a religious or a secular character, whether formed in response to the revealed Torah or made up on the spot by a private individual as his or her own opinion. The distinction between the ethnic and the religious, spelled out in *The Way of Torah*, is carried forward in this anthology.

religion. Specifically, it is the Jews' religion, Judaism, that has formed their world and framed their realities, and not the world of politics, culture, society.

From the fourth century in Christendom, and from the seventh in Islam, Judaism therefore enjoyed remarkable success in that very world that it both created and also selected for itself—the world of Israel, the Jewish people. Both Islam and Christendom presented a single challenge: the situation of subordination coupled with toleration. The power of Judaism lay in its capacity to do two things in this context.

First, Judaism in its classical statement, shaped in the fourth-century Talmud of the Land of Israel and then fully articulated by the sixth-century Talmud of Babylonia, presented doctrines both to explain and to draw renewal from the condition of subordination and toleration, so that the facts of everyday life served to reenforce the claims of the system.

Second, that same Judaism taught an enduring doctrine of the virtues of the heart that did more than make Israel's situation acceptable, it shaped the inner life of Israel so as to define virtue in the very terms imposed by politics. Century after century, Israel recreated within itself that exact condition of acceptance of humility and accommodation that the people's political circumstance imposed from without. Consequently, the enduring doctrine of virtue not only made it possible for Israel to accept its condition, it recreated in the psychological structure of Israel's inner life that same condition, so bringing political facts and psychological fantasies into exact correspondence.

This brings us to the point at which classical Judaism intersects with our contemporary sensibility. In today's classroom we are acutely concerned with issues specifically important to women as well as to men. You will note that sages have their own way of defining what is masculine and what is feminine, and, by their own word, they have chosen as virtues for all of holy Israel the traits they impute to women in particular. So here we learn that it was the feminization of Rabbinic Judaism that accounts for its success, its holding in the balance deeply masculine and profoundly feminine traits. Judaism triumphed in Christendom and Islam because of its power to bring into union both heart and mind, inner life and outer circumstance, psychology and politics. The Judaism of the dual Torah not only matched the situation of Israel the conquered but (ordinarily) tolerated people. That Judaism created, within the psychological heritage of Israel, the same condition: the condition of acceptance of a subordinated but tolerated position while awaiting the superior one.

Let us not lose sight of the remarkable power of this religion of humility, which endures not in books from a faraway time and place, but in the lives of nearly everybody who practices a Judaism today. It is a religion of mind and heart, but also of family and community, one that asks entire devotion to God— not only the parts of life that God can command, the life of the people together in community, but especially the secret places of existence not subject to God's will but only one's own. Beyond the objective facts of evidence, the analysis of theories of the social order and their unfolding, we should not miss the defining fact. It comes not from the theorizing of refined intellects but from the hard, coarse reality that, for the whole of their history from the formation of this Judaism to the present moment—wherever they lived, whatever their circumstances—the people, Israel, drew nourishment from these ideas and found in this system the power to endure.

Now the world did not make life easy, affording to the faith of Israel no honor, and to the Israelite no respect by reason of loyalty to that vocation. But through conversion, which is to say, apostasy, both Islam and Christianity offered Israel easy access to an honored place. At the sacrifice of home and property, even at the price of life itself, Israel resisted them and reaffirmed its eternal calling. For whatever the choice of private persons, that social order formed by Israel endured, against it all, despite it all, through all time and change. And, in the lifetime of many who read these pages, even beyond the gates of hell, the surviving remnants determined to be Israel. They chose once more to form—in a precise sense, to embody—the social order of that one whole Torah that God taught to Our Rabbi, Moses, at Sinai, that publicly revealed Torah that rests on the private, personal, and profoundly, deeply feminine, and intimate virtue of *zekhut.*

Whether in Poland or Algeria, Morocco or Iraq and Iran, whether in the land called the Land of Israel or in distant corners of the exile, Israel kept the faith, abided by the covenant, lived in stout hope and perfect trust in God. That fact defines the power of this Judaism, this dual Torah. The act of defying fate in the certainty of faith in God's ultimate act of grace is the one thing God cannot have commanded at Sinai.

God could have said, and many times in the Torah did say, "Serve me," but God could only beseech, "And trust me too." For even God cannot coerce trust. To give or withhold trust is left up to us. Only Israel could give what God could only ask, but not compel: the gifts of the heart, love and trust, for which the loving God yearns, which only the much-loved Israel can yield freely, of its own volition. And that is what Israel, in response to Sinai, willingly gave, and by its loyal persistence in its life as Israel, whether in the Land or in the patient exile, freely gives today.

The selections that give substance to the everyday reality of Classical Judaism stress the inner life of the faithful, the emotions that the Torah inculcates, the responses to crisis and challenge that the Torah means to elicit. We begin with a picture of virtue—the doctrine of emotions—that Classical Judaism sets forth. This is set forth in tractate Abot, the Sayings of the Fathers, from c. 250 C.E. We proceed to a Rabbinic exegesis of Scripture, as exemplified by Genesis Rabbah, Judaism's reading of the book of Genesis. In this reading we see how Rabbinic Judaism expressed its ideas by writing with Scripture, by using Scripture as the principal language of thought and expression.

Classical Judaism concerns itself not only with feelings but with attitudes and appeals to reason to persuade people to keep the faith. Hence we review Maimonides' rationalist reading of the reasons behind the commandments. From there we move to three accounts, from diverse periods in the history of Classical Judaism, on the critical issue of every human life: the confrontation with death that comes to us all. Here we begin with the rules that govern visiting the sick, dying, and burying the dead, as these rules are codified for everyday life. We proceed to a moralistic account of how to die, and then turn to how the exemplary twentieth-century rabbi, Milton Steinberg, who died young and lived knowing that he would, writes about death. From the personal we move to the public, and ask about how mystical life and experience figures in classical Judaism. The account comes from the premier theologian of Judaism in the twentieth century.

Why does a religion succeed when it does, and why does it fail and lose credibility when it does? Every religion has its successful moments, and at some point every religion faces a time of retrenchment, even decline. A single theory has to explain why a religion works when it works and does not work when it fails, and here we deal with a specific case. We conclude with an effort to explain why a single Judaic religious system, Rabbinic or Classical Judaism, succeeded for so long in winning the allegiance of nearly all Jews who practiced Judaism. Until the nineteenth century, that Judaism met little important and sustained competition, and its definition of the Torah governed. Why was that so? This is the question introduced at the end of Part One. Here is the point at which students can exercise their own taste and judgment in forming a theory of why a religion succeeds in accomplishing its goals when and where it does, and why that same religion fails to achieve its purposes where and when it does. For until we can explain both phenomena—the success and the failure, of a religious system—and do so within a single theory, we cannot claim to understand that religion, or any religion.

3 Sayings of the Founders: Tractate Abot

TRANSLATED BY JACOB NEUSNER

1. Why is this reading important?

After the Written Torah and the Daily Prayerbook (Hebrew *Siddur*), the tractate Abot, c. 250 C.E. (= A.D.) is the single most important document in the lives of those who practice Judaism. It is studied among the pious, read in synagogue worship through a season of the year, and discussed in everyday life. Instead of a story together with laws, as in the Five Books of Moses, or prophecy and poetry, as in Psalms, the tractate Abot presents a collection of wise sayings. The authorities who are cited are not identified, so the entire weight of authority rests upon the wisdom of what is said. These are the teachings that all Jews who practice Judaism live by.

2. What should you notice as you proceed?

While the sayings appear random, they do form clusters from which you can derive an idea of doctrines. But what doctrines? Perhaps the single most important doctrine concerns right relationships with both God and other people. Out of what is said in particular terms, try to identify the basic attitudes and feelings that people are supposed to cultivate—an important chapter in the life of piety in Judaism. Above all, ask yourself what kind of people are to be nurtured, and what sort of society is to be formed, by sayings such as these, which are memorized and repeated and applied in ordinary affairs.

3. How should you frame a question for class discussion in response to what you have read?

Pick out the saying, or set of sayings, you think would make the deepest impact upon the personality of the pious Jews, and explain why that is your choice, including reasons for rejecting some other saying or set of sayings in favor of your choice. Treat the sayings as choices made among various alternatives: Why do you think sages have favored one saying and rejected its opposite?

1:1 A. Moses received Torah at Sinai and handed it on to Joshua, Joshua to elders, and elders to prophets.

 B. And prophets handed it on to the men of the great assembly.

 C. They said three things:

 (1) "Be prudent in judgment.

 (2) "Raise up many disciples.

 (3) "Make a fence for the Torah."

1:2 A. Simeon the Righteous was one of the last survivors of the great assembly.

 B. He would say: "On three things does the world stand:

 (1) "On the Torah,

 (2) "and on the Temple service,

 (3) "and on deeds of loving kindness."

1:3 A. Antigonos of Sokho received [the Torah] from Simeon the Righteous.

 B. He would say,

 (1) "Do not be like servants who serve the master on condition of receiving a reward,

 (2) "but [be] like servants who serve the master not on condition of receiving a reward.

 (3) "And let the fear of Heaven be upon you."

1:4 1 A. Yosé b. Yoezer of Seredah and Yosé b. Yohanan of Jerusalem received [it] from them.

 B. Yosé b. Yoezer says,

 (1) "Let your house be a gathering place for sages.

 (2) "And wallow in the dust of their feet.

 (3) "And drink in their words with gusto."

1:5 A. Yosé b. Yohanan of Jerusalem says,

 (1) "Let your house be wide open.

 (2) "And seat the poor at your table ["make the poor members of your household"].

 (3) "And don't talk too much with women."

 B. (He spoke of a man's wife, all the more so is the rule to be applied to the wife of one's fellow. In this regard did sages say, "So long as a man talks too much with a woman, (1) he brings trouble on himself, (2) wastes time better spent on studying Torah, and (3) ends up an heir of Gehenna.")

1:6 A. Joshua b. Perahiah and Nittai the Arbelite received [it] from them.

 B. Joshua b. Perahiah says,

 (1) "Set up a master for yourself.

 (2) "And get yourself a fellow disciple.

 (3) "And give everybody the benefit of the doubt."

1:7 A. Nittai the Arbelite says,

 (1) "Keep away from a bad neighbor.

 (2) "And don't get involved with a wicked man.

 (3) "And don't give up hope of retribution."

1:8 A. Judah b. Tabbai and Simeon b. Shatah received [it] from them.
　　　B. Judah b. Tabbai says,
　　　　(1) "Don't make yourself like one of those who make advocacy before judges [while you yourself are judging a case].
　　　　(2) "And when the litigants stand before you, regard them as guilty.
　　　　(3) "And when they leave you, regard them as acquitted (when they have accepted your judgment)."

1:9 A. Simeon b. Shatah says,
　　　　(1) "Examine the witnesses with great care.
　　　　(2) "And watch what you say,
　　　　(3) "lest they learn from what you say how to lie."

1:10 A. Shemaiah and Abtalion received [it] from them.
　　　　B. Shemaiah says,
　　　　(1) "Love work.
　　　　(2) "Hate authority.
　　　　(3) "Don't get friendly with the government."

1:11 A. Abtalion says,
　　　　(1) "Sages, watch what you say, 'lest you become liable to the punishment of exile, and go into exile to a place of bad water, and disciples who follow you drink [bad water] and die, and the name of heaven be thereby profaned."

1:12 A. Hillel and Shammai received [it] from them.
　　　　B. Hillel says,
　　　　(1) "Be disciples of Aaron, loving peace and pursuing peace, loving people and drawing them near to the Torah."

1:13 A. He would say [in Aramaic],
　　　　(1) "A name made great is a name destroyed.
　　　　(2) "And one who does not add subtracts.
　　　　(3) "And who does not learn is liable to death.
　　　　(4) "And the one who uses the crown passes away."

1:14 A. He would say,
　　　　(1) "If I am not for myself, who is for me?
　　　　(2) "And when I am for myself, what am I?
　　　　(3) "And if not now, when?"

1:15 A. Shammai says,
　　　　(1) "Make your learning of Torah a fixed obligation.
　　　　(2) "Say little and do much.
　　　　(3) "Greet everybody cheerfully."

1:16 A. Rabban Gamaliel says,
　　　　(1) "Set up a master for yourself.
　　　　(2) "Avoid doubt.
　　　　(3) "Don't tithe by too much guesswork."

1:17 A. Simeon his son says,
　　　　(1) "All my life I grew up among the sages, and I found nothing better for a person [the body] than silence.

(2) "And not the learning is the main thing but the doing.

(3) "And whoever talks too much causes sin."

1:18 A. Rabban Simeon b. Gamaliel says, "On three things does the world stand:

(1) "on justice,

(2) "on truth,

(3) "and on peace,

B. "as it is said, Execute the judgment of truth and peace in your gates [Zech. 8:16]."

2:1 A. Rabbi says, "What is the straight path which a person should choose for himself? Whatever is an ornament to the one who follows it, and an ornament in the view of others.

B. "Be meticulous in a small religious duty as in a large one, for you do not know what sort of reward is coming for any of the various religious duties.

C. "And reckon with the loss [required] in carrying out a religious duty against the reward for doing it,

D. "and the reward for committing a transgression against the loss for doing it.

E. "And keep your eye on three things, so you will not come into the clutches of transgression:

F. "Know what is above you:

G. "(1) An eye which sees, and (2) an ear which hears, and (3) all your actions are written down in a book."

2:2 A. Rabban Gamaliel, son of R. Judah the Patriarch, says, "Fitting is learning in Torah along with a craft, for the labor put into the two of them makes one forget sin.

B. "And all learning of Torah which is not joined with labor is destined to be null and cause sin.

C. "And all who work with the community—let them work with them for the sake of Heaven.

D. "For the merit of their fathers strengthens them, and their [fathers'] righteousness stands forever.

E. "And as for you, I credit you with a great reward, as if you had done [all of the work required by the community on your own merit alone]."

2:3 A. "Be wary of the government, for they get friendly with a person only for their own convenience.

B. "They look like friends when it is to their benefit, but they do not stand by a person when he is in need."

2:4 A. He would say, "Make his wishes into your own wishes, so that he will make your wishes into his wishes.

B. "Put aside your wishes on account of his wishes, so that he will put aside the wishes of other people in favor of your wishes."

C. Hillel says, "Do not walk out on the community.

D. "And do not have confidence in yourself until the day you die.

E. "And do not judge your fellow until you are in his place,

F. "And do not say anything which cannot be heard, for in the end it will be heard.

G. "And do not say, 'When I have time, I shall study,' for you may never have time."

2:5 A. He would say, (1) "A coarse person will never fear sin, (2) nor will an am haares [ignoramus] ever be pious, (3) nor will a shy person learn, (4) nor will an intolerant person teach, (5) nor will anyone too busy in business get wise.

B. "In a place in which there are no men, try to act like a man."

2:6 A. Also: he saw a skull floating on the water and said to it, "Because you drowned others, they drowned you, and in the end those who drowned you will be drowned."

2:7 A. He would say, "(1) Lots of meat, lots of worms; (2) lots of property, lots of worries; (3) lots of women, lots of witchcraft; (4) lots of slave girls, lots of lust; (5) lots of slave boys, lots of robbery.

B. "(6) Lots of Torah, lots of life; (7) lots of discipleship, lots of wisdom; (8) lots of counsel, lots of understanding; (9) lots of righteousness, lots of peace."

C. "[If] one has gotten a good name, he has gotten it for himself.

D. "[If] he has gotten teachings of Torah, he has gotten himself life eternal."

2:8 A. Rabban Yohanan b. Zakkai received [it] from Hillel and Shammai.

B. He would say, "(1) If you have learned much Torah, (2) do not puff yourself up on that account, (3) for it was for that purpose that you were created."

C. He had five disciples, and these are they: R. Eliezer b. Hyrcanus, R. Joshua b. Hananiah, R. Yosé the priest, R. Simeon b. Netanel, and R. Eleazar b. Arakh.

D. He would list their good qualities:

E. R. Eliezer b. Hyrcanus: A plastered well, which does not lose a drop of water.

F. R. Joshua: Happy is the one who gave birth to him.

G. R. Yosé: A pious man.

H. R. Simeon b. Netanel: A man who fears sin.

I. And R. Eleazar b. Arakh: A surging spring.

J. He would say, "If all the sages of Israel were on one side of the scale, and R. Eliezer b. Hyrcanus were on the other, he would outweigh all of them."

K. Abba Saul says in his name, "If all of the sages of Israel were on one side of the scale, and R. Eliezer b. Hyrcanus was also with them, and R. Eleazar [b. Arakh] were on the other side, he would outweigh all of them."

2:9 A. He said to them, "Go and see what is the straight path to which someone should stick."

B. R. Eliezer says, "A generous spirit."

C. R. Joshua says, "A good friend."

D. R. Yosé says, "A good neighbor."

E. R. Simeon says, "Foresight."

F. R. Eleazar says, "Good will."

G. He said to them, "I prefer the opinion of R. Eleazar b. Arakh, because in what he says is included everything you say."

H. He said to them, "Go out and see what is the bad road, which someone should avoid."

 I. R. Eliezer says, "Envy."

J. R. Joshua says, "A bad friend."

K. R. Yosé says, "A bad neighbor."

L. R. Simeon says, "Defaulting on a loan."

M. (All the same is a loan owed to a human being and a loan owed to the Omnipresent, blessed be he, as it is said, The wicked borrows and does not pay back, but the righteous person deals graciously and hands over [what he owes] [Psalm 37:21].)

N. R. Eleazar says, "Bad will."

O. He said to them, "I prefer the opinion of R. Eleazar b. Arakh, because in what he says is included everything you say."

2:10 A. They [each] said three things.

B. R. Eliezer says, "(1) Let the respect owing to your fellow be as precious to you as the respect owing to you yourself.

C. "(2) And don't be easy to anger.

D. "(3) And repent one day before you die.

E. "And (1) warm yourself by the fire of the sages, but be careful of their coals, so you don't get burned.

F. "(2) For their bite is the bite of a fox, and their sting is the sting of a scorpion, and their hiss is like the hiss of a snake.

G. "(3) And everything they say is like fiery coals."

2:11 A. R. Joshua says, "(1) Envy, (2) desire of bad things, and (3) hatred for people push a person out of the world."

2:12 A. R. Yosé says, "(1) Let your fellow's money be as precious to you as your own.

B. "And (2) get yourself ready to learn Torah,

C. "for it does not come as an inheritance to you.

D. "And (3) may everything you do be for the sake of Heaven."

2:13 A. R. Simeon says, "(1) Be meticulous in the recitation of the shema and the Prayer.

B. "And (2) when you pray, don't treat your praying as a matter of routine.

C. "But let it be a [plea for] mercy and supplication before the Omnipresent, blessed be he.

D. "As it is said, For he is gracious and full of compassion, slow to anger and full of mercy, and repents of the evil [Joel 2:13].

E. "(3) And never be evil in your own eyes."

2:14 A. R. Eleazar says, "(1) Be constant in learning of Torah.

B. "(2) And know what to reply to an Epicurean.

C. "(3) And know before whom you work,

D. "for your employer can be depended upon to pay your wages for what you can do."

2:15 A. R. Tarfon says, "(1) The day is short, (2) the work formidable, (3) the workers lazy, (4) the wages high, (5) the employer impatient."

2:16 A. He would say, "It's not your job to finish the work, but you're not free
to walk away from it.

    B. "If you have learned much Torah, they will give you a good reward.

    C. "And your employer can be depended upon to pay your wages for what
       you do.

    D. "And know what sort of reward is going to be given to the righteous in
       the coming time."

3:1 A. Aqabiah b. Mehallalel says, "Reflect upon three things and you will not
fall into the clutches of transgression:

    B. "Know (1) from whence you come, (2) whither you are going, and
       (3) before whom you are going to have to give a full account [of yourself].

    C. "From whence do you come? From a putrid drop.

    D. "Whither are you going? To a place of dust, worms, and maggots.

    E. "And before whom are you going to give a full account of Yourself?
       Before the King of kings of kings, the Holy One, blessed be he."

3:2 A. R. Hananiah, Prefect of the Priests, says, "Pray for the welfare of the
government.

    B. "For if it were not for fear of it, one man would swallow his fellow
       alive."

    C. R. Hananiah b. Teradion says, "[If] two sit together and between them
       do not pass teachings of Torah, lo, this is a seat of the scornful,

    D. "as it is said, Nor sits in the seat of the scornful [Ps. 1:2].

    E. "But two who are sitting, and words of Torah do pass between them—
       the Presence is with them,

    F. "as it is said, Then they that feared the Lord spoke with one another,
       and the Lord hearkened and heard, and a book of remembrance was
       written before him, for them that feared the Lord and gave thought to
       His name [Mal. 3:16]."

    G. I know that this applies to two.

    H. How do I know that even if a single person sits and works on Torah, the
       Holy One, blessed be he, sets aside a reward for him?

    I. As it is said, Let him sit alone and keep silent, because he has laid it
       upon him [Lam. 3:28].

3:3 A. R. Simeon says, "Three who ate at a single table and did not talk about
teachings of Torah while at that table are as though they ate from dead sacrifices [Ps. 106:28],

    B. "As it is said, For all tables are full of vomit and filthiness [if they are]
       without God [Ps. 106:28].

    C. "But three who ate at a single table and did talk about teachings of
       Torah while at that table are as if they ate at the table of the Om-
       nipresent, blessed is he,

    D. "as it is said, And he said to me, This is the table that is before the Lord
       [Ez. 41:22]."

3:4 A. R. Hananiah b. Hakhinai says, "(1) He who gets up at night, and (2) he
who walks around by himself, and (3) he who turns his desire to emptiness—
lo, this person is liable for his life."

3:5 A. R. Nehunya b. Haqqaneh says, "From whoever accepts upon himself the yoke of Torah do they remove the yoke of the state and the yoke of hard labor.

>   B. "And upon whoever removes from himself the yoke of the Torah do they lay the yoke of the state and the yoke of hard labor."

3:6 A. R. Halafta of Kefar Hananiah says, "Among ten who sit and work hard on Torah the Presence comes to rest,

>   B. "as it is said, God stands in the congregation of God [Ps. 82:1].

>   C. "And how do we know that the same is so even of five? For it is said, And he has founded his group upon the earth [Am. 9:6].

>   D. "And how do we know that this is so even of three? Since it is said, And he judges among the judges [Ps. 82:1].

>   E. "And how do we know that this is so even of two? Because it is said, Then they that feared the Lord spoke with one another, and the Lord hearkened and heard [Mal. 3:16].

>   F. "And how do we know that this is so even of one? Since it is said, In every place where I record my name I will come to you and I will bless you [Ex. 20:24]."

3:7 A. R. Eleazar of Bartota says, "Give him what is his, for you and yours are his.

>   B. "For so does it say about David, For all things come of you, and of your own have we given you [I Chron. 29:14]."

>   C. R. Simeon says, "He who is going along the way and repeating [his Torah tradition] but interrupts his repetition and says, 'How beautiful is that tree! How beautiful is that ploughed field!'—Scripture reckons it to him as if he has become liable for his life."

3:8 A. R. Dosetai b. R. Yannai in the name of R. Meir says, "Whoever forgets a single thing from what he has learned—Scripture reckons it to him as if he has become liable for his life,

>   B. "as it is said, Only take heed to yourself and keep your soul diligently, lest You forget the words which your eyes saw [Dt. 4:9]."

>   C. Is it possible that this is so even if his learning became too much for him?

>   D. Scripture says, Lest they depart from your heart all the days of your life.

>   E. Thus he becomes liable for his life only when he will sit down and actually remove [his learning] from his own heart,

3:9 A. R. Haninah b. Dosa says, "For anyone whose fear of sin takes precedence over his wisdom, his wisdom will endure,

>   B. "And for anyone whose wisdom takes precedence over his fear of sin, his wisdom will not endure."

>   C. He would say, "Anyone whose deeds are more than his wisdom—his wisdom will endure.

>   D. "And anyone whose wisdom is more than his deeds—his wisdom will not endure."

3:10 A. He would say, "Anyone from whom people take pleasure—the Omnipresent takes pleasure.

B. "And anyone from whom people do not take pleasure, the Omnipresent does not take pleasure."

C. R. Dosa b. Harkinas says, "(1) Sleeping late in the morning, (2) drinking wine at noon, (3) chatting with children, and (4) attending the synagogues of the ignorant drive a man out of the world."

3:11 A. R. Eleazar the Modite says, "(1) He who treats Holy Things as secular, and (2) he who defiles the appointed times, (3) he who humiliates his fellow in public, (4) he who removes the signs of the covenant of Abraham, our father, (may he rest in peace), and (5) he who exposes aspects of the Torah not in accord with the law,

B. "even though he has in hand learning in Torah and good deeds, will have no share in the world to come."

3:12 A. R. Ishmael says, "(1) Be quick [in service] to a superior, (2) efficient in service [to the state], and (3) receive everybody with joy."

3:13 A. R. Aqiba says, "(1) Laughter and lightheadedness turn lewdness into a habit.

B. "(2) Tradition is a fence for the Torah.

C. "(3) Tithes are a fence for wealth.

D. "(4) Vows are a fence for abstinence.

E. "(5) A fence for wisdom is silence."

3:14 A. He would say, "Precious is the human being, who was created in the image [of God].

B. "It was an act of still greater love that it was made known to him that he was created in the image [of God],

C. "as it is said, For in the image of God he made man [Gen. 9:6].

D. "Precious are Israelites, who are called children to the Omnipresent.

E. "It was an act of still greater love that they were called children to the Omnipresent,

F. "as it is said, You are the children of the Lord your God [Dt. 14:1].

G. "Precious are Israelites, to whom was given the precious thing.

H. "It was an act of still greater love that it was made known to them that to them was given that precious thing with which the world was made,

I. "as it is said, For I give you a good doctrine. Do not forsake my Torah [Prov. 4:2]."

3:15 A. "Everything is foreseen, and free choice is given.

B. "In goodness the world is judged.

C. "And all is in accord with the abundance of deed[s]."

3:16 A. He would say, "(1) All is handed over as a pledge,

B. "(2) And a net is cast over all the living.

C. "(3) The store is open, (4) the storekeeper gives credit, (5) the account book is open, and (6) the hand is writing.

D. "(1) Whoever wants to borrow may come and borrow.

E. "(2) The charity collectors go around every day and collect from man whether he knows it or not.

F. "(3) And they have grounds for what they do.

G. "(4) And the judgment is a true judgment.

H. "(5) And everything is ready for the meal."

3:17 A. R. Eleazar b. Azariah says, "If there is no learning of Torah, there is no proper conduct.

B. "If there is no proper conduct, there is no learning in Torah.

C. "If there is no wisdom, there is no reverence.

D. "If there is no reverence, there is no wisdom.

E. "If there is no understanding, there is no knowledge.

F. "If there is no knowledge, there is no understanding.

G. "If there is no sustenance, there is no Torah learning.

H. "If there is no Torah learning, there is no sustenance."

I. He would say, "Anyone whose wisdom is greater than his deeds—to what is he to be likened? To a tree with abundant foliage, but few roots.

J. "When the winds come, they will uproot it and blow it down,

K. "as it is said, He shall be like a tamarisk in the desert and shall not see when good comes but shall inhabit the parched places in the wilderness [Jer. 17:6].

L. "But anyone whose deeds are greater than his wisdom—to what is he to be likened? To a tree with little foliage but abundant roots.

M. "For even if all the winds in the world were to come and blast at it, they will not move it from its place,

N. "as it is said, He shall be as a tree planted by the waters, and that spreads out its roots by the river, and shall not fear when heat comes, and his leaf shall be green, and shall not be careful in the year of drought, neither shall cease from yielding fruit [Jer. 17 :8]."

3:18 A. R. Eleazar Hisma says, "The laws of bird offerings and the beginning of a woman's menstruation period—they are indeed the essentials of the Torah.

B. "Calculations of the equinoxes and reckoning the numerical value of letters are the savories of wisdom."

4:1 A. Ben Zoma says, "Who is a sage? He who learns from everybody,

B. "as it is said, From all my teachers I have gotten understanding [Ps. 119:99].

C. "Who is strong? He who overcomes his desire,

D. "as it is said, He who is slow to anger is better than the mighty, and he who rules his spirit than he who takes a city [Prov. 16:32].

E. "Who is rich? He who is happy in what he has,

F. "as it is said, When you eat the labor of your hands, happy will you be, and it will go well with you [Ps. 128:2].

G. ("Happy will you be—in this world, and it will go well with you—in the world to come.")

H. "Who is honored? He who honors everybody,

I. "as it is said, 'For those who honor me I shall honor, and they who despise me will be treated as of no account [I Sam. 2:30]."

4:2 A. Ben Azzai says, "Run after the most minor religious duty as after the most important, and flee from transgression.

B. "For doing one religious duty draws in its wake doing yet another, and doing one transgression draws in its wake doing yet another.

C. "For the reward of doing a religious duty is a religious duty, and the reward of doing a transgression is a transgression."

4:3 A. He would say, "Do not despise anybody and do not treat anything as unlikely.

B. "For you have no one who does not have his time, and you have nothing which does not have its place."

4:4 A. R. Levitas of Yabneh says, "Be exceedingly humble, for the hope of humanity is the worm."

B. R. Yohanan b. Beroqah says, "Whoever secretly treats the Name of Heaven as profane publicly pays the price.

C. "All the same are the one who does so inadvertently and the one who does so deliberately, when it comes to treating the name of Heaven as profane."

4:5 A. R. Ishmael, his son, says, "He who learns so as to teach—they give him a chance to learn and to teach.

B. "He who learns so as to carry out his teachings—they give him a chance to learn, to teach, to keep, and to do."

C. R. Sadoq says, "Do not make [Torah teachings] a crown with which to glorify yourself or a spade with which to dig.

D. (So did Hillel say [M. 1:13], "He who uses the crown perishes.")

E. "Thus have you learned: Whoever derives worldly benefit from teachings of Torah takes his life out of this world."

4:6 A. R. Yosé says, "Whoever honors the Torah himself is honored by people.

B. "And whoever disgraces the Torah himself is disgraced by people."

4:7 A. R. Ishmael, his son, says, "He who avoids serving as a judge breaks off the power of enmity, robbery, and false swearing.

B. "And he who is arrogant about making decisions is a fool, evil, and prideful."

4:8 A. He would say, "Do not serve as a judge by yourself, for there is only One who serves as a judge all alone.

B. "And do not say, 'Accept my opinion.'

C. "For they have the choice in that matter, not you."

4:9 A. R. Yonatan says, "Whoever keeps the Torah when poor will in the end keep it in wealth.

B. "And whoever treats the Torah as nothing when he is wealthy in the end will treat it as nothing in poverty."

4:10 A. R. Meir says, "Keep your business to a minimum and make [your] business Torah.

B. "And be humble before everybody.

C. "And if you treat the Torah as nothing, you will have many treating you as nothing.

D. "And if you have labored in Torah, [God] has a great reward to give you."

4:11 A. R. Eliezer b. Jacob says, "He who does even a single religious duty gets himself a good advocate.

    B. "He who does even a single transgression gets himself a prosecutor.

    C. "Penitence and good deeds are like a shield against punishment."

    D. R. Yohanan Hassandelar says, "Any gathering which is for the sake of Heaven is going to endure.

    E. "And any which is not for the sake of Heaven is not going to endure."

4:12 A. R. Eleazar b. Shammua says, "The honor owing to your disciple should be as precious to you as yours.

    B. "And the honor owing to your fellow should be like the reverence owing to your master.

    C. "And the reverence owing to your master should be like the awe owing to Heaven."

4:13 A. R. Judah says, "Be meticulous about learning,

    B. "for error in learning leads to deliberate violation [of the Torah]."

    C. R. Simeon says, "There are three crowns: the crown of Torah, the crown of priesthood, and the crown of sovereignty.

    D. "But the crown of a good name is best of them all."

4:14 A. R. Nehorai says, "Go into exile to a place of Torah, and do not suppose that it will come to you.

    B. "For your fellow disciples will make it solid in your hand.

    C. "And on your own understanding do not rely."

4:15 A. R. Yannai says, "We do not have in hand [an explanation] either for the prosperity of the wicked or for the suffering of the righteous."

    B. R. Matya b. Harash says, "Greet everybody first,

    C. "and be a tail to lions.

    D. "But do not be a head of foxes."

4:16 A. R. Jacob says, "This world is like an antechamber before the world to come.

    B. "Get ready in the antechamber, so you can go into the great hall."

4:17 A. He would say, "Better is a single moment spent in penitence and good deeds in this world than the whole of the world to come.

    B. "And better is a single moment of inner peace in the world to come than the whole of a lifetime spent in this world."

4:18 A. R. Simeon b. Eleazar says, "(1) Do not try to make amends with your fellow when he is angry,

    B. "or (2) comfort him when the corpse of his beloved is lying before him,

    C. "or (3) seek to find absolution for him at the moment at which he takes avow,

    D. "or (4) attempt to see him when he is humiliated."

4:19 A. Samuel the Small says, "Rejoice not when your enemy falls, and let not your heart be glad when he is overthrown, lest the Lord see it and it displease him, and he turn away his wrath from him [Prov. 24:17]."

4:20 A. Elisha b. Abuyah says, "He who learns when a child—what is he like? Ink put down on a clean piece of paper.

    B. "And he who learns when an old man—what is he like? Ink put down on a paper full of erasures."

C. R. Yosé b. R. Judah of Kefar Habbabli says, "He who learns from children—what is he like? One who eats sour grapes and drinks fresh wine.

D. "And he who learns from old men—what is he like? He who eats ripe
grapes and drinks vintage wine."

E. Rabbi says, "Do not look at the bottle but at what is in it.

F. "You can have a new bottle full of old wine, and an old bottle which has
not got even new wine."

4:21 A. R. Eliezer Haqqappar says, "Jealousy, lust, and ambition drive a person
out of this world."

4:22 A. He would say, "Those who are born are [destined] to die, and those
who die are [destined] for resurrection.

B. "And the living are [destined] to be judged—

C. "so as to know, to make known, and to confirm that (1) he is God,

D. "(2) he is the one who forms,

E. "(3) he is the one who creates,

F. "(4) he is the one who understands,

G. "(5) he is the one who judges,

H. "(6) he is the one who gives evidence,

I. "(7) he is the one who brings suit,

J. "(8) and he is the one who is going to make the ultimate judgment.

K. "Blessed be he, for before him are not (1) guile, (2) forgetfulness,
(3) respect for persons, (4) bribe taking,

L. "for everything is his.

M. "And know that everything is subject to reckoning.

N. "And do not let your evil impulse persuade you that Sheol is a place of
refuge for you.

O. "For (1) despite your wishes were you formed, (2) despite your wishes
were you born, (3) despite your wishes do you live, (4) despite your
wishes do you die, and (5) despite your wishes are you going to give a
full accounting before the King of kings of kings, the Holy One, blessed
be he."

5:1 A. By ten acts of speech was the world made.

B. And what does Scripture mean [by having God say "say" ten times]?
And is it not so that with a single act of speech [the world] could have
been brought into being?

C. But it is to exact punishment from the wicked, who destroy a world
which was created through ten acts of speech,

D. and to secure a good reward for the righteous, who sustain a world
which was created through ten acts of speech.

5:2 A. There are ten generations from Adam to Noah, to show you how long-
suffering is [God].

B. For all those generations went along spiting him until he brought the
water of the flood upon them.

C. There are ten generations from Noah to Abraham, to show you how
long-suffering is [God].

D. For all those generations went along spiting him, until Abraham came
along and took the reward which had been meant for all of them.

5:3 A. Ten trials were inflicted upon Abraham, our father, may he rest in peace, and he withstood all of them,
>   B. to show you how great is His love for Abraham, our father, may he rest in peace.

5:4 A. Ten wonders were done for our fathers in Egypt, and ten at the Sea.
>   B. Ten blows did the Holy One, blessed be he, bring upon the Egyptians in Egypt, and ten at the Sea.
>   C. Ten trials did our fathers inflict upon the Omnipresent, blessed be he, in the Wilderness,
>   D. as it is said, Yet they have tempted me these ten times and have not listened to my voice [Num. 14:22].

5:5 A. Ten wonders were done for our fathers in the Temple:
>   B. (1) A woman never miscarried on account of the stench of the meat of Holy Things. (2) And the meat of the Holy Things never turned rotten. (3) A fly never made an appearance in the slaughterhouse. (4) A high priest never suffered a nocturnal emission on the eve of the Day of Atonement. (5) The rain never quenched the fire on the altar. (6) No wind ever blew away the pillar of smoke. (7) An invalidating factor never affected the omer, the Two Loaves, or the Show Bread. (8) When the people are standing, they are jammed together. When they go down and prostrate themselves, they have plenty of room. (9) A snake and a scorpion never bit anybody in Jerusalem. (10) And no one ever said to his fellow, "The place is too crowded for me [Is. 49:20] to stay in Jerusalem."

5:6 A. Ten things were created on the eve of the Sabbath [Friday] at twilight, and these are they:
>   B. (1) the mouth of the earth [Num. 16:32]; (2) the mouth of the well [Num. 21:16–18]; (3) the mouth of the ass [Num. 22:28]; (4) the rainbow [Gen. 9:13]; (5) the manna [Ex. 16:15]; (6) the rod [Ex. 4:17]; (7) the Shamir; (8) letters, (9) writing, (10) and the tables of stone [of the ten commandments, Ex. 32:15f.].
>   C. And some say, "Also the destroyers, the grave of Moses, and the tamarisk of Abraham, our father."
>   D. And some say, "Also: the tongs made with tongs [with which the first tongs were made]."

5:7 A. There are seven traits to an unformed clod, and seven to a sage.
>   B. (1) A sage does not speak before someone greater than he in wisdom.
>   C. (2) And he does not interrupt his fellow.
>   D. (3) And he is not at a loss for an answer.
>   E. (4) He asks a relevant question and answers properly.
>   F. (5) And he addresses each matter in its proper sequence, first, then second.
>   G. (6) And concerning something he has not heard, he says, "I have not heard the answer."
>   H. (7) And he concedes the truth [when the other party demonstrates it].
>   I. And the opposite of these traits apply to a clod.

5:8 A. There are seven forms of punishment which come upon the world for seven kinds of transgression.

B. (1) [If] some people give tithes and some people do not give tithes, there is a famine from drought.

C. So some people are hungry and some have enough.

D. (2) [If] everyone decided not to tithe, there is a famine of unrest and drought.

E. (3) [If all decided] not to remove dough offering, there is a famine of totality.

F. (4) Pestilence comes to the world on account of the death penalties which are listed in the Torah but which are not in the hands of the court [to inflict];

G. and because of the produce of the Seventh Year [which people buy and sell].

H. (5) A sword comes into the world because of the delaying of justice and perversion of justice, and because of those who teach the Torah not in accord with the law.

5:9 A. (6) A plague of wild animals comes into the world because of vain oaths and desecration of the Divine Name.

B. (7) Exile comes into the world because of those who worship idols, because of fornication, and because of bloodshed,

C. and because of the neglect of the release of the Land [in the year of release].

D. At four turnings in the years pestilence increases: in the Fourth Year, in the Seventh Year, in the year after the Seventh Year, and at the end of the Festival [of Tabernacles] every year:

E. (1) in the Fourth Year, because of the poor man's tithe of the Third Year [which people have neglected to hand over to the poor];

F. (2) in the Seventh Year, because of the poor man's tithe of the Sixth Year;

G. (3) in the year after the Seventh Year, because of the dealing in produce of the Seventh Year;

H. and (4) at the end of the Festival every year, because of the thievery of the dues [gleanings and the like] owing to the poor [not left for them in the antecedent harvest].

5:10 A. There are four sorts of people.

B. (1) He who says, "What's mine is mine and what's yours is yours"—this is the average sort.

C. (And some say, "This is the sort of Sodom.")

D. (2) "What's mine is yours and what's yours is mine"—this is a boon.

E. (3) "What's mine is yours and what's yours is yours"—this is a truly pious man.

F. (4) "What's mine is mine and what's yours is mine"—this is a truly wicked man.

5:11 A. There are four sorts of personality:

B. (1) easily angered, easily calmed—he loses what he gains;

C. (2) hard to anger, hard to calm—what he loses he gains;

D. (3) hard to anger and easy to calm—a truly pious man;

E. (4) easy to anger and hard to calm—a truly wicked man.

5:12 A. There are four types of disciples:
   B. (1) quick to grasp, quick to forget—he loses what he gains;
   C. (2) slow to grasp, slow to forget—what he loses he gains;
   D. (3) quick to grasp, slow to forget—a sage;
   E. (4) slow to grasp, quick to forget—a bad lot indeed.

5:13 A. There are four traits among people who give charity:
   B. (1) he who wants to give but does not want others to give—he begrudges what belongs to others;
   C. (2) he wants others to give, but he does not want to give—he begrudges what belongs to himself;
   D. (3) he will give and he wants others to give—he is truly pious;
   E. (4) he will not give and does not want others to give—he is truly wicked.

5:14 A. There are four sorts among those who go to the study house:
   B. He who goes but does not carry out [what he learns]—he has at least the reward for the going.
   C. He who practices but does not go [to study]—he has at least the reward for the doing.
   D. He who both goes and practices—he is truly pious.
   E. He who neither goes nor practices—he is truly wicked.

5:15 A. There are four traits among those who sit before the sages:
   B. a sponge, a funnel, a strainer, and a sifter.
   C. A sponge—because he sponges everything up;
   D. a funnel—because he takes in on one side and lets out on the other;
   E. a strainer—for he lets out the wine and keeps in the lees;
   F. and a sifter—for he lets out the flour and keeps in the finest flour.

5:16 A. [In] any loving relationship which depends upon something, [when] that thing is gone, the love is gone.
   B. But any which does not depend upon something will never come to an end.
   C. What is a loving relationship which depends upon something? That is the love of Amnon and Tamar [11 Sam. 13:15].
   D. And one which does not depend upon something? That is the love of David and Jonathan.

5:17 A. Any dispute which is for the sake of Heaven will in the end yield results, and any which is not for the sake of Heaven will in the end not yield results.
   B. What is a dispute for the sake of Heaven? This is the sort of dispute between Hillel and Shammai.
   C. And what is one which is not for the sake of Heaven? This the dispute of Korach and all his party.

5:18 A. He who brings merit to the community never causes sin.
   B. And he who causes the community to sin—they never give him a sufficient chance to attain penitence.
   C. Moses attained merit and bestowed merit on the community.
   D. So the merit of the community is assigned to his [credit],

E. as it is said, He executed the justice of the Lord and his judgments with Israel [Dt. 33:21).

F. Jeroboam sinned and caused the community to sin.

G. So the sin of the community is assigned to his [debit],

H. as it is said, For the sins of Jeroboam which he committed and where-with he made Israel to sin [I Kings 15:30].

5:19 A. Anyone in whom are these three traits is one of the disciples of Abraham, our father;

B. But if he bears three other traits, he is one of the disciples of Balaam, the wicked:

C. [1] a generous spirit, [2] a modest mien, and [3] a humble soul—he is one of the disciples of Abraham, our father.

D. A grudging spirit, [2] an arrogant mien, and [3] a proud soul—he is one of the disciples of Balaam, the wicked.

E. What is the difference between the disciples of Abraham our father and the disciples of Balaam the wicked?

F. The disciples of Abraham our father enjoy the benefit of their learning in this world and yet inherit the world to come, as it is said, "That I may cause those who love me to inherit substance, and so that I may fill their treasures" [Prov. 8:21].

G. The disciples of Balaam the Wicked inherit Gehenna and go down to the Pit of Destruction, as it is said, "But you, O God, shall bring them down into the pit of destruction; blood thirsty and deceitful men shall not live out half their days" [Ps. 55:24].

5:20 A. Judah b. Tema says, "Be strong as a leopard, fast as an eagle, fleet as a gazelle, and brave as a lion, to carry out the will of your father who is in heaven."

B. He would say, "The shameless go to Gehenna and the diffident to the garden of Eden.

C. "May it be found pleasing before you, Lord our God, that you rebuild your city quickly in our day and set our portion in your Torah."

5:21 A. He would say, "At five to Scripture, ten to Mishnah-study, thirteen to re-ligious duties, fifteen to Talmud-study, eighteen to the wedding canopy, twenty to responsibility for providing for a family, thirty to fullness of strength, forty to understanding, fifty to counsel, sixty to old age, seventy to ripe old age, eighty to remarkable strength, ninety to a bowed back, and at a hundred he is like a corpse who has already passed and gone from this world."

5:22 A. Ben Bag Bag says, "Turn it over and over because everything is in it. And reflect upon it and grow old and worn in it and do not leave it,

B. "for you have no better lot than that."

5:23 A. Ben He He says, "in accord with the effort is the reward."

4   How Judaism Reads Scripture: Genesis Rabbah

TRANSLATED BY JACOB NEUSNER

1. Why is this reading important?

Christians commonly identify Judaism as the "religion of the Old Testament," meaning pretty much the same as Christianity, only without the New Testament. They then assume that Judaism reads just as Christianity does the Hebrew Scriptures of Ancient Israel (called in Hebrew *Tanakh*, which stands for Torah, Pentateuch, Nebiim [prophets], and Ketubim [writings]; also called the Written Torah). But that is a mistake. Christianity reaches the Old Testament through the New. Judaism receives the Written Torah along with its complement and completion, called the Oral Torah. How, then, does the Written Torah find its way into Judaism? It is through a set of interpretive writings called Midrash, meaning exegesis or explanation. Many of these writings are organized around books of Scripture. Through what they say about particular verses of those books, they set forth a basic, encompassing viewpoint. Comments on particular verses, therefore, allow the commentators to make a large and general statement. To see how this works, we turn to Genesis Rabbah, the sages' commentary on the book of Genesis, which reached closure c. 500 C.E. It is the single most important, and most representative, compilation of Midrash comments from the formative age of Judaism.

2. What should you notice as you proceed?

Midrash reads one thing in light of another, Scripture in light of the large, theological conception that shaped the sages' reading of Scripture. Notice how in the details, sages repeat their main point over and over. Try to pick out points at which a particular incident in the life of a patriarch is transformed into a general, exemplary rule. You will see how the sages turn cases into principles of conduct. Notice also how much sages discover in a given verse. That is because they bring so much to the reading of that verse. The great Catholic theologian Joseph Cardinal Ratzinger says that first comes hermeneutics, then exegesis—that is, first you frame your encompassing view of how and why the text is going to make sense, then you turn to the text and make sense of the details in accord with your theory. See whether you can find a basis for Cardinal Ratzinger's theory of Scripture in the way the sages read Genesis Rabbah.

3. How should you frame a question for class discussion in response to what you have read?

In what ways can contemporary Bible-believing Christians identify with the sages' reading of Scripture, and in what ways (apart from doctrine) will they part company? How about contemporary literary critics, who read Scripture without the mediation of faith: in what way will they find valuable the sages' reading of particular verses, and how will they prefer to ignore that reading? Finally, what about everyday Bible readers, neither Bible believing nor academic, but ordinary Jews and ordinary Christians and ordinary secular folk—how will each group come to grips with the mode of reading Genesis, and the distinctive message derived from Genesis, that the sages set forth? Here is a work of comparison and contrast that is made possible by imagining the different approaches to the same thing. When you consider how influential Genesis is in contemporary culture, you will see what is at stake.

In Genesis Rabbah, which reached closure c. 450 C.E., about a century and a half after Christianity became the official religion of the Roman empire, the entire narrative of Genesis is formed to point toward the sacred history of Israel, the Jewish people: its slavery and redemption; its coming Temple in Jerusalem; its exile and salvation at the end of time. In the rereading by the authors of Genesis Rabbah, Genesis proclaims the prophetic message that the world's creation initiated a single, straight line of significant events—that is, history—leading in the end to the salvation of Israel and, through Israel, of all humanity. The single most important proposition of Genesis Rabbah is that the story of the beginnings of creation, humanity, and Israel contains the message of the meaning and end of the life of the Jewish people in the fifth century. The deeds of the founders supply signals for the children about what will come in the future. In this way the biography of Abraham, Isaac, and Jacob also constitutes a projected account of the history of Israel to come.

Genesis Rabbah is a composite document. Some of the materials can be shown to have preexisted the compilation. Many times a verse of Genesis has been joined to a set of comments in no way pertinent to the verse at hand. Proof for a given syllogism, furthermore, will derive from a verse of Genesis as well as from numerous verses of other books of the Bible. The verse itself is not the focus of discourse; it has not generated the comment but has merely provided a proof for a syllogism. That is what it means to say that a proposition yields an exegesis. The fundamental proposition, displayed throughout Genesis Rabbah, that yields the specific exegeses of many of the verses of the book of Genesis and even whole stories, is that the beginnings point toward the endings and the meaning of Israel's past points toward the message that lies in Israel's future. What happened to the fathers and mothers of the family Israel provides a sign for what will happen to the children later on.

At stake is the discovery, among the facts provided by the written Torah, of the social rules that govern Israel's history. As with the Mishnah, the governing mode of thought is natural philosophy. It involves the classification of data by shared traits, yielding descriptive rules, the testing of propositions against the facts of data, the whole aimed at the discovery of underlying rules out of a multiplicity of details—in all, the proposing and testing, against the facts provided by Scripture, of the theses of Israel's salvation that demanded attention at that time. The issues, however, were not so much philosophical as religious. While philosophy addressed questions of nature and rules of enduring existence, religion asked about issues of history and God's intervention in time. Specifically, we may classify the document before us and its successors and companions as works of profound theological inquiry into God's rules for history and society in the here and now and for salvation at the end of historical time.

Genesis Rabbah in its final form emerges from that momentous century in which the Roman empire passed from pagan to Christian rule and in which, in the aftermath of Julian's abortive reversion to paganism, c. 360, which endangered the empire's Christian character, Christianity adopted that politics of repression of paganism that rapidly engulfed Judaism as well. The issue confronting Israel in the Land of Israel therefore proved immediate: the meaning of the new and ominous turn of history, the implications of Christ's worldly triumph for the other-worldly and supernatural people, Israel, whom God chooses and loves. The message of the exegete-compositors addressed the circumstance of historical crisis and generated remarkable renewal, a rebirth of intellect in the encounter with Scripture, now in quest of the rules not of sanctification—these had already been found—but of salvation. So the book of Genesis, which portrays how all things began, would testify to the message and the method of the end: the coming salvation of patient, hopeful, enduring Israel.

That is why Genesis Rabbah presents a deeply *religious* view of Israel's historical and salvific life, in much the same way that the Mishnah provides a profoundly *philosophical* view of Israel's everyday and sanctified existence. Just as the main themes of the Mishnah evoke issues of being and becoming, potential and actual, and mixtures of other problems of physics all in the interest of philosophical analysis, so Genesis Rabbah presents its cogent and coherent agendum. That program of inquiry concerns the way in which God set forth to Moses in the book of Genesis the entire scope and meaning of Israel's history among the nations and salvation at the end of days. The mode of thought by which the framers of Genesis Rabbah work out their propositions dictates the character of their exegesis: according to rhetoric, logical principles of cogent and intelligible discourse, and even topic. In their reading of Scripture a given story will bear a deeper truth about what it means to be Israel, on the one side, and what in the end of days will happen to Israel, on the other. True, their reading makes no explicit reference to what, if anything, had changed in the age of Constantine. But we do find repeated references to the four kingdoms of Babylonia, Media, Greece, Rome—and beyond the fourth will come Israel, fifth and last. So the sages' message, in their theology of history, was that the present anguish prefigured the coming vindication, of God's people.

It follows that the sages read Genesis as the history of the world with an emphasis on Israel. So the lives portrayed in that work, the domestic quarrels and petty conflicts with the neighbors, all serve to yield insight into the future as well as the past. The deeds of the patriarchs taught lessons about how the children were to act, and the lives of the patriarchs signaled the history of Israel. Israel constituted one extended family, and the metaphor of the family, serving the nation as it did, imparted to the stories of Genesis the character of a family record. History become genealogy conveyed the message of salvation. These propositions laid down the same judgment, one for the individual and the family, the other for the community and the nation, since there was no differentiating one from the other. Every detail of the narrative therefore served to prefigure what was to be, and Israel found itself, time and again, in the revealed facts of the history of the creation of the world, the decline of humanity down to the time of Noah, and, finally, its ascent to Abraham, Isaac, and Israel.

As a corollary to the view that the biography of the fathers prefigures the history of the descendants, the sages maintained that the deeds of the children—the holy way of life of Israel—follow the model established by the founders long before. So they looked in Genesis for the basis for what they held to be God's will for Israel. And they found ample proof. The sages invariably searched the stories of Genesis for evidence of the origins not only of creation and of Israel, but also of Israel's cosmic way of life, its understanding of how, in the passage of nature and the seasons, humanity worked out its relationship with God. The holy way of life that Israel lived through the seasons of nature would therefore make its mark upon the stories of the creation of the world and the beginning of Israel.

Part of the reason the framers of Genesis Rabbah pursued the interest at hand derived from polemic. From the first Christian century, theologians of Christianity maintained that salvation did not depend upon keeping the laws of the Torah. Abraham, after all, had been justified and he did not keep the Torah, which, in his day, had not yet been given. So time and again the sages maintained that Abraham indeed kept the entire Torah even before it had been revealed. They further attributed to Abraham, Isaac, and Jacob rules of the Torah enunciated only later on—for example, the institution of prayer three times a day. But the reading before us bears a different charge. It is to Israel to see how deeply embedded in the rules of reality were the patterns governing God's relationship to Israel. That relationship, one of human sin and atonement, divine punishment and forgiveness, expresses the most fundamental laws of human existence.

One rule of Israel's history is yielded by the facts at hand. Israel is never left without an appropriate hero or heroine, and the relevance of the long discourse becomes clear at the end. Each story in Genesis may forecast the stages in Israel's history later on, beginning to end. A matter of deep concern focused the sages' attention on the sequence of world empires to which, among other nations, Israel was subjugated: Babylonia, Media, Greece, and Rome—Rome above all. What will follow? The sages maintained that beyond the rule of Rome lay the salvation of Israel:

XLII:IV.

1.   A. "And it came to pass in the days of Amraphel" [Gen. 14:1]:

4.   A. Another matter: "And it came to pass in the days of Amraphael, king of Shinar" [Gen. 14:1] refers to Babylonia.

   B. "Arioch, king of Ellasar" [Gen. 14:1] refers to Greece.

C. "Chedorlaomer, king of Elam" [Gen. 14:1] refers to Media.

D. "And Tidal, king of Goiim [nations]" [Gen. 14:1] refers to the wicked government [Rome], which conscripts troops from all the nations of the world.

E. Said R. Eleazar bar Abina, "If you see that the nations contend with one another, look for the footsteps of the king-messiah. You may know that that is the case, for lo, in the time of Abraham, because the kings struggled with one another, a position of greatness came to Abraham."

Obviously, section 4 presents the most important reading of Gen. 14:1, since it links the events of the life of Abraham to the history of Israel and even ties the whole to the messianic expectation. The process of history flows in both directions. Just as what Abraham did prefigured the future history of Israel, so what the Israelites later on were to do imposed limitations on Abraham. Time and again events in the lives of the patriarchs prefigure the four monarchies, among which the fourth, last, and most intolerable was Rome.

Genesis is read as if it portrayed the history of Israel and Rome. For that is the single obsession binding the framers of Genesis Rabbah to common discourse with the text before them. Why Rome in the form it takes here? And why the obsessive character of the sages' disposition of the theme of Rome? Were their picture merely of Rome as tyrant and destroyer of the Temple, we should have no reason to link the text to the contemporary problems of redaction and closure. But now it is Rome as Israel's brother, counterpart, and nemesis, Rome as the one thing standing in the way of Israel's, and the world's, ultimate salvation. So the stakes are different, and much higher. It is not a political Rome but a Christian and messianic Rome that is at issue: Rome as surrogate for Israel, Rome as obstacle to Israel. Why? It is because Rome now confronts Israel with a crisis, and, I argue, the program of Genesis Rabbah constitutes a response to that crisis. Rome in the fourth century became Christian. The sages responded by facing that fact squarely and saying: "Indeed, it is as you say, a kind of Israel, an heir of Abraham as your texts explicitly claim. But we remain the sole legitimate Israel, the bearer of the birthright—we and not you. So you are our brother: Esau, Ishmael, Edom." And the rest follows.

By rereading the story of the beginnings, the sages discovered the answer and the secret of the end. Rome claimed to be Israel, and indeed, sages conceded, Rome shared the patrimony of Israel. That claim took the form of the Christians' appropriation of the Torah as the "Old Testament," so sages acknowledged a simple fact in acceding to the notion that, in some way, Rome too formed part of Israel. But it was the rejected part, the Ishmael and the Esau, not the Isaac and the Jacob. The advent of Christian Rome precipitated the sustained polemical and, I think, rigorous and well-argued rereading of beginnings in light of the end. Rome marked the conclusion of human history as Israel had known it. Beyond lay the coming of the true Messiah, the redemption of Israel, the salvation of the world, the end of time. So the issues were not inconsiderable, and when the sages spoke of Esau/Rome, as they did so often, they confronted the life-or-death decision of the day.

We consider a single example of how ubiquitous is the shadow of Ishmael/Esau/Edom/Rome. Whenever the sages reflected on future history, their minds turned to their own day. They found the hour difficult, because Rome, now Christian, claimed that very birthright and blessing they had understood to be theirs alone. Christian Rome posed a threat without precedent. Now another dominion besides Israel's claimed the rights and blessings that sustained Israel. Wherever in Scripture they turned, the sages found comfort in the iteration that the birthright, the blessing, the Torah, and the hope—all that belonged to them and to none other.

GENESIS RABBAH *PARASHAH* LXX TO GENESIS 28:20–29:30

LXX:I.

1.   A. "Then Jacob made a vow, saying, 'If God will be with me and will keep me in this way that I go and will give me bread to eat and clothing to wear, so that I come again to my father's house in peace, then the Lord shall be my God. And this stone, which I have set up for a pillar, shall be God's house; and of all that you give me, I will give the tenth to you'" [Gen. 28:20–22]:
      B. "I will perform for you my vows, which my lips have uttered and my mouth has spoken when I was in distress" [Ps. 66:13–14].
      C. Said R. Isaac the Babylonian, "One who takes a vow carries out a religious duty [if he does so in time of stress]."
      D. What is the meaning of the statement, "Then Jacob made a vow, saying"? "Saying" to the future generations, so that they too will take vows in a time of stress.

What attracts the exegete's attention in Gen. 28:20 is the simple fact that Jacob has taken a vow, and the intersecting verse, Ps. 66:13–14, then underlines that fact. R. Isaac evaluates vow taking, subjected to criticism, by saying that it can represent a meritorious action. Paragraph D repeats the basic syllogism of Genesis Rabbah: What the founders do, the children carry on, and what happens to the founders tells what will happen to the children, and, finally, the merit accumulated by the founders serves the children later on as their inheritance and source of protection. The amplification of the opening encounter of base verse and intersecting verse follows. This order—base verse, then intersecting verse—will be reversed in the later compilations, which will begin in the distant reaches of Scripture and only slowly and unpredictably recover the point articulated in what becomes the base verse.

2.   A. Jacob was the first to take a vow, therefore whoever takes a vow should make it depend only upon him.
      B. Said R. Abbahu, "It is written, *'How he swore to the Lord and vowed to the mighty one of Jacob'* [Ps. 132:2].
      C. "What is written is not, 'how he [David] swore to the Lord and vowed to the mighty one of Abraham' or 'of Isaac,' but 'of Jacob.'
      D. "He made the vow depend upon the first person ever to take a vow."

The theme of the passage, taking vows, produces two important points. First is that of section 1, that, while vowing in general does not meet the sages' approval, in times of stress it does, and Jacob is the example of that fact. Then, in section 2, Jacob is the one who started the practice of vowing, so Jacob is the one to whom vows are referred as in the cited passage from Psalms. These two intersecting verses do not receive detailed exegesis on their own; they contribute themes and propositions. So the passage is not like those in which a long sequence of comments either brings the intersecting verse back to the base verse or reads the intersecting verse as an expression of the views of the principle of the base verse. Later on Jacob's failure to keep his vow promptly elicits comment.

LXX:II.

1.   A. R. Yudan in the name of R. Idi: "It is written. *'Then the people rejoiced, for they offered willingly. Wherefore David blessed the Lord before all the congregation, and David said, "Blessed be you, O Lord, the God of Israel our father"'* (1 Chr. 29:9–10).

   B. "It was because they were engaged in carrying out religious duties that were acts of free will and that matters were successful that they rejoiced.

   C. "What is the meaning of the statement, *'Wherefore David blessed the Lord before all the congregation, and David said, "Blessed be you, O Lord, the God of Israel our father"'*? Specifically, we note that what is written is not, 'the God *of Abraham, Isaac,* and Israel,' but only 'God of Israel'?

   D. "He made the vow depend upon the first person ever to take a vow."

   E. Said R. Yudan, "From the document at hand [the Torah, not merely the Writings] we do not lack further proof of that same fact. For example, *'And Israel vowed'* [Num. 21:2], meaning, our father, Israel.

   F. "*'Then Jacob made a vow.'*"

The same point now recurs, with a different set of proof texts. The rhetorically noteworthy point is at F, where we revert to the base verse. This will form a bridge to the systematic exposition of that base verse, which now begins.

LXX:III.

1.   A. *"Then Jacob made a vow:"*

   B. Four made a vow, two vowed and lost out, and two vowed and benefited.

   C. Israel took a vow and Hannah took a vow, and they benefited.

   D. Jephthah took a vow and lost out, Jacob took a vow and lost out. [Freedman, *Genesis Rabbah,* p. 637, n. 2: His (Jacob's) vow was superfluous, since he had already received God's promise and therefore he lost thereby.]

The fragmentary comment serves the purpose of removing the impression that the text of Scripture goes over the same ground twice and contradicts itself. This same problem will be solved in a different way in what follows. Since, as we know, the Pentateuchal books, including Genesis, are composed of a number of prior strands, some of which go over the same ground two or more times, the text itself, read by the sages as single, linear, and unitary, presents its own problems for their attention.

LXX:IV.

1. A. R. Aibu and R. Jonathan:
    B. One of them said, "The passage states matters out of the proper order."
    C. The other said, "The passage is entirely in the proper order."
    D. The one who has said, "The passage states matters out of the proper order" points to the following: *"And lo, I am with you"* [Gen. 28:15] contrasts to the statement, "Then Jacob made a vow, saying, *'If God will be with me.'"*
    E. The other who has said, "The passage is entirely in the proper order" has then to explain the statement, "If God will be with me" in light of the statement already at hand.
    F. His point is this: "If he will be with me" means "if all of the conditions that he has stipulated with me will be carried out," [then I will keep my vow].

2. A. R. Abbahu and rabbis:
    B. R. Abbahu said, " 'If God will be with me and will keep me in *'this way'* refers to protection from gossip, in line with this usage: *'And they turn their tongue in the way of slander* [Freedman, p. 637, n. 4], *their bow of falsehood'* [Jer. 9:2].
    C. " '. . . *will give me bread to eat'* refers to protection from fornication, in line with this usage: *'Neither has he kept back any thing from me, except the bread which he ate'* [Gen. 39:9], a euphemism for sexual relations with his wife.
    D. " '. . . *so that I come again to my father's house in peace'* refers to bloodshed.
    E. " '. . . *then the Lord shall be my God'* so that I shall be protected from idolatry.' "
    F. Rabbis interpreted the statement *"this way"* to speak of all of these.
    G. [The rabbis' statement now follows:] "Specifically: *'If God will be with me and will keep me in this way that I go'* [by referring only to 'way'] contains an allusion to idolatry, fornication, murder, and slander.
    H. " '*Way'* refers to idolatry: *'They who swear by the sin of Samaria and say, As your god, O Dan, lives, and as the way of Beersheba lives'* [Amos 8:14].
    I. " '*Way'* refers to adultery: *'So is the way of an adulterous woman'* [Prov. 30:20].
    J. " '*Way'* refers to murder: *'My son, do not walk in the way of them, restrain your foot from their path, for their feet run to evil and they make haste to shed blood'* [Prov. 1:15–16].
    K. " '*Way'* refers to slander: *'And he heard the words of Laban's sons, saying, "Jacob has taken away [everything that belonged to our father]"'* [Gen. 31:1]."

Section 1 goes over the problem of the preceding and makes it explicit. Section 2 then subjects the verse to a close exegesis, with the standard repertoire of mortal sins—murder, fornication, slander—now read into the verse. Jacob asks God's protection to keep himself from sinning. That interpretation rehabilitates Jacob, since the picture in Scripture portrays a rather self-centered person, and now Jacob exhibits virtue.

LXX:V.

1. A. ". . . *will give me bread to eat and clothing to wear:*"

B. Aqilas the proselyte came to R. Eliezer and said to him, "Is all the gain that is coming to the proselyte going to be contained in this verse: '. . . *and loves the proselyte, giving him food and clothing'* [Deut. 10:18]?"

C. He said to him, "And is something for which the old man [Jacob] beseeched going to be such a small thing in your view, namely, '. . . *will give me bread to eat and clothing to wear'*? [God] comes and hands it over to [a proselyte] on a reed [and the proselyte does not have to beg for it.]"

D. He came to R. Joshua, who commenced by saying words to appease him: "'*Bread*' refers to Torah, as it is said, '*Come, eat of my bread*' [Prov. 9:5]. '*Clothing*' refers to the cloak of a disciple of sages.

E. "When a person has the merit of studying the Torah, he has the merit of carrying out a religious duty. [So the proselyte receives a great deal when he gets bread and clothing, namely, entry into the estate of disciples.]

F. "And not only so, but his daughters may be chosen for marriage into the priesthood, so that their sons' sons will offer burnt-offerings on the altar. [So the proselyte may also look forward to entry into the priests' caste. That statement will now be spelled out.]

G. "'*Bread*' refers to the show-bread."

H. "'*Clothing*' refers to the garments of the priesthood."

I. "So lo, we deal with the sanctuary.

J. "How do we know that the same sort of blessing applies in the provinces? '*Bread*' speaks of the dough-offering [that is separated in the provinces] while '*clothing*' refers to the first fleece [handed over to the priest]."

The interpretation of "bread" and "clothing" yields its own message, intersecting only at one point with the passage at hand. So at issue in this composition is not the exegesis of our base verse but the meaning of "bread" and "clothing" as applied to the proselyte. We now see how the components of the base verse are reread in terms of the base values of sages themselves: Torah and cult. The sages regarded study of Torah as equivalent to a sacrifice, and the sage as equivalent to the priest. This typological reading of Israel's existence would then guide the sages' interpretation of such specific passages as the one before us.

LXX:VI.

1.   A. ". . . *so that I come again to my father's house in peace, then the Lord shall be my God*" [Gen. 28:20–22]:

B. R. Joshua of Sikhnin in the name of R. Levi: "The Holy One, blessed be he, took the language used by the patriarchs and turned it into a key to the redemption of their descendants.

Now comes the main event in our passage: the reading, in the light of Israel's future history—that is, the story of Israel's salvation—of the deeds of the matriarchs and patriarchs and of God's love for them

C. "Said the Holy One, blessed be he, to Jacob, 'You have said, "*Then the Lord shall be my God.*" By your life, all of the acts of goodness, blessing, and consolation which I am going to carry out for your descendants I shall bestow only by using the same language:

D. "' "*Then in that day, living waters shall go out from Jerusalem*" [Zech. 14:8].
"*Then in that day a man shall rear a young cow and two sheep*" [Is. 7:21].
"*Then, in that day, the Lord will set his hand again the second time to recover
the remnant of his people*" (Is. 11:11). "*Then, in that day, the mountains shall
drop down sweet wine*" [Joel 4:18]. "*Then, in that day, a great horn shall be
blown and they shall come who were lost in the land of Assyria*" [Is. 27:13].' "

This section unites Jacob's biography and Israel's history. The explicit details,
rather conventional in character, are less interesting than the basic syllogism,
which is implicit and ubiquitous.

Another approach to the interpretation of Scripture that this document's
framers pioneered is the imputation to a single verse of a wide variety of coherent,
alternative readings. Later on, this exegetical mode would be given its own form,
introduced by Hebrew words meaning "another matter," and a long sequence of
"other matters" would be strung together. In fact, all of the "other matters" turn
out to say the same thing, only in different ways, or convey a single, coherent attitude, emotion, sentiment, or conception. In the following, however, we find the substance of the hermeneutics, but not the form it would ultimately be given.

LXX:VIII.

1.   A. "*Then Jacob lifted up his feet*" [Gen. 29:1]:
      B. Said R. Aha, "'*A tranquil heart is the life of the flesh*' [Prov. 14:30].
      C. "Since he had been given this good news, his heart carried his feet.
      D. "So people say: 'The stomach carries the feet.'"

What captures attention is the happiness expressed in the description of Jacob's
onward journey. The good news carried him forward. But what does this good
news ("gospel") represent? What follows more than fills the gap. It is the gospel
of Israel: its salvation, worked out in the principal components of its holy way of
life of sanctification. So the base and intersecting verses prepare the way for a
powerful and sustained statement. In the following protracted, six-part interpretation of the simple verse about seeing a well in the field, we see the full power
of Midrash as proposition yielding exegesis. Elements of both sanctification and
salvation are joined in a remarkable message.

2.   A. "*As he looked, he saw a well in the field:*"
      B. R. Hama bar Hanina interpreted the verse in six ways [that is, he di-
         vides the verse into six clauses and systematically reads each of the
         clauses in light of the others and in line with an overriding theme]:
      C. "'*As he looked, he saw a well in the field:*' this refers to the well [of water in
         the wilderness, Num. 21:17].
      D. "'. . . *and lo, three flocks of sheep lying beside it:*' specifically, Moses, Aaron,
         and Miriam.
      E. "'. . . *for out of that well the flocks were watered:*' from there each one drew
         water for his standard, tribe, and family."
      F. "*And the stone upon the well's mouth was great:*"
      G. Said R. Hanina, "It was only the size of a little sieve."
      H. [Reverting to Hama's statement:] "'. . . *and put the stone back in its place
         upon the mouth of the well:*' for the coming journeys.

Thus the first interpretation applies the passage at hand to the life of Israel in the wilderness. The premise is the prevailing syllogism: Israel's future history is lived out, the first time around, in the lives of the patriarchs and matriarchs.

3.   A. " *'As he looked, he saw a well in the field:'* refers to Zion.
     B. " *'. . . and lo, three flocks of sheep lying beside it:'* refers to the three festivals.
     C. " *'. . . for out of that well the flocks were watered:'* from there they drank of the holy spirit.
     D. " *'. . . The stone on the well's mouth was large:'* this refers to the rejoicing of the house of the water-drawing."
     E. Said R. Hoshaiah, "Why is it called 'the house of the water drawing'? Because from there they drink of the Holy Spirit."
     F. [Resuming Hama b. Hanina's discourse:] " *'. . . and when all the flocks were gathered there:'* coming from *'the entrance of Hamath to the brook of Egypt'* [1 Kgs. 8:66].
     G. " *'. . . the shepherds would roll the stone from the mouth of the well and water the sheep:'* for from there they would drink of the Holy Spirit.
     H. " *'. . . and put the stone back in its place upon the mouth of the well:'* leaving it in place until the coming festival.

Thus the second interpretation reads the verse in light of the Temple celebration of the Festival of Tabernacles.

4.   A. " *'. . . As he looked, he saw a well in the field:'* this refers to Zion.
     B. " *'. . . and lo, three flocks of sheep lying beside it:'* this refers to the three courts, concerning which we have learned in the Mishnah: There were three courts there, one at the gateway of the Temple mount, one at the gateway of the courtyard, and one in the chamber of the hewn stones [M. San. 11:2].
     C. " *'. . . for out of that well the flocks were watered:'* for from there they would hear the ruling.
     D. " *'The stone on the well's mouth was large:'* this refers to the high court that was in the chamber of the hewn stones.
     E. " *'. . . and when all the flocks were gathered there:'* this refers to the courts in session in the Land of Israel.
     F. " *'. . . the shepherds would roll the stone from the mouth of the well and water the sheep:'* for from there they would hear the ruling.
     G. " *'. . . and put the stone back in its place upon the mouth of the well:'* for they would give and take until they had produced the ruling in all the required clarity."

The third interpretation reads the verse in light of the Israelite institution of justice and administration. The intrusion of the cited passage of the Mishnah alerts us to the striking difference between our document and Sifra and Sifré to Numbers. The Mishnah passage serves as mere illustration. It does not generate the question to be answered, nor does it come under detailed amplification itself. It is in no way a focus of interest.

5.   A. " *'As he looked, he saw a well in the field:'* this refers to Zion.
     B. " *'. . . and lo, three flocks of sheep lying beside it:'* this refers to the first three kingdoms [Babylonia, Media, Greece].

C. *"'. . . for out of that well the flocks were watered:'* for they enriched the treasures that were laid up in the chambers of the Temple.

D. *"'. . . The stone on the well's mouth was large:'* this refers to the merit attained by the patriarchs.

E. *"'. . . and when all the flocks were gathered there:'* this refers to the wicked kingdom, which collects troops through levies from all the nations of the world.

F. *"'. . . the shepherds would roll the stone from the mouth of the well and water the sheep:'* for they enriched the treasures that were laid up in the chambers of the Temple.

G. *"'. . . and put the stone back in its place upon the mouth of the well:'* in the age to come the merit attained by the patriarchs will stand [in defense of Israel]."

So the fourth interpretation interweaves the themes of the Temple cult and the domination of the four monarchies.

6.   A. *"'As he looked, he saw a well in the field:'* this refers to the sanhedrin.

B. *"'. . . and lo, three flocks of sheep lying beside it:'* this alludes to the three rows of disciples of sages that would go into session in their presence.

C. *"for out of that well the flocks were watered:'* for from there they would listen to the ruling of the law.

D. *"'. . . The stone on the well's mouth was large:'* this refers to the most distinguished member of the court, who determines the law-decision.

E. *"'. . . and when all the flocks were gathered there:'* this refers to disciples of the sages in the Land of Israel.

F. *"'. . . the shepherds would roll the stone from the mouth of the well and water the sheep:'* for from there they would listen to the ruling of the law.

G. *"'. . . and put the stone back in its place upon the mouth of the well:'* for they would give and take until they had produced the ruling in all the required clarity."

The fifth interpretation again reads the verse in light of the Israelite institution of legal education and justice.

7.   A. *"'As he looked, he saw a well in the field:'* this refers to the synagogue.

B. *"'. . . and lo, three flocks of sheep lying beside it:'* this refers to the three who are called to the reading of the Torah on weekdays.

C. *"'. . . for out of that well the flocks were watered:'* for from there they hear the reading of the Torah.

D. *"'. . . The stone on the well's mouth was large:'* this refers to the impulse to do evil.

E. *"'. . . and when all the flocks were gathered there:'* this refers to the congregation.

F. *"'. . . the shepherds would roll the stone from the mouth of the well and water the sheep:'* for from there they hear the reading of the Torah.

G. *"'. . . and put the stone back in its place upon the mouth of the well:'* for once they go forth [from the hearing of the reading of the torah] the impulse to do evil reverts to its place."

The sixth and last interpretation turns to the twin themes of the reading of the Torah in the synagogue and the evil impulse, temporarily driven off through the hearing of the Torah.

The six themes read in response to the verse cover (1) Israel in the wilderness, (2) the Temple cult on festivals with special reference to Tabernacles, (3) the judiciary and government, (4) the history of Israel under the four kingdoms, (5) the life of sages, and (6) the ordinary folk and the synagogue. The whole is an astonishing repertoire of fundamental themes of the life of the nation, Israel: at its origins in the wilderness, in its cult, in its institutions based on the cult, in the history of the nations, and, finally, in the twin social estates of sages and ordinary folk, matched by the institutions of the master-disciple circle and the synagogue. The vision of Jacob at the well thus encompassed the whole of the social reality of Jacob's people, Israel. The labor of interpreting this passage in the profound typological context already established now goes forward.

LXX:IX.

1. A. R. Yohanan interpreted the statement in terms of Sinai:
    B. "'*As he looked, he saw a well in the field:*' this refers to Sinai.
    C. "'*. . . and lo, three flocks of sheep lying beside it:*' these stand for the priests, Levites, and Israelites.
    D. "'*. . . for out of that well the flocks were watered:*' for from there they heard the Ten Commandments.
    E. "'*. . . The stone on the well's mouth was large:*' this refers to the Presence of God."
    F. "*. . . and when all the flocks were gathered there:*"
    G. R. Simeon b. Judah of Kefar Akum in the name of R. Simeon: "All of the flocks of Israel had to be present, for if any one of them had been lacking, they would not have been worthy of receiving the Torah."
    H. [Returning to Yohanan's exposition:] "'*. . . the shepherds would roll the stone from the mouth of the well and water the sheep:*' for from there they heard the Ten Commandments.
    I. "'*. . . and put the stone back in its place upon the mouth of the well:*' 'You yourselves have seen that I have talked with you from heaven*' [Ex. 20:19]."

Yohanan's exposition adds what was left out, namely, reference to the revelation of the Torah at Sinai. As though the demonstration of the ubiquitous syllogism that Israel's history is the story of the lives of the founders, we now go over the same proposition again with utterly fresh materials. Doing so shows that the proposed syllogism states the deep structure of reality, the syntax that permits words to make diverse yet intelligible statements. Once we have taken up the challenge of the foregoing, a still greater task requires us to make the same basic point in utterly different cases, allowing us definitively to demonstrate that syllogism as it is tested against diverse cases presented by Scripture's facts.

LXX:X.

1. A. "Jacob said to them, '*My brothers, where do you come from?*' They said, '*We are from Haran*'" [Gen. 29:40]:
    B. R. Yosé bar Haninah interpreted the verse at hand with reference to the Exile.
    C. "'Jacob said to them, "*My brothers, where do you come from*"' They said, "*We are from Haran:*" that is, 'We are flying from the wrath of the Holy One,

blessed be he.' [Here there is a play on the words for "Haran" and "wrath," which share the same consonants.]

D. " '*He said to them, "Do you know Laban the son of Nahor?"* ' The sense is this, 'Do you know him who is destined to bleach your sins as white as snow?' [Here there is a play on the words for "Laban" and "bleach," which share the same consonants.]

E. " '*They said, "We know him." He said to them, "Is it well with him?" They said, "It is well."* ' On account of what sort of merit?

F. [Yosé continues his interpretation:] " '[The brothers go on,] "*. . . and see, Rachel his daughter is coming with the sheep*" ' [Gen. 29:6–7].

G. "That is in line with this verse: '*Thus says the Lord, "A voice is heard in Ramah, lamentation and bitter weeping, Rachel weeping for her children. She refuses to be comforted." Thus says the Lord, "Refrain your voice from weeping . . . and there is hope for your future," says the Lord, and your children shall return to their own border*" ' [Jer. 31:15–16]."

Now the history of the redemption of Israel is located in the colloquy between Jacob and Laban's sons. The themes pour forth in profusion, forming subordinate propositions.

LXX:XI.

1.   A. ["*He said to them, 'Is it well with him?' They said, 'It is well; and see, Rachel his daughter is coming with the sheep'*" (Lev. 29:6–7)]: "*He said to them, 'Is it well with him?'* " "*Is there peace between him and you?*"

   B. "*They said, 'It is well.'* And if it is gossip that you want, "*see, Rachel his daughter is coming with the sheep.*" ' "

   C. That is in line with this saying: "*Women like gossip.*"

2.   A. "*He said, 'Behold, it is still [high day, it is not time for the animals to be gathered together; water the sheep and go, pasture them.' But they said, 'We cannot until all the flocks are gathered together, and the stone is rolled from the mouth of the well; then we water the sheep']*" [Gen. 29:7–8]:

   B. He said to them, "If you are hired hands, '*it is still high day.*' [You have no right to water the flock so early in the day.]

   C. "*If you are shepherding your own flock: 'It is not time for the animals to be gathered together.'* [It is not in your interest to do so.]"

3.   A. "*They said, 'We cannot. . . .' While he was still speaking with them, Rachel came*" [Gen. 29:9]:

   B. Said Rabban Simeon b. Gamaliel, "Come and note the difference between one neighborhood and the next.

   C. "Elsewhere [in Midian, when the daughters of Jethro came to water their flocks,] there were seven women, and the shepherds wanted to give them a hard time, as it is said, '*And the shepherds came and drove them away*' [Ex. 2:17].

   D. "Here, by contrast, there was only one woman, and yet not one of them laid a hand on her, because '*The angel of the Lord encamps around about those who fear him and delivers them*' [Ps. 34:8].

   E. "This refers to those who live in a neighborhood of those who fear him."

Sections 1 and 2 articulate the conversation between Jacob and the shepherds. Section 3 draws a more general conclusion, using the verse at hand to demonstrate the contrast necessary for the syllogism: It is safer to live in a Jewish neighborhood.

LXX:XII.

1.   A. *"Now when Jacob saw Rachel, the daughter of Laban his mother's brother, and the sheep of Laban, his mother's brother, Jacob went up and rolled the stone [from the well's mouth and watered the flock of Laban his mother's brother. Then Jacob kissed Rachel and wept aloud. And Jacob told Rachel that he was Rebecca's son, and she ran and told her father]"* [Gen. 29:10–12]:

    B. Said R. Yohanan, "He did it without effort, like someone who takes a stopper out of a flask."

2.   A. *"Then Jacob kissed Rachel:"*

In Genesis Rabbah the sages show in detail the profound depths of the story of the creation of the world and Israel's founding family. Bringing their generative proposition about the character of the Scripture to the stories at hand, they systematically found in the details of the tales the history of the people Israel portrayed in the lives and deeds of the founders, the fathers and the mothers of this book of the Torah. It is no accident that the exegetes of the book of Genesis invoke large-scale constructions of history to make fundamental judgments about society—Israel's society. Nor is it merely happenstance that the exegetes bring into juxtaposition distinct facts—passages—of scriptural history or appeal to a metaphorical reading of the humble details of the scriptural tale, the simple statement that the shepherds had brought their flocks to the well, for example. A large proposition has governed the details of exegesis, and the individual verses commonly, though not always, address their facts in the proof of an encompassing hypothesis, a theorem concerning Israel's fate and faith.

5 Imitating God: Virtue and the Doctrine of Emotions

JACOB NEUSNER

1. Why is this reading important?

This reading deepens our understanding of the Judaism of the dual Torah, which is set forth in terms of doctrine and practice in *The Way of Torah*. But religion affects how people feel as much as, perhaps more than, they think. Religion also takes an interest in the emotions that move people, and many religions set forth doctrines of virtuous emotions and sinful ones as well. Emotions, moreover, spill over into attitudes, and religions catalogue the attitudes to be cultivated—generosity, humility—and those to be suppressed—envy, lust. So no picture of Judaism is complete without the doctrine of virtue expressed in emotions, and a view of a religion that stresses what people (are supposed to) believe but not how they are supposed to live their everyday lives is grossly incomplete. Here you will find a review of what you saw in Tractate Abot.

2. What should you notice as you proceed?

Three facts are striking: First you will notice how much weight is placed upon right attitude and feeling. Second, you will find how unchanging the doctrine of emotions is as we move from one writing to its successor. (Other doctrines, such as the Messiah theme, show considerable variation over time.) Third, you will see that, beginning to end, the Judaism of the dual Torah has a few simple lessons to teach on this subject. That is a sign that you are at the very center of a religious system.

3. How should you frame a question for class discussion in response to what you have read?

Why does Judaism place the highest value on humility and restraint? Can you translate that doctrine of emotions into (1) public policy? What sort of foreign policy would this theoretical model of Israel define for itself? How do you think people who live in accord with this doctrine of emotions would conduct themselves in public places? What sort of

(2) family life would emerge among people raised in these patterns? Once you have defined the kind of social order and personal life nurtured in these pages, ask yourself two further questions: (1) at what cost? and (2) for what end? Do you think these teachings work for ordinary folk, not saints? What kind of community do the sages envisage for their holy Israel to embody?

The Ethics of the Right Attitude

The sages' Judaism for a defeated people prepared the nation for a long future. The vanquished people, the brokenhearted nation that had lost its city and its Temple—that had, moreover, produced another nation from its midst to take over its Scripture and much else—could not bear too much reality. That defeated people, in its intellectuals, as represented in the Rabbinic sources, found refuge in a mode of thought that trained vision to see things otherwise than as the eyes perceived them. That is the vision of Midrash, as we saw in Genesis Rabbah. Among the diverse ways by which the weak and subordinated accommodate to their circumstance, the way of iron-willed pretense in life is most likely to yield the mode of thought that maintains that things never are, because they cannot be, what they seem. The uniform tradition on emotions persisted intact because the social realities of Israel's life proved permanent, until they changed in our own time. Rabbinic Judaism's Israel was instructed on how to tame its heart and govern its wild emotions, to accept with resignation, to endure with patience, and above all, to value the attitudes and emotions that made acceptance and endurance plausible.

The sages of Rabbinic Judaism taught not only what Israel was supposed to do or not do, but also what Israel was supposed to feel. And that was how they accomplished their most difficult task, the transformation of the Jews to conform to the picture of "Israel" that the sages set forth and proposed to bring into being. From beginning to end, the documents of Rabbinic Judaism set forth a single, consistent, and coherent doctrine: the true Israelite was to exhibit the moral virtues of subservience, patience, endurance, and hope. These virtues would translate into the emotional traits of humility and forbearance. And they would yield to social virtues of passivity and conciliation. The hero was one who overcame impulses; the truly virtuous person was the one who reconciled others by giving way before their opinions.

All of these acts of self-abnegation and self-denial, accommodation rather than rebellion, required at the outset the right attitudes, sentiments, emotions, and impulses. The single most dominant motif of the Rabbinic writings, start to finish, is its stress on the right attitude's leading to the right action, the correct intentionality's producing the besought decision, above all, accommodating in one's heart to what could not be changed by one's action. And that meant, the world as it was. The sages prepared Israel for the long centuries of subordination and alienation by inculcating attitudes that best suited people who could govern little more than how they felt about things.

The notion that the sages taught feelings is hardly puzzling. Since Israelites are commanded to love God, it follows that an emotion, love, becomes holy when it is directed to God. The same emotion may become not only profane but sinful when it is directed to the wrong objects—self or power, for example. Accordingly, "our sages" in the definitive holy books of Judaism make plain their conviction that feelings too come to the surface as matters of judgment. Emotions constitute constructions for which we bear responsibility.

The repertoire of approved and disapproved feelings remains constant through the half-millennium of the unfolding of the canon of Judaism from the Mishnah through the Talmud of Babylonia. The emotions that are encouraged, such as humility, forbearance, accommodation, and a spirit of conciliation, exactly correspond to the political and social requirements of the Jews' condition in that time. The reason that the same repertoire of emotions persisted with no material change throughout the writings of the sages of that formative age was the constancy of the Jews' political and social condition. In the view of these sages, emotions fit together with the encompassing patterns of society and culture, theology and the religious life.

So the affective rules form an integral part of the way of life and worldview put forward to make sense of the existence of a social group. For sages, it follows that how I am supposed to feel in ethos matches what I am expected to think. In this way, as an individual, I link my deepest personal emotions to the cosmic fate and transcendent faith of that social group of which I form a part. Emotions lay down judgments. They derive from rational cognition. The individual Israelite's innermost feelings, the microcosm, correspond to the public and historic condition of Israel, the macrocosm.

What Rabbinic Judaism teaches the private person to feel links her or his heart to how that same Judaism describes the condition of Israel in history and of God in the cosmos. All form one reality, in supernatural world and nature, in time and in eternity wholly consubstantial (so to speak). In the innermost chambers of deepest feelings, the Israelite therefore lives out the public history and destiny of the people, Israel. The genius of Rabbinic Judaism, the reason for its resilience and endurance, lies in its power to teach Jews to feel in private what they also must think in public about the condition of self and nation alike. The world within, the world without are so bonded that one is never alone. The individual's life always is lived with the people.

The notion of the centrality of human feelings in the religious life of Israel presents no surprises. Scripture is explicit on both sides of the matter. The human being is commanded to love God. In the biblical biography of God, the tragic hero God will despair, love, hope, feel disappointment or exultation. The biblical record of God's feelings and God's will on the feelings of humanity—wanting human love, for example—leaves no room for doubt. Nor does the Judaism that emerges from Late Antiquity ignore or propose to obliterate the datum that "the merciful God wants the heart." The Judaism of the rabbis of Late Antiquity makes explicit that God always wants the heart. God commands that humanity love God with full heart, soul, mind, and might. That is the principal duty of humanity.

So without the rabbinic canon and merely on the basis of knowledge that that canon begins in the written Torah of Scripture, the facts about the critical place of religious affections in Israel's religion would still prove clear and one sided. Just as the sages framed matters of the Written Torah in a fresh and original way, all the time stating in their own language and categories the teachings of the Written Torah, so here too we ask where, when, how, and for what purpose did rabbinical authorships draw upon the legacy of the Written Torah in concluding, as they did, "the Merciful God wants the heart"?

Emotion as Tradition

In the unfolding components of the canon of Judaism, emotions form part of an iron tradition. From the first to the final document, a single doctrine and program dictated what people had to say on how Israel should tame its heart. That is, the matter of feelings was governed by a repertoire of rules and relationships handed on from the past, always intact and ever unimpaired. The labor of the generations meant to receive the repertoire and recipe for feeling proved one of only preserving and maintaining that tradition. Successive documents added improvements while leaving the structure basically the same. Like a cathedral that takes a thousand years to build but always looks uniform throughout construction as well as at the end, so the view of the affective life over centuries remained not only cogent but essentially uniform.

The sources, read sequentially, do not. Even though the formative centuries of the history of Judaism overall mark a period of remarkable growth and change, with sequenced developments in various substantial ideas and generative conceptions, here, in the matter of emotions, it does not. The single fact emerging from a canonical survey is that the sages' doctrine of affections remained a constant in an age of change.

The Mishnah casually refers to emotions—for example, tears of joy, tears of sorrow—but always in a public and communal context. For one important example, where there is an occasion of rejoicing, one form of joy is not to be confused with some other, or one context of sorrow with another. Accordingly, marriages are not to be held on festivals (M.M.Q. 1:7); likewise, mourning is not to take place at such times (M.M.Q. 1:5, 3:7–9). Where emotions play a role, it is because of the affairs of the community at large, rejoicing on a festival, mourning on a fast day (M. Suk. 5:1–4). Emotions are to be kept in hand, as in the case of the relatives of an executed felon (M. San. 6:6). If one had to specify the single underlying principle governing all displays of emotion in the Mishnah, it is that feelings must be kept under control, never fully expressed without reasoning about the appropriate context. Emotions must always lay down judgments.

We see in most of those cases in which emotions play a systemic, not merely a tangential, role, that we can, and must, frame our feelings to accord with the appropriate rule. In only one case does emotion play a decisive role in settling an issue, and that has to do with whether or not a farmer was happy that water came upon his produce or grain. That case underlines the conclusion just now drawn. If people feel a given sentiment, it is a matter of judgment and therefore invokes the law's penalties. So in this system emotions are not treated as spontaneous, but as significant aspects of a person's judgment. It would be difficult to find a more striking example of that view that at M. Makh. 4:5 and related passages. The very fact that the law applies comes about because the framers judged the farmer's feelings to constitute, on their own and without associated actions or even conceptions, final and decisive judgments on what happened.

The reason that emotions form so critical a focus of concern in Rabbinic Judaism is that God and the human being share traits of attitude and emotion. They want the same thing, respond in the same way to the same events, share not only ownership of the Land of Israel but also a viewpoint on the value of its produce. For example, in the law of tithing, the produce becomes liable to tithing—that is, giving to God's surrogate God's share of the crop of the Holy Land—when the farmer deems the crop to be desirable. Why is that so? When the farmer wants the crop, so does God. When the householder takes the view that the crop is worthwhile, God responds to the attitude of the farmer by forming the same opinion. The theological anthropology that brings God and the householder into the same continuum prepares the way for understanding what makes the entire Mishnaic system work.

The intention and will of the human being is critical as we move from theological to philosophical thought in the Mishnah's system. "Intention" stands for attitude, and, as we have already noted, attitude cannot be distinguished from emotion. For the discussion on intention works out several theories concerning not God and God's relationship to humanity but the nature of the human will. Unlike beasts and, as a matter of fact, angels (who do not, in fact, figure in the Mishnah at all), the human being is defined not only as a sentient but also as a volitional being, who can will with effect. Only the human being, in the person of the farmer, possesses and also exercises the power of intentionality. And it is the power that intentionality possesses that forms the central consideration. Because a human being forms an intention, consequences follow, whether or not they are given material expression in gesture or even in speech. The Mishnah and the law flowing from it impute extraordinary power to the will and intentionality of the human being.

How does human will bear practical consequences? The attitude of the farmer toward the crop, like that of the Temple priest toward the offering that he carries out, affects the status of the crop. It classifies an otherwise unclassified substance. It changes the standing of an already classified beast. It shifts the status of a pile of grain, without any physical action whatsoever, from one category to another. Moreover, the attitude or will of a farmer can override the effects of the natural world—as in keeping in the status of what is dry and so unsusceptible to cultic uncleanness a pile of grain that in fact has been rained upon and wet down. An immaterial reality, shaped and reformed by the householder's attitude and plan, overrides the material effect of a rainstorm.

That example brings us to the remarkable essay on theories of the relationship between action and intention worked out in the Mishnah tractate Makhshirin and exemplified by chapter 4 of that tractate. In this tractate Judah and his son, Yosé, take up the position that ultimate deed or result is definitive of intention. What happens is retrospectively deemed to decide what one wanted to happen (M. Makhshirin 3:5–7). Other mid-second-century sages, Yosé in particular (M. Makhshirin 1:5), maintain the view that while consequence plays a role in the determination of intention, it is not exclusive and definitive. What a person wanted to make happen affects the assessment of what actually has happened.

Two positions on the interplay of action and intention suffice to make the point relevant to our inquiry. Judah has the realistic notion that a person changes his mind and his feelings shift, and therefore we adjudge a case solely by what he does and not by what he says he will do, intends, or has intended to do. If we turn Judah's statement around, we come up with the conception predominant throughout his rulings: *A case is judged solely in terms of what the person does.* We know it is not subject to the original intention, because the person's action has not accomplished the original intention or has placed limits upon the original intention. What is done is wholly determinative of what was originally intended, and that is the case whether the result is that the water is deemed capable or incapable of imparting susceptibility to uncleanness. Action defines emotion. Yosé at M. Makhshirin 1:5 expresses the contrary view. He rejects the view that what is done is wholly determinative of what is originally intended. We sort things out by appeal to nuances of effect.

The Doctrine of Emotions in Tractate Abot

Tractate Abot presents the single most comprehensive account of religious affections. The reason is that in this document above all, how we feel defines a critical aspect of virtue. The issue proves central, not peripheral. The doctrine emerges fully exposed. A simple catalogue of permissible feelings comprises humility, generosity, self-abnegation, love, a spirit of conciliation of the other, and eagerness to please. A list of impermissible emotions is made up of envy, ambition, jealousy, arrogance, sticking to one's opinion, self-centeredness, a grudging spirit, vengefulness, and the like. People should aim at eliciting from others acceptance and goodwill and should likewise avoid confrontation, rejection, and humiliation of others. This they do through conciliation and giving up their own claims and rights. So both catalogues form a harmonious and uniform whole, aiming at the cultivation of the humble and malleable person, one who accepts everything and resents nothing. Here are some representative sentiments:

TRACTATE ABOT

2:4 A. He would say, "Make his wishes into your own wishes, so that he will make your wishes into his wishes.

B. "Put aside your wishes on account of his wishes, so that he will put aside the wishes of other people in favor of your wishes."

3:10 A. He would say, "Anyone from whom people take pleasure—the Omnipresent takes pleasure.

B. "And anyone from whom people do not take pleasure, the Omnipresent does not take pleasure."

4:1 A. Ben Zoma says, "Who is a sage? He who learns from everybody,

B. "as it is said, From all my teachers I have gotten understanding [Ps. 119:99].

C. "Who is strong? He who overcomes his desire,

D. "as it is said, He who is slow to anger is better than the mighty, and he who rules his spirit than he who takes a city [Prov. 16:32].

E. "Who is rich? He who is happy in what he has,

F. "as it is said, When you eat the labor of your hands, happy will you be, and it will go well with you [Ps. 128:2].

G. ("Happy will you be in this world, and it will go well with you in the world to come.")

H. "Who is honored? He who honors everybody,

I. "as it is said, 'For those who honor me I shall honor, and they who despise me will be treated as of no account' [I Sam. 2:30]."

4:18 A. R. Simeon b. Eleazar says, "(1) Do not try to make amends with your fellow when he is angry,

    B. "or (2) comfort him when the corpse of his beloved is lying before him,

    C. "or (3) seek to find absolution for him at the moment at which he takes a vow,

    D. "or (4) attempt to see him when he is humiliated."

4:19 A. Samuel the Small says, "Rejoice not when your enemy falls, and let not your heart be glad when he is overthrown, lest the Lord see it and it displease him, and he turn away his wrath from him [Prov. 24:17]."

True, these virtues, in this tractate as in the system as a whole, derive from knowledge of what really counts, which is what God wants. But God favors those who please others. The virtues appreciated by human beings prove identical to the ones to which God responds as well. And what single virtue of the heart encompasses the rest? Restraint, the source of self-abnegation and humility, serves as the antidote for ambition, vengefulness, and, above all, arrogance. It is restraint of our own interest that enables us to deal generously with others, humility about ourselves that generates a liberal spirit towards others.

So the emotions prescribed in Tractate Abot turn out to provide variations of a single feeling, which is the sentiment of the disciplined heart, whatever affective form it may take. And where does the heart learn its lessons, if not in relationship to God? So: "Make his wishes yours, so that he will make your wishes his" [Abot 2:4]. Applied to the relationships between human beings, this inner discipline of the emotional life will yield exactly those virtues of conciliation and self-abnegation, humility and generosity of spirit, that the framers of Tractate Abot spell out in one example after another. Imputing to Heaven exactly those responses felt on earth, such as "Anyone from whom people take pleasure, God takes pleasure" (Abot 3:10), makes the point at the most general level.

Humility and Accommodation in the Tosefta and the Yerushalmi

When the authors or compilers of the Tosefta finished their labor of amplification and complement, they had succeeded in adding only a few fresh and important developments of established themes. What is striking is first of all the stress upon the communal stake in an individual's emotional life. Still more striking is the Tosefta's authors' explicit effort to invoke an exact correspondence between public and private feelings. In both realms emotions are to be tamed, kept in hand and within accepted proportions. Public sanctions for inappropriate, or disproportionate, emotions entail emotions, such as shame. It need hardly be added that feeling shame for improper feelings once again underlines the social and judgmental character of those feelings. For shame is public, guilt private. People are responsible for how they feel as much as for how, in word or deed, they express feeling. Hence an appropriate penalty derives from the same aspect of social life, that is, the affective life.

There is no more stunning tribute to the power of feeling than the allegation, surfacing in the Tosefta, that the Temple was destroyed because of vain hatred. That sort of hatred, self-serving and arrogant, stands against the feelings of love that characterize God's relationship to Israel. Accordingly, it was improper affections that destroyed the relationship embodied in the Temple cult of old. Given the critical importance accorded to the Temple cult, sages could not have made more vivid their view that how a private person feels shapes the public destiny of the entire nation. So the issues came to expression in a context in which the stakes are very high. But the basic position of the authors of the Mishnah, inclusive of their first apologists in Abot, seems entirely consistent. What Tosefta's authors accomplished is precisely what they claimed, which was to amplify, supplement, and complement established principles and positions.

The principal result of this survey of the present topic in the Yerushalmi has confirmed the one dominant result throughout. Emotions not taken up earlier did not come under discussion now. Principles introduced earlier enjoyed restatement and extensive exemplification. Some principles of proper feelings might even generate secondary developments of one kind or another. But nothing not present at the outset drew sustained attention later on. The system proved essentially complete in the earliest statement of its main points. Everything that followed for four hundred years served to reinforce and restate what had emerged loud and clear to begin with. What, then, do the authors or compilers of the Yerushalmi contribute? That temper marks the ignorant person, restraint and serenity the learned one. In general, where the Mishnah introduces into its system issues of the affective life, the Yerushalmi's authors and compilers will take up those issues. But they rarely create them on their own and never say much new about those they do treat. What we find is instruction to respect public opinion and cultivate social harmony.

What is most interesting in the Yerushalmi is the recognition that there are rules for feelings as much as for other facts of life. These rules tell us how to dispose of cases in which feelings make a difference. The effects of emotions, as much as of opinions or deeds, come within the rule of law. It must follow, in the view of sages, that the affective life once more proves an aspect of society. People are assumed to frame emotions, as much as opinions, in line with common and shared judgments. In no way do emotions form a special classification, one expressive of what is private, spontaneous, individual, and beyond the law and reason.

The Bavli's Recapitulation

The Bavli carried forward with little change the now traditional program of emotions, listing the same ones catalogued earlier and no new ones. The authors said about those feelings what had been said earlier: A leader must be someone acceptable to the community. God then accepts him, too. People should be ready to give up quarrels and forgive. Social and personal virtues correspond; the community must forbear, the individual must forgive. Communal tolerance for causeless hatred destroyed the Temple; individual vendettas yield miscarriages. The two coincide. In both cases people nurture feelings that express arrogance. Arrogance is what permits the individual to express emotions without discipline, and arrogance is what leads the community to undertake what it cannot accomplish.

A fresh emphasis in the Bavli favored mourning and disapproved of rejoicing: Excessive levity marks arrogance, deep mourning characterizes humility. The nurture of an attitude of mourning should mark both the individual and the community, both in mourning for the Temple and also in mourning for the condition of nature, including the human condition, signified in the Temple's destruction.

A mark of humility is humble acceptance of suffering. This carried forward the commonplace view that suffering now produces joy later on. The ruin of the Temple, for example, served as a guarantee that just as the prophetic warnings came to realization, so too would prophetic promises of restoration and redemption. In the realm of feelings, the union of opposites came about through the same mode of thought. Hence God's love comes to fulfillment in human suffering, and the person who joyfully accepts humiliation or suffering will enjoy the appropriate divine response of love.

The basic motif—theological as much as affective—encompassing all materials is simple. Israel is estranged from God and therefore should exhibit the traits of humility and uncertainty, acceptance and conciliation. When God recognizes the proper feelings in Israel's heart, as much as in the nation's deeds and deliberation, God will respond by ending that estrangement that marks the present age. So the single word encompassing the entire affective doctrine of the canon of Judaism is alienation. No contemporary, surviving the Holocaust, can miss the psychological depth of the system, which joins the human condition to the fate of the nation and the world and links the whole to the broken heart of God.

We therefore find ourselves where we started, in those sayings that state that if one wants something, he or she should aspire to its opposite. Things are never what they seem. To be rich, accept what you have. To be powerful, conciliate your enemy. To be endowed with public recognition in which to take pride, express humility. So, too, the doctrine of the emotional life expressed in law, scriptural interpretation, and tales of sages alike turns out to be uniform and simple. Emotions well up uncontrolled and spontaneous. Anger, vengeance, pride, arrogance—these people feel by nature. So feelings as much as affirmations and actions must become what by nature they are not. If one wants riches, seek the opposite; if honor, pursue the opposite. But how do people seek the opposite of wealth? It is by accepting what they have. And how to pursue humility, if not by doing nothing to aggrandize oneself?

So the life of the emotions, in conformity to the life of reflection and of concrete deed, will consist in the transformation of what things *seem* into what they *ought* to be. No contemporary psychologists or philosophers can fail to miss the point. Here we have an example of the view—whether validated by the facts of nature or not—that emotions constitute constructs, and feelings lay down judgments. So the heart belongs, together with the mind, to the human being's power to form reasoned viewpoints. Coming from sages, intellectuals to their core, such an opinion surely coheres with the context and circumstance of those who hold it.

Seeing Things as if They Were Not What They Seem

This theory of the emotional life, persistent through the unfolding of the canonical documents of Judaism, fits into a larger way of viewing the world. How shall we describe this mode of thought? We may call it an *as-if* way of seeing things. That is to say, it is *as if* a common object or symbol really represented an uncommon one. Nothing says what it means. Everything important speaks symbolically. All statements carry deeper meaning, which inheres in other statements altogether. So, too, each emotion bears a negative and a positive charge, as each matches and balances the other: humility, arrogance, love, hate. If a negative emotion is natural to the heart, then the individual has the power to sanctify that negative, sinful feeling and turn it into a positive, holy emotion. Ambition then must be tamed, so transformed into humility; hatred and vengeance must change into love and acceptance.

What we see is an application of a large-scale, encompassing exercise in analogical thinking—something is like something else; it stands for, evokes, or symbolizes that which is quite outside itself. It may be the opposite of something else, in which case it conforms to the exact opposite of the rules that govern that something else. The reasoning is analogical or it is contrastive, and the fundamental logic is taxonomic. The taxonomy rests on those comparisons and contrasts we should call parabolic. In that case, what lies on the surface misleads. What lies beneath or beyond the surface—there is the true reality. People who see things this way constitute the opposite of ones who call a thing as it is. Self-evidently, they have become accustomed to perceiving more—or less—than is at hand. Perhaps that is a natural mode of thought for the Jews of this period (and not then alone), so long used to calling themselves God's first love, yet now seeing others with greater worldly reason claiming that same advantaged relationship.

Not in mind only, but still more in the politics of the world, the people who remembered its origins along with the very creation of the world and founding of humanity—who recalled how it alone served, and serves, the one and only God— for hundreds of years had confronted a quite different existence. The radical disjuncture between the way things were and the way Scripture said things were supposed to be (and would some day become) surely imposed an unbearable tension. It was one thing for the slave born to slavery to endure. It was another for the free man sold into slavery to accept that same condition. The vanquished people, the brokenhearted nation that had in 586 B.C.E. and again in 70 B.C.E. lost its city and its Temple, that had, moreover, in the fourth century produced another nation from its midst to take over its Scripture and much else, could not bear too much reality. That defeated people, in its intellectuals, as represented in the sources we have surveyed, then found refuge in a mode of thought that trained vision to see things otherwise than as the eyes perceived them. Israel is to tame its heart so that it will feel that same humility within, that Israel's worldview and way of living demand in life, at large. Submit, accept, conciliate, stay cool in emotion as much as in attitude, inside and outside—and the Messiah will come.

Forbearance or Aggression

The profound program of emotions, the sages' statement of how people should feel and why they should take charge of their emotions, remained remarkably constant. No one can imagine that Jews in their hearts felt the way sages said they should. The repertoire of permissible and forbidden feelings can hardly have defined the broad range of actual emotions, whether private or social, of the community of Israel. In fact, we have no evidence about how people really felt. We see only a picture of what sages thought they should, and should not, feel. Writings that reveal stunning shifts in doctrine, teleology, and hermeneutical method form from beginning to end the one picture of the ideal Israelite. It is someone who accepts, forgives, conciliates, makes the soul "like dirt beneath other people's feet." These kinds of people receive little respect in the world we now know; they are called cowards. Self-assertion is admired, conciliatory attitudes despised. Ours is an age that admires the strong-minded individual, the uncompromising hero, the warrior whether on the battlefield or in the intellect. Courage takes the form of confrontation, which therefore takes precedence over accommodation in the order of public virtue.

Why the sages counseled a different kind of courage is clear enough. Given the situation of Israel, vanquished on the battlefield, broken in the turning of history's wheel, we need hardly wonder why wise men advised conciliation and acceptance. Exalting humility made sense, there being little choice. Whether or not these virtues found advocates in other contexts for other reasons, in the circumstance of the vanquished nation, for the people of broken heart, the policy of forbearance proved instrumental, entirely appropriate to both the politics and social condition at hand. If Israel had produced a battlefield hero, the nation could not give him an army. If Jewry cultivated the strong-minded individual, it sentenced such a person to a useless life of ineffective protest. The nation required not strong-minded leadership but consensus.

The social virtues of conciliation moreover reinforced the bonds that joined the nation lacking frontiers, the people without a politics of its own. For all there was to hold Israel together would have to issue from inner strength. Bonding emerged mainly from within. So consensus, conciliation, self-abnegation and humility, the search for acceptance without the group—these defined appropriate emotions in that literary culture because they dictated wise policy and shrewd politics.

Vanquished Israel therefore would nurture not merely policies of subordination and acceptance of diminished status among nations. Israel also would develop, in its own heart, the requisite emotional structure. The composition of individuals' hearts would then comprise the counterpart virtues. A policy of acceptance of the rule of others dictated affections of conciliation to the will of others. A defeated people meant to endure defeat would have to get along by going along. How to persuade each Jew to accept what all Jews had to do to endure? Persuade the heart, not only the mind. Then each one privately would feel what everyone publicly had in any case to think.

That accounts for the persistence of the sages' wise teachings on temper, their sagacious counsel on conciliating others and seeking the approval of the group. Society, in the canonical writings, set the style for the self's deepest sentiments. So the approved feelings retained approval for so long because emotions in the thought of the sages of the canon followed rules. They formed public, not personal and private, facts. Feelings laid down judgments. Affections therefore constituted not mindless effusions but deliberate constructions. Whether or not the facts then conformed to the sages' view (or now with the frameworks of psychology, philosophy, and anthropology) we do not know. But the sages' view did penetrate deeply into what had to be. And that is so whether or not what had to be ever corresponded with what was.

The sages of the formative age of Judaism proposed for Israel the formation of exactly that type of personality that could and did endure the condition and circumstance of the Exile. The doctrine of the Messiah makes this point as well. In rejecting the heroic model of Bar Kokhba for the Messiah general's arrogance and affirming the very opposite, the sages who defined Judaism in the first seven centuries C.E. and whose heirs expanded and developed the system they had defined made the right choice. From the end of the second revolt against Rome in 135 to the creation of the state of Israel in 1948, Israel, the Jewish people, faced a different task. Living in other peoples' countries and not in their own land meant for Israel, as Judaism conceived Israel, a long span of endurance, a test of patience to end only with the end of time. That required Israel to live in accord with the will of others. Under such circumstances the virtues of the independent citizen, sharing command of affairs of state, the gifts of innovation, initiative, independence of mind, proved beside the point.

The human condition of Israel therefore defined a different heroism, one filled with patience, humiliation, self-abnegation. To turn survival into endurance, pariah status into an exercise in Godly living, the sages' affective program served full well. Israel's hero saw power in submission, wealth in the gift be grateful, wisdom in the confession of ignorance. Like the cross, ultimate degradation was made to stand for ultimate power. Like Jesus on the cross, so Israel in exile served God through suffering. True, the cross would represent a scandal to the nations and foolishness to some Jews. But Israel's own version of the doctrine endured and defined the nation's singular and astonishing resilience. For Israel did endure and endures today.

If, then, as a matter of public policy, the nurture of the Israelite as a person of forbearance and self-abnegation proved right, within the community too the rabbis were not wrong. The Jewish people rarely enjoyed instruments of civil coercion capable of preserving social order and coherence. Governments at best afforded Jews limited rights over their own affairs. When, at the start of the fifth century, the Christian Roman government ended the existence of the patriarchate of the Jews of the Land of Israel, it created a parlous state of affairs. A government in charge of itself and its subjects, a territorial community able routinely to force individuals to pay taxes and otherwise conform where necessary—these political facts of normality rarely marked the condition of Israel between 429 C.E. and 1948. What was left was another kind of power, civil obedience generated by force from within. The stress on pleasing others and conforming to the will of the group, so characteristic of the sayings of the sages, the emphasis that God likes people whom people like—these substitutes for the civil power of political coercion imparted to the community of Israel a different power of authority.

Both sources of power, the one in relationship to the public world beyond, the other in respect to the social world within, gained force in the sages' rules through the primal energy of emotion. Enough has been said to require little explication of that fact. A system that made humility a mark of strength and a mode of gaining God's approval, a social policy that imputed ultimate virtue to feelings of conciliation, restraint, and conformity to social norms, had no need of the armies and police it did not have. The heart would serve as the best defense, inner affections as the police who are always there when needed. The remarkable inner discipline of Israel through its exacting condition in history from the beginnings of the sages' system to today began in those feelings that laid down judgments, that construction of affections, coherent with beliefs and behavior, that met the match of misery with grandeur of soul. So the vanquished nation every day would overcome the onetime victors. Israel's victory would come through the triumph of the broken heart, now mended with the remedy of moderated emotion. That union of private feeling and public policy imparted to the Judaic system of the dual Torah its power, its status as self-evidence, for the long centuries to come.

6 *The Reasons for the Commandments*

MOSES MAIMONIDES

1. Why is this reading important?

Rabbinic Judaism must be seen as a single, continuous religious system
from its initial statement in the documents of the Oral Torah of the first
six centuries C.E. to our own day. The same worldview, the same way of
life, and the same theory of who and what is Israel that was defined in
antiquity endured and continued to define normative Judaism. That is
why it is important for us to see how the great intellects of later times expressed their ideas within the ongoing and always vital tradition. Among
them the greatest was Moses Maimonides, 1135–1204, who was born in
Cordoba, Spain, fled a Muslim persecution and found refuge in more tolerant Muslim countries—first in Fez, Morocco, and later in Cairo, Egypt.
Maimonides is important because he mastered the entire legal system of
ancient times and restated its main points in two forms: theology, in his
Guide to the Perplexed, and law, in his code of the law laid out along rationalist lines, *The Repetition of the Torah (Mishneh Torah).* This reading is important because it shows how a well-trained philosophical mind looks at
the practices of the faith and explains the reasons behind them.

2. What should you notice as you proceed?

What does a philosopher want to know about the details of the law? Notice how Maimonides is trying to state a general rule that unifies and or-
ganizes the details. He picks out fundamental purposes that he thinks
the laws together are meant to accomplish. See the principles of organization that he takes for granted and ask yourself why he thinks that he
will persuade thoughtful people to keep the laws of the Torah through
this kind of presentation. The interesting question is: What does Maimonides take for granted are the main traits of the holy Israel, the Jewish community, to whom he is writing?

3. How should you frame a question for class discussion in response to what you have read?

Two questions—one historical, the other contemporary—may prove engaging. First, the historical one: How would you define Maimonides'
principal concerns, the things he thinks count most of all, in explaining
the point of the laws? These could well be listed. When you compare the

values he implicitly stresses—maintaining a just social order—with those of Moses in the Torah or with those of the rabbis of the Mishnah, do you think they are continuous and unpacked received teachings? Or does Maimonides innovate?

The contemporary question is: Do you think the emphasis on the maintenance of a stable and just society make sense for contemporary society? And do you think that these are the same answers to the question "Why keep the faith?" that other religions would give? Finally, compare and contrast these reasons set forth for Judaism with the rationale offered for a life of faith set forth by Islam, Christianity, Buddhism, and other world religions.

By the way, do you think Maimonides is right?

The Law Has a Two-Fold Intention; the Perfection of the Mind and the Welfare of the Body

The general intention of the Law is two-fold., viz.—the soundness of the body, and of the mind. *Soundness of Mind,*—that the people, according to their capacities, may obtain just sentiments of religious matters. On this account some things are declared clearly and openly, but others in parables, because of the incorrect apprehension of the unskilful multitude. *Soundness of Body,*—produced by the disposition and ordering of the food which ministers to its support; and perfected, first, by the prevention of violence, so that no one may do just what he pleases, or desires, or it is possible for him to do, but that every one may regard the public good;—and, secondly, by teaching men the virtues necessary and useful for the government of the commonwealth.

It must be acknowledged, however, that one intention of the Law excels the other, for *Soundness of Mind,* which embraces matters of belief, is certainly first in dignity, though *Soundness in Body,* as referring to the government of the commonwealth and the administration of its affairs, is first in nature and time;—and being necessary first, is therefore, with all its parts, treated the most exactly and minutely in the Law; for it is impossible to arrive at the first intention without having previously secured the second. This is demonstrable, for man is capable of a *two-fold perfection.* The first perfection is of the body;—the second perfection is of the mind.

The *first Perfection* consists in health, and the best bodily dispositions. But this cannot take place unless there be at all times a supply of necessaries, as food, and other things relating to the regimen of the body, as habitations, baths, and similar conveniences. Nor can this be effected by one man alone; (for no man's capacity is sufficient for them all;) but by the political association of a whole region or city, as it has been said—"Man is, by nature, a political animal."

The *second Perfection* is mental, and comprehends the vigorous exercise of the intellectual powers, and the knowledge of every thing possible to be known by man in his most perfect state. This perfection, therefore, includes neither works, nor qualities, nor virtues, but those of science, the result of observation and diligent inquiry. To this last and noblest perfection, it is evident, none can arrive, but through the medium of the first; for no man can attain the knowledge of all that is possible to be known, even when assisted by the instructions of others, and much less by himself, whilst he is daily affected and depressed by grief, and hunger, and thirst, and heat, and cold; but when he has gained the former perfection, he may pursue and obtain the latter:—a perfection in every way the most excellent, and especially so, because it leads to Life Eternal. The *true* Law, I mean the Law of Moses, inculcates this two-fold perfection, and even indicates that it is the design of the Law to lead men to the attainment of them. Thus it is said, "And the Lord commanded us to do all these statutes, to fear the Lord our God for our good always, that he might preserve us alive, as it is this day;" where the latter perfection is placed first because of its dignity and excellence, which is what is intimated by the words, "For our good always," agreeably to the expressions of our wise men, who say, "That it may be well with thee in that world which is *altogether* good, and *always* lasting." So, of what is here said, "That it may be for our good always," the sense is, "That thou mayest arrive at that world, which is all goodness and all duration," subsisting for ever.—But when it is said, "That he might preserve us alive, as it is this day," it is to be understood of the first and corporeal subsistence, which is only of temporary duration, and can only be perfected by the association of a whole province or city, as we have already shown.

The Mosaic Precepts Are Rational, Tending Either to the Well-Being of the Soul or of the Body

The Law designs the final perfection of man, it therefore commands us to believe in the existence and unity of God, and in his knowledge, power, will and eternity, which are all final ends, and can only be attained by various previous knowledge. It also enjoins the belief of certain principles necessary to the welfare of civil and political institutions, as "that God is angry with the wicked," and therefore ought to be feared, and wickedness cautiously avoided. But of other speculations or realities, as for instance, those reasonings by which the opinions constituting the final end are verified, the Law commands nothing expressly but only generally, as when it says, "Thou shalt love the Lord."—But how strenuously this duty is enjoined, is evident from its being added, "Thou shalt love Him with all thy heart, and with all thy soul, and with all thy strength." In our Talmudical work we have shown that no love to God is rightly established, but that which is founded on a clear and extensive view of the Divine Existence and Perfections.

The sum of this reasoning is, that every precept of the Law, whether affirmative or negative is intended, first, to prevent the exercise of violence, and encourage those virtuous habits which are necessary to the existence and preservation of Political Society; and, then, to inculcate just notions of those things where are to be believed, especially such as are useful in the prevention of violence, and the promotion of virtue. Of such precepts it may be safely affirmed, that the reason and utility of them are manifest, and that there can be no doubt of their final design; for no one can doubt or inquire, why we are commanded to believe the Unity of God; or why murder, theft, or revenge are forbidden; or why we are commanded to love one another. But those which perplex the mind, and about which men dispute,—some asserting that they have no particular utility, but are mere positive commands,—and others that they have an utility, though not always discovered by us,—are those which do not appear on the face of them to have any direct relation, either to the prevention of vice, or the promotion of virtue, or the inculcation of truth, and consequently affording no assistance to the well-being of the mind, by instruction in matters of faith, nor to the well-being of the body, by instruction in the science of Political or General Economy; such are, for instance, those precepts relating to mixed garments of linen and woollen; to divers seeds; to seething a kid in its mother's milk; to covering blood; to the decollation of the calf; to the redemption of the first-born of the ass; and other similar injunctions. The true reasons, however, of these and many other precepts of like nature, I will develop, by demonstrating, that, with the exception of some particular circumstances, and a few precepts not understood by us at present, they are all necessary either to the welfare of the Soul or Body; the latter especially being produced by the prevention of lawless violence, and the formation of virtuous habits. But let not what we have already said respecting the dogmas of faith be forgotten,—that sometimes a precept solely regards an article of belief, and has no other reference as in the case of the precepts respecting the Unity, Eternity, and Spirituality of God; but that at other times, the precept is to be believed in order to banish vice and encourage virtue; as when it is declared, that God is angry with the man who injures another; as it is said, *My wrath shall wax hot, and I will kill you with the sword;* and again, that God will speedily hear the cry of the oppressed and afflicted.

7 *Visiting the Sick, Dying, Burying the Dead: From the* Shulhan Arukh

TRANSLATED BY CHAIM N. DENBURG

1. Why is this reading important?

The Shulhan Aruch, "prepared table," is a code of the law of Judaism written by Joseph Caro. It is a synopsis of the law, guiding these topics: observance of everyday rules and those for Sabbaths and festivals; dietary laws, usury, purity, mourning; marriage and divorce; civil and criminal law. The Shulhan Arukh first appeared in 1565 in Venice and over time became the handbook of everyday observance for the world of Judaism. Like Maimonides, it is an important reading because it demonstrates the unity and continuity of Rabbinic Judaism from ancient to modern times. Most of the laws originate in Scripture or in the Mishnah and Talmud; the newer laws are mere amplifications or improvements on those laws, the whole forming a single, unitary tradition of law and theology. I have chosen the laws of burial because these are very widely observed today; Jews who do not keep other chapters of the law of Judaism very commonly wish to conduct funerals and burials in accord with the law.

2. What should you notice as you proceed?

Especially interesting is the fact that there are rules that cover matters we should not expect to be subject to fixed laws at all. How, when, and why to visit the sick; the ritualization of the act of dying; defining the prayer to be said by the dying person—all of these rules show that the most private and personal chapter of life, how we die, is made public and subject to the sanctification of the community. Notice details that indicate a certain restraint and refinement, matters you might hear discussed in a contemporary hospital. Also consider how the law of Judaism deals with the treatment of the corpse, paying enormous respect to the dying person and to the corpse afterward. You might contrast these customs with the treatment of the corpses of the Jews murdered by the Germans and their allies in World War II.

3. How should you frame a question for class discussion in response to what you have read?

The laws take up details but express a philosophy of life, and one of the interesting problems for class discussion will focus upon translating details into encompassing convictions. Why, for example, does the law of Judaism stress the simplicity of burial? What conclusion do you draw from the details that the funeral procession makes way for the bridal procession and the marriage takes priority over the burial? What are the reasons behind the rules about what a mourner may not do, and why are these rules deemed important?

[From Chapter 335: When to visit the sick, which sick persons should be visited, and how to pray for the sick.]

1. It is a religious duty to visit the sick. Relatives and close friends should enter at once, others after three days. If the illness is serious, both groups can visit him at once.

2. Even a distinguished person should visit a humble one. The more one visits the more praiseworthy it is, provided only that the visits do not become a burden to the patient.

Gloss: Some say that an enemy may not visit a sick person. However, this does not seem plausible to me. But he should not visit a sick person whom he hates lest the patient think that he is rejoicing at his misfortune and become depressed.

3. One who visits the sick should not sit upon a bed or upon a chair or upon a stool but should sit in front of the patient, for the Divine Presence rests above a sick person.

Gloss: This applies only if the patient lies upon the ground, but if the patient lies upon a bed then it is permissible for the visitor to sit upon a chair or a stool. And this is our custom.

4. One should not visit the sick during the first three hours of the day, for every patient's illness is alleviated in the morning, and consequently he will not trouble himself to pray for him; and not during the last three hours of the day, for then his illness grows worse and one will give up hope to pray for him.

Gloss: One who visited a sick person and did not pray for him has not fulfilled his religious duty.

5. When one prays for him, if in his presence, one may pray in any language; if not in his presence, one should pray in Hebrew.

6. When praying for a sick person one should combine him with all the others who are ill by saying: "May the Omnipresent have mercy upon you together with all the rest of the sick in Israel." On the Sabbath one should say: "This is the Sabbath when one must not cry and yet may recovery come soon."

7. The sick person should be advised to look over his affairs and to see if he has any debts or credits outstanding. He should be reassured that this is only a precaution and that it does not mean that he is about to die.

8. One should not visit those who are suffering from those diseases where a visit will cause the patient embarrassment or discomfort. If a person is so ill

that conversation is a strain to him, he should not be visited, but instead one should stand in the antechamber and inquire about him, and offer whatever household or nursing help he may need, and sympathize with him, and pray for him.

[From Chapter 338: The sick person's confessional.]

1. When death draws near he is advised to confess. And we reassure him: "Many have confessed and then not died just as many have not confessed and died." If he is unable to confess aloud let him confess in his heart. If he does not know what to say we instruct him to say: "May my death be an expiation for all my sins." This is not done in the presence of women and children lest they cry and break his heart.

2. The order of the confessional for a terminally ill person is set.

Gloss: But if he wishes he has the right to say more, even as much as the long confessional of the Day of Atonement.

[From Chapter 339: Laws concerning one who is dying.]

1. One who is dying is considered a living being in all respects. We may not tie up his jaws, nor remove the pillow from under him, nor place him on sand, nor summon the town on his behalf, nor close his eyes before his soul departs. And whoever closes his eyes before death, is regarded as a murderer. One may not rend garments nor make a lamentation for him nor bring a coffin into the house for him before he dies.

Gloss: Some say that we may not dig grave for him before he dies even though this is not done in his presence and he would not be aware of it. It is likewise forbidden to hasten the death of a dying man—e.g., if one has been moribund for a long time and continues to linger on, we may not remove the pillow or the mattress from under him or do anything overt to hasten his death. However, if there is anything external that prevents his release from his death pangs, such as a clattering noise near the patient's house, or if there is salt on his tongue, and these hinder the departure of the soul, it is permitted to remove them, for this is no direct act but only the removal of a hindrance.

4. When a person is about to die one should not leave him so that he does not depart this life alone.

Gloss: It is a *mitzvah* to stand by a person during the departure of his soul.

[From Chapter 340: The laws of cutting *keriah*.]

1. Whoever has suffered a bereavement for which he is required to observe the mourning rites must cut his garments. One must do so standing, and if he did so while sitting he has not fulfilled his duty.

2. The region for rending is all along the neck of the garment in the forepart. If he rent in the back part or in the lower part of the garment or on the side, he has not discharged his duty.

3. The extent of rending is a handbreadth. If he rent his garment upon suffering a bereavement and then extended the rent on sustaining another bereavement, if the second bereavement is after the seven days of mourning, then the additional tear may be as small as he wishes.

[From Chapter 343: The duty of attending the dead to the grave.]

1. So long as there is a dead person in town awaiting burial all the townspeople are forbidden to engage in work. And whoever sees a corpse and does not attend to its needs is subject to being placed under a ban. However, if there are

associations in town, each one of which attends to the burial needs of the dead on its particular day, then it is permissible for the others who are not required to attend to the burial needs to engage in work on the day which is not appointed for it.

[From Chapter 360: In case of a conflict between the religious duty of escorting a corpse and the religious duty of honoring a bride.]

1. If a funeral procession and a bridal procession meet each other on the way, the funeral procession should make way for the bridal procession. Likewise, if there are not enough people in the city to attend both, they bring the bride under the canopy first and then they bury the dead. But after the wedding ceremony, if a man has the duty to comfort the mourner and to gladden the bride and groom, comforting the mourner comes first. Similarly, the mourner's meal takes precedence over the wedding feast. When does this rule apply? When he has the means to fulfill both obligations; but if he does not possess the means to fulfill both, then the wedding feast comes first.

In the case of a corpse and a circumcision, circumcision comes first. If, however, he is a corpse that has no attendants at all, then he has priority over all else.

[From Chapter 376: On how to behave at the house of mourning.]

1. The comforters should not speak until the mourner initiates the conversation. When the mourner nods his head, indicating that he dismisses the comforters, they should not remain with him any longer.

Gloss: A mourner is not required to rise in honor of any distinguished visitor even if it be the leader of all Israel.

[From Chapter 378: The laws of the mourner's meal.]

1. A mourner is forbidden to eat of his own food at the first meal upon return from the burial. Some explain that this is because sometimes the mourner refuses to eat and prefers death; the meal provided by the neighbors is thus an act of assisting the bereaved toward reaccepting life.

10. A great number of people should not assemble to eat with the mourner, for this would necessitate that they overflow into two groups.

[From Chapter 380. Things forbidden to the mourner.]

1. The following are the things forbidden to the mourner: He is forbidden to engage in work, to bathe, to anoint himself, to put on shoes, to have marital intercourse, to read the Pentateuch, to greet one, to wash his garments during the first seven days of mourning and to cut his hair, to rejoice, and to resew a rent during the whole of the thirty days of mourning.

2. To what extent is a mourner forbidden to engage in work? During the first three days he is forbidden to engage in work even if he is a poor man who is supported from charity. Thereafter, if he is a poor man and has nothing to eat, he may work in the privacy of his house. But the Sages say: May poverty come upon his community who by not providing his maintenance at such a time were the cause of his needing to engage in work.

6. A woman should not paint her eyelids nor rouge her face during the days of her mourning. A married woman is forbidden to do this only during the seven days, but after this she is permitted everything so that she will not become repulsive in the sight of her husband. A bride whose mourning befell within the thirty days subsequent to her marriage is permitted to adorn herself even within the first seven days. A girl who has reached adolescence whom mourning befalls

is permitted to paint her eyelids and apply rouge to her face but does not bathe her entire body in warm water. A girl who has not reached adolescence and who becomes a mourner is forbidden even painting of the eyelids and applying rouge to her face.

8 *How to Die:*
From the Histalkut Hanefesh

TRANSLATED BY SAMUEL H. DRESNER

1. Why is this reading important?

The laws of dying make a statement of theory. In the stories of how Hasidic masters died you see another way in which the same laws are represented—now they are embodied in everyday life, but in the persons of
exemplary figures of a subdivision of Rabbinic Judaism (which we shall
meet again in Chapter 14). Here we see how the great masters made use
of the law; here the law serves as the concrete expression of the theology. Without examining stories such as these, you might conclude that
Judaism is a religion for robots, people who say: Tell me my duty and I
shall do it. Now you see the Torah (that is, Judaism) as a supple instrument of expression, a remarkable way of responding to God's presence
in life in all of the diverse ways that humanity can invent for personal
and individual response.

2. What should you notice as you proceed?

How the great Hasidic rabbis turn the moment of death into an occasion
for affirming God emerges in the several stories. Notice how brief the stories are, and identify the details that the writers, great artists one and all,
think important to supply as well as the details they do not think they
need to tell us at all. Notice how the great masters convey what it means
to live in God's presence and to die in a manner appropriate to that Presence. The Torah—that is, Judaism—has defined how to die as much as
how to live, and here you have a chance to see that definition embodied
by the greatest holy men of Hasidic Judaism. If you were to describe a
death scene that you thought worth reporting and remembering, what
details would strike you as worth preserving and handing on, and why
would you choose those details? Try to invent a basis for comparison and
contrast between the stories before you here and other stories of the same
event that you can imagine or that you yourself have witnessed.

3. How should you frame a question for class discussion in response to what you have read?

Compare the death scenes of exemplars of faith and culture—the death of Socrates in the *Phaedo*, for example, or that of Jesus in the Passion narratives, or that of the sages of Hasidism. How does each world of sensibility and wisdom make its definitive statement through the representation of the death of its great exemplary figure (Socrates), founder (Jesus), or saint, as in the present case. One of the points of stress in *The Way of Torah* is how a system makes a single coherent statement, which it repeats in countless detailed ways. Can you identify the main statement that Hasidism wishes to make through the representation of the deaths of its saints?

When the hour arrived for Rabbi Simhah Bunan of Psyshcha to depart from the world, his wife stood by his bedside and wept bitterly. He said to her, "Be silent— why do you cry? My whole life was only that I might learn how to die." He died on the twelfth day of Elul, 1827.

Before the death of Rabbi Abraham Joshua Heschel of Apt, he moaned bitterly over the exile of his people and over the fact that the Messiah tarried in coming. Finally he cried out, "The Rabbi of Berditchev said before he died that when he arrived up there he would not rest nor be silent, nor would he allow any of the holy ones to rest or be silent until the Messiah would come. But when he came there, the beauties and wonders of heaven overwhelmed him, so that he forgot about this. But I"—concluded the Rabbi of Apt—"I shall not forget."

Afterward he said: "Master of the world, I know that I am not worthy to be allowed to enter heaven with the other righteous men. Perhaps you will permit me to enter Gehenna with the wicked. But you, O Master of the World, you know how much I hate those who transgress your will. You know I cannot bear to be with them. How should I then make my dwelling among them? Therefore, I beg of you that you remove all the wicked of Israel from Gehenna in order that you might be able to bring me there." He died on the fifth of Nissan, 1825.

Rabbi Sussya of Plozk raised his head at midnight and said, "At midnight I rise to praise Thee," and with these words his soul departed from him. He died in the year 1840.

Rabbi Mayer, the son of Eliezer of Dzikov, died while he was sitting on his chair with his pipe in his mouth. He said, "The soul is Thine and the body is Thy work. Have mercy upon Thy craft." And when he had finished these words, his pure soul departed. He died on the eighth day of Tammuz, 1876.

It is told that Rabbi Abi of Olinov was among the greatest admirers of Rabbi Naphtali of Ropshitz. He died on Simchat Torah in Olinov. At that time, the Hasidim in Ropshitz were dancing in their fashion before the window of their Rabbi. Rabbi Naphtali stood by the window and watched. Suddenly he raised his hand as a sign that they should stop. And he stood as if in confusion for some time. Afterward he roused himself and said, "If they go out to war and one of the captains falls, should the soldiers flee? No. The battle must go on. Rejoice and dance." Then he gave a sign that they should begin to dance. Afterward it was made known that this was the precise moment when Rabbi Abi had died.

In the year 1831 a terrible plague raged in the world, and many letters were sent to Rabbi Zvi Hirsch of Ziditchov, from many distant places, saying: "O Rabbi, save us." One day when many of these letters were handed to him, and he was robed in his tallit, while he stood in his house of study, he grieved greatly, put his hand upon the *mezzuzah*, and said, "Behold, I shall be a *kapparah* [atonement] for all Israel." On the next Sabbath, when he put on his tallit, he saw that one fringe was torn and said, "It needs to be renewed." On the next Sabbath, his wife died. Then he himself fell ill and was no longer able to rise from his bed. On the tenth of Tammuz, a serious illness seized him. He asked his son-in-law if it was permissible for a man to look for a virtue within himself. His son-in-law said that, according to the Torah, it was permissible. He said, "I have served through the length of my days and I have only found one virtue among them: that I married off forty orphans. Each time I married off one of my own children, grandchildren, nieces, or nephews, I married off an orphan girl and provided her with a dowry and food at my own table."

At the hour of the death of the Ari, all of his students gathered around him with the exception of Rabbi Hayim Vital. Rabbi Isaac Hacohen [the priest] cried out, "Is this to be our hope, for all of us have waited to see great goodness and Torah and wisdom in the world while you yet live?" The Ari answered, "If I had found even one true zaddik among you, I would not depart." Afterward he inquired, "Where is Rabbi Hayim Vital?" And he seemed troubled. It was evident from the manner of his words that he wanted to hand over some secret to him. Later on, they inquired of him, "What shall we do from this time forth?" The Ari said, "You shall say to the disciples, in my name, that from this time forth they should not study Cabbala at all, for they have not understood it properly, and they might come, God forbid, to doubt and even to the destruction of their souls. Only Rabbi Hayim Vital may study it, in secret." The disciples asked, "Is there then no hope for us?" "If you merit it," he replied, "I myself shall come and teach you." Rabbi Isaac Hacohen asked, "How shall our Rabbi come to teach us after he has departed from the world?" He said, "It is not for you to delve into secret things, how I shall come—whether by night or by day, or in a vision. And now rise up quickly and leave this house for you are a priest [and forbidden to be in the same room with a dead man]; the time has come and I cannot speak more about this matter."

Rabbi Isaac rose to take leave at once, but before he had gone out of the door, the Ari opened his mouth and his soul departed with a kiss. He died on the fifth of Ab, 1605.

When the Baal Shem Tov fell ill shortly before his death, he would not take to bed. His body grew weak, his voice faint, and he would sit alone in his room meditating. On the eve of Shabuot, the last evening of his life, his intimates were gathered around him and he preached to them about the giving of the Torah. In the morning he requested that all of them gather together in his room and he taught them how they should care for his body after death. Afterward he asked for a Siddur [prayer book] and said, "I wish to commune yet a while with *Hashem Yitbarakh* [the Name, may He be blessed]."

Afterward they heard him talking to someone and they inquired with whom he was speaking. He replied, "Do you not see the Angel of Death? He always flees from me, but now he has been given permission to come and flaps his wings and is full of joy." Afterward all the men of the city gathered together to greet him on the holiday and he spoke words of Torah to them. Afterward he said, "Until now I have treated you with *hesed* [loving kindness]. Now you must treat me with *hesed*." [The burial is considered the truest act of *hesed*, because there is no repayment.] He gave them a sign that at his death the two clocks in the house would stop.

While he was washing his hands, the large clock stopped and some of the men immediately stood in front of it so that the others should not see it. He said to them, "I am not worried about myself, for I know clearly that I shall go from this door and immediately I shall enter another door." He sat down on his bed and told them to stand around him. He spoke words of Torah and ordered them to recite the verse—"And let Thy graciousness, O Lord our God, be upon us; establish Thou also the work of our hands for us; Yea the work of our hands establish Thou it." He lay down and sat up many times and prayed with great *kavvanah* and devotion, until the syllables of his words could no longer be distinguished. He told them to cover him with blankets and began to shake and tremble as he used to do when he prayed the Silent Prayer. Then little by little he grew quiet. At that moment they saw that the small clock too had stopped. They waited and saw that he had died. He died on Shabuot, 1760.

Before the great Maggid, Rabbi Dov Ber of Mezritch, departed from the world, there stood before him his son Rabbi Abraham, "the Angel," Rabbi Judah Leib, the priest, and Rabbi Shneer Zalman, the Rabbi from Ladi. He said to them, "My children, hold fast to one another in unity, for by this you will overcome everything. Go forward and not backward. Afterward the zaddik, Rabbi Zussya of Hanipol, entered, and he intimated to him with a gesture of his finger that he come close. He took his right hand and said to him, "You, Zussya, were mine in this world and there, too, you shall be close to me." Later on he inquired whether Rabbi Mendel of Vitebsk was there and groaned when he learned that he was not. He asked whether Rabbi Leib Cohen was there. When he saw him he said to him, "You, too, shall be with me." Later he uttered these words, "Zalman, Zalman, you alone shall remain, but I shall take you out of your suffering and cause you to rejoice in the end." Then he said, "Abraham, you shall live. Only you shall be silent and conduct yourself as you have until now and serve Zalman—and it shall be good for you. The main thing is that you should not mortify yourself, for if you take from the strength of your body, you take also from the strength of your soul."

Then he said goodnight and he slept away. May his merit guard us all. He died on the nineteenth day of Kislev, 1774.

Many months before the death of Rabbi Nachman of Bratzlav—who already had achieved a rung so lofty that it seemed impossible to ascend higher while clothed with flesh—he said that he yearned to be free of his body. It was impossible for him to remain upon one rung for any length of time, for all of his days he had never stood still upon one rung even when he ascended to the highest point. He constantly yearned to go higher and higher. And so it was that a long time before he died he began to seek out a place of burial for himself, since for reasons he would not reveal, he did not wish to be buried in Bratzlav. At last he chose the city of Oman (where the Baal Shem, his grandfather, was born). He said that many deliverances could be brought about there and that there were many mysteries there which he could reveal to no one. When he settled in Oman, he had already grown very weak. On the Sabbath following Tishah-b'Ab, many Hasidim came to him and before they washed their hands for the meal, he said, "Why have you all come here? I do not know you at all, for I have now become a simple man."

On the last night of his life, he spoke again about the soul. He commanded his disciples that immediately after he had died, while he yet lay upon the earth, they should take all of his writings that were in his desk and burn them. He insisted that they carry out his command. They stood about in confusion and despair and whispered among themselves while he was already preparing himself to depart. Then he said to them, "Perhaps you are speaking about your own concerns. But why do you worry that I depart from you? If these souls who know me not at all, look to me for deliverance, how much the more so need you not fear." In the morning he gathered his tallit around him, prayed, took the ethrog and lulav, completed saying the Hallel in a strong voice, and used the siddur of the Ari, which rested upon his knees. Then he ordered them to dress him and wash him. And he took some wax and rubbed it between his fingers and mediated great thoughts, as was the custom of the great men; when they would meditate about something they would turn over in their fingers some wax. Thus at the last hour his mind was occupied with matters deep and most wonderful.

And when they saw that it was close to the end, they began to recite the verses which are said at the time of the death of the righteous. When it appeared that he had died, they began to cry out, "Our Rabbi—our Rabbi—with whom have you left us?" At that moment he stirred, raised his head and his wonderful face as if to say, "I am not leaving you." They he expired and was gathered to his people in holiness and in purity. He died on the eighteenth day of Tishri, 1810.

9   To Hold with Open Arms

MILTON STEINBERG

1. Why is this reading important?

Comparing how great Hasidic rabbis addressed death with how an
American rabbi prepared for the same moment allows us to see continu-
ities and points of change in the unfolding of a single, linear, coherent
religious tradition. Milton Steinberg, the most gifted and brilliant rabbi
of the first half of the twentieth century in the United States, died before
his time, leaving a legacy of writing of enduring interest. A Conservative rabbi, able to translate the classical writings into the idiom of contemporary thought and sensibility, Steinberg here allows us to compare
and contrast the premodern with the modern Judaic way of delivering
an essentially uniform message. The challenge to you is to identify how
a single theology, embodied in concrete deeds in the law and carried on
in the exemplary deaths of Hasidic masters, permeates the remarkable
spirit of a man of the same world of discourse we now share: Western
speech and Western values. Here, recovering in Texas from a long illness, Steinberg writes about Texas sun on a midwinter day in Dallas.
Then and there, he finds the whole of life's meaning in the Torah's version. I chose this reading because I could find none better to express
what it means for an individual to practice the religion Judaism.

2. What should you notice as you proceed?

When you review in your mind the laws and stories already examined,
you will want to know how Steinberg participates in a tradition and
how he innovates within it. As you read, ask this question: How does
Steinberg's message embody in his language and idiom the same messages that you identified in the law of dying on one side and in the stories of Hasidic masters' deaths on the other? And how do you think he
is saying something in which the tradition is not simply repeated but renewed with fresh insight? This remarkable essay, deeply responsive to
the rules of essay writing that you may learn in a course in English and
American literature, states a rabbi's view of the Torah's message. But
the medium is so vastly different from the media of law and exemplary
story that we have to wonder what the three pieces of writing have in
common.

3. How should you frame a question for class discussion in response to what you have read?

Given Steinberg's remarkable power to speak in common language about experiences with which anyone can identify, do you think that his is a message that is unique to Judaism? Could a Christian saint write in these terms, or a Muslim holy man? In more general terms, as you read ask what makes a religion special and different from other religions when it sets down its particular message about an experience common to all humanity. When we consider the differences between and among religious traditions, we must also take account of their points in common. On one side, some hold, what you believe does not matter so long as you're a good human being. On the other side, others maintain, religions divide people and define difference. Here is a good chance to consider both perspectives and to frame a discussion on how Judaism is special among religions and how it is common.

It is a sound convention which requires that a sermon begin with a text—some verse from Scripture, or from Rabbinic literature, which summarizes the theme. But it is well to understand that a text is, after all, only the soul-experience of some man boiled down to the size of an epigram. At some time in the past a prophet or a saint met God, wrestled with good or evil, tasted of life and found it bitter or sweet, contemplated death, and then distilled the adventure into a single line, for those that would come after him. That is a text.

But it is not only the great, the saints, the prophets, and the heroes who contemplate God, life, and death. We, too, the plainer folk of the world, live, love, laugh, and suffer, and by no means always on the surface. We, too, catch glimpses of eternity and the things that people do. Not only of Moses, but of us, too, it may be said, as Lowell put it:

Daily with souls that cringe and plot
We Sinais climb and know it not.

There are texts in us, too, in our commonplace experiences, if only we are wise enough to discern them.

One such experience, a *textual* experience, so to speak, fell to my lot not so long ago. There was nothing dramatic about its setting nor unusual in its circumstances. And yet to me it was a moment of discovery, almost of revelation.

Let me recount it very briefly, as befits a text. After a long illness, I was permitted for the first time to step out-of-doors. And as I crossed the threshold sunlight greeted me. This is my experience—all there is to it. And yet, so long as I live, I shall never forget that moment. It was mid-January—a time of cold and storm up North, but in Texas, where I happened to be, a season much like our spring. The sky overhead was very blue, very clear, and very, very high. Not, I thought, the *shamayim*, heaven, but *shemei shamayim*, a heaven of heavens. A faint wind blew from off the western plains, cool and yet somehow tinged with warmth—like a dry, chilled wine. And everywhere in the firmament above me,

in the great vault between the earth and sky, on the pavements, the buildings—
the golden glow of the sunlight. It touched me, too, with friendship, with warmth,
with blessing. And as I basked in its glory there ran through my mind those wonderful words of the prophet about the sun which someday shall rise with healing on its wings.

In that instant I looked about me to see whether anyone else showed on his
face the joy, almost the beatitude, I felt. But no, there they walked—men and
women and children, in the glory of the golden flood, and so far as I could detect, there was none to give it heed. And then I remembered how often I, too, had
been indifferent to sunlight, how often, preoccupied with petty and sometimes
mean concerns, I had disregarded it. And I said to myself, How precious is the
sunlight but alas, how careless of it are men. How precious—how careless. This
has been a refrain sounding in me ever since.

It rang in my spirit when I entered my own home again after months of absence; when I heard from a nearby room the excited voices of my children at play;
when I looked once more on the dear faces of some of my friends; when I was
able for the first time to speak again from my pulpit in the name of our faith and
tradition, to join in worship of the God who gives us so much of which we are
so careless.

And a resolution crystallized within me. I said to myself that at the very first
opportunity I would speak of this. I knew full well that it is a commonplace truth,
that there is nothing clever about my private rediscovery of it, nothing ingenious
about my way of putting it. But I was not interested in being original or clever
or ingenious. I wanted only to remind my listeners, as I was reminded, to spend
life wisely, not to squander it.

I wanted to say to the husbands and wives who love one another: "How precious is your lot in that it is one of love. Do not be, even for a moment, casual
with your good fortune. Love one another while yet you may."

And to parents: "How precious is the gift of your children. Never, never be
too busy for the wonder and miracle of them. They will be grown up soon enough
and grown away, too."

We human beings, we frail reeds who are yet, as Pascal said, *thinking* reeds,
feeling reeds, how precious are our endowments—minds to know, eyes to see,
ears to listen, hearts to stir with pity, and to dream of justice and of a perfected
world. How often are we indifferent to all these!

And we who are Jews and Americans, heirs of two great traditions, how fortunate our lot in both, and how blind we are to our double good fortune.

This is what struggled in me for utterance—as it struggled in Edna St. Vin-
cent Millay when she cried out:

O world I cannot hold thee close enough.

I want to urge myself and all others to hold the world tight—to embrace life
with all our hearts and all our souls and all our might. For it is precious, ineffably
precious, and we are careless, wantonly careless of it.

And yet, when I first resolved to express all this, I knew that it was only a
half-truth.

Could I have retained the sunlight no matter how hard I tried? Could I have
prevented the sun from setting? Could I have kept even my own eyes from be-

coming satiated and bored with the glory of the day? That moment had to slip away. And had I tried to hold on to it, what would I have achieved? it would have gone from me in any case. And I would have been left disconsolate, embittered, convinced that I had been cheated.

But it is not only the sunlight that must slip away—our youth goes also, our years, our children, our senses, our lives. This is the nature of things, an inevitability. And the sooner we make our peace with it the better. Did I urge myself a moment ago to hold on? I would have done better, it now begins to appear, to have preached the opposite doctrine of letting go—the doctrine of Socrates who called life a *peisithanatos,* a persuader of death, a teacher of the art of relinquishing. It was the doctrine of Goethe who said: *Entsagen sollst, du sollst entsagen,* Thou shalt renounce. And it was the doctrine of the ancient rabbis who despite their love of life said: He who would die, let him hold on to life.

It is a sound doctrine.

First, because, as we have just seen, it makes peace with inevitability. And the inevitable is something with which everyone should be at peace. Second, because nothing can be more grotesque and more undignified than a futile attempt to hold on.

Let us think of the men and women who cannot grow old gracefully because they cling too hard to a youth that is escaping them; of the parents who cannot let their children go free to live their own lives; of the people who in times of general calamity have only themselves in mind.

What is it that drives people to such unseemly conduct, to such flagrant selfishness, except the attitude which I have just commended—a vigorous holding on to life? Besides, are there not times when one ought to hold life cheap, as something to be lightly surrendered? In defense of one's country, for example, in the service of truth, justice, and mercy, in the advancement of mankind?

This, then, is the great truth of human existence. One must not hold life too precious. One must always be prepared to let it go.

And now we are indeed confused. First we learn that life is a privilege—cling to it! Then we are instructed: Thou shalt renounce!

A paradox, and a self-contradiction! But neither the paradox nor the contradiction are of my making. They are a law written into the scheme of things—that a man must hold his existence dear and cheap at the same time.

Is it not, then, an impossible assignment to which destiny has set us? It does not ask of us that we hold life dear at one moment, and cheap at the next, but that we do both simultaneously. Now I can grasp something in my fist or let my hand lie open. I can clasp it to my breast or hold it at arm's length. I can embrace it, enfolding it in my arms, or let my arms hang loose. But how can I be expected to do both at once?

To which the answer is: With your body, of course not. But with your spirit, why not?

Is one not forever doing paradoxical and mutually contradictory things in his soul?

One wears his mind out in study and yet has more mind with which to study. One gives away his heart in love and yet has more heart to give away. One perishes out of pity for a suffering world and is the stronger therefor.

So, too, it is possible at one and the same time to hold on to life and let it go, provided—well, let me put it this way:

We are involved in a tug-of-war: Here on the left is the necessity to renounce life and all it contains. Here on the right, the yearning to affirm it and its experiences. And between these two is a terrible tension, for they pull in opposite directions.

But suppose that here in the center I introduce a third force, one that lifts upward. My two irreconcilables now swing together, both pulling down against the new element. And the harder they pull, the closer together they come.

God is the third element, that new force that resolves the terrible contradiction, the intolerable tension of life.

And for this purpose it does not especially matter how we conceive God. I have been a great zealot for a mature idea of God. I have urged again and again that we think through our theology, not limping along on a child's notion of God as an old man in the sky. But for my immediate purpose, all of this is irrelevant. What is relevant is this: that so soon as a man believes in God, so soon indeed as he wills to believe in Him, the terrible strain is eased; nay, it disappears, and that for two reasons.

In the first place, because a new and higher purpose is introduced into life, the purpose of doing the will of God, to put it in Jewish terms, of performing the *mitzvot*. This now becomes the reason for our existence. We are soldiers whose commander has stationed us at a post. How we like our assignment, whether we feel inclined to cling to it or to let it go, is an irrelevant issue. Our hands are too busy with our duties to be either embracing the world or pushing it away.

That is why it is written: "Make thy will conform to His, then His will be thine, and all things will be as thou desirest."

But that, it might be urged, only evades the problem. By concentrating on duty we forget the conflicting drives within ourselves. The truth is, however, that, given God, the problem is solved not only by evasion but directly; that it is solved, curiously enough, by being made more intense. For, given God, everything becomes more precious, more to be clung to, more embraceable; and yet at the same time easier to give up.

Given God, everything becomes more precious.

That sunshine in Dallas was not a chance effect, a lucky accident. It was an effect created by a great Artist, the master Painter of Eternity. And because it came from God's brush it is more valuable even than I had at first conceived.

And the laughter of children, precious in itself, becomes infinitely more precious because the joy of the cosmos is in it.

And the sweetness of our friends' faces is dearer because these are fragments of an infinite sweetness.

All of life is the more treasurable because a great and Holy Spirit is in it.

And yet, it is easier for me to let go.

For these things are not and never have been mine. They belong to the universe and the God who stands behind it. True, I have been privileged to enjoy them for an hour, but they were always a loan due to be recalled.

And I let go of them the more easily because I know that as parts of the divine economy they will not be lost. The sunset, the bird's song, the baby's smile, the thunder of music, the surge of great poetry, the dreams of the heart, and my own being, dear to me as every man's is to him, all these I can well trust to Him who made them. There is poignancy and regret about giving them up, but no anxiety. When they slip from my hands they will pass to hands better, stronger, and wiser than mine.

This then is the insight which came to me as I stood some months ago in a blaze of sunlight: Life is dear, let us then hold it tight while we yet may; but we must hold it loosely also!

And only with God can we ease the intolerable tension of our existence. For only when He is given, can we hold life at once infinitely precious and yet as a thing lightly to be surrendered. Only because of Him is it made possible for us to clasp the world, but with relaxed hands; to embrace it, but with open arms.

10 *The Mystical Element in Judaism*

ABRAHAM J. HESCHEL

1. Why is this reading important?

By *mysticism* in Judaism, people mean doctrines and practices that embody a direct, unmediated encounter with God and God's presence in the here and now. Certainly the greatest modern interpreter of mysticism in Judaism was Abraham J. Heschel, 1907–1972, who wrote both within that tradition and about it. There is no better way of introducing the mystical experience that Judaism affords than through Heschel's account of the mystic experience embodied in the Torah. Heschel writes from his own encounter, not about what third parties tell him. He speaks of *cabbalists,* meaning those who study texts that convey knowledge of the direct encounter with God and practice mystical religious rites of prayer and encounter. Heschel defines what he means by mysticism through what he says about cabbalists: people to whom God is as real as life, who are not content to prove that there is a God but to feel and to enjoy him, not only to obey but to approach him. No study of Judaism would be complete without a clear statement of what it means to seek and find God in the Torah, and within the diverse formulations of Rabbinic Judaism mysticism takes priority. I have chosen passages in which Heschel describes mystic experience directly and also shows how mystic study of the Torah is to be accomplished. In this way we see mysticism both in concrete and in intellectual terms.

2. What should you notice as you proceed?

Especially noteworthy is the tone that Heschel establishes for his account. Does he write the way Milton Steinberg writes, and, if not, what are the telling features of his prose? Heschel has in mind to deliver the message through the medium as well, and you will want to notice how he does this. In what way does he want the reader to join him in the experiences that he describes, and how does he accomplish his goal? Second, pay attention to how Heschel describes the mystic union with God. He is using the special terminology of the Torah, but he is trying to convey to any reader, not only the insider, the substance of his message. Finally, notice the redefinition of the Torah, from a statement of how holy Israel is to live a sanctified life to a source of direct encounter with God. How do you think Jewish mysticism accomplishes the redefinition of the Torah, as Heschel explains the matter?

3. How should you frame a question for class discussion in response to what you have read?

As we noticed when we studied the Judaic encounter with death in law, in narratives of holy men, and in the profound reflections of a great contemporary figure, so here, too, we have to wonder: What makes Judaism special? Even though it uses its own language in speaking of the Torah and referring to holy Israel and to Scripture, in the end the writings of Jewish mysticism describe an encounter with God that is not particular to holy Israel and the Torah at all. So we have to wonder in what way is mysticism—the direct encounter with God in the here and now—going to be special in a given religious setting (here Judaism), and in what way is mysticism going to speak of an experience common to all religious people? If you know about great Christian or Muslim mystics, you will wonder what distinguishes the Judaic, Christian, and Muslim approach to the same fundamental encounter and what they have in common.

The Meaning of Jewish Mysticism

There are people who take great care to keep away from the mists produced by fads and phrases. They refuse to convert realities into opinions, mysteries into dogmas, and ideas into a multitude of words, for they realize that all concepts are but glittering motes in a sunbeam. They want to see the sun itself. Confined to our study rooms, our knowledge seems to us a pillar of light; but when we stand at the door that opens out to the Infinite, we see how insubstantial is our knowledge. Even when we shut the door to the Infinite and retire to the narrow limits of notions our minds cannot remain confined. Again, to some people explanations and opinions are a token of wonder's departure, like a curfew after which they may not come abroad. In the cabbalists, the drive and the fire and the light are never put out.

Like the vital power in ourselves that gives us the ability to fight and to endure, to dare and to conquer, which drives us to experience the bitter and the perilous, there is an urge in wistful souls to starve rather than be fed on sham and distortion. To the cabbalists God is as real as life, and as nobody would be satisfied with mere knowing or reading about life, so they are not content to suppose or to prove logically that there is a God; they want to feel and to enjoy Him; not only to obey, but to approach Him. They want to taste the whole wheat of spirit before it is ground by the millstones of reason. They would rather be overwhelmed by the symbols of the inconceivable than wield the definitions of the superficial.

Stirred by a yearning after the unattainable, they want to make the distant near, the abstract concrete, to transform the soul into a vessel for the transcendent, to grasp with the senses what is hidden from the mind, to express in symbols what the tongue cannot speak, what the reason cannot conceive, to experience as a reality what vaguely dawns in intuitions. "Wise is he who by the power of his own contemplation attains to the perception of the profound mysteries which cannot be expressed in words."

The cabbalist is not content with being confined to what he is. His desire is not only to *know* more than what ordinary reason has to offer, but to *be* more than what he is; not only to comprehend the Beyond but to concur with it. He aims at the elevation and expansion of existence. Such expansion goes hand in hand with the exaltation of all being.

The universe, exposed to the violence of our analytical mind, is being broken apart. It is split into the known and unknown, into the seen and unseen. In mystic contemplation all things are seen as one. The mystic mind tends to hold the world together: to behold the seen in conjunction with the unseen, to keep the fellowship with the unknown through the revolving door of the known, "to learn the higher supernal wisdom from all" that the Lord has created and to regain the knowledge that once was in the possession of men and "that has perished from them." What our senses perceive is but the jutting edge of what is deeply hidden. Extending over into the invisible, the things of this world stand in a secret contact with that which no eye has ever perceived. Everything certifies to the sublime, the unapparent working jointly with the apparent. There is always a reverberation in the Beyond to every action here: "The Lord made this world corresponding to the world above, and everything which is above has its counterpart below . . . and yet they all constitute a unity"; "there being no object, however small, in this world, but what is subordinate to its counterpart above which has charge over it; and so whenever the thing below bestirs itself, there is a simultaneous stimulation of its counterpart above, as the two realms form one interconnected whole."

Opposed to the idea that the world of perception is the bottom of reality, the mystics plunge into what is beneath the perceptible. What they attain in their quest is more than a vague impression or a spotty knowledge of the imperceptible. "Penetrating to the real essence of wisdom . . . they are resplendent with the radiance of supernal wisdom." Their eyes perceive things of this world, while their hearts reverberate to the throbbing of the hidden. To them the secret is the core of the apparent; the known is but an aspect of the unknown. "All things below are symbols of that which is above." They are sustained by the forces that flow from hidden worlds. There is no particular that is detached from universal meaning. What appears to be a center to the eye is but a point on the periphery around another center. Nothing here is final. The worldly is subservient to the otherworldly. You grasp the essence of the here by conceiving its beyond. For this world is the reality of the spirit in a state of trance. The manifestation of the mystery is partly suspended, with ourselves living in lethargy. Our normal consciousness is a state of stupor, in which our sensibility to the wholly real and our responsiveness to the stimuli of the spirit are reduced. The mystics, knowing that we are involved in a hidden history of the cosmos, endeavor to awake from the drowsiness and apathy and to regain the state of wakefulness for our enchanted souls.

It is a bold attitude of the soul, a steadfast quality of consciousness, that lends mystic character to a human being. A man who feels that he is closely enfolded by a power that is both lasting and holy will come to know that the spiritual is not an idea to which one can relate his will, but a realm which can even be affected by our deeds. What distinguishes the cabbalist is the attachment of his entire personality to a hidden spiritual realm. Intensifying this attachment by means of active devotion to it, by meditation upon its secrets, or even by perception of its reality, he becomes allied with the dynamics of hidden worlds. Sensitive to the imperceptible, he is stirred by its secret happenings.

Attachment to hidden worlds holds the cabbalist in the spell of things more basic than the things that dominate the interest of the common mind. The mystery is not beyond and away from us. It is our destiny. "The fate of the world depends upon the mystery." Our task is to adjust the details to the whole, the apparent to the hidden, the near to the distant. The passionate concern of the cabbalist for final goals endows him with the experience of surpassing all human limitations and powers. With all he is doing he is crossing the borders, breaking the surfaces, approaching the lasting sources of all things. Yet his living with the infinite does not make him alien to the finite.

Mystic Experience

The ultimate goal of the cabbalist is not his own union with the Absolute but the union of all reality with God; one's own bliss is subordinated to the redemption of all: "we have to put all our being, all the members of our body, our complete devotion, into that thought so as to rise and attach ourselves to the *En Sof*, and thus achieve the oneness of the upper and lower worlds."

What this service means in terms of personal living is described in the following way:

> Happy is the portion of whoever can penetrate into the mysteries of his Master and become absorbed into Him, as it were. Especially does a man achieve this when he offers up his prayer to his Master in intense devotion, his will then becoming as the flame inseparable from the coal, and his mind concentrated on the unity of the lower firmaments, to unify them by means of a lower name, then on the unity of the higher firmaments, and finally on the absorption of them all into that most high firmament. Whilst a man's mouth and lips are moving, his heart and will must soar to the height of heights, so as to acknowledge the unity of the whole in virtue of the mystery of mysteries in which all ideas, all wills and all thoughts find their goal, to wit, the mystery of *En Sof*.

The thirst for God is colored by the awareness of His holiness, of the endless distance that separates man from the Eternal One. Yet, he who craves for God is not only a mortal being, but also a part of the Community of Israel, that is, the bride of God, endowed with a soul that is "a part of God." Shy in using endearing terms in his own name, the Jewish mystic feels and speaks in the plural. The allegory of the Song of Songs would be impertinent as an individual utterance, but as an expression of Israel's love for God it is among the finest of all expressions. "God is the soul and spirit of all, and Israel calls Him so and says: (My soul), I desire Thee in order to cleave to Thee and I seek Thee early to find Thy favor."

Israel lives in mystic union with God and the purpose of all its service is to strengthen this union: "O my dove that art in the clefts of the rock, in the covert of the cliff" (Song of Sol. 2:14). The "dove" here is the Community of Israel, which like a dove never forsakes her mate, the Holy One, blessed be He. "In the clefts of the rock": these are the students of the Torah, who have no ease in this world. "In the covert of the steep place": these are the specially pious among them, the saintly and God-fearing, from whom the Divine Presence never departs. The Holy One, blessed be He, inquires concerning them of the Community of Israel, saying, "Let me see thy countenance, let me hear thy voice, for sweet is thy voice"; "for above only the voice of those who study the Torah is heard. We have learned that the likeness of all such is graven above before the Holy One, blessed be He, Who delights Himself with them every day and watches them and that voice rises and pierces its way through all firmaments until it stands before the Holy One, blessed be He."

The concepts of the cabbala cannot always be clearly defined and consistently interrelated. As the name of Jewish mysticism, "cabbala" (lit.: "received lore"), indicates, it is a tradition of wisdom, supposed to have been revealed to elect Sages in ancient times and preserved throughout the generations by an initiated few. The cabbalists accept at the outset the ideas on authority, not on the basis of analytical understanding.

Yet the lips of the teachers and the pages of the books are not the only sources of knowledge. The great cabbalists claimed to have received wisdom directly from the Beyond. Inspiration and Vision were as much a part of their life as contemplation and study. The prayer of Moses: "Show me, I pray Thee, Thy glory" (Ex. 33:18) has never died in the hearts of the cabbalists. The conception of the goal has changed but the quest for immediate cognition remained. The Merkaba-mystics, following perhaps late prophetic traditions about the mysteries of the Divine Throne, were striving to behold the celestial sphere in which the secrets of creation and man's destiny are contained. In the course of the centuries the scope of such esoteric experiences embraced a variety of objectives. The awareness of the cabbalists that the place whereon they stood was holy ground kept them mostly silent about the wonder that was granted to them. Yet we possess sufficient evidence to justify the assumption that mystic events, particularly in the form of inner experiences, of spiritual communications rather than that of sense perceptions, were elements of their living. According to old Rabbinic teachings, there have always been Sages and saints upon whom the Holy Spirit rested, to whom wisdom was communicated from heaven by a Voice, through the appearance of the spirit of Elijah or in dreams. According to the *Zohar,* God reveals to the saints "profound secrets of the Holy Name which He does not reveal to the angels." The disciples of Rabbi Simeon ben Yohai are called prophets, "before whom both supernal and terrestrial beings tremble in awe." Others pray that the inspiration of the Holy Spirit should come upon them. The perception of the unearthly is recorded as an ordinary feature in the life of certain Rabbis. "When R. Hamnuna the Ancient used to come out from the river on a Friday afternoon, he was wont to rest a little on the bank, and raising his eyes in gladness, he would say that he sat there in order to behold the joyous sight of the heavenly angels ascending and descending. At each arrival of the Sabbath, he said, man is caught up into the world of souls." Not only may the human mind receive spiritual illuminations; the soul also may be bestowed upon higher powers. "Corresponding to the impulses of a man here are the influences which he attracts to himself from above. Should his impulse be toward holiness, he attracts to himself holiness from on high and so he becomes holy; but if this tendency is toward the side of impurity, he draws down toward himself the unclean spirit and so becomes polluted."

Since the time of the prophet Joel the Jews have expected that at the end of days the Lord would "pour out His spirit upon all flesh" and all men would prophesy. In later times, it is believed, the light of that revelation of mysteries could already be perceived.

The mystics absorb even in this world "something of the odor of these secrets and mysteries." Significantly, the Torah itself is conceived as a living source of inspiration, not as a fixed book. The Torah is a voice that "calls aloud" to men; she calls them day by day to herself in love . . . "The Torah lets out a word and emerges for a little from her sheath, and then hides herself again. But she does this only for those who understand and obey her. She is like unto a beautiful and stately damsel, who is hidden in a secluded chamber of a palace and who has a lover of whom no one knows but she. Out of his love for her he constantly passes by her gate, turning his eyes toward all sides to find her. Knowing that he is always haunting the palace, what does she do? She opens a little door in her hidden palace, discloses for a moment her face to her lover, then swiftly hides it again. None but he notices it; but his heart and soul, and all that is in him are drawn to her, knowing as he does that she has revealed herself to him for a moment because she loves him. It is the same with the Torah, which reveals her hidden secrets only to those who love her. She knows that he who is wise of heart daily haunts the gates of her house. What does she do? She shows her face to him from her palace, making a sign of love to him, and straightaway returns to her hiding place again. No one understands her message save he alone, and he is drawn to her with heart and soul and all his being. Thus the Torah reveals herself momentarily in love to her lovers in order to awaken fresh love in them."

11 *The Jew Who Wasn't There:* Halakhah *and the Jewish Woman*

RACHEL ADLER

1. Why is this reading important?

By one of the principal theorists of feminism in Judaism, this essay asks how the law or *halakhah* deals with one half of holy Israel, the women. Adler asks why the exposition of the subject appeals to norms of belief (in compilations of exegeses of Scripture called *Midrashim*, or in stories called *aggadot*) but not norms of behavior, such as, we realize now, *halakhah* sets forth. She calls various classes of persons "peripheral," not the center of interest, and then sets forth a program for making women integral to the life of the law. I chose this selection because after a quarter of a century it still carries a powerful message of commitment and concern. While much has changed—women are now accepted as rabbis by Reform, Reconstructionist, and Conservative Judaisms, and some components of Orthodoxy are making provision for women's participation in central religious activities—in religion things change slowly, and not always in the direction people plan or even want.

2. What should you notice as you proceed?

The essay lays out a bill of particulars, ways in which the received tradition conventionally defines women's place. Based on your knowledge of Judaism to this point, with special reference to the position of women in the law of the Mishnah set forth in *The Way of Torah*, notice how through its details the law spells out an entire philosophy and program for the regulation of women's lives as much as for men's—one that might be characterized as separate but equal in concern. Then ask whether the tradition can accommodate itself to the aspirations of women for a religious role identical to that of men without completely changing its character. Some of the changes Adler proposes—inclusion of women in study programs—have now been achieved by all organized Judaisms (separate Orthodox yeshivot, or study centers, have been organized for women only). But the problems that Adler identifies, such as allowing women to be judges and leaders of religious services, have not been solved. In reading this essay, ask whether feminist and Judaic aspirations are compatible.

3. How should you frame a question for class discussion in response to what you have read?

In the world of religion, Adler's program meets head on with others within Judaism, and we can point to parallel conflicts in Roman Catholic Christianity (on ordaining women, for one example) and in some Protestant denominations, in the Mormon Church, in Islam, and elsewhere. Are we, as people who aspire to be enlightened and reasonable, able to consider the case against feminism (or its counterparts in other sectors of sexual politics)? Can we even construct a case for a different sexual policy from that of revolution, not reform, that feminists in general are thought to advocate? A challenge to academics awaits: Can we see the viewpoint of the other, the outsider to the established norm? Or is learning the same thing as advocacy, and scholarship another mode of politics? These questions await our attention.

It is not unusual for committed Jewish women to be uneasy about their position as Jews. It was to cry down our doubts that rabbis developed their pre-packaged orations on the nobility of motherhood; the glory of childbirth; and modesty, the crown of Jewish womanhood. I have heard them all. I could not accept those answers for two reasons. First of all, the answers did not accept *me* as a person. They only set rigid stereotypes which defined me by limiting the directions in which I might grow. Second, the answers were not really honest ones. Traditional scholars agree that all philosophies of Judaism must begin with an examination of Jewish law, Halacha, since, in the Halacha are set down the ways in which we are expected to behave, and incontestably our most deeply engrained attitudes are those which we reinforce by habitual action.

Yet scholars do not discuss female status in terms of Halacha—at least not with females. Instead, they make lyrical exegeses on selected Midrashim and Agadot which, however complimentary they may be, do not really reflect the way in which men are expected to behave toward women by Jewish law. I think we are going to have to discuss it, if we are to build for ourselves a faith which is not based on ignorance and self-deception. That is why I would like to offer some hypotheses on the history and nature of the "woman problem" in Halacha.

Ultimately our problem stems from the fact that we are viewed in Jewish law and practice as peripheral Jews. The category in which we are generally placed includes women, children, and Canaanite slaves. Members of this category are exempt from all positive commandments which occur within time limits.[1] These commandments would include hearing the shofar on Rosh HaShanah, eating in the Sukkah, praying with the lulav, praying the three daily services, wearing tallit

---

[1]Kiddushin 29a.

and t'fillin, and saying Sh'ma.[2] In other words, members of this category have been "excused" from most of the positive symbols which, for the male Jew, hallow time, hallow his physical being, and inform both his myth and his philosophy.

Since most of the mitzvot not restricted by time are negative, and since women, children and slaves are responsible to fulfill all negative mitzvot, including the negative time-bound mitzvot, it follows that for members of this category, the characteristic posture of their Judaism is negation rather than affirmation.[3] They must not, for example, eat non-kosher food, violate the Shabbat, eat chametz on Pesach, fail to fast on fast days, steal, murder, or commit adultery. That women, children, and slaves have limited credibility in Jewish law is demonstrated by the fact that their testimony is inadmissible in a Jewish court.[4] The minyan—the basic unit of the Jewish community—excludes them, implying that the community is presumed to be the Jewish males to whom they are adjuncts. Torah study is incumbent upon them only insofar as it relates to "their" mitzvot. Whether women are even permitted to study further is debated.[5]

All of the individuals in this tri-partite category I have termed peripheral Jews. Children, if male, are full Jews *in potentio*. Male Canaanite slaves, if freed, become full Jews, responsible for all the mitzvot and able to count in a minyan.[6] Even as slaves, they have the b'rit mila, the covenant of circumcision, that central Jewish symbol, from which women are anatomically excluded. It is true that in Jewish law women are slightly more respected than slaves, but that advantage is outweighed by the fact that only women can never grow up, or be freed, or otherwise leave the category. The peripheral Jew is excused and sometimes barred from the acts and symbols which are the lifeblood of the believing community, but this compliance with the negative mitzvot is essential, since, while he cannot be permitted to participate fully in the life of the Jewish people, he cannot be permitted to undermine it either.

To be a peripheral Jew is to be educated and socialized toward a peripheral commitment. This, I think, is what happened to the Jewish woman. Her major mitzvot aid and reinforce the life-style of the community and the family, but they do not cultivate the relationship between the individual and God. A woman keeps kosher because both she and her family must have kosher food. She lights the Shabbat candles so that there will be light, and hence, peace, in the household. She goes to the mikva so that her husband can have intercourse with her and she bears children so that, through her, he can fulfill the exclusively male mitzvah of increasing and multiplying.[7]

Within these narrow confines, there have been great and virtuous women, but in several respects the tzidkaniot (saintly women) have been unlike the tzaddikim. Beruria, the scholarly wife of Rabbi Meir, the Talmudic sage, and a few ex-

---

[2]Ibid., but see also Mishna Sukkah 2:9 and Mishna Brachot 3:3.

[3]Kiddushin 29a.

[4]Sh'vuot 30a. See also Rosh HaShanah 22a.

[5]Sotah 20a.

[6]It must be admitted that Canaanite slaves were only to be freed if some overriding mitzvah would be accomplished thereby. The classic case in which Rabbi Eliezer frees his slave in order to complete a minyan is given in Gittin 38b.

[7]Mikva is not itself a mitzvah. It is a prerequisite to a permitted activity, just as shechita is prerequisite to the permitted activity of eating meat. See Sefer HaChinuch, Mitzvah 175.

ceptional women like her stepped outside the limits of the feminine role, but legend relates how Beruria came to a bad end, implying that her sin was the direct result of her "abnormal" scholarship.[8] There is no continuous tradition of learned women in Jewish history. Instead there are many tzidkaniot, some named, some unnamed, all of whom were pious and chaste, outstandingly charitable, and, in many cases, who supported their husbands. In contrast, there are innumerable accounts of tzaddikim, some rationalists, some mystics, some joyous, some ascetics, singers, dancers, poets, halachists, all bringing to God the service of a singular, inimitable self.

How is it that the tzaddikim seem so individualized and the tzidkaniot so generalized? I would advance two reasons. First of all, the mitzvot of the tzadeket are mainly directly toward serving others. She is a tzadeket to the extent that she sacrifices herself in order that others may actualize themselves spiritually. One has no sense of an attempt to cultivate a religious self built out of the raw materials of a unique personality. The model for the tzadeket is Rachel, the wife of Rabbi Akiva, who sold her hair and sent her husband away to study for twenty-four years, leaving herself beggared and without means of support; or the wife of Rabbi Menachem Mendel of Rymanov (her name incidentally, goes unremembered) who sold her share in the next world to buy her husband bread.

Frequently there is a kind of masochism manifest in the accounts of the acts of tzidkaniot. I recall the stories held up to me as models to emulate, of women who chopped holes in icy streams to perform their monthly immersions. A lady in the community I came from, who went into labor on Shabbat and walked to the hospital rather than ride in a taxi, was acting in accordance with this model. Implicit is the assumption that virtue is to be achieved by rejecting and punishing the hated body which men every morning thank God is not theirs.[9]

Second, as Hillel says, "an ignoramus cannot be a saint."[10] He may have the best of intentions, but he lacks the disciplined creativity, the sense of continuity with his people's history and thought, and the forms in which to give Jewish expression to his religious impulses. Since it was traditional to give women cursory religious educations, they were severely limited in their ways of expressing religious commitment. Teaching, the fundamental method of the Jewish people for transmitting religious insights, was closed to women—those who do not learn, do not teach.[11] Moreover, expressions of spiritual creativity by women seem to have been severely limited. Religious music written by women is virtually non-existent. There are no prayers written by women in the liturgy, although there were prayers written in Yiddish by women for women who were unable to pray in Hebrew.

It was, perhaps, most damaging that the woman's meager mitzvot are, for the most part, closely connected to some physical goal or object. A woman's whole life revolved around physical objects and physical experiences—cooking, cleaning, childbearing, meeting the physical needs of children. Without any independent

---

[8]Avoda Zara 18b. See Rashi.

[9]In the Traditional Prayerbook see the morning blessing, "Blessed are You, Lord our God, King of the universe, who has not created me a woman."

[10]Avot 2:6.

[11]Exactly this expression is used in Kiddushin 29b, where it is asserted that the mitzvah of teaching one's own offspring the Torah applies to men and not to women.

spiritual life to counterbalance the materialism of her existence, the mind of the average woman was devoted to physical considerations; marriages, deaths, dinners, clothes and money. It was, thus, natural that Jewish men should have come to identify women with *gashmiut* (physicality) and men with *ruchniut* (spirituality).

The Talmudic sages viewed the female mind as frivolous and the female sexual appetite as insatiable.[12] Unless strictly guarded and given plenty of busywork, all women were potential adulteresses.[13] In the Jewish view, all physical objects and experiences are capable of being infused with spiritual purpose; yet it is equally true that the physical, unredeemed by spiritual use, is a threat. It is therefore easy to see how women came to be regarded as semi-demonic in both Talmud and Kabbalah. Her sexuality represented a temptation, or perhaps a threat which came to be hedged ever more thickly by law and custom.[14] Conversing with women was likely to result in gossip or lewdness.[15] Women are classed as inadmissible witnesses in the same category with gamblers, pigeon-racers and other individuals of unsavory repute.[16]

Make no mistake; for centuries, the lot of the Jewish woman was infinitely better than that of her non-Jewish counterpart. She had rights which other women lacked until a century ago. A Jewish woman could not be married without her consent. Her ketubah (marriage document) was a legally binding contract which assured that her husband was responsible for her support (a necessity in a world in which it was difficult for a woman to support herself), and that if divorced, she was entitled to a monetary settlement. Her husband was not permitted to abstain from sex for long periods of time without regard to her needs and her feelings.[17] In its time, the Talmud's was a very progressive view. The last truly revolutionary ruling for women, however, was the Edict of Rabbenu Gershom forbidding polygamy to the Jews of the Western world. That was in 1000 C.E. The problem is that very little has been done since then to ameliorate the position of Jewish women in observant Jewish society.

All of this can quickly be rectified if one steps outside of Jewish tradition and Halacha. The problem is how to attain some justice and some growing room for the Jewish woman if one is committed to remaining *within* Halacha. Some of these problems are more easily solved than others. For example, there is ample precedent for decisions permitting women to study Talmud, and it should become the policy of Jewish day schools to teach their girls Talmud. It would not be difficult to find a basis for giving women aliyot to the Torah. Moreover, it is both feasible and desirable for the community to begin educating women to take on the positive time-bound mitzvot from which they are now excused; in which case, those

---

[12]Kiddushin 80b contains the famous statement, "The rational faculty of women weighs lightly upon them." Interestingly enough, the Tosafot illustrate this with an ancient mysogynistic fabliau whose written source is the Satryicon of Petronius Arbiter. See also Sotah 20a.

[13]Mishna Ketubot 5:5.

[14]This is the context in which one may understand the statement of the Kitzur Shulchan Aruch, "A man should be careful not to walk between two women, two dogs, or two swine." Ganzfried, Rabbi Solomon, Code of Jewish Law I, trans. Hyman E. Goldin, 2nd ed., New York: 1961, p. 7.

[15]Avot 1:5. See also the commentaries of Rashi, Rambam, and Rabbenu Yonah.

[16]Rosh HaShanah 22a.

[17]Mishna Ketubot 5:6.

mitzvot would eventually become incumbent upon women. The more difficult questions are those involving minyan and mechitza (segregation at prayers). There are problems concerning the right of women to be rabbis, witness in Jewish courts, judges and leaders of religious services. We need decisions on these problems which will permit Jewish women to develop roles and role models in which righteousness springs from self-actualization, in contrast to the masochistic, self-annihilating model of the post-Biblical tzadeket. The halachic scholars must examine our problem anew, right now, with open minds and with empathy. They must make it possible for women to claim their share in the Torah and begin to do the things a Jew was created to do. If necessary we must agitate until the scholars are willing to see us as Jewish souls in distress rather than as tools with which men do mitzvot. If they continue to turn a deaf ear to us, the most learned and halachically committed among us must make halachic decisions for the rest. That is a move to be saved for desperate straits, for even the most learned of us have been barred from acquiring the systematic halachic knowledge which a rabbi has. But, to paraphrase Hillel, in a place where there are no menschen, we may have to generate our own menschlichkeit. There is no time to waste. For too many centuries, the Jewish woman has been a golem, created by Jewish society. She cooked and bore and did her master's will, and when her tasks were done, the Divine Name was removed from her mouth. It is time for the golem to demand a soul.[18]

Postscript: "The sort of *piskei halacha* requested in the text of this article are *genuine* decisions based on sources and understanding of the halachic process made by people who understand and observe the Torah. Rationalizations will not do." [R.A.]

---

[18]There is a famous folk tale that the scholar Rabbi Loewe of Prague created a golem or robot, using the Kabbalah. The robot, formed from earth, came to life and worked as a servant when a tablet engraved with the Divine Name was placed in its mouth. When the tablet was removed, the golem reverted to mindless clay.

12 Explaining the Success of Classical Judaism as a Religion

JACOB NEUSNER

1. Why is this reading important?

Here I offer a theory of why a particular Judaism, the Rabbinic system, worked for so long and so well as it did, and continues to work today. By *work,* I mean persuading people to accept the worldview of a given system and organizing and conducting life, both public and private, within that system's way of life. Among the options that Jews have confronted over time, Rabbinic Judaism succeeded for a long time without significant competition from other Judaisms, and it succeeds today in diverse formulations. So this Judaism works in the sense that a functioning community of Jews regard themselves as constituting that "Israel" of which Scripture speaks, God's people, and live their lives and conduct their community in accord with the Oral and Written Torah, defined by "our sages of blessed memory," or rabbis. Over the past two hundred years, however, that Judaism has met competition from other systems, each with its own way of life, worldview, and theory of the social entity ("Israel") formed by the faithful. Moreover, this Judaism and indeed all Judaisms have been abandoned entirely in favor of secularism or even other religions by persons born of a Jewish mother and hence "Jewish" within the framework of ethnic sensibility and Judaic or Israelite within the definition of the Torah of Rabbinic Judaism. For those Jews, this Judaism does not work—in the sense of this essay. The same theory that explains why a religion works when it works has to explain why that same religion does not work when it does not work. That is the intellectual challenge facing this essay.

2. What should you notice as you proceed?

Among diverse sources of explanation, what does the writer deem a suitable source of explanation for the facts at hand? Consider alternatives that are not taken up at all—for example, a theological explanation or a psychological one. Feminism is a consideration here, with the argument that Rabbinic Judaism is androgynous and that this trait forms part of the success of that Judaism. The fundamental theory of success also includes the conviction that a religious system that is found irrelevant by half of its intended communicants cannot succeed. The condition of the Jews in world politics—as a subordinated group in some ways, a privileged group in others—is invoked. The author proposes a theory that shows how the shape and structure of Rabbinic Judaism exactly match the social world in which Jews lived. Finally, the competing religions and their challenges to this system are addressed: Why this, not that, for those who chose this, not that? That is a third mode of explanation in play in this essay. But you may well pick up others.

3. How should you frame a question for class discussion in response to what you have read?

The academic study of religion, also called the history of religion, within which *The Way of Torah* and the series of which it is a part find their place, forms an academic field of learning, with its program of questions and methods, its selected corpus of sources of evidence, its distinctive modes of analysis and argument—its way of seeing things. But the history of religion forms only one approach to learning among many well grounded in the academy. Questions are formulated and answered in accord with other rules besides those that implicitly govern this essay. The social sciences—the fields of learning devoted to the systematic study of society—address the same data with different questions and different ways of answering them. To gain perspective on what we do in the study of religion, you might try to reconsider the issues taken up in this essay in a different way. How would a political scientist, a psychologist, a sociologist, or an anthropologist frame and answer the same question? Students who major in other fields of the humanities or the social sciences besides the study of religion should take the lead. In dealing with the success of Classical or Rabbinic Judaism, they might try to spell out their conception of asking and answering basic questions of explanation.

Did—and, today, does—Classical or Rabbinic Judaism accomplish its goals? Certainly one question that every religious tradition ought to be asked to answer is: Is this a successful religion, and if so, why does it work? If it is not a successful religion, then why does it not work? Do people find its claims implausible, its demands excessive, its rewards trivial? This part of the book makes possible a discussion of how a religion defines the life of the faithful and whether that definition—in students' judgment—makes sense. To begin with, we have to define what constitutes success for religion, past or present. The criterion for the success of a religious system for a given social order may be set forth in these questions:

1. Has that religious system long governed the social order that it first shaped and addressed, or do holy books, not the character of society, form the principal evidence of the theory?

2. Does that religious system define the character of its enemies—for example, does it identify heresy—or does the social group produce

heresies out of phase with that religious system? That is, does the Judaism of the dual Torah so govern the imagination of all Jews, not only the participants in that Judaism, that other Judaisms, as they take shape, respond to the points of emphasis of the dominant one? Or do other Judaisms take shape that pay no attention to the Judaism of the dual Torah, which would suggest that the dominant Judaism made little difference outside its own boundaries?

3. Does that religious system exhibit the power to take over new ideas, rites, myths?

4. Does that religious system possess the inner resources to produce— in line with its single mythic system and symbolic structure, and in communication with its canonical writings—continuators and secondary developments over time? Or does the original statement appear to have delivered the entire message? Is its canon closed or open? The criterion of success here is simple: Does the system continue to shape the world and exercise formative influence, or does the system stand off from the world around it and influence only the faithful? Again, does the system possess an inner logic, an interior dynamic, that evolves over time, or is it essentially static and one dimensional?

The answers to all four questions (and many like them that can be fabricated) point in one direction and to one conclusion: Rabbinic Judaism takes its place among the most successful religious systems of the social order ever put forth in humanity. From the time the Talmud of Babylonia reached closure to our own day, that document formed the court of final appeal among nearly all Jews who practiced a Judaism. The heresies produced by Jews—such as Karaism of the ninth and tenth centuries, with its rejection of the oral part of the Torah, and Sabbateanism, of the seventeenth century, with its rejection of the doctrine of the Messiah as a sage—took as their principal issues the definitive convictions of this Judaism, and no recorded heresies stood entirely beyond the framework of this Judaism. Rabbinic Judaism made its own both the philosophical and the mystical approaches to thought and religious experience, deriving greatest strength from the modes of inquiry of the former and the modes of knowing God of the latter. And, of greatest interest, Rabbinic Judaism maintained an open canon, classifying as Torah those teachings, writings, and public statements of even the most current generation of sages (though diverse groups within Rabbinic Judaism certainly fight out their differences on which sages teach authentic Torah).

One final criterion of success finally validates the claim that in Rabbinic Judaism we meet a truly remarkable religious system of the social order. This was not a Judaism for a triumphant nation, but for a defeated people; not one for a nation secure in its own territory, but for a disenlandised and dispossessed people; not one for a society uniform and coherent in its indicative traits, but for a vast number of societies, each with its own customs and traditions, language, and economic system and setting. This Judaic system commanded no politics of its own to support its position with power, and found sustenance in no economy of its own to sustain its communicants with comfort.

Here the composite character of this Judaism—with its profoundly exclusionary male character, but its deeply feminine core of valued attitudes and emotions—comes to the surface. For if there is a single social form that this Judaism chose for itself, it is the family: the governing metaphor for what, after all, Israel is. Israel was imagined in accord with the metaphor not of kingdom of priests and holy people, nor of the inheritor nation to form the final world order, nor even of the realm of kings and priests, though the literature of this Judaism refers here and there to all of these metaphors for the social entity. Israel was first and foremost a family, and its frontiers were marked by genealogy, its passport provided through marriage, and its future defined in the act of procreation and nurture. What formed the Israel that found its life and strength in this Judaism was only the family and the composite of families in a given place, and what nourished and succored those families and formed of them a community, a society, a people, a holy nation—Israel—was this Judaism's Torah.

The strength of that religious system, in its language, that Torah, then finds its full measure in its enduring and compelling power to persuade precisely those to whom the sages intended to teach their Torah and offer their model of what it means to know God and to enter into communion with God. Knowing God through Torah study ordinarily excluded women; living in accord with the Torah nearly entirely depended upon the government, not just the nurture, of women: the religion of home and hearth, of sanctification of the here and now, of transactions marked by humility, generosity, and forbearing, was framed in the language of men but realized in the conduct of women.

In this context—evaluating and explaining success—we need not rehearse the painful history of subordination, contumacy, and humiliation that tells the tale of the world in which this Israel gave itself over to the life that the Torah sets forth as the Godly way. So far as a successful religious theory of the social order persuades individuals to stick it out and stay the course, before us is the documentary account of the founding of a religious system with scarcely a peer. For under ordinary conditions, it was easier to remain a Christian, whether Latin or Greek, or a Muslim, than to become something else; and the opportunities for change, such as conversion, were few and distant. Not a day went by, from the formation of this Judaism to our own time, in which, for individual Jews, the easier way did not lead outward, and the distance covered by the step was only down the street, to a nearby church or mosque.

Nor was the movement to an alien world. It was actually toward a different but entirely congruent social order, whether Muslim or Christian. Both religions defined orders of being that spoke of the same God and appealed to the same Scriptures (in the case of Christianity) or at least to the same God in the line of Abraham and Moses, not to mention Christ (in the case of Islam), and neither was unintelligible to or uncomprehending of Israel. Moreover, often the choice was not one or another way to God, but life of exile or even death; when faced with the choice of death or apostasy, entire communities of Israel chose to leave their homes and all they had or even to die. This is a truly successful religious system, one that exacted that last full measure of devotion that, in the name of God, a theory of the social order can demand.

What accounts for the success of Rabbinic Judaism is its power to address the challenges that Christianity and Islam set for the Israel that sustained that Judaism. When Christianity became the religion of the Roman empire in the fourth century, and Christians plausibly claimed that the remarkable success in converting the known world proved that what they said was so, Judaism met the challenge. We see how that happened when we ask precisely how the Christianization of Rome affected the formation of the Judaism of the dual Torah—and how it did not. The answer derives from the political facts that changed and those that did not change when Constantine became Christian at the beginning of the fourth century. When Rome became Christian and when Christianity became first licit, then established, and finally triumphant, the condition of Israel changed in some ways but not in others. What remained the same? The politics and social context of a defeated nation. Israel in the land of Israel/Palestine/the Holy Land had long ago lost its major war as an autonomous political unit of the Roman empire. In the year 70, the Romans had conquered the capital and destroyed the Temple there. In 132, a war broke out with the evident expectation that after three generations God would call an end to the punishment, as God had done in the time of the destruction of the first Temple, in 586 B.C.E., and its restoration some seventy years later. But that is not what happened. Israel again suffered defeat, this time worse than before. With Jerusalem now transformed into a forbidden city to Jews and the Temple now in permanent ruins, Israel, the Jewish people, took up the task of finding an accommodation with enduring defeat. Whether Rome accepted pagan or Christian rule had no bearing on the fundamental fact of Israel's life: a beaten nation.

Then what changed? The political situation of Israel did not change, but rather the circumstance and context of the religious system of Judaism. The political situation of Christianity did—and therefore, also, that of Judaism. Israelites in the Land of Israel persisted as a subject people. That is what they had been, that is what they remained. But Judaism now confronted a world in which its principal components confronted an effective challenge in the corresponding components of the now-triumphant faith in Christ. The Judaism that emerged dealt with that challenge in a way particular to Christianity. The doctrines that assumed central significance, those concerning the Messiah on one side and the character of God's revelation in the Torah to Moses at Sinai on the other, took up questions addressed to Judaism by Christianity and only by Christianity. So what changed changed because of the distinctive claims of Christianity, and what remained intact out of the antecedent heritage endured because Israel continued as a subjugated people.

Now, as we know, the Hebrew Scriptures, the Written Torah, in Christian view demanded a reading as the Old Testament predicting the New. Why? Because history now proved that Scripture's prophetic promises of a king-Messiah to begin with had pointed toward Jesus, now Christ enthroned. Concomitantly, the teleology of the Israelite system of old, focused as it was on the coming of the Messiah, now found confirmation and realization in the rule of Jesus, again, Christ enthroned. And the symbol of the whole—hermeneutics, teleology alike— rose in heaven's heights: the cross that had triumphed with Constantine's victory at the Milvian Bridge. No wonder, then, that the critical components of the prior system of Judaism were reviewed and sharply revised, as follows:.

1. The Written Torah found completion in the Oral Torah. So Judaism's extrascriptural traditions found legitimacy.

2. The system as a whole was now made to point toward an eschatological teleology, to be realized in the coming of the Messiah when Israel's condition, defined by the one whole Torah of Sinai, itself warranted. And it would necessarily follow that

3. The symbol of the Torah would expand to encompass the new teleology and hermeneutics. Therefore salvation comes from the Torah,
   not the cross.

Point by point, the principles of Judaism turn out in the fresh reading of the
Talmud to respond to the particular challenge of the principal event. The fourth
century C.E. marked the first century of Judaism as it would flourish in the West.
It further indicated the first century of Christianity as Christianity enthroned
would define and govern the civilization of the West.

Christianity's explicit claims, validated in world-shaking events of the age,
demanded a reply, and the sages of the Talmud of the Land of Israel provided it.
What did Israel have to present to the cross? The Torah—in the doctrine, first, of
the status, as oral and memorized revelation, of the Mishnah and, by implication,
of other rabbinical writings. The Torah, moreover, in the encompassing symbol
of Israel's salvation. The Torah, finally, in the person of the Messiah who would
be a rabbi. The Torah in all three modes confronted the cross, with its doctrine of
the triumphant Christ, Messiah and king, ruler now of earth as of heaven. What
changed? Those components of the sages' worldview that now stood in direct
confrontation with counterparts on the Christian side. What remained the same?
Doctrines governing fundamental categories of Israel's social life to which the triumph of Christianity made no material difference.

Every detail of the Judaic religious system set forth in the two Talmuds exhibits essentially the same point of insistence, captured in the simple notion of
the Torah as the generative symbol, the total, exhaustive expression of the system
as a whole. That is why the definitive ritual of this Judaism consisted in studying the Torah in these terms. That is why the definitive myth explained that one
who studied Torah would become holy, like Moses "our rabbi," and like God, in
whose image humanity was made and whose Torah provided the plan and the
model for what God wanted of a humanity created in his image.

As we saw in *The Way of Torah*, the issue of the Messiah and the meaning of
Israel's history framed through the Messiah myth convey in their terms precisely
the same position that we find in all other symbolic components of the Rabbinic
system and canon. The heart of the matter, then, is Israel's subservience to God's
will, as expressed in the Torah and embodied in the teachings and lives of the
great sages. When Israel fully accepts God's rule, then the Messiah will come. Until Israel subjects itself to God's rule, the Jews will be subjugated to pagan domination. Since the condition of Israel governs, Israel itself holds the key to its own
redemption. But this it can achieve only by throwing away the key!

The paradox must be crystal clear: Israel acts to redeem itself through the opposite of self-determination—namely, by subjugating itself to God. Israel's power
lies in its negation of power. Its destiny lies in giving up all pretense at deciding
its own destiny. Weakness is the ultimate strength, forbearance the final act of
self-assertion, passive resignation the sure step toward liberation. (The obvious
parallel here is the crucified Christ.) Israel's freedom is engraved on the tablets
of the commandments of God: to be free is freely to obey. That is not the meaning associated with these words in the minds of others who, like the sages of the
rabbinical canon, declared their view of what Israel must do to secure the coming of the Messiah. The kings of the Gentiles do not qualify, for they are arrogant.

The counterpart, the sages of Israel, will qualify, through humility and conciliation and acceptance of God's will. The upshot is a simple and strikingly relevant message: "Do not despair but hope, do not rebel but accept and humbly submit, do not mistake the present for the end, which, even now, we may attain by fulfilling, by embodying the Torah."

In all, therefore, we find a systematic confrontation on a program confronting both parties for a single reason. And that reason? The political revolution accomplished by Constantine's Christian continuators. The fact that Judaic sages conceived doctrines on a program of issues shared with Christianity would shape the future history of the Judaism formed by those sages. For as Christianity continued to harp on the same points, as it did, the Judaic party to the dispute for centuries to come could refer to the generative symbols and determinative myths of the sages' Judaism, which, to begin with dealt with these very issues. The Christian challenge, delivered through instruments of state and society, demanded a Judaic response, one involving not merely manipulation of power but exercise of intellect. Jews, continuing as a distinct society, took to heart the negative message of Christianity—"the Messiah has already come, you have no hope in the future, you are not Israel anyhow, and history proves we are right."

The sages produced responses to these questions, with doctrines of the meaning of history, the conditions in which the Messiah will come to Israel, and the definition of Israel. The symbolic system of the sages' Judaism, with its stress on Torah; the eschatological teleology of that system, with its stress on the Messiah-sage coming to obedient Israel; the insistence on the equivalence of Israel and Rome, Jacob and Esau, with Esau penultimate and Israel at the end of time—these constituted Israel's powerful responses to the Christian question.

The success of Judaism derives from this reciprocal process. On one side, the Judaism of the dual Torah restated for Israel in an acutely contemporary form, in terms relevant to the situation of Christendom and Islam, that generative experience of loss and restoration, death and resurrection, that the first Scripture had set forth. The people thus found a renewed sense of its own distinctive standing among the nations of the world. At the same time, Judaism taught the Jews the lesson that their subordinated position itself gave probative evidence of the nation's true standing: the low would be raised up, the humble placed into authority, the proud reduced, the world made right.

But the Judaism of the dual Torah did more than react, reassure, and encourage. It acted upon and determined the shape of matters. For a long time that Judaism defined the politics and policy of the community. It instructed Israel, the Jewish people, on the rules for the formation of the appropriate world, and it laid forth the design for those attitudes and actions that would yield an Israel both subordinate and tolerated on one side, but also proud and hopeful on the other. The Judaism of the dual Torah began in the encounter with a successful Christianity and persisted in the face of a still more successful Islam.

For Israel, the Jewish people, that Judaism persevered because, long after the conditions that originally precipitated the positions and policies deemed normative had passed, that same Judaism not only reacted to, but also shaped Israel's condition in the world. Making a virtue of a policy of subordination that was not always necessary or even wise, the Judaism of the dual Torah defined the Jews' condition and set the limits to its circumstance.

As the religion of a small, weak group, Judaism more than held its own against the challenge of triumphant Christendom and world-conquering Islam. The reason for the success of the Judaism of the dual Torah was that that system answered the question of why God's people, in exile, held a subordinated but tolerated position within the world framed by the sibling-rivals, Ishmael and Isaac, Esau and Jacob. The appeal to exile accounted for the dissonance of present unimportance and promised future greatness: "today if only you will. . . ." Therefore the question was urgent, the answer self-evidently true, in its appeal to the holy way of life explained by the received worldview addressed to the Israel consisting of the believers throughout the world. Here was the family of Abraham, Isaac, and Jacob: Israel. Now tolerated, sometimes oppressed, in exile, the family will ultimately come home to its own land. With the road back fully mapped out, people had now to remember who they were, where they were going, and what they had to do—or not do—to get from here to there.

The framing of the world as a system of families, with Israel *sui generis* and Israel's siblings part of its genus, admirably accounted for the state of the people, Israel. The way of life of the Judaism of the dual Torah, with its stress on the ongoing sanctification of the everyday; the worldview, with its doctrine of the ultimate salvation of the holy people—these realized the fundamental system in concrete and acutely relevant form. The consequence was total and enduring success. So long as Christianity defined the civilization of the West and Islam that of North Africa, the Near and Middle East, and Central Asia, Judaism in its fourth-century, classical statement triumphed in Israel, the Jewish people, located within Christendom and Islam. The questions deemed urgent, the answers found self-evidently true for Israel defined the world.

In a profound sense, therefore, the Judaism that reached canonical expression in the late fourth century C.E. succeeded in Israel because it dealt in a strikingly relevant way with both the issues and the politics of the Christian world within which Jews lived. The issues carried intellectual weight, the politics imparted urgency and power to those issues. Because of politics, the issues demanded attention. Had the doctrines focused on matters not at issue at all, and had the points of direct confrontation not elicited response within Judaism, then that Judaism would have proved itself simply irrelevant and died of the attrition of sheer lack of interest. When we deal with a later world that confronted Israel, the Jewish people, with other challenges enjoying self-evident urgency, we will see how the Judaism of the sages lost its standing as self-evidently true and right in large sectors of Israel.

The world beyond works out its affairs to accommodate God's will for Israel, and Israel's relationship to that larger world remains wholly within the control and subject to the power of Israel—but in a paradoxical way. For what Israel must do is accept, submit, accommodate, and receive with humility the will and word of God in the Torah. The power to govern the fate of the nation rested with the nation, but only so far as the nation accorded that power to God alone. Were people perplexed about who Israel is? The Torah answered the question: Israel is God's people, living out, here and now, the holy life prescribed by God. Did people wonder how long that people had to endure the government of Gentiles? The Torah addressed that issue: so long as God willed. The very God who had created the heavens and the earth dictated the fate of Israel—but also cared what each Jew ate for breakfast and responded to the conduct of every collectivity of Israel, each pool of the sacred formed by even a handful of Jews. The Judaism of the dual Torah in its distinctive idiom recapitulated the principle of the Judaism of the Torah of Moses. The system laid emphasis upon the everyday as a sequence of acts of sanctification. It promised remission and resolution—salvation—in consequence of the correct and faithful performance of those acts of sanctification. The subordinate position of Israel therefore served to attest to the true status of Israel, small and inconsequential now, but holy even now and destined for great reward at the end of time.

PART TWO

Classical Judaism
in Modern Times

13 Introduction

When we come to modern times, I aim at two separate goals. First, I add to the treatment of Judaism in modern times in *The Way of Torah*, where the focus was on what took place in Central and Western Europe and the United States—the advent of Reform, Orthodox, and Conservative Judaism in response to the political changes of the eighteenth and nineteenth centuries. Here we add consideration of a critical moment in the history of Judaism in Eastern Europe—the development of Hasidism. Hasidism is one of those mystical Judaisms within the large framework of Rabbinic Judaism to which Heschel makes reference, and we already have met its masters. The movement developed in the second half of the eighteenth century, but its first publications reached print at the same time that Reform and Orthodox Judaism were taking the form that would become familiar to us. Both before and after World War II, moreover, Hasidism successfully competed for the loyalty of Jews practicing a Judaism in the United States and Western Europe as much as in the state of Israel. It is a Judaism of modern times as much as is Reform Judaism; some argue, as we see later in the book, that it is as modern a Judaism as Reform Judaism. Hasidism has shown the power to frame a Rabbinic Judaism capable of meeting the human challenges of modern secularism and resisting the impulse to accommodate change that characterizes other Judaisms of modern times.

People use the term *modern* to refer to modernized religions—that is, religions that accommodate change. But in light not only of Hasidism but of other, powerful and popular versions of classical Rabbinic Judaism—whether organized in communities around yeshivot or study centers, formed into entire townships in the state of Israel, or neighborhoods elsewhere—we cannot accept that limited usage. A classroom discussion on what we can possibly mean by *modern, modernization, modernity,* and other terms that express the idea of the inevitability of change in the direction of a more secular order ought to take place. The discussion will do well to call upon the ideas set forth by Martin Buber, the greatest scholar of Hasidism as a religious movement (not just a set of ideas), who is amply represented in these pages.

But Reform, integrationist-Orthodox, and Conservative Judaisms compete alongside Hasidism, and these demand attention. They represent alternatives found "successful" (in the sense defined in essay 12) by millions of Jews from the nineteenth century onward—80 percent of practicing Jews in the United States and Canada, for example—and (taking account of the popularity of integrationist Orthodoxy there) the same proportion in Britain. The second point of addition takes up the personalties of principal figures in the formation of Reform, Orthodox, and Conservative Judaism. In *The Way of Torah* I focus upon the main issues and ideas of the new Judaisms within the Rabbinic sector. Here I call attention to the lives and ideas of the founders of those Judaisms, and students may want to ask questions about the role of the hero, the influential or charismatic personality, in religion and how that personality both embodies the problems of the day and also influences their solution.

In addition, here we encounter in their own words important modern and contemporary voices of Reform, integrationist-Orthodox, and Conservative Judaisms. The first, Eugene Borowitz, is the principal theologian of Reform Judaism in the second half of the twentieth century and speaks to acutely contemporary matters. Alongside his work we encounter the critique of Reform Judaism set forth by an important figure in the recent past, Jakob J. Petuchowski. Among important integrationist-Orthodox voices, I have selected the man who attained the position of moral authority for much of integrationist-Orthodox Judaism in the United States and who, as chancellor of Bar Ilan University in the state of Israel, achieved influence overseas as well. In the recent past, Conservative Judaism has found its voices among a new generation of rabbis, and I have identified in their ideas what seems to be a challenge of a fundamental character.

What, in fact, has taken place in the history of Judaism from the eighteenth century onward? Two powerful European movements, one intellectual, the other political, shook the foundations of the received social structure of the Judaism of the dual Torah.

Intellectual Modernization

The intellectual movement was the Enlightenment, a movement of intellectuals who maintained that reason was the measure of all things and that through rational planning and action humanity could attain perfection through its own best efforts. All things, then, had to withstand the test of reason. The political movement closely allied to the Enlightenment was the Emancipation, which recognized the rights of individuals as citizens not differentiated by reason of ethnic or religious origin, but which did not recognize the standing of the caste, ethnic group, or quasiofficial community, that the Jewish community had enjoyed for so long. Reform, then Orthodox, then Conservative Judaisms responded to the challenges of the Enlightenment and the Emancipation. So, too, in a very different way, did Hasidism, and, further, Zionism.

To the end of the eighteenth century, when the "modern period" of the history of Judaism begins, Jewish society was corporate, segregated, and collective in emphasis. Jews in Europe spoke a common language—Yiddish—and regarded themselves as a separate nation, living within other nations and awaiting their ultimate return to their own land. The central social ideal was study of Torah, which would result in heavenly reward. The obligation to study the Torah, leading to an intense appreciation for intellectualism, prevented the sanctification of economic activity as an ultimate goal and ensured effective control over the people's value structure for the tradition—study of which was the chief purpose of living. The community itself was governed by its own classical legal tradition, with the rabbi as judge and community official.

The *kehillah* (structure of community government) controlled economic activities, relations with non-Jews, family and social life, and matters of religion—including, of course, all aspects of culture and education. It was the structural embodiment of the corporate community. How did this community disintegrate so that the focus of Judaism came to center upon the individual, and the emphasis of Jewish thought upon the individual's personal religious needs and convictions? *It was not the result of external catastrophes.* Jewish society was badly shaken by the massacres of 1648–49, but the response of the community did not deviate from the traditional pattern. It took the form of fasting, prayer, severe sumptuary laws, and rededication to study and observance of the Torah.

During the eighteenth century, Hasidism in Eastern Europe and *Haskalah* (Enlightenment) in the West undermined traditional society. These movements shattered the framework of the community—which had formerly been able to reconstitute itself following banishments and migrations—in the several localities. Hasidism, a pietist movement recalling the contemporary Methodism of Britain and the Great Awakening of mid-eighteenth-century New England, weakened the fidelity of the people to the rabbinic lawyer's leadership by stressing the importance *not* of learning in the law, but of religious charisma—the capacity to say particularly effective prayers, tell evocative stories, and engage in acts of a theurgic character. Existing institutions seemed to have lost their hold on large numbers of people. The situation was ripe for new social groups to take shape among people who had lost faith in the old ones. The Hasidic rabbi, called *Tzaddik* (literally, righteous one), won the loyalty of such people through the force of his personality. He was regarded not as a mere wonder worker, but as an intermediary between heaven and earth.

Hasidism was more than an adjustment to new social conditions or a movement of protest. In content, value, and structure, it was a revolution that set in a new light all preceding faith. One achieved holiness through Torah or through the *Tzaddik* (by celebrating his holiness), but not through both. A movement within the community, Hasidism created sects in the traditional corporate society. Some followed the charismatic leader; others did not. The consequence of these doctrines and policies was a religious and social revolution based upon a new requirement for leadership—not learning but personality. It resulted in the formation, within the body of the old community, of new and limited societies; in consequence, the traditional *kehillah* was destroyed.

Political Modernization

The second force for modernization of traditional society was the Emancipation, which in France and Germany altogether revolutionized the basis of Jewish society by destroying both its legal and its philosophical foundation. External rather than internal in its impact, the Emancipation withdrew the political basis of Jewry by extending to the Jews the rights of citizens and at the same time denying Judaism the authority over Jews it had formerly exercised. It furthermore encouraged the development within Jewry of a new type of person, the *maskil* (illumined man), who mastered areas of human erudition formerly thought to be irrelevant to Jews. So the Enlightenment's processes of intellectual dissolution and the Emancipation's revision of the Jews' political status and condition reinforced one another. Because of the Emancipation the *kehillah* lost its legal standing, and because of the Enlightenment some of its subjects opted out of it at the same time.

Now individual members of Jewish society began to interest themselves in the opinion of the Gentile world and to seek the esteem of non-Jews on the basis of Gentile values. Had Jews merely converted to Christianity, it would hardly have affected traditional society; but many left that society and *yet* chose to remain Jews. They plunged into a crisis of identity that has yet to find resolution.

As part of the Jewish community—though perhaps on its fringes—the *maskilim* held up to the tests of reason, intelligence, and nature the artifacts of the tradition that had formerly been accepted as part of the given—the revealed reality—of the world. And they did so aggressively and derisively. The values they projected were those of the neutral society, which they saw as the wave of the future. They criticized the economic structure of Jewish society, its occupational one-sidedness, the traditional organizations (whose compulsory authority they rejected), and the traditional system of education, which did nothing to prepare young people to participate in the new world then seen to be opening up.

They did not propose to abandon Jewish society but to "modernize" it. Values formerly held to be ends in themselves now came to be evaluated in terms of their usefulness and rationality—a usefulness measured not within the Jewish framework at all. The synagogue was seen as the locus of assemblage of the faithful for prayer rather than, as in former times, the focus for community life, society, and culture. The content and language of prayer, the architecture of the synagogue and its ritual were among the earliest objects of a reformation. Most significantly, the traditional modes of social control—denunciation and excommunication—ceased to operate effectively. Deviants no longer saw themselves as sinners. They did not justify themselves by traditional values at all.

The Extent of Intellectual and Political Modernization in the Nineteenth and Twentieth Centuries

Modernization was hardly a broad, widespread phenomenon. It mattered in only a few places—and even there unevenly—to almost the present time. Though the *kehillah* in its late medieval form underwent vast changes, the traditional personality and pattern of living of Jews in many places did not. The Enlightenment's impact, even in Germany until well into the nineteenth century, was limited to the upper classes. Hasidism was a mostly regional phenomenon, and after two generations its fervor was directed into more or less traditional channels. Today, while remaining highly sectarian, Hasidism has become a bastion of the "tradition" in its least malleable forms.

More broadly still, the Jews in French-ruled Moslem countries—apart from the Frenchified urban upper classes—remained deeply a part of the traditional culture, not so much affirming intellectual *reasons* for remaining so, as *practicing* the faith in its classical forms into the twentieth century. For many, arriving in the state of Israel also signified arrival in the twentieth century as we know it. The political changes we grouped under the category of emancipation had hardly reached Polish, Hungarian, Rumanian, and Russian Jewry before the Holocaust of 1933 to 1945. Furthermore, for many Jews in Western countries, the experience of modernization was objectionable; and, as we shall see, many rejected it. If a tradition changes, it is only for some; it never disintegrates for all.

It would be impossible to offer a fully adequate delimitation of the modernization of Judaism for three reasons. First, substantial parts of the Jewish people never underwent such a process—not only the Jews in Moslem countries, but also very large segments of Eastern European Jewry. Second, even in the great cities—to which the majority of Central and Western European Jews had come by 1900—significant populations of traditionalists existed to the time of the Holocaust during World War II; in the Western countries groups of traditionalists continue to exist to the present day. Whether they are traditional in the way in which the seventeenth-century Jew was traditional is not the issue. The fact is that those qualities we have associated with traditionalism apply without qualification to large parts of Jewry and therefore to significant segments of Judaism in Israel, the United States, Great Britain, continental Europe, and elsewhere. Third, the inner dynamism of a living tradition is such that at no point may we arbitrarily arrest its development for purposes of definition and conclude that a given form is the tradition from which all that changes thereby deviates and therefore constitutes "modernization." Within the circles of the most traditional Jews, cultural phenomena are today accepted that a century ago would have been regarded as unacceptable; yet should we call such Jews modernists, the term would be deprived of any meaning whatever. In context, they think of themselves and are thought of by others as living within the classic tradition.

The Complexity of the Notion of Modernity

By this point in the discussion, we can begin to see some of the complexity of the problem of modernity in the history of Judaism. On one hand, we have reviewed some of the climactic moments and experiences of the life of the Jew. We have seen that the Judaic religious tradition exercises a majestic force—a power—over the imagination and feeling, the mind and the soul, of the Jew. So we must ask how it was possible for large numbers of people to break the bonds that tied them to so glorious a world as that constructed by Judaism.

On the other hand, the political status of the Jew radically changed; the Jews no longer formed a fairly closed social group but wanted to relate to non-Jews and get to know and live with them. In Western countries—the United States, Britain, France, Holland, Belgium, Canada, and Germany—Jews were granted full civil rights and were able to exercise them in some measure. The wonder is, then, why anyone should have held to the old way of life at all. How could anyone have resisted the appeal of the new age? But Zionism recognized that the new age contained within itself unprecedented dangers to the physical security of the Jews and presented the foundation of a Jewish state as the sole means of escaping the catastrophe that modernity was bringing.

Tradition and Change

This is the paradox: the power of the tradition versus the force of modernity. The two spent themselves, to be sure, in the disasters of World War II. But by then the changes were mostly in place. Western Jews (in the United States, France, Britain, and Canada, for example) had clearly found their way into the larger societies in which they were born and grew up. Few wanted to live on the fringes of culture and in tight little communities of faith. On the other hand, these same Jews clearly wanted not only to remain Jewish, but to remain Jewish in a religious way. Many aspired to regain access to that which their grandparents and great-grandparents had rejected. Indeed, as the great historian of American immigration, Marcus Lee

Hansen, put it: "What the child [the first-generation American] wants to forget, the grandchild [the third generation] tries to remember." To state Hansen's perception in terms of the religious history of contemporary Jews: The native-born Jew of the third and fourth and fifth generations past the immigration times (or "emancipation") are fully acculturated—so much so that they, too, are in search of their roots.

The question becomes, then, whether or not the majesty of an alien worldview may once more exert its reality-constructing power. To phrase the question in the language with which we began: Has the context, the natural system, of the Jewish people so vastly changed that that old, world-constructing system—Judaism—that made sense for so long can make sense no longer? Are the ecological data so new and unprecedented that a way of seeing the world that worked for so many generations of moderately skeptical, moderately optimistic people today can work no more? These are the issues of the future that is now.

14 *Hasidism*

MARTIN BUBER

1. Why is this reading important?

In the academic study of mysticism in Judaism, two great pioneers defined the tradition of scholarship, Abraham J. Heschel and Martin Buber. Their success rested on intellectual, not political, power. We have already encountered Heschel's exposition of the mysticism within Rabbinic Judaism, and here we address Buber's way of introducing the Hasidic component of mysticism. Buber chooses as his focus the principal medium of Hasidism, which is the story of a holy man. I have given an excerpt to allow full exposure of Buber's remarkable power of formulation and recapitulation. Through his combination of scholarship and empathy with his subject, Buber not only sets the stage, he also acts out the play. But he never loses sight of us, his readers, who are onlookers and not participants; everything is explained, in a deft way, so that we are never lost because of unfamiliar details. Buber's remains the single most effective and reliable account of Hasidism as an alternative within Rabbinic Judaism. In his day he had his critics; they are forgotten, the achievement of learning and art endures. This reading is the most important single statement about Hasidism available in the English language for the general reader. It is exemplary of the finest kind of scholarly reading on religion that Judaism put forth in the twentieth century.

2. What should you notice as you proceed?

Notice how Buber first explains the importance of the story, and only then tells the story. Ask yourself the question: What choices has Buber made in explaining matters in this way and not in some other? To consider the alternatives, you might look up "Hasidism" in an encyclopedia or examine a book on Hasidism in your college or university library. There you will see that others have chosen a more "historical" mode of defining and explaining Hasidism. They tell us what came first and what happened then; they examine the setting in which Hasidism took shape and try to relate the distinctive emphases of Hasidism—upon piety rather than learning, for example—to the world in which Hasidism found itself. That forms a mode of explanation imposed upon the very characterization of the phenomenon. But this is not Buber's way. Because he believes that everything is captured in the story, he introduces, then tells, the stories. Ask yourself whether the stories contain the power that Buber attributes to them: Are you affected by them? Can people be changed by hearing them?

3. How should you frame a question for class discussion in response to what you have read?

Religions excel in diverse media, and no religion uses all the available media of human expression with equally powerful effect. Some religions come to expression in dance, some in song, some in plastic and graphic arts, some in theological articulation, some in political activity. And in their choice of media in which to excel, religions make a statement not only about their media but also about their messages. A stimulating discussion will address the question: Why does Hasidism find in the story about the holy man the ideal medium for conveying its message? What is it about the story that the Hasidim regard as particularly effective? Hasidism not only tells stories but emphasizes joyful activities in song and dance. But it does not stress disciplined learning, and its rabbis, then and now, are famous in the world of Judaism for their ignorance of the really demanding intellectual exercises of Rabbinic Judaism—Talmud study, for example. That outcome is in line with the saying, "You pay your money and you make your choice." What choices do other religions make? Why, for example, do Catholic and Orthodox Christianities lay heavy emphasis upon the character of buildings, producing in the Catholic case impressive cathedrals and in the Orthodox case remarkable churches as well? What do the Reformation churches put in place of the cathedral? Abraham J. Heschel described the Sabbath in Judaism as "a cathedral in time." What are the counterparts in other religions? Here again, an exercise in comparison and contrast should shed light on the choices religions make.

One of the most vital aspects of the hasidic movement is that the hasidim tell one another stories about their leaders, their "zaddikim." Great things had happened, the hasidim had been present, they had seen them, and so they felt called upon to relate and bear witness to them. The words used to describe these experiences were more than mere words; they transmitted what had happened to coming generations, and with such actuality that the words in themselves became events. And since they serve to perpetuate holy events, they bear the consecration of holy deeds. It is told that the "Seer" of Lublin once saw a pillar of light rise out of a klaus; when he entered he saw hasidim telling one another about their zaddikim. According to hasidic belief, the primeval light of God poured into the zaddikim; from them it poured into their works, and from these into the words of the hasidim who relate them. The Baal Shem, the founder of hasidism, is supposed to have said that when a hasid spoke in praise of the zaddikim, this was equivalent to dwelling on the mystery of the divine Chariot which Ezekiel once saw. And a zaddik of the fourth generation, Rabbi Mendel of Rymanov, a friend of the "Seer," added in explanation: "For the zaddikim *are* the chariot of God." But story is more than a mere reflection. The holy essence it testifies to lives on in it. The miracle that is told, acquires new force; power that once was active, is propagated in the living word and continues to be active—even after generations.

A rabbi, whose grandfather had been a disciple of the Baal Shem, was asked to tell a story. "A story," he said, "must be told in such a way that it constitutes help in itself." And he told: "My grandfather was lame. Once they asked him to tell a story about his teacher. And he related how the holy Baal Shem used to hop and dance while he prayed. My grandfather rose as he spoke, and he was so swept away by his story that he himself began to hop and dance to show how the master had done. From that hour on he was cured of his lameness. That's the way to tell a story!"

Side by side with the oral transmission went a written transmission which began far back in the history of the movement, but of the written recollections of the first generations only very few uncorrupted texts have been preserved. In their youth a number of zaddikim wrote down the deeds and utterances of their masters, but apparently for their own use rather than for the public at large. Thus we know from a reliable source that the rabbi of Berditchev, of all rabbis the closest to the people, noted down everything his teacher, Dov Baer of Mezritch, the Great Maggid, said and did, including everyday utterances, and read and re-read the pages, straining his soul to the utmost in the effort to understand the meaning of every word. But his notebook has been lost and very few similar notations have been preserved. . . .

2.

The core of hasidic teachings is the concept of a life of fervor, of exalted joy. But this teaching is not a theory which can persist regardless of whether it is translated into reality. It is rather the theoretic supplement to a life which was actually lived by the zaddikim and hasidim, especially in the first six generations of the movement.

The underlying purpose of all great religions and religious movement is to beget a life of elation, of fervor which cannot be stifled by any experience, which, therefore, must spring from a relationship to the eternal, above and beyond all individual experiences. But since the contacts a man makes with the world and with himself are frequently not calculated to rouse him to fervor, religious concepts refer him to another form of being, to a world of perfection in which his soul may also grow perfect. Compared to this state of perfect being, life on earth seems either only an antechamber, or mere illusion, and the prospect of a higher life has the task of creating fervor in the face of disappointing outer and inner experiences, of creating the fervent conviction that there is such a higher life, and that it is, or can gradually become accessible to the human soul, under certain conditions beyond the bounds of earthly existence. Although faith in a life hereafter is integral to Judaism, there has always been a strong tendency to provide an earthly residence for perfection. The great Messianic concept of coming perfection on earth which everyone can actively help prepare for, could not, in spite of the power it exerted over souls, endow daily life with that constant, undaunted and exalted joy in the Now and Here, which can spring only from fulfilment in the present, not from hope in a future fulfilment. This was not altered when the Kabbalistic teaching of the transmigration of souls made it possible for everyone to identify his soul with that of a person of the Messianic generation, and thus have the feeling of participating in it. Only in the Messianic movements themselves, which always were based on the belief that perfection was just on the verge of being realized, did the fervor break through and permeate all of life. When the last of these movements, the Sabbatian movement, and its after-effects ended in renegacy and despair, the test for the living strength of religion had come, for here no mere softening of sorrow, but only a life of fervent joy could aid the Jew to survive. The development of hasidism indicates that the test was passed.

The hasidic movement did not weaken the hope in a Messiah, but it kindled both its simple and intellectual followers to joy in the world as it is, in life as it is, in every hour of life in this world, as that hour is. Without dulling the prick of conscience or deadening the sense of chasm between the ideal pattern of the individual limned by his Creator, and what he actually is, hasidism shows men the way to God who dwells with them "in the midst of their uncleannesses," a way which issues forth from every temptation, even from every sin. Without lessening the strong obligation imposed by the Torah, the movement suffused all the traditional commandments with joy-bringing significance, and even set aside the walls separating the sacred and the profane, by teaching that every profane act can be rendered sacred by the manner in which it is performed. It had nothing to do with pantheism which destroys or stunts the greatest of all values: the reciprocal relationship between the human and the divine, the reality of the I and the You which does not cease at the rim of eternity. Hasidism did, however, make manifest the reflection of the divine, the sparks of God that glimmer in all beings and all things, and taught how to approach them, how to deal with them, how to "lift" and redeem them, and re-connect them with their original root. The doctrine of the Shekhinah, contained in the Talmud and expanded in the Kabbalah, of the Shekhinah as the Divine Presence which resides in this world, receives a new and intimate significance and applicability. If you direct the undiminished power of your fervor to God's world-destiny, if you do what you must do at this moment—no matter what it may be!—with your whole strength and with kavvanah, with holy intent, you will bring about the union between God and Shekhinah, eternity and time. You need not be a scholar or a sage to accomplish this. All that is necessary is to have a soul united within itself and indivisibly directed to its divine goal. The world in which you live, just as it is and not otherwise, affords you that association with God, which will redeem you and whatever divine aspect of the world you have been entrusted with. And your own character, the very qualities which make you what you are, constitutes your special approach to God, your special potential use for Him. Do not be vexed at your delight in creatures and things! But do not let it shackle itself to creatures and things; through these, press on to God. Do not rebel against your desires, but seize them and bind them to God. You shall not stifle your surging powers, but let them work at holy work, and rest a holy rest in God. All the contradictions with which the world distresses you are only that you may discover their intrinsic significance, and all the contrary trends tormenting you within yourself, only wait to be exorcised by your word. All innate sorrow wants only to flow into the fervor of your joy.

But this joy must not be the goal toward which you strive. It will be vouchsafed you if you strive to "give joy to God." Your personal joy will rise up when you want nothing but the joy of God—nothing but joy in itself.

3.

But how was man, in particular the "simple man," with whom the hasidic movement is primarily concerned, to arrive at living his life in fervent joy? How, in the fires of temptation, was he to recast the Evil Urge into an urge for what is good? How, in the wonted fulfilling of the commandments was he to develop the rapturous bond with the upper worlds? How, in his meeting with creatures and things, grow aware of the divine sparks hidden within them? How, through holy kavvanah, illumine everyday life? We do, indeed, know that all that is necessary is to have a soul united within itself and indivisibly directed to its divine goal. But how, in the chaos of life on our earth, are we to keep the holy goal in sight? How to retain unity in the midst of peril and pressure, in the midst of thousands of disappointments and delusions? And once unity is lost, how recover it? Man needs counsel and aid, he must be lifted and redeemed. And he does not need all this only in regard to his soul, for in some way or other, the domains of the soul are intertwined with the big and little cares, the griefs and despairs of life itself, and if these are not dealt with, how shall those loftier concerns be approached? A helper is needed, a helper for both body and soul, for both earthly and heavenly matters. This helper is called the zaddik. He can heal both the ailing body and the ailing soul, for he knows how one is bound up with the other, and this knowledge gives him the power to influence both. It is he who can teach you to conduct your affairs so that your soul remains free, and he can teach you to strengthen your soul, to keep you steadfast beneath the blows of destiny. And over and over he takes you by the hand and guides you until you are able to venture on alone. He does not relieve you of doing what you have grown strong enough to do for yourself. He does not lighten your soul of the struggle it must wage in order to accomplish its particular task in this world. And all this also holds for the communication of the soul with God. The zaddik must make communication with God easier for his hasidim, but he cannot take their place. This is the teaching of the Baal Shem and all the great hasidim followed it; everything else is distortion and the signs of it appear relatively early. The zaddik strengthens his hasid in the hours of doubting, but he does not infiltrate him with truth, he only helps him conquer and reconquer it for himself. He develops the hasid's own power for right prayer, he teaches him how to give the words of prayer the right direction, and he joins his own prayer to that of his disciple and therewith lends him courage, an increase of power—wings. In hours of need, he prays for his disciple and gives all of himself, but he never permits the soul of the hasid to rely so wholly on his own that it relinquishes independent concentration and tension, in other words, that striving-to-God of the soul without which life on this earth is bound to be unfulfilled. Not only in the realm of human passions does the zaddik point over and over to the limits of counsel and help. He does this also in the realm of association with God; again and again he emphasizes the limits of mediation. One man can take the place of another only as far as the threshold of the inner sanctum.

Both in the hasidic teachings and in the tales, we often hear of zaddikim who take upon themselves the sorrow of others, and even atone for others by sacrificing their own lives. But on the very rare occasions (as in the case of Rabbi Nahman of Bratzlav) when we read that the true zaddik can accomplish the act of turning to God for those nearest and dearest to him, the author immediately adds that this act done in place of the other, facilitates the hasid's own turning to God. The zaddik helps everyone, but he does not relieve anyone of what he must do for himself. His helping is a delivery. He even helps the hasid through his death; those near him in the hour of his death receive "a great illumining."

Within these limits the zaddik has the greatest possible influence not only on the faith and mind of the hasid, but on his active everyday life, and even on his sleep, which he renders deep and pure. Through the zaddik, all the senses of the hasid are perfected, not through conscious directing, but through bodily near-ness. The fact that the hasid looks at the zaddik perfects his sense of sight, his lis-tening to him, his sense of hearing. Not the teachings of the zaddik but his existence constitute his effectiveness; and not so much the circumstance that he is present on extraordinary occasions as that he is there in the ordinary course of days, unemphatic, undeliberate, unconscious; not that he is there as an intellec-tual leader but as the complete human being with his whole worldly life in which the completeness of the human being is tested. As a zaddik once said: "I learned the Torah from all the limbs of my teacher." This was the zaddik's influence on his true disciples. But his mere physical presence did not, of course, suffice to ex-ert influence on the many, on the people at large, that influence which made ha-sidism a popular movement. To achieve this, he had to work with the people until they were ready to receive what he had to give them, to present his teachings in a form the people could accept as their own, he must "participate in the multi-tude." He had to mix with the people and, in order to raise them to the rung of what perfection they were capable of, he had to descend from his own rung. "If a man falls into the mire," says the Baal Shem, "and his friend wants to fetch him out, he must not hesitate to get himself a little dirty."

There are many distorted aspects of hasidism which are by no means inher-ent only in the later stages of the movement. Side by side with the fervent love for the zaddik we find a coarsened form of reverence on the part of those who regard him as a great magician, as one who is an intimate of heaven and can right all that is wrong, who relieves his hasidim of straining their own souls and se-cures them a desirable place in the hereafter. Though the hasidim of a zaddik were often united by a feeling of true brotherliness, they frequently held aloof from and sometimes were even hostile to the followers of other zaddikim. A like contrast obtained between the free life in religion of a hasidic community and their thick-skinned opportunism in regard to the powers of the state. Sometimes, dull superstition settled down side by side with the innocent fantasy of the elated spirit and made shallows of its depths, and sometimes crass fraud made its ap-pearance and abused it. Most of these phenomena are familiar to us through the history of other religious movements that sprang from the vitality of the people, others become understandable when we consider the pathological premises of life in exile. My aim was not to go into all this, but to show what it was that made hasidism one of the most significant phenomena of living and fruitful faith that we know, and—up to this time—the last great flowering of the Jewish will to serve God in this world and to consecrate everyday life to him.

In the very beginnings of the movement, hasidism disintegrated into sepa-rate communities whose inner life had small connection, and early in its history individual zaddikim display problematic traits. But every hasidic community still contains a germ of the kingdom of God, a germ—no more than that, but no less, and often this germ lives and grows even in substance which has fallen prey to decay. And even the zaddik who has squandered the spiritual inheritance of his forbears has hours in which his forehead gives forth a glow as though the pri-mordial light had touched it with radiance.

Israel ben Eliezer The Baal Shem Tov

THE TREE OF KNOWLEDGE

They say that once, when all souls were gathered in Adam's soul, at the hour he stood beside the Tree of Knowledge, the soul of the Baal Shem Tov went away, and did not eat of the fruit of the tree.

THE SIXTY HEROES

It is said that the soul of Rabbi Israel ben Eliezer refused to descend to this world below, for it dreaded the fiery serpents which flicker through every generation, and feared they would weaken its courage and destroy it. So he was given an escort of sixty heroes, like the sixty who stood around King Solomon's bed to guard him against the terrors of night—sixty souls of zaddikim to guard his soul. And these were the disciples of the Baal Shem.

THE TEST

It is told:

Rabbi Eliezer, the Baal Shem's father, lived in a village. He was so hospitable that he placed guards at the outskirts of the village and had them stop poor wayfarers and bring them to his house for food and shelter. Those in Heaven rejoiced at his doing, and once they decided to try him. Satan offered to do this, but the prophet Elijah begged to be sent in his stead. In the shape of a poor wayfarer, with knapsack and staff, he came to Rabbi Eliezer's house on a sabbath afternoon, and said the greeting. Rabbi Eliezer ignored the desecration of the sabbath, for he did not want to mortify the man. He invited him to the meal and kept him in his house. Nor did he utter a word of reproof the next morning, when his guest took leave of him. Then the prophet revealed himself and promised him a son who would make the eyes of the people of Israel see the light.

HIS FATHER'S WORDS

Israel's father died while he was still a child.

When he felt death drawing near, he took the boy in his arms and said: "I see that you will make my light shine out, and it is not given me to rear you to manhood. But, dear son, remember all your days that God is with you, and that because of this, you need fear nothing in all the world."

Israel treasured these words in his heart.

VAIN ATTEMPTS

After the death of Israel's father, the people looked out for the boy for the sake of Rabbi Eliezer, whose memory was dear to them, and sent his son to a melammed.

Now, Israel studied diligently enough, but always only for a few days running. Then he played truant and they found him somewhere in the woods and alone. They ascribed this behavior to the fact that he was an orphan without proper care and supervision, and returned him to the melammed over and over, and over and over the boy escaped to the woods until the people despaired of ever making an honest and upright man of him.

THE FIRST FIGHT

When the boy grew up, he hired himself out as teacher's assistant. Early in the morning, he called for the children in their homes and brought them to school and the House of Prayer. In a clear and moving voice, he recited to them those words of prayer which are said in chorus, such as "Amen, let His great name be blessed forever and in all eternity." While he walked with them, he sang to them and taught them to sing with him. And when he took them home, he went by way of fields and woods.

The hasidim say that those in heaven rejoiced in these songs every morning, just as they had once rejoiced in the song of the Levites in the Temple of Jerusalem. The hours when the hosts of Heaven gathered to listen to the voices of mortals, were hours of grace. But Satan was there too. He knew very well that what was in the making down there would threaten his power on earth. So he entered into the body of a sorcerer who could change himself into a werewolf.

Once when Israel was walking through the woods and singing with the little ones in his care, the monster fell on them, and the children screamed and scattered in all directions. Some of them fell ill from the shock and the parents decided to put a stop to the doings of the young school assistant. But he remembered what his father had said as he lay dying, went from house to house, promised the people to protect their children, and succeeded in persuading them to entrust them to him once more. The next time he shepherded them through the wood, he took a sound stick with him and when the werewolf attacked again, he struck him between the eyes, so that he was killed on the instant. The following day they found the sorcerer dead in his bed.

CONJURING

After this, Israel was employed as a servant in the House of Study. Since he had to be there day and night, but felt that Heaven wished him to keep secret his fervor and intentness, he made a habit of sleeping while those in the House of Study were awake, and to pray and study while they slept. But what they thought was that he slept all night and on into the day. The hasidim tell of wonderful happenings that occurred in those days.

Before the time of the Baal Shem Tov—so they say—a wonder-working man by the name of Adam lived, no one knows just where, but it was probably in the imperial city of Vienna. Like the succession of wonder-working men before him, Adam was called Baal Shem, that is the Master of the Name, because he knew the secret, full name of God, and could say it in such a way that—with its help—he was able to effect strange things and especially to heal men in body and soul. When this man knew he was about to die, he did not know to whom to leave the age-old writings from which he had learned his secrets, the writings which had been handed down from Abraham, the patriarch. While his only son was a man both learned and devout, he was not worthy of a heritage such as this. And so Adam, in his dream, asked Heaven what he should do and was told to have the writings given to Rabbi Israel ben Eliezer in the city of Okup, who would then be fourteen years old. On his death-bed, Adam entrusted his son with the errand.

When his son reached Okup, he first found it difficult to believe that the servant in the House of Study, who was generally regarded as a crude and ignorant boy, could be the person he was looking for. He let the boy wait on him in the

House of Study, observed him closely and secretly and soon realized that Israel was hiding his true character and preoccupations from the world. Now he told him who he was, gave him the writings and only asked that he might participate in studying them under the boy's direction. Israel consented on condition that their agreement remain secret and that he continue to serve the stranger. Adam's son rented a small house outside the city and apart from others, and the people were only too glad to give him Israel for his servant. They thought, indeed, that this devout and learned man was willing to put up with the boy only because his father had been a person of such merit.

Once Rabbi Adam's son asked the boy to conjure up the Prince of the Torah with the aid of the directions given in the writings, so that they might ask him to solve certain difficulties in the teachings. For a long time, Israel refused to undertake so great a venture, but in the end he let himself be persuaded. They fasted from sabbath to sabbath, immersed themselves in the bath of purification, and—at the close of the sabbath—fulfilled the rites prescribed. But, probably because Adam's son did not fix his soul utterly on the teachings themselves, an error crept in. Instead of the Prince of the Torah, the Prince of Fire appeared and wanted to burn up the entire town. It was only by a great effort that it was saved.

After a long time, Adam's son urged the boy to make another attempt. Israel steadfastly refused to do again what was obviously displeasing to Heaven. But when his companion called on him in the name of his father, who had bequeathed the miraculous writings to the boy, he consented. Again they fasted from one sabbath to the next. Again they immersed themselves in the bath of purification and, at the close of the sabbath, fulfilled the rites prescribed. Suddenly the boy cried out that they were condemned and would die unless they watched through the night with unflagging spiritual intentness. All night they remained standing. But when day was just dawning, Rabbi Adam's son could not fight his drowsiness any longer and fell asleep on his feet. In vain Israel tried to wake him. They buried him with great honors.

HIS MARRIAGE

In his youth, Israel ben Eliezer was an assistant teacher in a small community not far from the city of Brody. No one knew anything much about him, but the children he taught were so eager and happy to learn, that their fathers also came to like him. Presently it was bruited about that he was wise, and people came to ask his advice. When a quarrel broke out, the young teacher was asked to mediate and this he did so well that a man against whom he decided was no less pleased than his opponent in whose favor he had spoken, and both went their ways serene and happy.

At that time, a great scholar, Rabbi Gershon of Kitov, lived in Brody. His father, Rabbi Efraim, was carrying on a law-suit with a member of the small community whose children the Baal Shem taught. He looked up his opponent and suggested that they both go to Brody to submit their disagreement to the rabbinical court. But the other man kept telling him about the wisdom and sense of justice of the young teacher until Rabbi Efraim agreed to put the matter up to him. When he entered his room and looked at him, he was startled, for shining from Israel's forehead, he saw a curved sign exactly like that he had seen for an instant—and never forgotten!—on the little forehead of his own daughter, when the midwife had shown him the new-born child. He lowered his gaze, his tongue was numb and he could hardly utter his request. When he raised his eyes again, the sign had vanished. Israel listened, put questions, listened again, and then pronounced judgment. Soon after, the hearts of both men were at peace, and it seemed to them that shining justice itself had blazed forth from the mists of their differences.

Later Rabbi Efraim went to the Baal Shem and asked him to take his daughter to wife. Israel consented but insisted on two conditions: that their agreement should remain secret for the time being, and that in the contract about to be drawn up, his scholarship should not even be mentioned; that he should be designated merely by name: Israel ben Eliezer, for—he added—"You want me and not my knowledge, as a husband for your daughter." Everything was done according to his wish.

When Rabbi Efraim returned from his trip, he fell suddenly ill and died after a few hours. His son, Rabbi Gershon Kitover, came to bury him. Among his father's papers he found the marriage contract and read that his sister had been promised to a man who had no learned title and who was not of a famous family. Not even the native town of the stranger was mentioned. He immediately informed his sister of this unheard-of arrangement, but she only replied that since this had been her father's wish, only this and nothing else could be right for her.

Israel waited until he had completed his year of teaching. The fathers of his pupils did not want him to go, but had did not let them hold him back. He put aside his robe and clothed himself in a short sheepskin with a broad leather belt, such as peasants wear, and he adopted their speech and gestures. Thus he came to Brody and to Rabbi Gershon's house. There he stood in the door, on the inner threshold. The scholar, who was just comparing various interpretations of a difficult passage in the Talmud, had them give a coin to the stranger who looked needy to him, but the man said he had something to tell him. They went into the adjoining room together and Israel informed the rabbi that he had come to fetch his wife. In great consternation, Gershon called his sister to see the man her father had chosen for her. All she said was: "If he has commanded this, then it is God's command," and bade them prepare for the wedding. Before they went to the marriage canopy, the Baal Shem talked to his wife and revealed his secret to her. But she had to promise never to breathe a word of it, no matter what might happen. He also told her that great misery and many troubles were in store for them. She only said that all this was as it should be.

After the wedding, Rabbi Gershon spent day after day trying to teach his ignorant brother-in-law the Torah, but it was impossible to get him to remember a single word of the teachings. Finally he said to his sister: "I am ashamed of your husband. It would be a good thing for you to divorce him. If you do not want to do this, I shall buy you horses and a carriage and you can go with him wherever you like." She was well satisfied with the second alternative.

They drove until they came to a little town in the Carpathian Mountains, where the woman found a place to live. Israel went to the nearby hills, built himself a hut, and quarried clay. Two or three times a week, she went to him, helped him load the clay in the wagon, took it into the town and sold it for a small sum. When Israel was hungry, he put water and flour into a little pit, kneaded the dough, and baked it in the sun.

15 Founders of Modern Judaism: Reform Abraham Geiger

JACOB NEUSNER

1. Why is this reading important?

The three accounts of the modern Judaisms—Reform, Orthodox, and Conservative—in each case focus upon principal founders. That is because religions not only constitute movements and produce institutions and affect communities, they also express the particular insight of persons, whom we might even regard as "religious geniuses," people of remarkable capacity to see the shape of matters and to impose upon them the imprint of their own minds, characters, and personalities. In the case of the founders of Judaisms in modern times, we ask what ideas they found absolutely obvious and self-evident. We want to identify what lies underneath the doctrines they put forth, justifying change and accommodating political aspirations hitherto unfelt by holy Israel, for example. Abraham Geiger was not the only important figure among the intellectual pioneers of Reform Judaism, but among the founders he was by far the most interesting and imaginative. That is why my account of his life and thought stresses issues important to history of religion. These are the ideas he put forth to justify change, to transform change into reform, and to transform a pattern of reform into Reform Judaism.

2. What should you notice as you proceed?

Geiger appeals to the past to justify change and thinks that History will transform change into Reform. Notice how he defines authority, finding validation in the past. Do you find an equivalent evaluation of the norm-setting character of the past, of history, in Rabbinic Judaism? Comparing Buber's view of Hasidism with Geiger's view of Judaism, we note an interesting contrast. Both tell stories, but for different purposes. If you were to characterize any Judaism as a storytelling religion, whether in the Hebrew Scriptures, in the Rabbinic literature of ancient times, or in Hasidism or in Reform Judaism, you would not be far off the mark. But how to explain the different types of stories that are told, and how to explain one choice over another? These are the questions that you might try to answer in reading about Geiger.

3. How should you frame a question for class discussion in response to what you have read?

It is no disrespect to point in this context to those figures accorded supernatural standing or believed to communicate directly with God— Moses, Jesus, or Muhammed, for example. The faithful deem them God's choices, but scholars of religion, not bound to the theological framework of the faithful, want to know about the biography, both personal and spiritual, of those persons and the many others who, through time, have helped define the this-worldly history of religion. In the context of Reform Judaism, you might wish to form a class discussion on the relationship of scholarship and theology—that is, scholarship about factual historical questions of what really happened on one side and systematic critical thought about religious truth on the other. Do facts settle questions of faith? Do the people who write books about the historical Jesus think so? If not, then why do they write those books? If so, then what do they expect to prove, and for whom are they writing? The entire relationship between historical ("scientific") fact and religious belief is now open for discussion.

Reform Judaism was the creation of a handful of intellectuals, and they had the advantage of possessing first-rate minds. Their sharpness of intellect and astuteness carried the day—that and the match between their ideas and the urgent issues of the hour. Abraham Geiger enjoyed the advantage of the finest argumentative mind in Jewry in the nineteenth century. If we want to understand the new Judaisms of the age, therefore, we turn to the leading intellect to show us how people reached their conclusions, not merely what they said or why they found self-evident the positions that they took. Geiger's life presents facts of less interest than his work, and, in his work his way of asking and answering questions tells us what matters in Reform Judaism. For that is the point at which we gain access to what people found self-evident on one side and urgent on the other.

The urgency accounts for the questions, the self-evidence, the mode of discovering the answer. To those two matters, everything else takes second place. The question Geiger found ineluctable takes simple form: How can we explain what has happened to us? The answer: What has taken place—change become Reform—forms the natural and necessary outcome of history. Geiger emphasized the probative status and value of the facts of history, those self-evident principles that lead us deep into the consciousness of the man and the Judaism he embodied.

What Geiger took for granted—in our terms, held as self-evident—is that history proved propositions of theology. Whatever the particular matter of conviction or custom takes a secondary place. The primary source of verification, therefore, of appropriate and inappropriate traits in Judaism—that is, the origin of the reliable definition of Judaism—emerges not in revealed records of God's will but in human accounts of humanity's works. To that principle, everywhere taken for granted, occasionally enunciated but never systematically demonstrated, Geiger's mode of argument and inquiry took second place.

Since the earliest changes turned into reforms, and reforms of Judaism into Reform Judaism, to Geiger we address our principal questions: old or new? And how did people explain themselves? Abraham Geiger presented in clearest form the argument that Reform carried forward the historical processes of Judaism. He posited both a single, linear Judaism and a Judaism affected by history, that is, by change. He appealed to the facts of history, beginning with the critical study of the Bible. The eminent Reform theologian Jakob J. Petuchowski summarizes Geiger's view as follows:

> Judaism is a constantly evolving organism. Biblical Judaism was not identical with classical rabbinic Judaism. Similarly, the modern age calls for further evolution in consonance with the changed circumstances. . . . The modern rabbis are entitled to adapt medieval Judaism, as the early rabbis had the right to adapt biblical Judaism. . . . He found traces of evolution within the Bible itself. Yet for Geiger changes in Judaism had always been organic. . . . The modern changes must develop out of the past, and not represent a revolutionary break with it.[1]

Geiger therefore recognized change as "traditional," meaning that changing represents the way things always have been and so legitimately now goes forward. The Jews change, having moved from constituting a nation to a different classification of social entity. The messiah idea, not only speaking of national restoration, now addresses the whole of humanity. Revelation then turns out to form a progressive, not a static fact. In these diverse ways Geiger—and with him, Reform Judaism through its history—appealed to history to verify its allegations and validate its positions. So facts turn into the evidence for faith.

Geiger was born in 1810 and died in 1874.[2] Growing up in Frankfurt, he undertook university studies at Heidelberg, then Bonn, with special interest in philosophy and Semitics. University study formed the exception, not the rule, for Jews. By definition, therefore, the change Geiger had to explain in fact came about through the decision of the former generation. Geiger explained change. His parents made it. But among the intellectual leaders in Geiger's day, not only he, but his arch-opponent Samson Raphael Hirsch, founder of Orthodox Judaism, also acquired a university education. So Orthodox Judaism too emerged as the result of the decision of the generation preceding the age of the founders.

To both sets of parents, therefore, the value of an education in the sciences of the West proved self-evident; the ways of harmonizing that education and its values with the education in the Judaic sciences considerably less clear. Earlier generations had not sent their sons to universities (and their daughters would have to wait until nearly our own day for a similar right). Before Geiger and Hirsch could reach the academy, then, their parents had to find self-evident the value of such an education. But before that generation, most parents found self-evident the value of education in the established institutions of the Judaism of the dual Torah—there alone. Knowledge of another sort, under other auspices, bore no value. Before the advent of the reformer, then, whether the great intellect

---

[1]*Encyclopaedia Judaica,* s.v. Geiger.

[2]Max Wiener, *Abraham Geiger and Liberal Judaism. The Challenge of the Nineteenth Century,* trans. Ernst J. Schlochauer (New York: Jewish Publication Society of America, 1962).

of Reform Judaism or the courageous leader of Orthodoxy, change had already characterized modes of self-evident truth.

Geiger led a parlous life in synagogue pulpits, not always appreciated for virtues he brought to them: flawless German and his questioning of routine.[3] What he did with most of his time, however, concerned not the local synagogue community but the constituency of Judaic learning. He produced a periodical, *The Scientific Journal for Jewish Theology*, from 1835 onward. The purpose of scientific knowledge Wiener epitomizes in the following statement: "They were convinced that, given the historical facts, it would be possible to draw the correct practical conclusions with regard to the means by which their religion could best be served and elevated to the level of contemporary culture."[4] That is, through systematic learning Judaism would undergo reform. Reform Judaism rested on deep foundations of scholarship of a certain sort, specifically of a historical character.

What Geiger had in mind was to analyze the sources of Judaism and the evolution of Judaism. If science (used in its German sense, systematic learning) could uncover the sources of the Jewish "spirit," then, in Wiener's words, "the genius of his people and . . . its vocation" would serve "as a guide to the construction of a living present and future." Geiger's principle of Reform remained fixed. Reform had to emerge from *Wissenschaft*, "a term which he equated with the concept of the understanding of historical evolution."[5] To him, "Judaism in its ideal form was religion per se, nothing but an expression of religious consciousness. Its outer shell was subject to change from one generation to another."[6] All things emerge out of time and of change. But when it comes to tracing the history of time and change, contemporary categories assuredly defined the inquiry. Thus Geiger produced, out of ancient times, portraits suspiciously congruent to the issues of his own day.

For example, in his account of the Sadducees and Pharisees—the former enjoying a bad press, the latter, in Judaism, a good one, he identified the former with "the strict guardians of traditional institutions, while the latter spoke out in behalf of progress in both religion and politics."[7] As Wiener explains:

> What Geiger sought to prove by this demonstration [that the text of Scripture was fluid] is quite obvious. It was not the Bible that created and molded the religious spirit of Judaism; instead, it was the spirit of Judaism that left the stamp of its own form and expression upon the Bible—Life, and its needs and strivings, change from age to age.[8]

What we learn from Wiener's and Petuchowski's accounts of Geiger concerns what Geiger found to be self-evident—truths beyond all appeal that formed the foundation of his life's work as the first and best historian of Judaism.

---

[3]Ibid., p. 11.

[4]Ibid., p. 13.

[5]Ibid., p. 40.

[6]Ibid., p. 42.

[7]Ibid., p. 50.

[8]Ibid., p. 51.

16 Contemporary Reform Judaism Speaks: Finding a Jewish View of the "Just Society"

EUGENE BOROWITZ

1. Why is this reading important?

The 1997 commencement address at Gratz College in Philadelphia, this essay shows how Reform Judaism formulates its best ideas. Professor Eugene Borowitz of the Hebrew Union College–Jewish Institute of Religion, New York City, has been teaching future Reform rabbis and scholars for an entire lifetime. Now in his seventies, Borowitz remains the principal systematic theologian of Reform Judaism and one of the handful of systematic and constructive theologians of Judaism in the world. This address represents the cutting edge of his, and therefore Reform-Judaic, theological thought. In it Borowitz tries to frame normative religious truths, articulating the mode of thought, the character of the evidence, and the shape of compelling arguments in the service of an important proposition meant to solve a critical problem. When important intellectuals undertake theological tasks in Judaism, this is what they do.

2. What should you notice as you proceed?

What does Borowitz take as his critical problem? Why does he find problematic the relationship in the thought of Jewish social activists between the language of Messiahism and the secular goal of social betterment? How does he propose to explain the disporportionate engagement of Jews with the politics of the left and not the right? Borowitz not only describes but also proposes to evaluate contemporary attitudes and policies. How does he conduct his critique? What is important here is the indicative character of Reform Judaism as an approach to the "tradition" or as a representation of the Torah. Borowitz turns to cutting-edge issues of the hour such as equal opportunity and equal pay for the same work, and he asks how, within Judaism, these issues ought to be sorted out. He embodies the intellectual aspirations of Reform Judaism.

3. How should you frame a question for class discussion in response to what you have read?

In any living religion, the theologian defines a task of unique importance: to stand for the religion in the framework of intelligible discourse, to translate the attitudes and feelings of the faith into a body of coherent doctrine, and to shape that doctrine to the acutely contemporary setting of the place, the hour, and the crisis. In this essay we see how a great figure does just that. Can we point, in class discussion, to counterpart figures in contemporary Christianity, Islam, and Buddhism? Among the black churches, who are the principal theological figures, where do they work, to what issues of general intelligibility do they respond, and how do they claim moral authority for their teaching? Take the case of Martin Luther King, Jr., and ask in what ways, in his life, he did the work of theology. From such an analysis, discussion may well shade over into the role of theology in religion, both in history and in our own day.

Most people devote their study time to Jewish texts, or Jewish history and community, or how to help Jews better understand and live by our tradition. I study Jewish belief, not just what Jews once believed (as important as that is), but what in this complicated, sophisticated life of ours, Jews ought to believe. Few people work on Jewish theology, but since I do, let me introduce you to my discipline. I want to spend some moments showing how understanding Jewish belief better might guide a caring Jew in responding to the troublesome, disputed contemporary issue of creating a just society.

Until about two centuries ago, Jews were not active participants in the shaping of their societies, even in the limited, predemocratic ways the will of the people then shaped their world. This led to what I shall describe, without substantiation here, as the somewhat passive, meliorative, microeconomically focused, theocentric approach of classic Judaism to economic relations. But this point of view underwent profound transformation with the rise of modernity—a development, however, that is true only for that vast proportion of Jews who modernized when given the opportunity. Some Jews never accepted the modern ethos and others never were truly emancipated. In due course, particularly in Europe and the United States, most Jews accepted modernism's emphasis on human creativity as self-evidently true and desirable. Yet like most other moderns, they did not become revolutionaries. Only significant minorities, the various Jewish communists and Marxist socialists, agreed with the Nietzschean proclamation that God was dead and so human beings should now, in full responsibility, radically refashion their economic destiny. Most Jews remained meliorists and regularly supported in great statistical disproportion their country's liberal parties. They did so, one may speculate, because they considered it their Jewish responsibility to reshape their social orders and wanted the kind of government that would provide leadership in this regard. Much of this history can easily be seen as the result of modernization's identification with secularization.

Two aspects of this development seem to call for theological analysis. The first of these is the way in which ethics provided a heavy ideological overlay for these movements. Jewish social activists often used the language of social betterment, asserting that they would accomplish by revolution or the ballot what pietists could never achieve by prayer and ritual. Moreover, they would do so with a universal reach which transcended the narrow purview of religion. They and all enlightened humankind would be the "Messiah"—the exaltation of human initiative went this far. But why did they need to be so moralistic (it being assumed, with some reason, that there was a considerable measure of sincerity in what they said)? This is nothing intrinsically ethical about secularization, or relying on human effort, or seeing economics as central to human relationships, or turning to politics as the means of effecting significant social change.

A second such anomaly may be seen in the continuing affinity of a disproportionate number of Jews for liberal political causes. The phenomenon can be observed in a number of countries and has lasted over a considerable period of time. To some extent this can be explained as political self-interest, the conservatives generally supporting the established social interests and thus traditional prejudices. Yet as Jews have risen in the socioeconomic scale and have been widely accepted in their societies, thereby acquiring class interests that would normally lead them to conservatism, they have largely remained liberals. Jewish apologists despise the locution of the "Jewish vote." Applied to modernized Jews, it still refers to that statistically unexpected number of Jews who continue to want government action to improve the effective reach of the economy and our social welfare generally.

These two phenomena are closely connected, and theologically they are a logical consequence of secularization's transformation of the traditional Jewish attitude toward the just economy. Modernized Jews did not utterly abandon the theology of their premodern days. While God and holiness no longer played an effective role in these Jewish lives, the goodness connected with God and holiness was still seen as fundamental to the structure of the universe. Thus, as modern Jews saw it, the essential human duty was to increase goodness, a duty still understood in a social, not merely interpersonal mode. God's revelation of duty was replaced by the ethics common to all rational people. This view, primarily in its neo-Kantian formulation or in versions derived from it, became the major plausibility structure for modern Jews. In this system, universal inclusiveness characterized rational injunctions so that humanity as a whole became the ideal field of social concern. As a result, the microeconomic horizon of premodern Jews expanded to embrace the host nation and thence the world. So, too, bringing the Messiah now rationally became the central task of humankind entire, one whose pursuit was the essence of humanhood. For enthusiastic modernized Jews, this course was best pursued through education and politics rather than via Talmud, Torah, and the observance of *mitzvot*.

The Emancipation—a personal or familial experience for modernized Jewry—gave this doctrine powerful reinforcement. After roughly 1,300 years of increasing segregation, degradation, and persecution, Jews were given social equality—by fits and starts, to be sure. As Jewish equality increasingly overcame ingrained prejudice and became reality, Jews had living confirmation that goodness was basic to the universe and humankind could indeed respond to it. They also saw efforts to extend benefits to other pariah groups as a reenactment of their own liberation and a reinforcement of the ethical activity that had given them opportunity and security. Theory and experience alike motivated a continual flow of Jews into activities for human betterment, and it is difficult to think of one in which they have been welcome where they have not also been overrepresented.

One further aspect of this transformation deserves emphasis. The Emancipation came about because of human action—that is, political change. Moreover, the radical shift in the status of the Jews resulted from decisive government leadership rather than a growing grassroots sentiment or as a direct outgrowth of market or other social forces. The effect of this moral leadership by government (regardless of what cynical motives accompanied it) has registered on the psyches of most Jews. They have benefited incredibly from national initiatives in social reconstruction and therefore remain committed to the critical importance of governmental action for the common good.

I do not consider it a great exaggeration—though surely its basis is more homiletic than empirical—to suggest that the experience of Emancipation has been something of a recapitulation of our Exodus experience and similarly has religiously transformed us. Because we were slaves in our segregated Egypt, the ghetto and shtetl, we know the heart of every stranger seeking effective equality in our society. And because with a strong hand and outstretched arm enlightened nations redeemed us from our pariah-hood, we accepted the secularized covenant of ethical concern for humankind. Something like that has served as modern Jewry's version of the classic Jewish covenant, and while it was and remains primarily a political vision, it could not help take on strong economic overtones as politics and economics grew ever more closely intertwined.

Alas, we expected too much of ourselves—that collectively we would be the Messiah. What a shock it has been to discover just how flawed we and our best plans are. The failure of communism, the economic inefficiency of the socialisms and the various problems connected with democratic welfare states have bankrupted the left—and the continuing human suffering brought on by doctrinaire Thatcherite reactions to the welfare state increasingly indicts the right. We have lost our confidence in our ability to manage our affairs as redemptively as modernity taught us we could. So privatism and cynicism often rule where once conscience did, and our new realism about the complexity and unresolveableness of our problems has paralyzed the morally healthy. In the face of these realities, hope has become an uncommon achievement and we tend to limit our investment of energy to the near at hand and personal projects.

In this bleak social ethical environment, many prefer the premodern ethos with its moral certainties and assurances to a modernity that knows the glory of freedom but not how to set its limits. Fundamentalisms have found new life all across Western civilization, teaching that revelation is more reliable than human reason and ingenuity. What, then, becomes of the role of human agency in our religious life and the possibilities of innovative social planning led by governmental initiative to help us carry out our ethical responsibilities? Does the collapse of messianic modernism require us realistically to reduce our reliance upon human creativity and inventiveness to the scope that our premodern tradition prescribes or permits? What "Judaism" has to say about a just economy would then become essentially: "What did the *halakhah* previously require or permit and what do recognized *poskim*, decision makers, rule it mandates today?"

I do not suggest that classic Jewish law lacks the means of moving in new directions to confront the issues that face us. I am only of the opinion that the history and ethos of those communities which most study and live by Jewish law—the ones in the best Jewish position to determine what is halakhically valid—makes any bold halakhic action in our time most unlikely. Those halakhists who do call for significant new action in the face of this traditionalistic refusal to act are themselves already committed to a positive, modernistic view of human agency. The only issue for them, then, is how much initiative to allow.

Let me now state what I take to be the other view, the one that roughly represents a large majority of the caring Jewish community (if their behavior can be taken as a criterion of their belief). Not unproblematically, to be sure, we non-Orthodox Jews do not understand why, in the face of compelling human need, contemporary Jews must limit themselves to what our law once commended or might now widely authoritatively advocate. The spiritual benefits of human creativity free to move outside the classic *halakhah* seem plain to those of us who love democracy and its pluralism, social arrangements created by essentially secularized modern types. Besides, it seems to us that on a number of critical issues Jewish law is wrongly restrictive.

Consider a single problem, one generally approached only from an ethical point of view but of equal interest as an economic problem. I refer to equal opportunity and equal payment for women in our society. Without substantial, sustained human initiative and government leadership, women in our society will remain unable to make a full contribution to society for reasons having nothing to do with interest or ability. With Jewish women, the most highly educated group of women in human history, our community, while emotionally unable to give up speedily its longstanding patterns of male dominance, increasingly recognizes that it must make place and pay for a change in our society's treatment of women. In the ongoing struggle for women's rights, Jewish law and its protagonists seem less part of the possible solution than of the continuing problem. And it is for this reason that most of the Jewish community finds conscience a better guide to what God wants of our community than is the classic halakhic tradition.

Two major factors often radically differentiate us from those Jewish communities for whom our law was elaborated. They lived in economies of scarcity and in societies that segregated and often oppressed them. Classic Jewish law spoke to their specific situation. It is most unlike ours, for we live in an economy of abundance, if not affluence, under conditions of tolerance and equality. And our different situation often suggests possibilities that would have seemed strange or undesirable to our tradition.

The issue before us is not whether we should seek to learn from our past and its experience in sanctifying existence under the most diverse circumstances. Where there are models in the past that still commend themselves or guidance that can direct us, we can, like prior generations, be its grateful recipients. But on issues like job creation for the unemployed, welfare for the needy, medical treatment available to everyone, and the regulation of interest and credit for the benefit of the society as a whole, having understood what our tradition says, shall we not then respond in creative respect to what we experience God demanding of us as Jews in our specific context? Jewish responsibility, then, must involve the free exercise of human imagination built upon reason and experience as well as the urging, idealism, and example of Jewish tradition. The specific plans and programs that might remedy our problems lie far beyond the capacity of experts in Jewish law or theology. Such matters test the competence and ingenuity of the area experts and the politicians whose lives have been devoted to studying and responding to them. Educating these people as best we can to what Judaism has taught about human responsibility, we can respect the God-given capacity of each generation, particularly as it faces new problems, to sense what God asks of Jews today and to respond to it in faithfulness. In that respect I remain a child of modern Judaism.

If I differentiate myself from my teachers, it is because I do not share their optimism about what human beings, essentially unaided, can accomplish. The work of righteousness remains our simple Jewish duty regardless of its long-range effect; of course, we pray that it may, indeed, make us all reflect more truly God's rule in our lives. But dearly bought realism has made my aspirations more meliorative than messianic. After all that we have seen of what the best and the brightest of us can do, after the chastening that has come with our finest institutions creating evil along with good, I do not expect that humankind is the Messiah or even that our spiritualized politics will bring the Messianic Age. If I have more faith in human initiative than Jewish tradition validated, I also have more faith in God and God's role in redeeming history than modern Judaism did. It is this sense of living partnership, of being summoned to action and endurance by the One behind every particular, of a personal humanhood defined by my people's ongoing, historic relationship with God that constitutes my postmodernity. God gives me, us, no rest from responsibility and no release from my complicity with the social sins that we might do something to rectify. God lifts me above my moods of cynicism, of fatalism, of selfishness and despair. God gives me hope that I, we, you, might find a better way to be human together, for I know that God's goodness has its own power and that one day it will be fully manifest on earth. And that gives me the courage to try once again, this time with your help, to face the daunting details. So my theology informs my life. And what, I ask, of yours?

17 *Contemporary Reform Judaism Speaks: The Limits of Liberal Judaism*

JAKOB J. PETUCHOWSKI

1. Why is this reading important?

The theologian not only undertakes a role of system building and problem solving, he or she also succeeds to the prophetic mantel and assumes responsibility to criticize. Borowitz's great constructive enterprise forms only half of the theological heritage of contemporary Reform Judaism. The other half derives from the criticism of Reform Judaism emanating from the late Jakob J. Petuchowski, a professor at Hebrew Union College–Jewish Institute of Religion, Cincinnati, who made his principal contribution in a perspicacious analysis of the intellectual problems facing Reform Judaism, and who proposed to solve those problems. Here is one of his most justly famed essays, a basic theoretical statement about what is wrong with Reform Judaism. Petuchowski asks whether change has its limits and wants to know whether Reform Judaism is merely a verb, as in *to reform, to change,* or also a noun, a body of coherent and enduring doctrine and practice that bears authority for more than one morning. He wants to know whether a Reform rabbi *must* believe in God and mocks the Rabbinical organization of Reform rabbis, the Central Conference of American Rabbis, for its latitudinarianism.

2. What should you notice as you proceed?

What sort of arguments appeals to Rabbi Petuchowski, and would these same arguments have enjoyed equal esteem from Rabbi Geiger a century earlier? Petuchowski clearly has in his mind a single definition of Judaism that he regards as fixed and firm. Can you identify the components of that Judaism, the propositions he takes for granted, and can you further explain why he holds that these truths indeed are self-evident? Petuchowski, like any other thinker about fundamental questions, identifies a critical issue in the definition of the faith accepted by converts to Judaism. That choice of ground-zero faith recalls the issue facing the earliest Christians when the apostle Paul addressed the question of whether converts had to be circumcised to become part of holy Israel. That fact alerts us to how basic a criticism of Reform Judaism

Petuchowski has framed. In reading his essay, look for other instances in which he has insisted upon a confrontation with the very grounds of a reformation of Judaism.

3. How should you frame a question for class discussion in response to what you have read?

When a new way of seeing the past takes shape within an ancient religion, what are the choices facing the critics of the past who legislate the future? Instances to consider include the Buddha, Jesus, Muhammed, Luther, Joseph Smith, and the like. In all cases they took up a heritage and recast it. What emerged was not a reformed heritage but a new religion altogether—Christianity distinct from Judaism or Protestantism from Catholicism, for example. In that context Petuchowski's critique of Reform Judaism takes on still greater weight for the history of religion. How would the Catholic Reformation (which Protestants call the Counterreformation) have formed an equivalent indictment of Protestantism, or Hindus in the old tradition of Buddhism? Or, to take a current example, how do contemporary Christians deal with Mormonism and its scripture, the Book of Mormon, in addition to the Bible? Religions change; some deem change to constitute Reform. But the critics not of change (all religions acknowledge change, each finding its own modes of legitimating it) but of deeming change to be Reform also have their say. What are the kinds of arguments meant to show the limits of Liberal Judaism that would serve a critic of the Reformation in Christianity or of Buddhism in the Hindu world?

In 1928, on the occasion of the Berlin Conference of the World Union for Progressive Judaism, some of the leaders of German Liberal Judaism presented a *festschrift* to the World Union's President, Claude G. Montefiore (*Festgabe für Claude G. Montefiore*, Berlin, Philo Verlag, 1928). In it, the leading figures of the movement are represented by scholarly and ideological contributions. Among the contributors are Leo Baeck, Ismar Elbogen, Hermann Vogelstein, Max Dienemann, Caesar Seligmann, Max Wiener and several others, both rabbis and lay leaders. It is an interesting document of the times. Appearing but two years after the World Union for Progressive Judaism had come into being, and written by German Jews who had no inkling of the fate which was to overtake them within the very next decade, this *festschrift* could be said to represent one of the most optimistic periods in the history of European Progressive Judaism.

All the more remarkable—and unexpected—is an essay by Felix Goldmann, entitled "The Limits of Liberalism." Goldmann was rabbi in Leipzig at the time, and was considered one of the leaders of Liberal Judaism in Germany. Yet, in his essay, he minces no words and is ruthless in his criticism. According to him, Judaism had always been recognizable through two characteristics: Revelation and Law. In modern times, these characteristics were exposed to the attacks of two opponents: rationalism, which undermined the belief in Revelation; and Christianity, which, if only indirectly, was responsible for a weakening of the concept of Law. This latter diagnosis is based on the fact that, in Liberal Judaism, *voluntary* deeds of kindness take the place of life "under the Law."

> The neglect of the Law is merely the consequence of an unconscious acceptance of Christianity as the supreme arbiter in all questions of ethics. Since Paul stamped Christianity with its antinomian character, Christianity has always stood in opposition to the principle of legality. The more powerful Christianity became, the more readily it sought to describe the Jewish point of view as morally inferior and incomplete. Its own position, however, it described as the deed of kindness, voluntarily performed and flowing from the depths of the soul. Such was the ideal of morality. But the half-sympathizing, half-condescending disdain with which one spoke about the "yoke of the Law," about its ossification of the spirit, about the externalization of the ethical deed, about the self-righteousness and the sinful pride to which it drove the Jew—this disdain was by no means confined to Christian circles. In many a *Jewish* view, too, the Jew living under the Law, the Pharisee of old, is looked upon as the product of a time which, after all, has been superseded by the spread of Christianity. This tendency is particularly strong in the Liberalism of the 19th century. Reform Judaism completely obliterates the Law as an obligatory factor, thereby consciously conceding the superiority of the foundations of Christian ethics. Moderate Liberalism—and [Hermann] Cohen proves to be no exception—seeks to comprehend the Law as an historical phenomenon which has had infinitely wholesome effects, and which, in view of these, deserves to be judged on the basis of extenuating circumstances. (pp. 54 ff.)

Yet Goldmann recognizes that "the denial of divine Revelation and freeing oneself from the Law constitute for every Jewish movement a striving away from the foundations of Judaism. This also applies to the individual Jew—even though, in periods when external hatred of the Jew strengthens internal attachment to the community, such consequences are not so visible" (p. 51). All of which is not to say that Orthodoxy escapes unscathed, for it, in turn, makes the mistake of overlooking the historical development which has taken place between the time of the Protestant Reformation and the French Revolution. Moreover, Orthodoxy has exchanged the concept of Revelation for a belief in Verbal Inspiration and for an unbending faith in the letter. The principle of legality has given way to the rule of law which demands obedience even in those instances where it has lost its meaning (p. 56). No, Goldmann does not consider Orthodoxy a live option. He remains the Liberal rabbi. But he does strive for a Liberal Judaism which does not forsake the basis of the Judaism of tradition, a basis circumscribed by belief in Revelation and the acceptance of the legal principle. Revelation, for Goldmann, means

> God's incursion into history. For its first coming-into-being the law of causality, in the sense of natural science, is excluded. Its origin does not lie in the sphere where logical proof is valid. For the concept of God, and for the morality flowing from it, there is only one justification: *faith!* And there is no authority which could examine its validity. (p. 53)

The efforts—even of Hermann Cohen—to regard Revelation as a product of Reason constitute "a subjugation to Rationalism and, thereby, a relativization of the Jewish basis."

> The pride, so often voiced, in the correspondence of Jewish dogma with the demands of Reason is really an indication of a lack of trust in the inherent certainty

of the presuppositions of Judaism. It is also dangerous, because it means that Judaism is dependent on a certain construction of thought which is rooted in the consciousness of the times and which, therefore, has temporary value only. (p. 53)

The analogy of the medieval Jewish philosophers does not apply, because in those days the principle of legality remained untouched. It therefore provided the protective wall which did not permit a destruction of Judaism from the inside (p. 54).

Since an historical Judaism is unthinkable without Revelation and the principle of legality, Goldmann concludes, Liberal Judaism, too, to the extent to which it really wants to be Jewish, cannot dispense with them. "To emphasize them more strongly, and more self-consciously, than has often been the case hitherto would afford Liberal Judaism a far greater inner security towards the outside, and a firm self-confidence inside" (p. 56).

What Goldmann had to say substantially is interesting enough. The fact that he said it thirty-seven years ago is even more interesting. But most interesting—and significant—of all is the fact that a leader of Liberal Judaism could bring himself to speak about "The *Limits* of Liberalism." He was not afraid that his very title would be laughed at as a *contradictio in adiecto,* though thirty-seven years later the suggestion that Liberalism has its "limits," if made on the floor of the Central Conference of American Rabbis or at a faculty meeting of the Hebrew Union College, would most certainly cause some raised eyebrows.

The case, recently given such publicity in the press, of the Reform rabbi in Michigan who openly proclaimed himself an atheist may be nothing more than a storm in a tea-cup. It may also mark a turning-point in the history of American Reform Judaism. For that young rabbi merely admitted in all frankness to a mental attitude which he is by no means alone in representing, though several of his peers would prefer the more innocuous designation of "humanist." When he furthermore claimed that there existed no machinery within Reform Judaism to discipline him, to expel him, or to revoke his rabbinical ordination, he also most probably spoke the truth. Nor would it seem altogether unlikely that there are in American Jewry laymen who cannot but welcome such "rabbinic" sanction of their own lack of Jewish religious commitment.

What remains doubtful as of this moment is whether the vast majority of the men and women who belong to, and support, the institutions of American Reform Judaism are likewise content to have the cause of atheism championed by Reform's rabbinical leadership. But if they are not, what channels do they have of making their predilections felt? None, it will have to be admitted. The atheist in the ranks of the Reform rabbinate considers himself to be there as a matter of right—of greater right, perhaps, than that of his theistic colleague, since it is now quite respectable to insist that theism has become an untenable position for the "thinking Jew." And nothing would bring a greater shudder to the spines of Reform Judaism's official leaders than the suggestion that religious "loyalty oaths" should be demanded of the religious functionaries of Progressive Judaism.

Atheism has, of course, been with us for a long time. But not so long ago, the Jewish atheist and the Jewish agnostic still had a certain sense of the fitness of things. They knew that they did not belong on the pulpit of a synagogue. They understood that the synagogue was a place where prayer was offered to the "God of Abraham, Isaac, and Jacob," and where the Torah was read as a document of

Revelation (be it ever so "unverbal"!). When Felix Adler discovered that morality was not dependent upon the theistic God-concept, he renounced the opportunity of becoming the rabbi of Temple Emanuel in New York, and founded the Ethical Culture movement instead. That was in 1876. Many kindred spirits followed him there. Today such a step is no longer deemed to be required. Historicism has run wild within the spacious contours of a limitless Liberalism. Nothing sacred has escaped the process of relativization. If one generation could give up the belief in the Messiah, and the next generation the belief in Verbal Inspiration, by what right should the present generation be denied the freedom to give up belief in God? So you can have your godlessness and the synagogue, too! Who can stop you? You may not like my definition of Judaism (without a God)—but, then, I do not like your definition of Judaism (with a God) either. Happily, Reform Judaism is broad enough to include us both. So, let's respect the legitimacy of each other's points of view. There is no Pope. There is no *sanhedrin*. The *Shulhan 'Arukh* is gone. And now, God, too, is dead. Long live the synagogue! Long live the rabbinate!

A century and a half ago, some of the militant Orthodox opponents seemed to overstate their case when they denounced the slightest aesthetic reforms of synagogue architecture and of the worship service as the thin end of the wedge which would lead to the ultimate rejection of the God of Israel. Today we must credit them with more perspicacity than was possessed by their Reform contemporaries who tried so hard to justify all their innovations by appealing to the authoritative sources of Rabbinic Judaism itself. The latter-day heirs of the Reformers all but retroactively justify the exaggerated invectives of the benighted medievalists. But are they really the latter-day heirs of the early Reformers? That is the question on which the whole problem turns.

To answer it we would need criteria. But the establishment of criteria is itself tantamount to essaying definitions, and definitions, in turn, operate with limits. And we are back to the apparent *contradictio in adiecto* of speaking about "The *Limits* of Liberalism."

Liberalism can have no limits. It cannot be bound by any fealty to dogma or authority. It cannot move along the grooves of preconceived notions, nor can it be held back by the fetters of tradition. Such is the nature of Liberalism: try to fence it in, and you have deprived it of its essence. Part of today's confusion may be traced back to the fact that not a few rabbis, and a not insignificant number of laymen, owe their allegiance to Liberalism. Liberalism is their philosophy, and Liberalism is their religion. Let it lead where it may. Such Liberalism may even go hand in hand with a proud affirmation of Jewishness. But it is a Jewishness of the ethnic and cultural variety, a Jewishness of admitted background rather than of religious affirmation.

What the early Reformers had in mind would seem to have been something entirely different. For that matter, the very syntactical construction of the phrase, "Liberal Judaism" indicates that it was not Liberalism *per se* which they were after, but Judaism. Their Liberalism was a matter of the adjective, not of the noun. If anything, the liberal agnostic, or the liberal atheist, would have fitted far less into a Holdheim's or a Geiger's definition of the Jew than into the quasi-biological definition maintained by the Halachah. It was not an espousal of Liberalism *per se* which marked the contribution of the pioneers of Reform Judaism, but a liberal approach to *Judaism*. Judaism was both the starting-point and the goal. Liberalism was to be employed in the service of Judaism; and, to that extent, it was Judaism itself which set limits to the free and unbridled iconoclasm of conventional Liberalism. It was, as we have seen, Felix Goldmann's criticism that those limits were not always sufficiently defined and adequately maintained by the Reformers of the nineteenth century. But of this there can be no doubt, that the early Reformers at least had the good intention of preserving the "eternal verities" of classical Judaism for a new age.

By now, however, the very forces which they helped to set in motion have, on occasion, been turned against them. The relativization of both content and form, and loyalty to the very historicism which they regarded as the key to the truth, have brought it about that some of those who, today, preach from their pulpits and lecture in their academies insist that there never was such a thing as a "Judaism" which, in matters of cardinal belief and legal interpretation, was the same in all ages and climes. How easy it is to contrast the supposed Aristotelianism of Maimonides with the supposed anthropomorphism of Rabbi Akiba! How uncomplicated the process of demonstrating that economic factors, rather than an inherent dynamic, have been responsible for the forms in which Halachah clothed itself in different ages and environments! How perfectly obvious the discovery that one and the same classical text—say, the Bible—meant two entirely different things when read by Maimonides, on the one hand, and by the Baal Shem Tov, on the other! And from all this it follows, or is said to follow, that what has been common to all the various "Judaisms" is merely a certain vocabulary, a number of well-worn clichés. In reality, so it is being claimed, people—for some reason known as "Jews"—always created their own religions to meet their particular convenience, seeking to establish a link with the past only by clinging to a traditional vocabulary.

Of course, it is not being denied that, in ages past, a "God-concept" (though never the identical one) figured in all of the various manifestations of—what was called—"Judaism." It could not have been otherwise. After all, those Jews all lived in environments where belief in God was taken for granted. They merely shared a common universe of discourse with Islam and Christianity. But all of this happened before Darwin, and before Freud, and before Logical Positivism. We are living in an entirely different world today. We have to create our own "Judaism," one that will fit into our world, and that will bring us our this-worldly "salvation." And, with this goal in mind, we consciously prefer the exclusion of the "God-concept" of our immediate or more remote predecessors. We pick those traditional insights which happen to suit our purposes. We can forget about all the others. After all, is it not enough that we identify ourselves as Jews, and that we even make use of the established "Jewish" institutions? We do call our assemblies "Jewish congregations," and our mentors, "rabbis." If Maimonides could pass off his Aristotelianism as Judaism, our humanism need fare no worse. Not to admit to our rejection of traditional superstitions would be intellectual dishonesty. We are committed to Truth and to Reason. What else do you want of us?!

Our latter-day humanists, agnostics, and atheists in the Central Conference of American Rabbis may thus deem themselves to be the heirs of a noble tradition. And, in a certain sense, that liberal tradition is noble. It contrasts favorably with the evidence of increased religious intolerance which of late has afflicted some of our brethren in the State of Israel and in England. In the ranks of the Central Conference, differences in basic religious orientation do not interfere with the forming of personal friendships, nor do they stand in the way of a joint pursuit of those aims and objectives which believers and non-believers do have in common.

But, when the ledger is consulted, there are entries also on the debit side. True, the humanists stand to gain by this arrangement. Membership in the Conference assures their status as Jewish spiritual leaders in the eyes of the American Jewish community, for whom a rabbi is, after all, still a rabbi. Were our humanists to designate themselves as leaders of Ethical Culture groups, or as functionaries of Rationalist Associations, they would find many a door closed which, as rabbis, they are now able to enter. It is the religionists (in the more traditional sense of that word) who are the real losers in this arrangement. Not that their views are not being tolerated. On the contrary! Toleration works both ways in the ranks of the Reform rabbinate. The anomaly of the situation lies in the fact that, within a rabbinical organization, the religious *weltanschauung* is being *tolerated!* It is *one* of the points of view represented! And, being represented in a democratic body, it has to take its chances in the compromises and in the give-and-take to which democratic procedures are always subject. It can never aspire to make the organization as such speak in its name. The theistic orientation thus becomes a point in the debate, and situations where mention of it cannot be avoided altogether have to be handled most tactfully—while the humanistic "opposition" is always entitled to "equal time."

In this connection, a study of the *Union Prayer Book* (published by the Central Conference of American Rabbis) becomes most enlightening. Even without attending the actual meetings of the Committee on Liturgy, one can, on the basis of the prayerbook itself, reconstruct the debates which must have taken place between theists and humanists. The God of Israel is indeed allowed His four cubits of space within the pages of the liturgy. But there are other pages which are clearly a concession to the humanists. Withal, the *Union Prayer Book* is still a theistic prayerbook. We say "still," because there is no telling what a new revision may produce once the humanists achieve numerical superiority.

Consider, for example, what has happened to the admission of proselytes—the one area where the Central Conference has never been able to shy away altogether from the creedal element. In the 1928 edition of the *Rabbi's Manual* (also published by the Central Conference), the prospective convert is required to declare his belief that "God is One, Almighty, Allwise and Most Holy," that "man is created in the image of God; that it is his duty to imitate the holiness of God; that he is a free-will agent, responsible to God for his actions; and that he is destined to everlasting life," that "Israel is God's priest-people, the world's teacher in religion and righteousness as expressed in our Bible and interpreted in the spirit of Jewish tradition," and, finally, that "God ruleth the world with justice and love, and in the fullness of time His kingdom will be established on earth" (pp. 31–32). Is it, then, merely a case of saving time and space that this declaration of belief is omitted from the "Conversion Service" of the 1961 revised edition of the *Rabbi's Manual?* Or was it omitted in order not to tread too heavily on humanist toes?

The time has come for the American Jewish community to be told—and in so many words—that mere membership in the Central Conference of American Rabbis does not *ipso facto* imply commitment to what are commonly considered to be the *religious* affirmations of Judaism. The case is somewhat similar to the membership in the A.F.L.-C.I.O., which does not, in and by itself, tell us anything about the philosophical and economic doctrines held by the member—unlike membership in any of the European Socialist trade unions. The community must learn to understand that the title "Rabbi," as used by members of the Central Conference, is no guarantee for any definite and specific religious views which the community might expect of the holder of such a title.

But the Jewish community is also entitled to have made available to them the leadership and the spiritual guidance of a body of rabbis uncompromisingly committed to the theistic position and the basic religious doctrines of Judaism. Since such a body does not exist, it ought to come into existence. It would consist of those Liberal and Reform rabbis (some Conservatives might want to be associated with it, too) for whom the belief in God and in Revelation is not a superseded tenet, at worst, or a possible "option," at best. They would be men who feel that the congregations deserve better than being fed secularism in (misleading) religious garb, and to whom such congregations could turn that are looking for a Liberal form of Judaism which has not ceased to be Judaism.

Lest we be misunderstood, let it be clearly stated that such a rabbinical body would not come into existence "in opposition" to the Central Conference of American Rabbis. On the contrary, it would come into existence precisely because it values the Central Conference and respects its Liberalism. And just because it has such a great respect for the Central Conference's Liberalism, it would not want to force the Central Conference into a theistic mold—whether the theists in the Conference are in the minority or (what, at present, is still most likely) in the majority. Religious commitments simply are not a matter of majority votes! The Central Conference would continue its present policy of religious neutrality and thus afford a common meeting ground, as heretofore, for all the diverse points of view which, in some limited areas, can combine in the striving for common goals. The various rabbinical organizations of pre-war Germany may serve as a model. There was an *Allgemeiner Rabbinerverband,* a "general" union of rabbis, comprising rabbis of all shades of opinion, dedicated to the welfare of Judaism as a whole, and to raising the status of the rabbinate. But, constitutionally, that rabbinical union barred the discussion and decision of questions in which the religious differences would come into play. Such questions were dealt with by the more "denominational" rabbinical associations (both Orthodox and Liberal) to which the members of the "general" union, in their individual capacities, likewise belonged. (Thus, for example, the late Leo Baeck was, at one and the same time, president of the "general" union of rabbis and a leading figure among the separately organized Liberal rabbis.)

It can easily be seen that several functions which seem incongruous in the present Central Conference of American Rabbis, or which cannot escape looking half-hearted and unconvincing, could more adequately and reasonably be performed by the new body of rabbis we have in mind. A revision of the liturgy on that level would indeed be preceded by lengthy discussions on creedal formulations, aesthetic considerations, the importance—or unimportance—of the Hebrew language for Jewish worship, and the relative authority of traditional usage. But it would not have to be concerned with the "diplomatic" question as to the amount of space to be allocated to theists and humanists respectively. Similarly, a Committee on Responsa on that level would be able to reach Halachic decisions within a definite theological context, and not, as at present, with a theological vacuum.

Nor do we want to be misunderstood as advocating sectarianism or heresy-hunts. Members of the new body we are contemplating would not presume to read non-members "out of the fold." Jewish status is guaranteed to the Jew by the Halachah itself—quite independently of any theological views he might hold. And there is no copyright protecting the brand names "Reform," "Liberal," or "Progressive"—a state of affairs which makes the use of such labels increasingly useless. Perhaps a new name will have to be invented for the particular orientation which we have in mind. Perhaps it might even be better to shun labels altogether. What does matter is that those who are committed to God, Torah, and a religious concept of Israel, make themselves heard in a united voice and offer authentic religious guidance where such guidance is sought.

Does all this mean that we are accepting limits for Liberalism? The answer is an unequivocal "Yes!" We have nothing but profound respect for true, even radical, Liberalism. We recognize it as a viable philosophy of life. But we also recognize that an acceptance of Liberalism entails a definite commitment—a commitment which, by the way, has its source and origin outside of the sphere of mere Reason, even as a commitment to Reason as one's sole guide is itself a commitment undertaken beyond the bounds of Reason.

The rabbis we have in mind, and the Jews who would turn to them, are people who are likewise committed to the ideal of personal freedom. But they have an even prior commitment to Judaism. Here, factors of tradition, personal experience, and of reasoning interact in such a way that no dogmatic historicism or sophisticated semantics can shatter the conviction that "our God" is the very One Who was the "God of our fathers." It is not a question of whether that conviction can be communicated to everybody and shared by everybody. Rather is it a *fact* that those who share that particular conviction do manage to understand one another and to relate their lives to that shared conviction. Our suggestion, therefore, that those who, for similar reasons, have made the same commitment now unite in a recognizable body is a suggestion which has been made for the purpose of greater effectiveness. It is liable to be fiercely opposed by all those who would feel threatened by any departure from the accustomed policy of "religious neutrality," by all those, that is to say, who now "feel at ease in Zion" on the strength of expanding membership rolls. The religious leaders of Judaism have weathered such storms before. They can do so again.

18 Founders of Modern Judaism: Orthodoxy Samson Raphael Hirsch

JACOB NEUSNER

1. Why is this reading important?

Hirsch founded integrationist Orthodoxy—that formulation of the Judaism of the dual Torah which affirms living not only among but in everyday communion with Gentiles. Many other voices of the Judaism of the dual Torah, opposed to Reform, took the view that Jews should continue to segregate themselves from the lives and culture of their neighbors, as they had for centuries. Hirsch's intellectual goal was to validate the givens of the social order; he confirmed the aspirations of those German Jews who wanted to preserve the life of the Torah and also participate in the life of German culture (just as nearly all American and Canadian Jews, whether Orthodox or Reform, want to organize their lives). How Hirsch set forth the case on behalf of integrationist Orthodoxy and against Reform Judaism forms the center of interest in this reading.

2. What should you notice as you proceed?

The issue that divided Reform from integrationist Orthodoxy was: What are the Jews—a religious community like the Methodists, a nation like the French or Germans, a people but not a nation, a cultural group, an ethnic group, a community sharing a common fate, or people who sustain a single historic memory—or all of the above? Notice how Hirsch faces that issue head on, just as the nineteenth-century Reformers did. But he appeals to history as much as to the revealed Torah for evidence on behalf of his position that the Jews are a people, a nation without a political structure, not merely a religious congregation. He adduces in evidence the Temple offerings and their symbolism and in other ways pursues a line of thought parallel to the Reformers'. As you read, think back to Geiger and ask yourself whether Hirsch and Geiger differ in their basic mode of thought or only in details. A further point of interest: In what way do you think Hirsch has learned from Maimonides' approach to the practice of the law of the Torah? Just as Maimonides aimed at showing the rationality of the laws, so Hirsch is trying to make the tradition reasonable and readily understandable.

3. How should you frame a question for class discussion in response to what you have read?

When religions meet a crisis, it is common for them to split into those who affirm the vitality of the "tradition," and those who wish to save the tradition by reforming it. The reaction against Reform Judaism on the part of integrationist Orthodoxy finds its parallel in other religions you may have studied, an already-familiar example being the Protestant Reformation and its counterpart, the Catholic Reformation. But to see integrationist Orthodoxy in its full context, we have also to remember Buber's account of Hasidism, taking shape in the Ukraine just before Reform Judaism came on the scene in Germany. Then we wonder: How would the faithful in Poland, Ukraine, Belarus, Hungary, and other areas of Central and Eastern Europe have responded to Hirsch's formulation of the Torah for the times? And, facing the many ways in which Hirsch's statement differed from that of the Baal Shem Tov or those of his own contemporaries in the East—one of whom said, "Everything new is forbidden by the Torah"—you must wonder how many Orthodox Judaisms we can identify. Clearly, there are more than a few. To frame a discussion of Judaism in the age of modernization, then, we need a different theory of matters from the simple one that posits traditionalists against reformers. Many types of traditionalism, many kinds of reformers have to be taken into account. That is because the categories we use—"Judaism" or "Islam" or "Christianity"—tend to homogenize diverse and complex bodies of the faithful. Even when we subdivide into "reformers" and "traditionalists," we also obscure important differences. Here is a chance to discuss the problem of defining a religion: how to deal with difference, how to construct an intelligible and appropriate account of the whole and its parts.

The importance of Samson Raphael Hirsch (1808–1888), the first great intellect of Integrationist Orthodoxy, derives from his philosophy of joining Torah with secular education, producing a synthesis of Torah and modern culture. Hirsch represents the strikingly new Judaism at hand, exhibiting both its strong tie to the received system but also its innovative and essentially new character. Sometimes called "neo-Orthodox,"[1] Hirsch's position, which laid stress on the possibility of living in the secular world and sustaining a fully Orthodox life, rallied the Jews of the counterreformation. But Hirsch and his followers took over one principal position of Reform, the possibility of integrating Jews in modern society. What made Hirsch significant was that he took that view not only on utilitarian grounds, as Samet says, "but also through the acceptance of its scale of values,

---

[1]Moshe Shraga Samet, "Neo-Orthodoxy," *Encyclopaedia Judaica* 12:956–958.

aiming at creating a symbiosis between traditional Orthodoxy and modern German-European culture; both in theory and in practice this meant abandonment of Torah study for its own sake and adopting instead an increased concentration on practical halakhah."[2] On that basis we rightly identify Orthodoxy as a distinct Judaism from the system of the dual Torah. Hirsch himself studied at the University of Bonn, specializing in classical languages, history, and philosophy.[3] So, as we noted, he did not think one had to spend all his time studying Torah, and in going to a university he implicitly affirmed that he could not define, within Torah study, all modes of learning. Gentile professors knew things worth knowing. But continuators of the Judaism of the dual Torah thought exactly the opposite: Whatever is worth knowing is in the Torah.

In his rabbinical posts, Hirsch published a number of works to appeal to the younger generation. His ideal for them was the formation of a personality that would be both enlightened and observant, educated in Western knowledge and observant of the Judaic way of life. This ideal took shape through an educational program that encompassed Hebrew language and holy literature and also German, mathematics, sciences, and the like. In this way he proposed to respond to the Reformers' view that Judaism in its received form constituted a barrier between Jews and German society. The Reformers saw the received way of life as an obstacle to the sort of integration they thought wholesome and good. Hirsch concurred in the ideal and differed on detail. Distinctive Jewish clothing, in Hirsch's view, enjoyed a low priority. Quite to the contrary, he himself wore a ministerial gown at public worship, which did not win the approbation of the traditionalists, and when he preached, he encompassed not only the law of the Torah but other biblical matters, equally an innovation. Hirsch argued that Judaism and secular education could form a union. This would require the recognition of externals, which could be set aside, and the emphasis on the principles, which would not change. This sounds suspiciously like Reform.

In his selections Hirsch included changes in the conduct of the liturgy, involving a choir, congregational singing, sermons in the vernacular—a generation earlier sure marks of Reform. He required prayers to be said only in Hebrew and Jewish subjects to be taught in that language. He opposed all changes in the Prayer Book. At the same time he sustained organizational relationships with the Reformers and tried to avoid schism. By mid-career, however, toward the middle of the century, Hirsch could not tolerate the Reformers' abrogation of the dietary laws and those affecting marital relationships, and he made his break, accusing the Reformers of disrupting Israel's unity. In the following decades he encouraged Orthodox Jews to leave the congregations dominated by Reform, even though, in the locale, such was the only synagogue. Separationist synagogues formed in the larger community.

We come now to Hirsch's framing of issues of doctrine. He constructed an affirmative system, not a negative one. His principal argument stressed that the teachings of the Torah constitute facts beyond all doubt, as much as the facts of nature do not allow for doubt. This view of the essential facticity—the absolute

---

[2]Ibid., p. 957.

[3]Simha Katz, "Samson (ben) Raphael Hirsch," *Encyclopaedia Judaica* (Jerusalem, 1971) 8: 508–515.

givenness—of the Torah led to the further conviction that human beings may not deny the Torah's teachings even when they do not grasp the Torah's meaning. Wisdom is contained within the Torah, God's will is to be found there. Just as the physical laws of nature are not conditioned by human search, so the rules of God's wisdom are unaffected by human search. The Torah constitutes an objective reality, and, in Katz's words, its laws form "an objective disposition of an established order that is not dependent on the will of the individual or society, and hence not even on historical processes."[4] Humanity nonetheless may through time gain religious truth.

What makes Israel different is that they gain access to the truth not through experience but through direct revelation. Gentile truth is truth, but it derives from observation and experience. What Israel knows through the Torah comes through a different medium. That people then stands outside of history and does not have to learn religious truth through the passage of history and changes over time. Israel then forms a supernatural entity, a view certainly in accord with the Judaism of the dual Torah. But when it came to explaining the way of life at hand, Hirsch went his own way. Hirsch pursued a theory of the practice of the religious life through concrete deeds—the commandments—in a highly speculative and philosophical way. What he maintained was that each of the deeds of the way of life represented something beyond itself, served as a symbol, not as an end in itself. So when a Jew carries out a holy deed, the deed serves to make concrete a revealed truth. This mode of thought transforms the way of life into an exercise in applied theology and practical, practiced belief.

Specifically, in Katz's words, "the performance of a commandment is not determined by simple devotion but by attachment to the religious thought represented in symbolic form by the commandment. Symbolic meanings must be attributed . . . particular to commandments which are described by the Torah itself as signs . . . and commandments which are established as pointing to historical events . . . and commandments whose entire content testifies to their symbolic character."[5] The diverse commandments all together stand for three principles: justice, love, and "the education of ourselves and others."

Hirsch's theory of who Israel is stood at the opposite pole from that of Geiger and the Reformers. To them, as we have seen, Israel fell into the classification of a religious community and that alone. To Hirsch, Israel constituted a people, not a religious congregation, and Hirsch spoke of "national Jewish consciousness: "The Jewish people, though it carries the Torah with it in all the lands of its dispersion, will never find its table and lamp except in the Holy Land." Israel performs a mission among the nations, to teach "that God is the source of blessing." Israel then falls between, forming its own category, because it has a state system, in the land, but also a life outside.[6] In outlining this position, Hirsch of course reaffirmed the theory of the supernatural Israel laid forth in the dual Torah. The power of the national ideal for Hirsch lay in its polemical force against the assimilationists and Reformers, whom he treated as indistinguishable:

---

[4]Ibid., pp. 512–513.

[5]Ibid., p. 513.

[6]Ibid., p. 514.

The contempt with which the assimilationists treat David's [fallen] tabernacle and the prayer for the sacrificial service clearly reveals the extent of their rebellion against Torah and their complete disavowal of the entire realm of Judaism. They gather the ignorant about them to whom the Book of Books, the Divine national document of their Jewish past and future, is closed with seven seals. With a conceit engendered by stupidity and a perfidy born from hatred they point to God's Temple and the Divine Service in Zion as the unholy center of the 'bloody cult of sacrifices.' Consequently, they make certain to eliminate any reference to the restoration of the Temple service from our prayers.... The 'cultured, refined' sons and daughters of our time must turn away with utter disgust from their 'prehistoric, crude' ancestors who worship their god with bloody sacrifices.

Hirsch reviews the long line of exalted leaders who affirmed sacrifice and who were not crude, such as Moses, Isaiah, Jeremiah, and others. Then he concludes:

The Jewish sacrifice expresses the highest ideal of man's and the nation's moral challenge Blood and kidney, head and limbs symbolize our service of God with every drop of blood, every emotion, every particle of our being. By performing the act of sacrifice at the place chosen by God as the site of His Law, we proclaim our determination to fulfill our lofty moral and ethical tasks to enable God to bless the site of the national vow with the presence of this glory and with the fullness of this love and grace.[7]

Hirsch's spiritualization of the sacrifices—in an ample tradition of precedent, to be sure—derives from the challenge of Reform. Demanding an acceptance at face value of the Torah as the revelation of God's wisdom, Hirsch nonetheless made the effort to appeal to more than the givenness of the Torah and its commandments.

On the contrary, he entered into argument in the same terms—spiritualization, lofty moral and ethical tasks—as did the Reformers. That marks his thought as new and responsive to a fresh set of issues. As for the Reformers, he met them on their ground, as he had to, and his principal points of insistence to begin with derived from the issues defined by others. That is why we may find for him a suitable place in the larger setting of discourse among the Judaisms of the nineteenth century, all of them products of the end of self-evidence and the beginning of a self-conscious explanation for what had formerly, and elsewhere in the age at hand, the authority of the absolutely given. We see that fact most clearly when we take up a single stunning instance of the possibility of locating the several Judaisms on a single continuum: the doctrine of the Torah, what it is, and where it comes from.

---

[7]Samson Raphael Hirsch, *Collected Writings* (New York and Jerusalem: Philipp Feldheim, 1984), vol. 1, pp. 388–389.

19 Contemporary Orthodox Judaism Speaks: A Challenge to Orthodoxy

EMANUEL RACKMAN

1. Why is this reading important?

When Rabbi Rackman wrote this paper thirty years ago, he set forth an enduring moral challenge to integrationist Orthodox Judaism, one that remains vivid today as much as the day he wrote it. People think of Orthodoxy as monolithic and always closed off from the world. Here is an authentic Orthodox voice—chancellor of Bar Ilan University, Israel's integrationist Orthodox university—to call that impression into doubt. Denying the division of Orthodoxy into "modern" and "traditional," Rackman insists that the same sources that sustain traditionalists govern the modernists as well. That explains why, with confidence in the tradition, Rackman writes dismissively about "reactionaries" in Orthodoxy, who, if anything, enjoy still greater authority today than three decades ago. He underscores the vitality and diversity of faith within Orthodoxy, which, if anything, also form dominant traits even now. Rackman's challenge is this: Can the Judaism of the dual Torah make a statement to the world of Judaism that is fair, reasonable, enlightened, and civil? He argues that freedom and the Torah are compatible, that the range of normative belief is limited and allows space for a variety of conflicting views on numerous important questions. His is the voice of Orthodoxy that is not heard much these days. I do not present him as typical, any more than Scripture presents the prophets as typical; I present him as exemplary, because his writing embodies one powerful stream within the Judaism of the dual Torah.

2. What should you notice as you proceed?

Try to identify the specific issues of public debate that divide Orthodox Jews. Rackman emphasizes the possibility of equally legitimate positions within much of the doctrine of the Torah. Where does he validate difference, and when does he declare a single doctrine or dogma infallible? On what basis does he know the one from the other? Like Hirsch, Rackman insists that Orthodox Judaism not only accommodates change but nurtures it. Then notice on what basis he advocates change and in what way he proposes to validate it. When Rackman speaks of areas of the law closed off to dissent, even here he identifies room for maneuver. On what basis would he open up a bit of wriggle space, and what distinctions does he make in order to do so? Finally, notice the role of history and historical precedent in his argument. In this aspect he carries forward the mode of argumentation from precedent (within the framework of the Torah) explored by Hirsch. But when Maimonides wishes to find reasons for the laws, he does not construct such an argument, and you will want to look back and find out what sorts of arguments work for Maimonides that do not work for Rackman, and vice versa.

3. How should you frame a question for class discussion in response to what you have read?

Clearly, Orthodox Judaism not only is divided against itself, but also finds no institutional means to resolve difference. That explains why Rackman can point to Orthodox Jews who condemn and curse other Orthodox Jews, so that people keeping the same laws, saying the same prayers, observing the same food taboos, hallowing the same Sabbath in the same way, can dismiss one another as heretics and traitors. So how are matters going to resolve themselves? A class discussion on the advantages that Catholics enjoy in the papacy would include speculation on what sort of institutional developments would help Orthodox Judaisms come to terms with one another. Britain has a Chief Rabbi, but his authority is at best tolerated by Orthodox Judaisms outside the institutional circle of those who stand behind the Chief Rabbinate. The liberal Judaisms reject his authority altogether. The state of Israel has two Chief Rabbis, one for Jews from Muslim countries, the other for Jews from European countries. However much they share, each rules only his own followers. Would a pope make a difference? Compare the situation also in the Muslim world, producing some facts on how Islamic authorities are recognized and the jurisdictions that they reach. How, finally, do other world religions deal with internal difference? Do institutional solutions, hierarchies at an ascending level to a final authority, such as the First Presidency of the Church of Jesus Christ of Latter-Day Saints (the Mormons) represents, hold promise. In all, how do institutions of governance work when they work, and why do they not work when they do not? Some classroom generalizing and theorizing would be very much in order now.

I

A group of Israeli intellectuals, orthodox in practice and commitment, addressed an inquiry to one of the world's most pious and learned of rabbis. In their work and thought they had embraced scientific theories which appeared to contradict passages of the Bible when literally interpreted. The age of the earth was one example. From another rabbi they had heard that Orthodoxy requires that one believe the earth to be only 5728 years old. Were they to be regarded as heretics because of their disagreement with this view?

The twenty-five-page reply prepared for them is not yet published. Its author (who prefers to be unnamed) sought the concurrence of three colleagues who had occasionally expressed progressive views. One declined to become involved because of advanced age and poor health; another declined concurrence because of fear of what he himself calls "McCarthyism" in Jewish Orthodoxy; the third felt that his status in the traditionalist community was not yet sufficiently secure to be of any value to the scholar soliciting approval, especially since the latter himself enjoyed so much more prestige than he.

The reply—with copious references to authorities—indicates that Orthodoxy is not monolithic: it requires acknowledgment of the divine origin of the Commandments and firm resolve to fulfill them; however, it also permits great latitude in the formulation of doctrines, the interpretation of Biblical passages, and the rationalization of *mitzvot*. It is not difficult to demonstrate that the giants of the Tradition held widely divergent views on the nature of God, the character of historic revelation, and the uniqueness of the Jewish faith. Not all of these views could possibly be true, and yet not one of them may be deemed heretical, since one respected authority or another has clung to it. The only heresy is the denial that God gave the Written and Oral Law to His people, who are to fulfill its mandates and develop their birthright in accordance with its own built-in methodology and authentic exegesis.

Often in the past, upon encountering new cultures or philosophical systems, Jewish scholars re-examined the Tradition and discovered new insights and interpretations. Their contemporary colleagues of a more conservative temperament resisted and attacked the creative spirits as heretics, though the impugned protested that they were deeply committed to the Tradition and had said nothing which was not supported by respected authorities who had preceded them. The resulting schisms were often no credit to the Jewish people and, in modern times, even yielded groupings among American Jews which are not based altogether on ideological differences.

Unfortunately, however, it is the reactionaries in Orthodoxy who bear much of the guilt for this tragic phenomenon. Their heresy is that they regard their own Biblical and Talmudic interpretation as canonized in the same measure as the texts themselves—which was never true. They are repeating this heresy again, in Israel and the Diaspora, so that already Jewish sociologists detect the possibility of further schisms in Orthodoxy. At least four groups are even now discernible,[1] and the "rightists" are exercising pressure to brand the "leftists" as heretics and to force them either to create a new sect or to identify with Conservative Judaism. The founder of Reconstructionism did break with the Tradition, and his views, insofar as they deny the divine origin of Torah and *mitzvot*, are heresy. But this was unequivocally clear to his own colleagues on the faculty of the Jewish Theological Seminary fifty years ago, and Solomon Schechter must have had him in mind when he poked fun at those who observe the *mitzvot* and yet deny their God-given character. However, this does not mean that all who have new approaches are *ipso facto* non-Orthodox and must affiliate elsewhere.

In more recent times Rabbi Abraham Isaac Kook, of blessed memory, was regarded as having expressed dangerous opinions. Dr. Joseph B. Soloveitchik and

---

[1]See Charles S. Liebman, "A Sociological Analysis of Contemporary Orthodoxy," *Judaism*, Summer 1964, p. 285 ff.

Dr. Samuel Belkin today are experiencing the same fate. The late Rabbi Aaron Kotler, dean of the "rightists," denied that those who receive a secular education can express authentic Torah views. The students of the Rabbi Isaac Elchanan Theological Seminary of Yeshiva University, whose graduates Dr. Belkin and Dr. Soloveitchik ordain, are taught by rabbis who are rightist, leftist, and centrist; and, while academic freedom is enjoyed by all, there prevails an uneasy tension among both faculty and seminarians which is also reflected in the rabbinical associations they subsequently join together with graduates of other Orthodox seminaries. Milton Himmelfarb has detected and written of this tension as it appears in the periodicals of Orthodox thought and opinion, like *Deot, Amudim, Jewish Observer, Tradition,* etc. It is even more pronounced in Israel in the sundry factions of several religious political parties and their daily, weekly, and monthly publications. The politicians there clamor for unity among the Orthodox, but the ideologists, especially in the religious collectives, insist that, before there can be unity even on an election slate, religious parties must at least unite on mutual respect for the legitimacy of their divergent religious views. But this is not forthcoming.

Two questions must needs be considered. Is the "right" correctly representing the Tradition? And is it wise even for them, from their point of view and certainly from the point of view of the survival of the Tradition, to deal with the "left" as they do?

One who undertakes to answer these questions must do so with fear and trepidation. Since he must deal with the totality of the law and creed known as Judaism, he ought not be so presumptuous as to regard himself as so much the master of the entire Tradition that he can offer definitive views on virtually every aspect. Furthermore, some of the views he must, of necessity, express will incur the wrath of colleagues and cause their exponent to share the fate of the very people whom he wants properly to reclaim as members of the community of the devout and committed. Like them he will be called a heretic whose ideas jeopardize the future and integrity of Torah.

Nonetheless, silence is not the alternative when one is convinced that precisely a measure of candor is the *desideratum,* not only because God wills that we speak the truth as we see it—for His name is Truth—but also because silence and its concomitant smugness are estranging Jewish intellectuals. Jewish intellectuals are becoming interested in the Tradition, but they will not accept the rigidity of most contemporary exponents of Orthodoxy. They crave more autonomy of the soul. Moreover, some effort ought to be expended to reaffiliate those who, principally because of the way in which Jews have organized themselves politically in Israel and socially and institutionally in the English-speaking countries, find themselves identified with groups whose ideology they do not truly share. For many reasons they cannot identify with the present leadership of Orthodoxy anywhere in the world, and yet they regard themselves as wholly within the Torah tradition. The time is ripe for a candid re-examination of fundamentals and a challenge to those whose principal claim to authority is that they have closed minds and secure their leadership by exacting a comparable myopia from their followers. One may not deny them their freedom of worship, but even as they want their views tolerated and respected so must they be prevailed upon to recognize that others are as devout and as committed as they, and that the Tradition has always permitted a considerable amount of diversity in thought and action. It was never proper to consolidate ranks by substituting fixity for dynamic religious creativity, and certainly in the contemporary open society with its emphasis on the open mind, it is hardly propitious to commit the error occasionally committed in the past when one group of Jews withdrew from their co-religionists, regarded the others as heretics, and sought to save themselves by severing contact with those with whom they disagreed.

Rightly or wrongly, one Jewish sociologist has named me as an ideologist of "modern Orthodoxy." However, one can hardly regard modern Orthodoxy as a movement: it is no more than a coterie of a score of rabbis in America and in Israel whose interpretations of the Tradition have won the approval of Orthodox intellectuals who are knowledgeable in both Judaism and Western civilization. None of the rabbis feels that he is articulating any position that cannot be supported by reference to authentic Jewish sources. None wants to organize a separate rabbinic body, and several have rejected an attempt to publish an independent periodical, because they did not want the remotest possibility that this form of separatism be interpreted as a schism in Orthodoxy. I, no less than they, deny any claim to innovation. Our choice of methods and values in the Tradition, our emphases, and our concerns, may be different. But the creation or articulation of shades and hues hardly warrants dignifying our effort with the terms "ideology" or "sect." We know that the overwhelming majority of Orthodox rabbis differ with us and that the faculties of most Orthodox day schools and rabbinical seminaries disapprove of some of our views and so instruct their pupils. It is not our mission to have them join our ranks. Rather do we seek to help Jewish intellectuals who are being alienated from the Tradition to realize that they can share a commitment to the faith which is acceptable to them and at least as authentic as the one they have received from their teachers but which they feel impelled to renounce. We reject the multiplication of dogmas and their precise formulation. Among Christians this notion is presently popular as "reductionism." In Judaism, however, "reductionism" is very ancient: the Midrash tells us of different prophets who sought to encapsulate the tradition in seven, three, or even one principle. Ours is a commitment which invites questioning and creativity in thought and practice, as applied not only to the Law but also to theology.

II

One must begin with the measure of freedom permitted in Jewish Law and commitment by the Tradition itself. When do one's thought and action place one beyond the circle of the devout? We discover that the range of diversity in creed, ritual, and law is so great that, no less than in a democracy, consensus is required on much less than is usually thought—in order to claim rightful status as an Orthodox Jew.

Must one who professes Orthodoxy be committed to the retention of the total Halachah insofar as it deals with civil law—the law of property and obligations, corporations, partnerships, sales, trusts, estates? According to the Halachah itself, there is a residual power to alter all property relationships in the *bet din* (court), and especially in a supreme legislative and judicial body such as the Sanhedrin once was and many hope will soon be reconstituted. The principle is known as *hefker bet din hefker*. A *bet din* has the power to declare property ownerless and in that way to divest a man of his rights, vesting them in another. This power was exercised whenever changes were made in the Halachah with regard to economic affairs. A man may thus be Orthodox and yet actively propagate changes in the law for the promotion of capitalism or socialism, bigness or smallness in economic enterprise, curbs on strikes, or greater freedom for organized labor.

The Halachah has many ethical norms and insights to offer on these subjects, but any Jew—committed to the Halachah—enjoys, on the basis of his interpretation of the Halachah, unlimited freedom to propose changes; if he were fortunate enough to be a member of the Sanhedrin and to prevail on his colleagues to embrace his point of view, he would be the creator of new Halachah. There may be instances where the changes are so radical that resort would have to be taken to legal fiction. Thus, when Hillel saw that Jews were not lending money to each other because of the fear that the sabbatical year would nullify the debts, he could have changed the rule by exercising the power of *hefker bet din hefker*, divesting debtors of their money and vesting it in their creditors, but this would have been an unequivocal nullification of a Biblical mandate. Instead he instituted the *pruzbul*—a legal fiction whereby the debts incurred prior to the sabbatical year were transferred to the court for collection. Perhaps he also hoped thereby to keep alive some memory of the Biblical rule and that one day it would be revived in practice. To alter the Biblical rule of inheritance in order to establish the equal rights of daughters to inherit with sons, or to abolish the last vestige of primogeniture in Jewish law, may also require resort to legal fictions—as the late Chief Rabbi Herzog once unsuccessfully proposed. In any case, one cannot be regarded as a heretic because of one's dissatisfaction with the present state of the Halachah with regard to economic matters and one's determination to effect change and development. Such change and development have always been, and must needs continue to be, achieved.

Is the Orthodox Jew any less free in connection with criminal law? Whether he wants to diminish the number of crimes and mitigate punishments or whether he wants to increase them, he can do so within the frame of the Halachah. He must be most circumspect, it is true, with regard to capital offenses—but even here he is by no means without power. Again, there are residual powers in the *bet din* and even in the king (the executive authority) which can be exercised to safeguard peace and order and promote the general welfare. Centuries after capital punishment had virtually been abolished, the Jewish community protected itself against informers by reviving capital punishment. It also altered the rules of evidence to make convictions more feasible. A devotee of the Halachah, therefore—even as he tries to fathom its spirit and especially the enormous regard it has for human life and freedom by comparison with its lesser regard for the right of property—need not feel impotent to propose and press, in fulfillment of that spirit, for the adoption of a new criminal law for a modern state, even for a state that professes to be committed to the Halachah.

Nor need he feel inhibited as he seeks within the spirit of the Halachah to urge upon his fellow citizens the consideration of specific proposals for the constitutional structure of the state. He will be able to justify unicameral and bicameral legislatures, proportional representation, popular election of judges and their appointment by the executive, a parliamentary and a presidential form of government, and sundry other forms of government which may be found in modern states. The more profound his commitment to the Halachah, and the more preoccupied he is with what God would have willed for a new Jewish State, the more tolerant will he be of all the proposals and the more will he resort to the will of the people except when that will flouts basic norms and ethics with regard to which majority rule is not to be countenanced. Thus, as neither civil nor criminal law is fixed and immutable in the Halachah, public law in general is an area in which commitment to the Halachah requires no general agreement among the devout.

Israel's victory in the Six-Day War made this abundantly clear. Shortly after the occupation of the new territory, Chief Rabbi Nissim held that, according to the Halachah, it would be forbidden to negotiate for peace as the *quid pro quo* for the return of any of these areas. Rabbi Joseph B. Soloveitchik questioned this decision and indicated that perhaps for an enduring peace it would be necessary to relinquish some of the land and that statesmen might be in a better position to render such a decision, which would be binding on rabbis precisely as the opinion of a doctor is binding on a rabbi in connection with the breaking of a fast on the Day of Atonement. Rabbi Nissim countered with the suggestion that there are certain commandments for which martyrdom is required. He was certainly justified in making that suggestion, since almost every conquest in the history of humanity has involved the loss of blood, and Jews, too, have been commanded to conquer. (In at least one situation this was even a *mitzvah*.) In a recent essay, a pupil of Rabbi Kook, Rabbi Yehuda Gershuni, documented his support of Dr. Soloveitchik's view. In any event, it is obvious that on so historic an issue, one so vital to the future of the people of Israel, a radical difference of opinion prevails among giants in the world of Halachah. And who will deny that all are Orthodox in commitment and practice!

In family law we encounter a more circumscribed area. Yet here, too, as a devotee of the Halachah one can propose and agitate for changes that will nullify almost every rule of the past. It might be the sheerest folly to do so. But the question under consideration is not whether one should write a new code for Jewish domestic relations but rather whether the power resides in the duly constituted authorities to do so. And it does. Therefore, he who thinks that changes are in order and proposes them for promulgation by the *bet din* or Sanhedrin cannot be regarded as a heretic. As in the case of property, the Rabbis ruled that all marriages have an implied condition that their validity and continuance are based on rabbinic consent. Rabbis in the past have differed as to how extensive this power is, but one cannot be deemed a heretic when he agrees with the most liberal views heretofore entertained. Exercising the power that rabbis have, they may one day reintroduce the annulment of Jewish marriages and the abolition of the last vestige of illegitimacy (except in the case of unequivocal proof that the child was born of an incestuous relationship). They may find ways to legislate an Enoch Arden law and make the incidence of the levirate law impossible. There are some limitations; but for any Orthodox group to brand as a heretic one who feels keenly that changes should be made—within the Halachic frame and by its own methodology—is to define heresy as it was never defined in the past. One can argue with the proponents of change because of policy considerations, but one may not challenge their loyalty to the faith. Indeed, they may be its most passionate champions as they try to relieve human distress.

III

The areas of personal religious observance and congregational or temple practice are quite different. There the *bet din* is not so free to act as in other spheres of the

Law. And he who would, for example, say that a Jew need not don the phylacteries or eat kosher food could be regarded as a heretic. However, one should not underestimate the extent to which rabbis may, in good faith, differ with each other within the frame of the Halachah without even recommending change. They may differ on policy considerations; they may differ on the steps that are required to nullify or modify earlier rabbinic legislation; they may differ on programs that are designed to guide people back to the Torah way of life. Even when they agree on what Orthodoxy requires in terms of normative practice, they can differ on policies and programs to achieve the goal they all envisage.

A few timely illustrations are in order. Should a rabbi use the microphone on the Sabbath in a synagogue where its use is required? The prohibition may be Biblical in origin. Others maintain that it is only rabbinic. Still others argue that the microphone may be used. Which is the better course for a rabbi to take—to rely on the more lenient view and serve the congregation so that it will not align itself with the non-Orthodox camp, or to decline to serve, thereby avoiding the compromise of one's own convictions and firmly presenting to that congregation a strict pattern of Jewish observance? In the final analysis, considerations of policy will dictate what one's decision will be, and Orthodox rabbis have been known to hold either view.

Similarly, Halachah dictates that men shall be separated from women in the synagogue. Some authorities hold that the most that can be Biblically supported is that they shall sit in separate sections. At least one authority holds that there is a Biblical requirement for a divider seventy-two inches high. But Biblical rules are also sometimes suspended in the face of greater needs of the community, especially in times of stress. Most often the suspension is temporary, but not necessarily so. Perhaps this explains why some of the policy-makers at Yeshiva University's theological seminary permit rabbis to serve congregations with mixed seating, in the hope that these congregations may one day revert to the traditional practice. They may be in error, but they are acting within the frame of a well-established Halachic principle that for God's sake one sometimes flouts Torah mandates. They are not to be regarded as diminished in their commitment. On the contrary, they may be more prophetic, and as they venture they may reclaim many, while others are saving only a remnant.

My last illustration is perhaps the one on which rabbinic opinion is most sharply divided. Most prohibitions are rabbinic in origin—they constitute the "fence around the Law." In modern times many of these rules have become onerous, and often meaningless. There are many ways to modify and even nullify their impact. Some rabbis seek the re-establishment of a Sanhedrin to accomplish this desired result. Others rely on a well-known principle that when the reason for the "fence" has disappeared the rule, too, automatically dies. What right does one have to question the integrity or commitment of an Orthodox Jew who proposes one way or the other? All have ample authority on which to rely. To what extent, for example, may electric power be used on the Sabbath, since the prohibition is at most rabbinic? Perhaps the use of musical instruments can also be liberalized. I personally may not agree, and in several instances I should like to see more "fences" added to safeguard Biblical rules (such as the prohibition against usury), but I cannot deny that there are reasons for modifying some established prohibitions. One ought not, in any case, pronounce bans against those who are pressing for conclusions with which one differs, provided that they make their proposals out of their commitment to the Law rather than their rejection of it.

If heresy is to be found anywhere, therefore, it must be in the areas of doctrine and creed rather than of law and practice.

IV

Even with regard to doctrine, such a divergence of opinion has prevailed among the giants of the Tradition that only one dogma enjoys universal acceptance: the Pentateuch's text was given to the Jewish people by God. However, what its mandates are, their number, application, and interpretation—this is part of the Oral Law, also God-given, but its guardians were rarely unanimous on its legal norms and less so on matters theological. That a majority prevailed on any particular issue in the past does not necessarily mean that the minority view is heretical, for, while one must continue to fulfill the law as the majority decided, one may propagate the minority point of view in the hope that it will one day be accepted by a new Sanhedrin. Maimonides is less liberal on this point than his critical glossator, Rabbi Abraham ben David, but even Maimonides accords this power to a Sanhedrin greater than its predecessors in quality and quantity. Therefore, how can one brand as a heretic anyone who in matters theological differs with his contemporaries and seeks to make normative a point of view once rejected or proscribed but for whose acceptance he continues to hope?

How many are the dogmas of Judaism? Maimonides said thirteen, but other scholars held that there were fewer. Even on so basic a point as to whether there can exist more than one divine law Albo differed with Maimonides. He denied that there is any evidence for Maimonides' contention that the immutability of the Mosaic Law is a pillar of the faith and opined that there may be a succession of divine laws, so that even Mosaic law is not beyond change or repeal.[2] Jews generally have agreed with Maimonides—at least until the Messiah will come, and upon his coming they believe with Albo that new divine laws may be promulgated. The collective experience of the Jewish people may warrant the conclusion that the Maimonidean view is the more prudent—pragmatically to be regarded as true—but who can gainsay the right of dissenter to agree with Albo or even a modification or extension of Albo's view and yet regard himself as a member of the family of the committed?

Agreement or even consensus is still more difficult to find in connection with such matters as the nature and mission of angels, the character of "the world-to-come" and how it differs from immortality of the soul, the precise role the Messiah will play when he comes and what events will be the most dependable credentials of his legitimacy, the form final judgment will take in a hereafter and the reward and punishments to be dispensed, the transmigration of souls, and a score of other issues with which ancient and medieval scholars were concerned. One discovers in their writings virtually every opinion known to man, ranging from the purest rationalism to the wildest fancy. Few Orthodox Jews try to be specific in formulating their own creeds. They are content with a few generalizations: that God endows every human being with a soul, which is His eternal spark

---

[2]*Book of Roots* 1, 3, 25: III, 13–16.

within us and immortal; the human being—body and soul—is responsible and accountable for his performance on earth; one day nature will be made perfect, and as God fulfills His promise to make it perfect He will also have to do justice to the dead, who are the most helpless victims of nature's imperfections. Details are not only avoided, they are unthinkable. Except in most elusive form these sentiments can hardly be regarded as dogmas; they leave too much room for the play of the imagination of the individual believer. Therefore, it is incredible that moderns, who are committed to faith and the Law, should be excluded from the fold because of limited credulousness in this sphere. Indeed, it would be impossible for reactionaries to ignore the giants of the past who were equally skeptical. (Only recently did I come upon a note of Strashoun proving that the Talmud did not subscribe to Kabbalistic notions of the transmigration of souls.)

But the range of the diversity involves doctrines even more basic to the faith. To what extent, for example, is there any binding authority on the nature of God and His attributes? Here, too, Maimonides and Rabbi Abraham ben David differed so radically on God's corporeality that, were Jews prone to create sects because of doctrinal disputes, as Protestants do, each would have been responsible for a new sect in Judaism. Even with regard to so integral a part of Judaism as God's role as Creator, Maimonides retained an open mind. He believed that the correct interpretation of the Bible required a belief in *creatio ex nihilo,* but he admitted that if it could be proven conclusively—as Aristotle had failed to do—that this was impossible, one would then only be required to re-examine and correct one's interpretation of the Bible to make it consonant with the demands of absolute truth. Judaism is very much at peace with a host of antimonies regarding God's nature—His imminence and His transcendence, His prescience and His becoming, His absolutism and His vacillation. To deny that God is a personal God who communicates with all men, and especially with Israel, would be heresy according to Judaism, but any description of Him by rationalists, empiricists, intuitionists, or existentialists would hardly be without some warrant in the writings of the Sages.

Similarly, there is no substantial agreement with regard to the manner in which God communicated with Israel, its Patriarchs and Prophets. Somehow the Tradition preferred never to demand of Jews more than that they believe the text of the Pentateuch to be divine in origin. Otherwise, the widest latitude in interpretation was not only permitted but often encouraged. Even the authorship of the Five Books of Moses was not beyond the scope of the diversity. Several Sages held that Moses himself wrote the book of *Deuteronomy* but God dictated its inclusion with the earlier books. Moreover, much in the earlier books started also as the work of man. In their dialogues with God the Patriarchs spoke their own words. Jacob composed his own prophecy for his offspring. Moses sang his own song of triumph on the Red Sea. In the final analysis, then, the sanctity of the Pentateuch does not derive from God's authorship of all of it but rather from the fact that God's is the final version. The final writing by Moses has the stamp of divinity—the kiss of immortality. So stated, the dogma is a much more limited one than one would be led to believe it is when one listens to many an Orthodox teacher today.

If this is the situation with regard to the Pentateuch, is it wise to add dogmas that the books of the Prophets and the Writings were all authored by the men to whom the Tradition attributes them? The Talmud itself was not dogmatic, but contemporary Orthodoxy always feels impelled to embrace every tradition as dogma. The Talmud suggests that perhaps David did not write all the Psalms. Is one a heretic because one suggests that perhaps other books were authored by more than one person or that several books attributed by the Tradition to one author were in fact written by several at different times? A volume recently published makes an excellent argument for the position there was but one Isaiah, but must one be shocked when it is opined that there may have been two or three prophets bearing the same name? No Sage of the past ever included in the articles of faith a dogma about the authorship of the books of the Bible other than the Pentateuch. What is the religious, moral, or intellectual need for adding dogmas now when it is well known with regard to many such issues that there always prevailed *noblesse oblige* among scholars? It may be heresy to deny the possibility of prophetic prediction, but it is not heresy to argue about authorship on the basis of objective historical and literary evidence. How material is it that one really believes that Solomon wrote all three Scrolls attributed to him? Is the value of the writings themselves affected? And if the only purpose is to discourage critical Biblical scholarship, then, alas, Orthodoxy is declaring bankruptcy: it is saying that only the ignorant can be pious—a reversal of the Talmudic dictum.

True, a pious man has *emunat hakhamim,* faith in the dicta of the Sages. Yet Orthodox Jews do not rely on this principle in connection with their physical well-being. They are willing to be treated in illness by physicians who hold views that differ radically from those expressed in the Talmud for the treatment of disease. Certainly the Tradition condones this. Is it less forgiving of one who in his study of the Bible feels impelled to arrive at conclusions on the basis of evidence unavailable to his forebears?

No more than with regard to the authorship of the Biblical books did the Sages canonize interpretations of the Bible. For the purpose of the Halachah one interpretation may have to be followed until the Halachah, within its own processes, is altered; but the Sages recognized, offered, and delighted in many alternative, frequently contradictory interpretations which had significance for their spiritual living. Especially was this true when they interpreted narrative portions of the Bible. Maimonides was the most revolutionary of all when he held that most Biblical history is allegorical. Whether Jacob only dreamed that he wrestled with an angel or actually did so was debated by sundry Sages. Nahmanides even held that it was God's intention that the *mitzvot* of the Torah were given for ultimate fulfillment in the Land of Israel, and our observance of them in the Diaspora is only preparation for our sojourn in the land of our fathers. Hardly any Orthodox rabbi agrees with him today—and perhaps none agreed with him in his day. Was he, therefore, deemed a heretic?

Even the historic fact of revelation was not specifically delineated. Whether God as much as spoke all the Decalogue so that everyone could hear it was controversial. One Rabbi dared to say that God did not descend to earth. Summing up the Talmudic and Midrashic texts available and the opinions of medieval philosophers, one modern scholar said that the best that could be said for the Jewish conception of revelation is that it is "elusive." Perhaps it is. But the net effect is a consensus on which the faith is founded. *Something* extraordinary happened—and the Jew begins with a text that is God's word. He may not always understand it. He may often question why God approved of much that He gave. Unlike Martin Buber, the Orthodox Jew does not reject any part of the text. If he finds it difficult to explain why the very God who ordered us never to take revenge also demanded the extermination of the Amalekites, he does not delete from the text the lines he does not fathom; he ponders them until divine illumination comes to him. He may discover that the Amalekites—unlike the Egyptians—merited destruction and continuing hate; he may regard Amalek as the symbol of militarism for the sake of militarism; or he may even conclude that what is meant is the id in every human being. Heresy begins not when interpretation is challenged but when the text is no longer considered divine. That is why Franz Rosenzweig did not consider himself un-Orthodox because of his theory of revelation but only because he could not bring himself to obey all the *mitzvot* until they spoke to him personally and became meaningful to his own existential situation. Unlike him, the Orthodox Jew obeys and does not wait. Obedience to God's will by itself is meaningful to his existential situation, and the more he obeys the more he discovers meaning and relevance.

If Jews differed with regard to their interpretation of the texts of Scripture, certainly they differed with regard to their interpretation of history. It has been demonstrated, for example, that Ashkenazim and Sephardim differed with regard to their positions on eschatology and the warrant that historical situations might provide for either activism or quiescence with regard to the coming of the Messiah.

Thus, even with respect to creed, the diversity is as legion as it is with respect to Law. To be counted among the devout and the committed never required unrelenting conformity in matters of the mind and heart. Judaism did not suffer as a result. On the contrary, it remained one of the most dynamic and spiritually satisfying of all religious traditions. In the last century and a half this magnificent Tradition was abandoned: in its encounter with the enormous diversity of the winds of doctrine prevailing in the modern world, Orthodoxy sought to guarantee its survival by freezing the Halachah and its theology. As a result, it now cannot realize its full potential in an age when more and more intellectuals are prepared for the leap of faith but hardly for a leap to obscurantism.

20 Founders of Modern Judaism: The Historical School Zechariah Frankel and Heinrich Graetz

JACOB NEUSNER

1. Why is this reading important?

Conservative Judaism in the United States began as the Critical-Historical School in Germany, a group of intellectuals—historians, not theologians—who sympathized with the goals of Reform Judaism and shared that Judaism's premises but who rejected as extreme its concrete policies for actual change. The moderate wing of reform, the Critical-Historical School, like the Reformers, appealed to what they called "history" to validate change and transform it into a reformation of Judaism. But they drew the line around the Hebrew Scriptures and conducted their historical study mainly of the Talmud and related writings of the first few centuries of the Common Era. To understand the Critical-Historical School, we need only to read books, not to examine the sociology or the theology of their Judaism. And the important books all appeared in the 1850s, a single decade marking the birth of this Judaism. What makes the subject important, not merely interesting, is the development, in the United States and Canada, of Conservative Judaism. That movement adopted the program and policies—as well as ambiguities—of the Critical-Historical School and, in a different environment altogether, made a huge success of religious historicism. The principal figures in Germany, Frankel and Graetz, themselves embody all the strengths and dilemmas of later North American Conservative Judaism. In the discussions of Conservative Judaism, readers will confront a number of different ways by which people refer to that Judaism: "Historical School," "Critical-Historical School," "Positive-Historical School," "Positive-Historical-Critical," and the like. Despite the variety of names, all refer to the same Judaism.

2. What should you notice as you proceed?

Three points of analysis should register. (1) The Critical-Historical School used "facts of history" to establish principles of faith. Why they appealed to historical fact rather than theological formulation of religious conviction is an important question to answer. (2) The Critical-Historical School privileged the Hebrew Scriptures of ancient Israel and exempted those writings from critical study. Why they made a distinction between ancient Israel's biblical writings and the somewhat-later rabbis' Talmudic ones defines a considerable problem. (3) The Critical-Historical School found the matter of biography in history to define their central interest. Why lives of great men should form the focus of their study is another question to consider.

3. How should you frame a question for class discussion in response to what you have read?

The Critical-Historical School in Judaism typifies what happens in an age of vast changes in politics and intellectual life. Such ages begin with a dramatic event of rejection of the old order. In response comes an equally articulate defense of the old order—but in the language of the new. Then a mediating effort tries to bridge the abyss between old and new. Take, for instance, the story of the Reformation, with its Catholic thesis, its Lutheran antithesis, and the settlements of the seventeenth century as the synthesis. Consider the progress of the Reformation in Britain, with its violent political attack on Roman Catholic Christianity, the formation of a moderate ("nonpapist") Catholic Christianity called Anglicanism, and the development of the Reformation Churches—Presbyterians in Scotland, Puritans in England at the outer extreme. But the interesting question for discussion is: Who defines change? When we consider an age of enormous religious conflict, such as the Reformation in the sixteenth and seventeenth centuries in Western Europe and the Reformation of Judaism in nineteenth-century Central Europe, who sets the issues for debate? When we identify the person who defines the agenda of change, we know who decides what is going to happen. In that setting, ask yourself: Which of the three Judaisms of the Judaic Reformation dictated the terms of discussion? In my view, the answer is: the most extreme and original of the three, which is Reform Judaism. That Judaism determined what would take place in the Judaisms of the West—Central and Western Europe, North America, and their offshoots in South Africa and Australia—from the Napoleanic Wars of the early nineteenth century through World War II. An interesting class discussion on the foundation of Reform Judaism's success and its principal ideas will seek cases for comparison and contrast in other ages of religious change—for instance, Protestant Christianity in the nineteenth-century United States.

If history, or rather, History, the chosen discipline for Judaic theological argument in the nineteenth century, gave its name to Conservative Judaism, the particular area of history that defined discourse by no means surfaced as a matter of accident. People made a very deliberate choice in the matter. What they studied—that is, subjected to critical processes of analysis, proof and disproof—was no more indicative than what they refrained from reading in that same detached and critical manner. They did not study Scripture in the critical way. They did study the documents of the Oral Torah in accord with the canons of contemporary academic scholarship. Why the difference? The principal theological issues under debate derived from the Judaism of the dual Torah. No one argued about whether or not Moses gave the Ten Commandments. But people did have to work out for themselves a relationship to the Judaism of the dual Torah—and, by definition, that meant to the documents of the Oral Torah. The historical question applied to that matter in particular, and, of course, people raised questions of origins (meaning authority) about the oral part of the dual Torah: where did it come from, is it part of the revelation of Sinai?

The Orthodox answers, we recall, left no ambiguity. The Torah came from God, not from mortal humanity; the Torah retains authority, such as it had from the very beginning; and, of course, the Talmud and the other rabbinic writings represented by it form part of the revelation of Sinai. The Reform answers took an opposite position. The Oral Torah forms part of the accidents of history; it comes from human authors; it is not part of the Torah of Sinai. Addressing these issues, then, would occupy scholars who thought that they could produce "positive, historical" knowledge, which would secure reliable facts in answer to the questions of faith. When history forms the arena for scholarship in the Judaic context, the history of the oral component of the dual Torah will attract attention and debate. That rule derives from the debates between Reform and Orthodox theologians. Both concurred on the divine origin of the Written Torah, but the former denied what the latter affirmed, which is the divine origin of the Oral Torah.

The Critical-Historical School's principal contribution to the debate derived from two historians, Zechariah Frankel and Heinrich Graetz, who founded the study of the rabbinic literature as a historical source. Since the theological motive for the work is now clear to us, we can understand that the beginnings of the study of the Talmud as history lie in nineteenth-century Germany. With Reform well defined and Orthodoxy coming to an articulate view of itself, the Critical-Historical School made its appearance third in line during the 1850s. The groundwork of the modern debate about the Talmud, in mostly historical terms, was supplied in that single decade, from 1851 to 1859. Four books published in less than ten years defined the way the work would be done for the next hundred years. Three of their four authors—Krochmal, Graetz, and Frankel—were identified (in Krochmal's case, posthumously) with the Critical-Historical School. These four books were Leopold Zunz's posthumous publication of Nahman Krochmal's *Moreh nebukhe hazzeman* ("guide to the perplexed of our times," a title meant to call to mind Maimonides' *Guide to the Perplexed*), 1851; Heinrich Graetz's fourth volume of his *History of the Jews from the Earliest Times to the Present*, which is devoted to the Talmudic period, 1853; Geiger's *Urschrift und Uebersetzungen der Bibel*, 1857; and Zechariah Frankel's *Darkhé hammishnah* ("ways of the Mishnah"), 1859. These four volumes—with Zunz and Geiger marking the Reform contribution, Graetz and Frankel the positive-historical school's contribution—placed the Talmud into the very center of the debates on the reform of Judaism and address the critical issues of the debate: the divine mandate of Rabbinic Judaism.[1] For three generations there would be no historical work on the Talmud deriving from Orthodoxy, and what came later on bore no constructive program at all.

The Talmudic period defines the arena of the struggle over reform because the Reform theologians made it so and because Conservative ones affirmed that same decision, for essentially the same reason. They had proposed that by exposing the historical origins of the Talmud and of the Rabbinic form of Judaism, they might "undermine the divine mandate of rabbinic Judaism."[2] As Schorsch points out, Geiger's work indicates the highwater mark of the attack on Rabbinic Judaism through historical study. Krochmal, Graetz, and Frankel presented a sympathetic and favorable assessment. That is the point at which, in historical work, they would take their leave of Reform Judaism and lay the foundations for the Historical School of Conservative Judaism. In so doing, however, they adopted the fundamental supposition of the Reformers: the Talmud can and should be studied historically. They conceded that the period in which the Talmud comes forth possessed a history, and the Talmud itself is a work of men in history.

The method of Graetz and of Frankel was essentially biographical. The two provided spiritual heroes, a kind of academic hagiography, imparting color and life to the names of the Talmudic canon. One-third of Frankel's book is devoted to biographies of personalities mentioned in the Talmud. Frankel collected the laws given in the name of a particular man and stated that this man appears in such and such tractates; his card file is neatly divided but yields no more than what is filed in it. Gereboff comments on Frankel as follows:

> For Frankel Rabbi was the organizer and the law-giver. He compiled the Mishnah in its final form, employing a systematic approach. The Mishnah was a work of art; everything was "necessary" and in its place. All these claims are merely asserted. Frankel gives citations from Mishnaic and Amoraic sources, never demonstrating how the citations prove his contentions. Frankel applied his theory of positive-historical Judaism, which depicted Jewish life as a process combining the lasting values from the past with human intelligence in order to face the present and the future, to the formation of the Mishnah. The Mishnah was the product of human intelligence and divine inspiration. Using their intelligence, later generations took what they had received from the past and added to it. Nothing was ever removed. Frankel's work has little lasting value. He was, however, the first to analyze the Mishnah critically and historically; and this was his importance.[3]

What is important is not what Frankel proves but what he implicitly concedes, which is that the Mishnah and the rest of the rabbinic literature are the work of men. Graetz likewise stresses the matter of great men. As Schorsch characterizes his work:

---

[1] Ismar Schorsch, *Heinrich Graetz: The Structure of Jewish History and Other Essays.* (New York, 1975: Jewish Theological Seminary of America), p. 48.

[2] Ibid., p. 48.

[3] Joel Gereboff, "The Pioneer: Zecharias Frankel," in *The Modern Study of the Mishnah*, ed. J. Neusner (Leiden, 1973: E. J. Brill), pp. 59–75.

> Graetz tried valiantly to portray the disembodied rabbis of the Mishnah and Tal-
> mud as vibrant men, each with his own style and philosophy and personal frail-
> ties, who collectively resisted the disintegrating forces of their age. . . . In the wake
> of national disaster, creative leadership forged new religious institutions to pre-
> serve and invigorate the bonds of unity. . . . He defended talmudic literature as a
> a great national achievement of untold importance to the subsequent survival of
> the Jews.[4]

Now it is clear why the biographies of great men should be deemed the principal work of history: historians of the day generally wrote biographies. History
was collective biography. Their conception of what made things happen is tied
to the theory of the great man as the maker of history. The associated theory of
history was as the story of politics—what great men did. Whether or not the Jewish historians of the Talmudic period do well, moderately well, or poorly, the sort
of history people did in general I cannot say. The important point is that history
meant biography to them. But we have to recall that the historians of the day did
not as a rule lay the foundations for religious movements, nor did they ordinarily engage in vigorous debate on theological questions. Graetz and Frankel, by
contrast, strongly opposed Reform and criticized not only the results of Reform
scholarship but the policies of Reform Judaism.

If we place the historical scholarship of Graetz and Frankel into the context
of the age, we realize that their program fit more comfortably into a theological
than a critical-historical classification, however much they invoked the status of
critical-historical and positive-historical knowledge for their results. And that fact
places a quite different construction on the Historical School. Measured by the
standards of its day, it proved far less critical, far less historical, and far more credulous and believing than its adherents admitted. For a broad range of critical
questions escaped the attention of the Historical School, questions having to do
with the reliability of sources.

Specifically, in both classical and biblical studies, long before the mid-
nineteenth century a thoroughgoing skepticism had replaced the gullibility of earlier centuries. Alongside the historicist frame of mind shaped in the aftermath of
the Romantic movement, there was an enduring critical spirit, formed in the Enlightenment and not to be eradicated later on. This critical spirit approached the
historical allegations of ancient texts with a measure of skepticism. For biblical
studies, in particular, the history of ancient Israel no longer followed the paths of
the biblical narrative from Abraham onward. In the work of writing about the life
of Jesus, the contradictions among the several gospels, the duplications of materials, the changes from one gospel to the next between one saying and story and
another version of the same saying and story, the difficulty in establishing a biographical framework—all of these and similar devastating problems had attracted
attention. The result was a close analysis of the character of the sources as literature—as, for example, the recognition before the nineteenth century that the Pentateuch consists of at least three main strands: JE, D, and P.

It was also well known that behind the synoptic Gospels is a source (called
Q, for source, in German, *Quelle*) containing materials assigned to Jesus, upon
which the three evangelists drew but reshaped for their respective purposes. The

---

[4]Schorsch, *Graetz*, p. 48.

conception that merely because an ancient storyteller says someone said or did something does not mean he really said or did it goes back before the Enlightenment. After all, the beginnings of modern biblical studies surely reach into the mind of Spinoza. He was not the only truly critical intellect in the field before Voltaire. But as a powerful, socially rooted frame of mind, historical-critical and literary-critical work on the ancient Scriptures is the attainment of the late eighteenth and nineteenth centuries. And for Graetz, Frankel, and Krochmal, the founders of Talmudic history, what had happened in biblical and other ancient historical studies was either not known or not found to be useful. And it was not used. We can understand their neglect of the critical program when we realize that the issues on which they worked derived from a religious and not an academic or narrowly scholarly debate.

And yet the model of German Protestant theological scholarship in biblical studies made slight impact. For a considerable critical program had already taken shape, so that scholarship on religion observed the critical norms worked out in other historical subjects. No German biographer of Jesus by the 1850s, for example, could have represented his life and thought by a mere paraphrase and harmony of the Gospels, in the way in which Graetz and Frankel and their successors down to the mid-twentieth century would paraphrase and string together Talmudic tales about rabbis and call the result "history" and biography. Nor was it commonplace, by the end of the nineteenth century, completely to ignore the redactional and literary traits of documents entirely, let alone their historical and social provenance. Whatever was given to a rabbi, in any document from any place or time, was forthwith believed to provide evidence of what that rabbi really said and did in the time in which he lived. So the claim of the positive Historical School to produce that same positivist data that historians in general claimed to present certainly failed, and the reason that fact matters is simple. The theologians of the Historical School claimed to present "mere" facts, but the bulk of the facts they did produce derived from a reading of sources in as believing, not to say credulous, a spirit as the Orthodox brought to Scripture. By the standards of their own day, the scholars proved not at all critical. What matters, then, is the theological program, not the scholarly outcome.

We therefore must wonder quite how much change the Historical School admitted. As I have said, it was less than people alleged. For while calling themselves "positive-Historical," none of these scholars could claim to contribute to history in the way in which critical historical work was generally carried on in their time. Yet the change, in the context of the received and available Judaisms, was nonetheless formidable. For the Conservatives took a delicately balanced position between Orthodox and Reform theologians. Admitting (1) that the Talmud and related writings came from mortals—an enormous reform—the historian-theologians then (2) took at face value—exactly as did the Orthodox—all of the tales and treated the document with a faith that in biblical studies settings would have earned the label "uncritical" or even "fundamentalist."

In this regard Orthodoxy cannot have objected to the results of historical study, only to its premises. Since the work of Talmudic history was methodologically obsolete by the critical standards of its own age, we must correct the notion that these scholars pursued an essentially secular and "objective" program and cannot be deemed the foundation of a Judaism. Quite to the contrary, the scholarship in historical sciences aimed at theological results. The worldview that would emerge in Conservative Judaism, with its stress on scholarship, simply insisted on the facticity of matters of faith—no less than did Hirsch, but with less reason. So the middle position emerged in a simple way. On one side, the historian-theologians of the Historical School chose to face the Orthodox with the claim that the Talmud was historical. On the other, they chose to turn their backs on the critical scholarship of their own day with that very same claim that the Talmud *was* historical.

That middle position formed a powerful weapon against Reform, and it was the weapon of the Reformers' own choice (as Geiger indicated, in so many words). As with the Reformers and the Orthodox, for the Conservatives the place and authority of the Oral Torah, embodied in the Talmud, formed the arena for debate. Facing one side, the Historical School treated the Talmud as a document of history, therefore a precedent for paying attention to context and circumstance, so to admit to the possibility of change. But facing the other side, the Historical School treated the Talmud as a uniformly reliable and inerrant source for historical information. The Talmud was the target of opportunity. The traditionalists trivialized the weapon, maintaining that history was essentially beside the point of the Talmud. They used an argument such as this: The historians can tell us what clothes Rab wore, and what he ate for breakfast. The Talmudists can report what he said and why it matters.

Two purposes—biography and theology—define the character of nearly all of the historical work done in Talmudic literature for the century from the decade of foundation onward. Graetz set the style for such history as was attempted; Frankel for biography. Schorsch's judgment of Graetz forms an epitaph for the whole enterprise of Talmudic history from the 1850s onward:

> Above all, Graetz remained committed to the rejuvenation of his people. His faith in God's guiding presence throughout Jewish history, as witnessed by two earlier instances of national recovery, assured him of the future. His own work, he hoped, would contribute to the revival of Jewish consciousness. He succeeded beyond measure. As a young man, Graetz had once failed to acquire a rabbinic pulpit because he was unable to complete the delivery of his sermon. There is more than a touch of irony in the remarkable fact that the reception accorded to Graetz's history by Jews around the world made him the greatest Jewish preacher of the nineteenth century.[5]

That none of this bears a narrowly historical task scarcely requires proof. In fact, we deal with a theological program, which resorts to facts to make its points and which imagines that history settles questions. The reliance on precedent, of course, will not have surprised proponents of the dual Torah. But the entire program, with its treating as this-worldly and matters of history what the received system of Judaism understood to form an entirely supernatural realm, surprised and deeply offended those proponents.

---

[5]Schorsch, *Graetz*, pp. 61–62.

21 Founders of Modern Judaism: Conservative Judaism in the United States

JACOB NEUSNER

1. Why is this reading important?

A religion is not a book, and the Critical-Historical School in Germany did not constitute a Judaism, only a group of like-minded scholars, some of them influential, most not. But ideas can and sometimes do change the world. More to the point, ideas make a difference when they respond with self-evidently valid answers to urgent and ineluctable questions. The program of the Critical-Historical School—scholarship as the medium of change, historical fact as the surrogate for religious conviction, ideology as replacement for theology—met its moment in North America in the twentieth century. For half a century after the end of World War I, Conservative Judaism would dominate among Judaisms in America. That is because its balance between tradition and change, its mediation between past and modern times responded to a very particular, if transient, crisis. This crisis came about because the children of immigrant Jews to the United States wanted to find a way of "being Jewish" that did not prevent them also from joining America. They came from homes where the way of life and worldview of the dual Torah governed. That Judaism, as we have seen, defined its Israel in terms of segregation and sanctification. How to maintain the tradition in an integrated society? Conservative Judaism, with its moderation and willingness to compromise, responded to that question, and the ideas of the Critical-Historical School explained and validated that response.

2. What should you notice as you proceed?

In what ways do the principal intellectuals of Conservative Judaism carry forward the ideas of the Critical-Historical School? Notice how Marx explains in autobiographical terms his special interest in biography. And in what ways do they sustain the emphases of integrationist Orthodoxy? Notice Ginzberg's insistence on punctilious observance of the laws of the Torah, with only some minor points of liberalization. Both men affirmed scholarly innovation and saw their own work as a break with the past. But Orthodoxy would and did accommodate the same range of interests. Try to identify the points at which Reform dominated and those at which Orthodoxy prevailed, in the formation of the Conservative Judaism of their times. Finally, you will notice that Conservative Judaism took a strong stand against theology in favor of history.

3. How should you frame a question for class discussion in response to what you have read?

Why the powerful bias against theology in Conservative Judaism? Here is a problem for sustained attention, since the other monotheisms, Islam and Christianity, and the Judaism of the dual Torah as well all lay enormous stress on religious belief, not only on religious behavior. What theological demons are being exorcised by the rites of history? And, along these same lines, what merit does Conservative Judaism find in the doctrine of orthopraxy? Can you imagine the characteristic traits of a Conservative synagogue in Judaism, its rabbi and its laymembers? What would you anticipate the members would want of the rabbi, and what would they demand of themselves? Finally, do you think that the Conservative success would sustain itself or prove transient?

That is one range of questions, those focused upon the topic. But what do we learn for the purpose of generalization—if we know about Conservative Judaism, what do we know about religion? Here a range of questions concerning the prospects and process of change in the other monotheisms should yield generalizations worth exploring. If you could predict the course of Muslim reform based on what you know about the reformation of the Judaism of the dual Torah, where do you think change will become reform? who do you think will sponsor and validate change? and what do you think the reformers within Islam will choose to emphasize? And, lest the questions mislead, if you take account of the actualities of Islamic reform today—the powerful return to rigorous and strict observance of the faith in place of what the reformers, who call themselves Islamists, perceive as laxity and compromise—you discover that reform (change raised to the status of the norm) leads in every direction and produces every result and its opposite. Taliban in Afghanistan are no less reformers than the Critical-Historical School and Conservative Judaism. So the issue of the reformation of historically long-lived religions proves extremely intriguing.

The Historical School represented a club of intellectuals, people who shared the same viewpoint. But in the United States, the ideas of the Historical School were realized in a very large and successful Judaism, Conservative Judaism. This was a Judaism that adapted Orthodox practice to form the liberal, integrationist wing of Orthodox Judaism but that accepted at the same time the premises of historical scholarship set forth by the Reformers, hence constituting the traditional sector of Reform Judaism. For all of the inconsistency represented by orthopraxy—keep the law, but think whatever you like—Conservative Judaism was and remains a wildly successful Judaism.

We therefore come to the question of who joined Historical Judaism in Europe and Conservative Judaism in America. Of particular interest are the system builders, the intellectuals: the historians, Talmudists, and other scholars. They are the ones, after all, who defined the ideas and expressed the values and the attitudes that made all of the Judaisms before us systems, whole and complete, each with its worldview, way of life, theory of an Israel—and powerful appeal to an Israel, too. Since nearly all of the first generations of Conservative Jews in America and adherents of the Historical School in Europe had made their way out of that received system of the dual Torah, the motivation for the deeply conservative approach to the received system requires attention. For that basis assuredly cannot emerge from matters of doctrine.

Indeed, once scholar-theologians maintained that the Oral Torah derived from mortals, not God, disagreements with Reformers on matters of change can have made little difference. For by admitting to the human origin and authority of the documents of the Oral Torah, the historian-theologians had accomplished the break with Orthodoxy as well as with the received system. After that, differences with Reform were of degree, not kind. But these differences sustained a Judaism for a very long time, a Judaism that would compose its worldview, its way of life, its audience of Israel, in terms that marked off that system from the other two successor Judaisms we have already considered. Where and how did the differences emerge? To answer the question, we look at two Europeans turned Americans who typify the first mature generation of Conservative Judaism.

Professors at the Jewish Theological Seminary of America for the first half of the twentieth century, important authorities in their fields of learning, Louis Ginzberg and Alexander Marx form the Conservative counterpart to Abraham Geiger and Samson Raphael Hirsch. Together they typify the principal points of emphasis of Conservative Judaism in its formative age, and they will serve as our interlocutors in pursuing the questions of this study. For what we want to find out—to remind ourselves—is not the sociology, or even the theology, of the successor Judaisms of the nineteenth century. We want to know, rather, where and how people made the passage from self-evidence to self-awareness, how we may identify what changed, and how we may specify what continued within the received way of life and worldview. The answers to these questions tell us how people identified and answered urgent questions and so constructed a social world in which to live out their lives.

In the case of the Historical School of Germany in the nineteenth century and Conservative Judaism in the United States, the answer is clear. Keeping the way of life of the received tradition, to which the Conservatives felt deep personal loyalty because of upbringing and association, would define the way of life of Conservative Judaism. Ignoring the intellectual substance of the received system and striking out in new directions would define the method of thought, the worldview. In *The Way of Torah* we have already met their cynical maxim, "Eat kosher and think *traif* (that is, unkosher food)," meaning keep the practical rules of the established way of life, but pursue your scholarly interests wherever they may lead you. Conservative Judaism began—and for many years persisted—as a blatant orthopraxy: Think what you like, but conform outwardly to the law. What we learn is that the inherited way of life exercised profound power over the heart of the Conservative Jew of the early generation. The received viewpoint persuaded no one, so keep what could not be let go, and relinquish what no longer possessed value. To justify both sides, historical scholarship would find reassuring precedents, teaching that change is not Reform after all. But no precedent could provide verification for orthopraxy, the most novel and interesting reform among the Judaisms of continuation.

In his *Essays in Jewish Biography,* Alexander Marx (1878–1953) introduces people he knows and loves, and his book presents a classic statement of the philosophy of the founders of Conservative Judaism. As such, Marx teaches us where Conservative Judaism came from—which, in his person, was out of the Westernized Orthodoxy of nineteenth-century Germany. Marx carried forward the legacy of his father-in-law, David Hoffmann, and Hoffmann's father-in-law, Rabbi Hildesheim—the two intellectual giants, after Hirsch, of Orthodoxy in Germany. So Marx explains the choices of those whom he provides with biographies: "The works of Rashi have attracted me since my early youth." "My interest in Saadia was aroused by the greatness and originality of his work and the unusual story of his life." The eight modern scholars were men he either knew personally or was deeply influenced by in his scholarly career. Hoffmann was his relative by marriage, and Schechter, the true founder of the Jewish Theological Seminary of America just after the turn of the twentieth century, was his friend.

But there is more to it than that. The notion that orthopraxy without a worldview characterized Conservative Judaism is wrong. As we have already noted, the mode of scholarship in the study of the Talmudic corpus, while different from that of Orthodoxy as well as of the system of the dual Torah called "traditional," in fact remained entirely within the programmatic and topical interests of the Orthodox and the traditionalists alike. In the case of Marx, this fact emerges clearly. His book is a party document—a work of theology masquerading as descriptive history. Orthopraxy contained its own worldview, remarkably like that of Orthodoxy—except where it differed. There are deep convictions in his book, beliefs about right and wrong as well as matters of fact. That is why Marx proves more interesting than people in his day might have predicted. He wrote an intellectual autobiography, expressed through the biographies of others—a powerful and subtle medium. In these pages a reticent but solid scholar reflects on himself through what he says about others, reveals his ideals through what he praises in others. Here is an authentic judgment on the nineteenth and twentieth century and its principal intellectual framers: Marx's masters, friends, and heroes.

Marx himself was born in Eberfeld, Germany. In his youth he served as a horseman in a Prussian artillery regiment. That hardly constituted a routine vocation for a rabbinical student any more than did Hirsch's attendance at university. Only later did he go to the Rabbinical Seminary in Berlin. There, in that center of Orthodoxy, Marx married David Hoffmann's daughter. Hoffmann himself was the son-in-law of the founder of that same seminary. So there is a continuity within the intellectual leadership of Western Orthodoxy: Hildesheim, Hoffmann, and then, via the Jewish Theological Seminary of America, Marx. But now comes the break: Who carried on the tradition in Conservative Judaism? While Hoffmann was an intellectual founder of Germany's Westernized Orthodoxy, Marx in 1903 accepted Solomon Schechter's call to come to America. Schechter, founding president of the Jewish Theological Seminary of America, brought major scholars from Europe, and Marx was one of them.

Perhaps Marx hoped that the Jewish Theological Seminary of America would reproduce the intellectual world of German Orthodoxy: intellectually vital and religiously loyal to tradition; in any case, he became professor of history and librarian there. Indeed, in his day, the Jewish Theological Seminary of America surely found a comfortable niche on the Western shores of Orthodoxy. To be Conservative in Judaism then meant to make minor changes in the law but to make much of them, at the same time making major innovations in the intellectual life of Judaism and minimizing them. Marx fit that pattern—but so did many of those about whom he writes. What were the consequences for learning? A kind of intellectual counterpart to orthopraxy yielded facts without much interpretation. In the case of Marx, the scholarship was erudite but not terribly original or productive. He formed a personal embodiment of a Judaism that made much of facts—observances—but did little with them.

In this way Marx carried on the intellectually somewhat arid tradition of Frankel and Graetz, collecting information and making up sermons about it, but engaging in slight analysis or sustained inquiry of a sophisticated character. He published in the areas of history and bibliography, and his most popular work was his *History of the Jewish People* (written with Max L. Margolis), published in 1927. The work, a one-volume history, must rank among the most boring of its uninspired genre, but it does provide an accurate catalogue of important facts. Marx's intellectual strength lay in his massive erudition, not in his powers of imagination and interpretation. To him, history was a sequence of facts of self-evident importance and obvious significance. That, of course, constituted a theological, not merely an academic, conviction. For the theological data of the Historical School derived from historical facts, which bore self-evident consequence.

But that view did not derive from Alexander Marx; it was a commonplace then and even today that the facts of history bear self-evident theological meaning. Because things once happened, today people find themselves compelled to do or not to do, to believe or to disbelieve. That is the view of theology to which Marx, as his entire generation of German and American scholars of Judaism, subscribed. Scholarship for Marx and his fellows was comprised of brief, topical, ad hoc, and unconnected papers—hence ideas, too. Graetz's history, made up of tales, and Frankel's biographies, thumbnail sketches based on paraphrases of Talmudic stories, fall into the same classification. Given the stress on the self-evident meaning of facts, we can understand why, in simply establishing a fact, Marx and his generation saw a message and derived a meaning. Brief ad hoc articles bore their self-evident importance, too. But even though even two of the three books are made up of short essays, they contain important statements of broad significance and general interest. The modern figures who interested Marx find a place at the center of the movement for the intellectual modernization of Judaism. All of them stood within the Western camp but also took a traditionalist position in that camp. When we reflect on those whom Marx does not choose as his subjects—for example, Zunz and Geiger, founders of Reform Judaism; or Zechariah Frankel, founder of the positive-historical school that yielded Conservative Judaism—we see his points of sympathy and concern.

That brings us to Louis Ginzberg (1873–1953), a still more typical and influential figure.[1] Ginzberg typifies this entire group of theologian-historians in that he grew up within the heartland of the Jewish world of Eastern Europe but left

[1]Arthur Hertzberg, "Louis Ginzberg," *EncyclopaediaJudaica* 7:584–586.

for the West. In that important respect he stands for the experience of departure and alienation from roots that characterized the generality of earlier Reformers, the earliest generations of Conservative theologians, and—if we substitute distance from alienation—the Orthodox of the age as well. Later on, some of these figures would lay down the rule that to be a scholar in Judaism, one had to grow up in a yeshiva—and leave! That counsel raised alienation to a norm, but it obviously bore no relationship whatsoever to the received system of the dual Torah. None of the representative figures in the early generations found urgent the replication of the way of life and worldview in which he grew up.[2] The policy of orthopraxy then formed a mode of mediating between upbringing and adult commitment—that is, of coping with change.

Ginzberg himself traced his descent to the Vilna Gaon, Elijah, a formidable and legendary figure in the life of the communities of the dual Torah. But though he was born and brought up in Lithuania, heartland of the intellectual giants of the received system, Ginzberg left for Berlin and Strasbourg, where he studied with Semitists, historians, and philosophers—practitioners of disciplines unknown in the sciences of the dual Torah. Ginzberg's next move brought him from the Central European universities to the United States, where he found employment at Hebrew Union College in 1899. But the appointment he had received was canceled when Ginzberg's position on biblical criticism became known. Specifically, he affirmed the validity of critical approaches to the Hebrew Scriptures, and that fact made him unacceptable at the Reform seminary. As we noted earlier, critical scholarship flourished within carefully circumscribed borders; within the frontier lay the Oral Torah, outside—and beyond permissible criticism—the Written Torah. That distinction, central to Reform and Conservative positive-historical scholarship, placed Ginzberg outside the camp for Reform seminaries.

Instead, he found employment at the Jewish Encyclopedia in 1900, and, in 1903, accepted an appointment in Talmud at the Jewish Theological Seminary of America, yet another of the founding faculty collected by Solomon Schechter. Why Schechter found Ginzberg's views on biblical scholarship acceptable I do not know, but, of course, Ginzberg taught Talmud, not Scriptures. At the Jewish Theological Seminary for fifty years, Ginzberg is called by Hertzberg simply, "a principal architect of the Conservative movement."[3]

Ginzberg's scholarly work covered the classical documents of the Oral Torah, with special interest in subjects not commonly emphasized in the centers of learning he had left. So the subject changed, and changed radically, but the mode of learning remained constant. Ginzberg's work emphasized massive erudition, a great deal of collecting and arranging, together with episodic and ad hoc solutions to difficult problems of exegesis. The work remained primarily textual and exegetical, and, when Ginzberg ventured into historical questions, the received mode of Talmudic discourse—deductive reasoning, ad hoc arguments—predominated. So, for example, he propounded the theory—famous in its day—that differences on issues of the law represented class differences. His 1929 essay "The Significance of the Halakhah for Jewish History" repeatedly enunciated this the-

---

[2]There were no women of note in this group; a century would have to pass before women found their rightful place in the life of Judaisms.

[3]Ibid., p. 584.

sis, then exemplified how the thesis might explain how differences of opinion took the place of rigorous analysis and cool testing of the thesis at hand. Ginzberg maintained that liberals expressed the class interests of the lower classes, conservatives of the upper classes. He then found in details of the law, as two parties debated it, ample exemplifications of this same theory. Just as in the yeshiva world Ginzberg had left, enthusiastic argument took the place of sustained analysis and critical exercise of testing, so in the world Ginzberg chose to build the same mode of thought persisted—changed in context, unchanged in character.

The claim to critical scholarship forms, for Conservative Judaism, the counterpart to Orthodoxy's appeal to the Torah as God's will. Much is made in the theologies of Conservative Judaism of historical fact, precedent, discovering the correct guidelines for historical change. But the essential mode of argument accords with the received patterns of thought of the yeshiva world from which Ginzberg took his leave. For Talmudists such as Ginzberg, who acquired a university training that included an interest in history, and who also continued to study Talmudic materials, never fully overcame the intellectual habits ingrained from their beginnings in *yeshivot.*

Characteristic of Talmudic scholarship is the search first, for underlying principles to make sense of discrete, apparently unrelated cases; second, for distinctions to overcome contradictions between apparently contradictory texts; and third, for *hiddushim,* or new interpretations of a particular text. That exegetical approach to historical problems which stresses deductive thought, while perhaps appropriate for legal studies, produces egregious results for history, for it too often overlooks the problem of evidence: How do we know what we assert? What are the bases in actual data to justify *hiddushim* in small matters, or, in large ones, the postulation of comprehensive principles (*shitot*) of historical importance? Ginzberg's famous theory that disputes reflect economic and social conflict is not supported by reference to archaeological or even extra-Talmudic literary evidence.

Having postulated that economic issues were everywhere present, Ginzberg proceeded to use this postulate to "explain" a whole series of cases. The "explanations" are supposed to demonstrate the validity of the postulate, but in fact they merely repeat and illustrate it. None of these theses bears much in common in their exposition and demonstration with then-contemporary humanistic learning. For humanistic history, even then, derives its propositions from inductive, not deductive, proof. In Ginzberg's case, what is lacking in each case is the demonstration that the data could not equally well—or even better—be explained by some other postulate or postulates. At best, we are left with "this could have been the reason," but with no concrete evidence that this was the reason. Masses of material perhaps originally irrelevant are built into pseudohistorical structures that rest on nothing more solid than "we might suppose that." The deductive approach to the study of law ill serves the historian.

We have dwelt at some length on Ginzberg's practice of historical scholarship so that we have a clear picture of the fresh and innovative approach he worked out. None of this, of course, in any way could find a point of compatibility with Orthodoxy. And that explains the orthopraxy of formative Conservative Judaism, captured in the saying, "Eat kosher and think *traif.*" While such inconsistency of belief and practice may strike some as difficult to sustain, for those who hold the position the worldview—imputing to religious practice enormous value, while ignoring the received mythic basis for the practice in favor of some other—provides ample explanation for their way of life. Ginzberg's son reports that when he visited Hebrew Union College, "they inquired of young Ginzberg whether he was observant and he replied affirmatively; they next asked whether he 'believed' and the reply was in the negative."[4] Both answers, in that context, were the wrong ones.

Ginzberg very explicitly stressed that Judaism "teaches a way of life and not a theology." At the same time, he conceded that theological systems do "expound the value and meaning of religion in propositional form," but doctrines follow practices: "Theological doctrines are like the bones of the body, the outcome of the life-process itself and also the means by which it gives firmness, stability, and definiteness of outline to the animal organism." Ginzberg rejected "the dogma of a dogma-less Judaism." Religious experience, in context meaning observance of the way of life, comes first and generates all theological reflection. The role of history: "Fact, says a great thinker, is the ground of all that is divine in religion and religion can only be presented in history—in truth it must become a continuous and living history."[5]

This extreme statement of the Positive Historical School will not have surprised Frankel and Graetz. It does provide a guide to the character of Conservative Judaism in the context of the changes of the nineteenth and twentieth centuries. The appeal to fact in place of faith, the stress on practice to the subordination of belief—these form responses to the difficult situation of sensitive intellectuals brought up in one world but living in another. Ginzberg's judgment placed experience prior to thought: "Religious phenomena are essentially reactions of the mind upon the experienced world, and their specific character is not due to the material environment but to the human consciousness."[6] Ginzberg's capacity for a lucid statement of his own theological views belied his insistence that theology followed upon, and modestly responded to, what he called "religious experience," but what, in fact, was simply the pattern of religious actions that he learned in his childhood to revere.

So orthopraxy eased the transition from one world to another. The next generation found no need to make such a move; it took as normal, not to say normative, the stress on deed to the near-exclusion of intellect that, for Ginzberg and the Positive Historical School, as much as for Orthodoxy, explained why and how to keep in balance a worldview now utterly beyond belief and a way of life very much in evidence. His address in 1917 to the United Synagogue of America, of which he served as president, provides a stunning statement of his system of Judaism:

> Looking at Judaism from an historical point of view, we become convinced that there is no one aspect deep enough to exhaust the content of such a complex phenomenon as Judaism, no one term or proposition which will serve to define it. Judaism is national and universal, individual and social, legal and mystic, dogmatic and practical at once, yet it has a unity and individuality just as a mathematical curve has its own laws and expression. By insisting upon historical

---

[4]Eli Ginzberg, *Keeper of the Law: Louis Ginzberg* (Philadelphia: Jewish Publication Society of America, 1966), p. 82.

[5]Ibid., p. 145.

[6]Ibid., p. 148.

> Judaism we express further our conviction that for us Judaism is no theory of the study or school, no matter of private opinion or deduction, but a fact. . . . If we look upon Jewish History in its integrity as a simple and uniform power, though marked in portions by temporary casual parenthetical interruptions, we find that it was the Torah which stood forth throughout the history of Israel as the guiding star of his civilization."[7]

While some may find this statement gibberish, affirming as it does everything and its opposite, we nonetheless discern a serious effort at a statement of deeply held convictions. The key to much else lies in the capital *H* assigned to the word History, the view that History possesses "integrity as a simple and uniform power." What we have is none other than the familiar notion that history—fact—proves theological propositions.

That position cannot surprise us when we remember that the facts of the way of life impressed Ginzberg far more than the faith that, in the context of the dual Torah, made sense of those facts and formed of the whole a Judaism. In fact, Ginzberg did not possess the intellectual tools for the expression of what he had in mind, which is why he found adequate resort to a rather inchoate rhetoric. Assuming that he intended no merely political platform, broad enough to accommodate everyone whom he hoped would stand on it, we reach a single conclusion. Conservative Judaism, in its formative century from Frankel to Ginzberg, stood for the received way of life, modified in only minor detail, along with the complete indifference to the received world view. To take the place of the missing explanation—theology—"Jewish History" would have to make do. That history, of course, supplied a set of theological propositions; but these demanded not faith but merely assent to what were deemed ineluctable truths of history: mere facts. At what price the positivism of the founding generation? The intellectual paralysis that would follow. But to what benefit? The possibility of defining a position in the middle, between the Reform, with its forthright rejection of the received way of life, and the Orthodox, with the equally forthright rejection of the new mode of thought.

---

[7]Ibid., pp. 159–160.

22 *Contemporary Conservative Judaism Speaks: Positive-Historical Judaism Exhausted: Reflections on a Movement's Future*

DANIEL H. GORDIS

1. Why is this reading important?

Just as Jakob Petuchowski addressed to Reform Judaism the critical issue at its very core—are there limits to liberalism?—so Daniel Gordis identifies the fundamental dilemmas that confront Conservative Judaism today. Like Petuchowski, Eugene Borowitz, and Emanuel Rackman, so Gordis intends by criticism to bring about renovation using fresh energies in a purposeful, well-crafted program of religious renewal. What makes Gordis's essay important is its systematic and fundamental program: He identifies the weaknesses of Conservative Judaism in its excessive deference to the preferences of ordinary folk. Conservative Judaism does not lead, it follows, in a politics of accommodation to the lowest common denominator. Gordis wants leadership. Conservative Judaism invokes historical precedent and calls it theology, but that historicistic theology no longer serves. Gordis proposes his own solutions to these problems. Others will do the same work in a different way, but none will plumb the depths of Judaic conscience and consciousness more daringly than Petuchowski, Borowitz, Rackman, and Gordis.

2. What should you notice as you proceed?

If Conservative Judaism is more of a sociology than a theology, then by "crisis" people will mean loss of adherents, a demographic concern. If it is more of a politics than a theology, then issues of contemporary political discourse, those of feminism and sexuality for example, will predominate. If it is more of a psychology than a theology, then experience will take priority, feeling will lead to action, and matters of belief will take second place. As you read his program-paper, ask Rabbi Gordis: What, in the end, do you define as the purpose of Conservative Judaism? And how do you propose to classify this Judaism? You may want to pick out the key words and classify them, too: Is this the language of religious discourse? Then where is God? Is it the language of theological inquiry? Then where is revelation, and how do I identify the logic that dictates right from wrong? Notice where Gordis uses a language of renewal to speak of very familiar concerns. When you find Gordis's own pro-gram—at the end of his essay—see whether you can differentiate what he says from what any Orthodox or Reform rabbi would want to main-tain. Then you will wonder: How different are the various integrationist Judaisms from one another?

3. How should you frame a question for class discussion in response to what you have read?

Can you compare the story of a religion (a Judaism, a Christianity) to the story of a person's life, with a beginning, middle, and end? If you can, then it is worth noting that Petuchowski's and Gordis's critiques of Reform and Conservative Judaism address a middle-aged person, just passing fifty, closer to decrepitude than to youthful vigor. The point of the metaphor is obvious: What happens in the second and later genera-tions of the faithful to reforming movements within religious traditions? The vitality deriving from renewing the old, the excitement of seeing everything fresh and all things as possible—these last for a generation or two. Then new institutions make permanent the moment of renewal. Describing a Conservative synagogue in Providence, Rhode Island, its most effective rabbi said, "Temple Emanu-El is too traditional and not Jewish enough"—that is, reform ossified. Innovations aiming at dig-nity—only wear black shoes when ascending the altar, ushers wear top hats—turned into pretentious customs. Leaving for a more vital pulpit, the rabbi remarked, "Temple Emanu-El has gone as far as it ever can. It has run out of leadership." That brings us back to the challenge facing all reformist movements: how to sustain the initial, generative policy and attitude that affirmed all things as possible? Today many would ar-gue that the most innovative and exciting developments in Judaism take place within segregationist Orthodoxy Judaisms (whether formed around Hasidic holy men or around Torah study), which attract the most enthusiastic and engaged Jews who wish to practice a Judaism. Has the reformation of Judaism run its course, as Petuchowski implies and Gordis states? Or does Borowitz show the way toward an ongoing engagement with tradition, so that, as Leonard Fein wrote in a report on the future of Reform Judaism, "Reform is a verb."

Conservative Judaism is in crisis.[1] On the eve of the twenty-first century, our Movement has lost its sense of direction. There is, of course, nothing new in this

---

[1]Though this paper focuses exclusively on the Conservative Movement, it should not be taken to imply that other movements are without their traumas and challenges. Reform, Recon-structionism, and Orthodoxy all face huge challenges as well.

claim. Many of us within the Movement have long feared a looming cataclysm. We have sensed a gradual erosion of the Movement's ability to lead and have watched with alarm as Conservative leaders have abdicated a responsibility to set an aggressive religious and spiritual agenda for the next millennium.

What may be new, however, is that this perception of Conservative Judaism adrift is spreading beyond the Movement itself. Take, for example, *The Jewish People in America*, a recently published five-volume social and cultural history of American Jews.[2] In the final volume of the series (a series with no particular denominational perspective), Edward Shapiro notes that in the years after World War II many observers believed that Conservative Judaism represented the wave of the future, but this optimism, he notes, gradually gave way to what he calls Conservative Judaism's enduring "plagu[e] of self-doubt, disquiet and gloom."[3]

Shapiro cites Marshall Sklare as a telling example of the gradual shift in how the Movement has been perceived. He notes that by the time the second edition of Sklare's study of the Movement was published in 1972,[4] Sklare referred to a "crisis" in Conservative Judaism. Shapiro cites the following from Sklare's scathing critique: "The belief among Conservative leaders that the Movement's approach to halakhah had the power to maintain observance, as well as to inspire its renewal, . . . proved illusory.[5] Indeed, Shapiro sees fit to quote Sklare's ultimate evaluation that in the arena of creating an observant laity, the Conservative Movement has been an "abysmal failure."[6]

Again, there is nothing new in this appraisal.[7] But the fact that a major historical review of American Judaism virtually "codifies" Sklare's critique ought to prod us to ask some far-reaching questions. What is the cause of this malaise? Why has our halakhic message not been heard? Is there anything that we can or should do differently?

---

[2]Edward S. Shapiro, ed., *The Jewish People in America* (Baltimore and London: Johns Hopkins University Press, 1992). The volume discussed below is Volume V, *A Time for Healing: American Jewry since World War II* and is authored by Shapiro. The project was sponsored by the American Jewish Historical Society.

[3]Shapiro attributes that phrase to Lawrence J. Kaplan, a faculty member at McGill University.

[4]Marshall Sklare, *Conservative Judaism: An American Religious Movement* (Glencoe, IL: Free Press, 1955). Second edition published by Jewish Publication Society of America, 1972.

[5]Cited in Shapiro, ibid., p. 171.

[6]Other movements share this problem, of course. Reconstructionism is still failing to grow, Reform cannot create Jewish behaviors, and even Orthodoxy, for all its successes and too frequent triumphalism, cannot ignore the reality that many of its adherents are effectively good Conservative Jews.

[7]Not everyone, to be sure, shares this assessment of the Movement. Chancellor Ismar Schorsch, in a paper presented to the Rabbinical Assembly's National Convention in May 1992 and which we will discuss, articulates a very different sense of the Movement's condition. He notes that the recent CJF population study suggests that fully 40.4% of American Jewish households define themselves as "Conservative." He also points to the predominance of Conservative leaders in the Federations of cities such as Boston, Philadelphia, and Detroit. And though Dr. Schorsch does not explicitly make this point in his paper, there can be no doubt that the Conservative Movement, primarily but not exclusively through the faculty of the Jewish Theological Seminary, has had tremendous impact on Jewish scholarship in America.

In this brief article, I will suggest that much of our problem stems from the central role that we have given to history in our Movement's ideology. The centrality of history in our theory of Conservative Judaism has had several pernicious effects. First, it has placed the laity at the helm of our halakhic odyssey; second, and perhaps more important, it has effectively precluded the possibility of our speaking with passion about an enduring mandate for halakhah. Something must change. Unless we can reconfigure the role that history plays in our identity and our description of Conservative Judaism's halakhic message, we will not recover our ability to speak with passion. And unless we begin to speak with passion, no one will listen.

Puk Hazei Run Amok: Who Sets Our Agenda?

Before we turn to the underlying issue of the over-reliance on history in Conservative ideology, it behooves us to note one of the most glaring symptoms of the problem. That symptom is the Movement's tendency to let our laity determine our religious and halakhic agenda.

The claim that both the halakhic agenda and the outcomes of halakhic discussions are now set by our laity requires little proof. For years, rather than simply acknowledging that our laity would fall short of the "halakhic mark" in some areas, we allowed their behavior to define our notion of what the halakhic mark should be. The Shabbat "driving responsum,"[8] which did very little to change the Shabbat observance of Conservative Jews, was motivated by the perceived need to lend halakhic justification to a practice we believed we could not alter. The same was true for a variety of other responsa, such as those legitimating the eating of broiled fish in non-kosher restaurants and the use of swimming pools instead of *mikva'ot*. Ultimately, the Movement felt a need to conform its halakhah to the behavior of its laypeople.

But this preoccupation with the laity as a focus of halakhic deliberations received what is probably its clearest expression in the recent debate between Rabbis Harold Schulweis and Ismar Schorsch at the Rabbinical Assembly Convention in March 1993. Though their papers address substantive issues beyond that of what the laity wants on the issue of homosexuality, it is striking that both of these radically opposing views see the *laity's* interest as a crucial factor in the Movement's decision-making process.[9]

---

[8] The most commonly cited reference to the *teshuvah* is Mordecai Waxman, ed., *Tradition and Change: The Development of Conservative Judaism* (New York: Burning Bush Press, 1958), pp. 351–74.

[9] Though these two men seem similar in their focus on the laity, we should note that their respective interests in the will of the people have very different sources. Schulweis, it seems, is most profoundly influenced by Mordecai Kaplan, for whom the will of the people was of tremendous importance. For Schorsch, however, a focus on the laity stems from Zechariah Frankel's work. Frankel, obviously, saw the Jewish world very differently than did Kaplan, though one could also argue that Kaplan was simply an accurate *talmid* of Frankel and took the latter's thought to its natural conclusion. Nonetheless, the fact that Schulweis and Schorsch both refer to the laity should in no way lead us to the conclusion that the roots of this concern are similar for the two.

Note Harold Schulweis' call to arms at the start of his talk. His argument could not be clearer: if Conservative halakhah is to survive, we will have to make the halakhah reflect more where our potential congregants are. Schulweis writes:

> Asked in the Lachman-Kosmin City University Study, "What is your religion, 1.1 million Jews answered: 'None.' These none-Jews are our constituency. . . . They are our sons and daughters. . . . They are our challenge. They must be won over. . . . [But t]hey will not be told what to eat, where to eat, when to eat; when to rest, where to rest; when to marry, whom to marry, where to marry; whom to mourn, how long to mourn, where to mourn."[10]

And what should be the primary pulse of the halakhah? Schulweis continues:

> My thesis is that the healing of our institutional schisms depends upon our integration of halakhah as a holistic moral and spiritual expression. For what we have in common, what unites us as a religious movement, is not our legal expertise but our moral sense.[11]

Schulweis' contention is that since our laity are not legalists, we need to find something else to unite us. That something-else, he suggests, ought to be a "moral sense." Yet while no one could reasonably argue that a moral sense ought to be divorced from the halakhic process, Schulweis seems to be saying more. He is saying that since our laity is not fundamentally halakhically oriented, we need to reconceptualize the halakhic process to conform to their strengths and interests.

One might have expected that Rabbi Schorsch, in his heated disagreement with Rabbi Schulweis, would have taken exception to this focus on the laity. But precisely the opposite is the case. Schorsch effectively agrees that the laity is a prime consideration; his only contention, however, is that Schulweis is wrong about what the laity wants.

Schorsch opens his discussion of the homosexuality issue as follows:

> Homosexuality is not the all-absorbing issue of Conservative laity. They did not rise in protest when the Committee on Jewish Law and Standards last year refused to redefine the basic Jewish institutions of marriage, the family and the rabbinate. They appear ready to heed the compassionate resolution of both the United Synagogue and the Rabbinical Assembly to fully welcome gays and lesbians into the local synagogue without sanctioning their lifestyle as equally normative. . . . And there is surely no ground swell to force us to bring Judaism into accord with the self-indulgence of American society on marital infidelity and premarital sex.[12]

What if there were such a ground swell? Would that change Rabbi Schorsch's view? Though one suspects not, it is instructive that his language gives such emphasis to the wishes of the laity that one might interpret the essay otherwise.

---

[10]Harold M Schulweis, "The Character of Halakhah Entering the Twenty-First Century," p. 6.

[11]Ibid., p. 12.

[12]Ismar Schorsch, "Marching to the Wrong Drummer," *Conservative Judaism*, 45:4 (Summer 1993), p. 16.

Schorsch's conclusion bolsters this point even further. He ends his entire discussion with the following warning:

> Through the miasma of ideological bathos, we need once again to hear the voice of our laity. It is telling us that they want more Judaism, not less. They want higher standards and clearer boundaries. They want a larger dose of religious intensity. . . . Above all, they seek a rabbinic leadership marked by exemplars of piety, learning and love, not halakhic revolutionaries.

But does Rabbi Schorsch mean that this is what they want, or that this is what they need? Again, his language is not clear, but the use of the verb *want* is instructive. Schorsch and Schulweis, while obviously motivated primarily by principle, seem to pay an inordinate amount of attention to their perceived sense of what the laity wants.[13]

But that is not leadership. None of our classic models of leadership based their religious vision upon an expanded conception of *puk hazei mai ama debar.*[14] That was certainly not the genius of the prophetic model, nor did the Rabbis— for all that we speak of their democratization of Jewish law—abdicate their responsibility to lead. And although modern scholarship has taken to illustrating the ways in which early modern *posekim* have taken a variety of sociological factors into consideration,[15] that is a far cry from the suggestion that *pesak* has to provide the laity with what they want. The Conservative Movement allows its laity to set its religious agenda; but that means that we do not lead, do not enrich, and do not challenge. What mandate is left for us?

How did this state of affairs come to be? Are there distinct root causes of our preoccupation with what the laity wants? Of course, one could point to many contributing factors, some rather technical, some more general.[16] Here, however, we will focus on one simple claim. We will suggest that our Movement's leadership allows the laity to shape our agenda because our attempts to shape the laity were doomed to failure and have in fact failed. Having found that we could not shape the laity, we have given them the helm.

---

[13]This point should not be taken out of context. Both Rabbis Schulweis and Schorsch see in the homosexuality issue matters of principle, both moral and legal. Each would undoubtedly maintain his position on the issue even if the feelings of the laity were to shift radically. I am in no way suggesting that their respective positions are born *exclusively* out of a sense that the laity's preferences need to be considered. Nonetheless, the fact that attention to the laity plays such a formidable role in their language seems worthy of both note and concern.

[14]Cf. B. T. *Berakhot* 45a, *Eruvin,* 14b and *Menahot* 35a.

[15]There is a growing body of work on this subject. Jacob Katz, David Ellenson, and Ira Robinson are among its most important representatives.

[16]On the technical side, for example, one could point to Schechter's notion of Catholic Israel as one of the main causes of the problem. The subject is complicated and subtle but can be briefly stated here: though Schechter saw Catholic Israel as a repudiation of Reform's emphasis on personal autonomy, implicit in the notion of Catholic Israel was tremendous power—even halakhic authority—for the laity. While Schechter saw the notion that the standards of legitimate Jewish religious behavior would be set by a core, committed group of traditional—but not necessarily rabbinic—Jews as a distinctly traditional claim, other Conservative thinkers understood that the Schechterian conception of Catholic Israel would inevitably be subversive of tradition. Some of them, Robert Gordis paramount among them, sought to reconfigure Schechter's notion in order to limit the potential damage of the concept. But even those reconfigurations did not work. Catholic Israel undermines Conservative Judaism's attempts to create traditional, halakhah-based communities; it is time to jettison the concept entirely.

If it is true that our attempts to shape a halakhic laity were misdirected from the outset, it is imperative that our Movement clarify precisely what was wrong with our message so that we can correct it. We need to find the courage to be honest about where we have gone wrong, and the creativity to chart a new course. The following discussion is intended as the beginning of such an ongoing conversation.

Positive-*Historical* Judaism: Exhausted Idiom

Many of Conservative Judaism's current difficulties may have been unavoidable, given the profound sociological and demographic changes in the American Jewish community. Nevertheless, we must admit that we have failed to make our case effectively.

Simply put, the problem is history. Conservative leadership for too long made its case for halakhah on the basis of a historical view of Jewish life, deeply informed by a nineteenth-century German conception of history. The problem, however, is that this historical vocabulary no longer speaks with any substantive power to the Jews we wish to reach. History no longer motivates everyday Jews. Therefore, as long as Conservative rhetoric is framed in historical terms, our arguments will fall on deaf ears.

This is not to suggest that compelling historical arguments for Conservative Judaism have not been made. Conservative Judaism has rightfully claimed for itself the mantle of being the most historically conscious of the modern movements in American Judaism. That role is in many respects an important one. But we err—perhaps fatally—when we assume that our historical arguments will bring about changes in the lives of the Jews who are our constituency.

For an example of this sense that history will redeem Conservative Judaism, we need only turn to Dr. Schorsch's Rabbinical Assembly address in 1991.[17] In a magnificent ode to the centrality of the notion of *klal yisrael* in Conservative thought and life, he pays particular attention to the role of history in Conservatism. He argues that the Movement's two academic centers in Breslau and New York endowed Conservative Judaism with "a profound sense of historical consciousness," and he suggests (with obvious approval) that for that reason it is no accident that "[t]he chancellors of JTS, judged by their scholarship, have all been historians."[18] He reminds us that the original name for the Movement was "not Conservative but Historical Judaism, implying an awareness of change as well as respect for the glory of past Jewish expressions."[19]

No one could reasonably argue with these assertions. But the problem is that Dr. Schorsch, like many Conservative theoreticians, expects these proclamations to shoulder more than mere historical weight. Indeed, Conservative Jewish historians have either implicitly or explicitly suggested that the historical roots of Conservative Judaism can—or will—provide the power behind our arguments for the future relevance of our brand of Jewish life. Thus, Schorsch writes, "[I]f

---

[17]Ismar Schorsch, "In Defense of the Common Good" (published as part of the Seminary's *Thoughts from 3080* Series).

[18]Ibid., p. 4

[19]Ibid.

Reform rested its case on reason and Orthodoxy on revelation, Conservatism reconceptualized Judaism in terms of history"[20]; he continues, "if the classical texts of Judaism were no longer seen as the product of pure revelation, they surely remained sacred by virtue of their antiquity, power and communal acceptance."[21]

Schorsch believes that the experience of Judaism as a *historical* tradition has the capacity to move modern American Jews and concludes this section of his paper by asserting:

> [I]t should be abundantly clear by now why the name of Conservative Judaism should have remained Historical Judaism. The German nomenclature gets much closer to the heart of its worldview. The discovery of the past elevated history to a countervailing force against the deleterious consequences of emancipation. It compelled a sense of awe and wonder for the ultimately inexplicable survival of the Jewish people. That record of fate and faithfulness, courage and creativity, suffering and sacredness denied any one generation or group the right to rupture the chain or rewrite the text. Continuity sanctified content; survival pointed to transcendence.[22]

History, Schorsch believes, can serve as the basis of our tradition's sanctity as we seek to reach our constituency.

But modern Conservative experience belies that claim. History *has* relativized our world-view, and the deep-seated historical ethic of Conservative Judaism has *not* had the spiritual impact to which Schorsch refers.[23] Except, perhaps, in the elite, continuity has *not* sanctified content; survival has *not* pointed to transcendence. Conservative Jews know full well that Conservative Judaism has provided the scholars who most eloquently revealed the beauty of the historical in Jewish life; but Conservative Jews have never internalized the sense that history "compelled a sense of awe and wonder for the ultimately inexplicable survival of the Jewish people [which therefore] denie[s] any one generation or group the right to rupture the chain or rewrite the text." Conservative Jews both recognize the historical quality of Conservative Judaism *and* rupture the chain. They do not even insist upon rewriting the text; it is precisely because the text has been shown to be a *historical* product that it seems virtually irrelevant to life in modernity.

Conservative ideologues erred profoundly—and with destructive consequences—when they assumed that demonstrating the deeply historical roots of the Conservative Jewish commitment would produce a response in terms of behavior. Perhaps Conservative Jews do not know as much history as they ought to. Perhaps what history they do know was not taught appropriately. Perhaps. But more likely, the root of the problem lies in the fact that our culture is much less oriented to the sanctity of history than was the culture of Breslau. In our congregants' world, what is sacred is not the ancient, but the potential of the new.

---

[20]Ibid., p. 5

[21]Ibid., p. 7.

[22]Ibid., p. 8.

[23]Elsewhere Dr. Schorsch makes clear that he recognizes the limitations of this approach. Cf., e.g., "The Limits of History" in *Proceedings of the 1989 Convention* (New York: Rabbinical Assembly of America, 1990), pp. 108–15.

They and their children are products of an academic enterprise which critiques the world of the traditional for the singleness of its voice and the absence of women in its chorus. Ours is a world in which the stamp of "tradition" can be an accusation rather than a support, and Jewish texts fall prey to precisely the same critique. Claims to sanctity in the world of modern American Conservative Jews will not emanate from historiography. History has lost its call upon them.[24]

This view of the reduced impact of history in modernity is no *da'at yahid*. Even historians themselves are aware of the drastically reduced role of history in the consciousness of the modern Jew. Hans Meyerhoff, speaking not of *Jewish* history but of general historical consciousness, notes the following paradox:

> The barriers of the past have been pushed back as never before; our knowledge of the history of man and the universe has been enlarged on a scale and to a degree not dreamed of by previous generations. At the same time, the sense of identity and continuity with the past, whether our own or history's, has gradually and steadily declined. Previous generations *knew* much less about the past than we do, but perhaps *felt* a much greater sense of identity and continuity with it.[25]

And Yosef Yerushalmi, who quotes the above passage in his well-known *Zakhor*, echoes a similar sentiment:

> The collective memories of the Jewish people were a function of the shared faith, cohesiveness and will of the group itself, transmitting and recreating its past through an entire complex of interlocking social and religious institutions that functioned organically to achieve this. The decline of Jewish collective memory in modern times is only a symptom of th[e] unraveling of that common network of belief and praxis through whose mechanisms . . . the past was once made present. Therein lies the root of the malady. Ultimately Jewish memory cannot be "healed" or rejuvenated. *But for the wounds inflicted upon Jewish life by the disintegrative blows of the last two hundred years the historian seems at best a pathologist, hardly a physician.*[26]

He is even more brutal several paragraphs later:

> Those Jews who are still within the enchanted circle of tradition, or those who have returned to it, find the work of the historian irrelevant. They seek, not the historicity of the past, but its eternal contemporaneity. Addressed directly by the text, the question of how it evolved must seem to them subsidiary, if not meaningless.[27]

---

[24]This is not an argument that disparages history as an academic discipline or as an important contribution to the worldview of committed and knowledgeable Jews. This is an argument *solely* about the nineteenth-century uses of history that some Conservative ideologues believe still can serve as a *motivator* for Jewish commitment. It is *that* view and use of history that have outlived their usefulness.

[25]Hans Meyerhoff, *Time in Literature,* cited in Yosef Hayim Yerushalmi, *Zakhor* (Philadelphia: Jewish Publication Society, 1982), p. 79.

[26]Yosef Yerushalmi, *Zakhor,* p. 94. Emphasis added.

[27]Ibid., p. 96.

For all its insight, history as the foundation of a Conservative sense of self cannot work.[28] Simply put, outside the world of academics, Historical Judaism has no constituency. Either we abandon it or we will sink with it.

Conservative Arguments Vitiating Conservative Claims

Perhaps because Conservative leadership has long recognized that history alone could not sustain the argument for a uniquely Conservative (read non-Orthodox) pattern of observance, we have tried to bolster history with a theology that endorses a historical view of Jewish life. But that, too, has failed.

Conservative publications have always been replete with references to a variety of rabbinic sources that seem to point to the very sort of halakhic enterprise Conservative Judaism claims to represent. We have expected, in what verges on magical thinking, that the constant references to aggadic material such as God's exclamation of *niẓḥuni banai, niẓḥuni banai,*[29] Moshe's ultimate sanguineness in Rabbi Akiva's house of study,[30] or the virtual incantation of halakhic material such as the ben *sorer u-moreh*[31] and prozbul[32] would do what history could not. We seem, as a Movement, to have believed that if only we could convince our congregants that *we* were the living incarnation of what the talmudic authorities were describing, our community would begin to take on the practices and commitments those rabbinic texts endorse.

But this tactic also has proved to be seriously flawed, for American Jews are no more motivated by classical theology than they are by history. If history will not engender commitment, "pure" theology will not either.[33] Theology as we normally construe it has always been a "second language" for Jews. We can learn the vocabulary of a second language and even the subtleties of some of the idioms, but we rarely think or dream in our second language. The same is true for Jews and theology. Most observant Jews live the way they do because halakhic living provides their lives with meaning. Patterns of Jewish life may be *justified* by theological arguments, but they are rarely motivated by the abstract and hyper-intellectualized concepts inherent in serious philosophy and theology.

---

[28]In fairness, we should note that not everyone agrees with Yerushalmi's perspective. Amos Funkenstein (*Perceptions of Jewish History,* Berkeley: University of California Press, 1993) disputes Yerushalmi's distinction between historical narrative and collective memory, and argues that while Judaism may not have consistently engaged in historiography, a sense of history always animated Jewish communities and contributed to their sense that they were part of something important and majestic. Ironically, even as he insists on the continuing importance of history and communal memory in the formation of Jewish identity, Funkenstein lends support to the underlying thesis of this article. He writes (p. 21): "[t]he distance between secular Jews (or secular Israeli culture) and traditional Judaism was created not by lack of historical knowledge and symbols, but by their alienation from texts and textual messages, the *halakha* and the *midrash* [italics original]."

[29]*Bava Mezi'a* 59b

[30]*Mehahot* 29b.

[31]*Sanhedrin* 71a–b is the most commonly cited reference.

[32]The *locus classicus* for this discussion is the Mishnah on *Gittin* 34b and the ensuing discussion on *Gittin* 36a–37b.

[33]Below we will argue that theology remains important, though in a dramatically reconceptualized fashion.

Yet the problem runs even deeper. Not only do the textually based theological arguments we have assembled not speak to today's potential Conservative Jews, those texts actually undermine our case. Conservative rhetoric as we have developed it thus far simply cannot do what we want it to, for it was designed for a generation that has come and gone, with agendas profoundly different from those of today's Jews.

A simple but important fact: even those Conservative ideologues who "created" these arguments were never personally swayed by them. Until relatively recently, the leadership and much of the laity of Conservative Judaism came from traditional backgrounds. They needed no arguments for personal observance; indeed, they could scarcely conceive of a Jewish life not centered around halakhah (in the case of the rabbinate) or serious Jewish observance (in the case of the laypeople). The arguments the Movement created using the *tanur shel akhnai* and similar texts served retroactively to buttress commitments the people had already made, and to justify the changes in halakhah that Conservative Judaism touted even in the face of halakhic seriousness. For that generation of Conservative leadership (and the elite of the laity), the theological subtleties implicit in these texts were a liberating, refreshing dimension of Jewish life long absent in the traditional world from which they hailed.

But today's rabbinic leadership and laity do not hail from those traditional communities. They did not grow up in homes in which a commitment to a halakhic lifestyle was synonymous with Jewish identity; Conservative congregants—and indeed, much of the younger leadership—find that they have to consciously *choose* observance. At one time, Conservative arguments needed only to justify the "change" element in our "tradition and change" mantra, but today it is the commitment to "tradition" that demands articulation, and the various *sugyot* we have spoken of for so many years are entirely the wrong choice.

The classic "Conservative" *sugyot* make the wrong claim for our purposes. They stress not the immutability and sanctity of halakhah, but its historicity and malleability. The lesson we have been taught to derive from *tanur shel akhnai* is that halakhah is God's will as determined by human beings. The chutzpah implicit in Rabbi Yehoshua's not only telling God that human beings will determine God's will (i.e., halakhah) but in proving their right to do so by consciously omitting the words *lo ta'aneh al rov lintot* from the verse that includes the famous quote *aharei rabim le-hatot*[34] is a chutzpah that we can no longer afford. That *sugya* works well when our goal is to "prove" that the tradition legitimates human activism in guiding the halakhic system. But that is not what we need to prove. Today we need to stress the element of submission to a higher authority that is also unquestionably part of the halakhic tradition. *That* is what our laity does not understand, and *tanur shel akhnai* only undermines us.

The same is true with Moses in Rabbi Akiva's *bet midrash*. We had every reason as a Movement to celebrate that *sugya* as long as what we needed to prove was that the halakhah could develop and still be considered part of one continuous, unfolding tradition. But again, our laypeople take that for granted. What they need to hear from us is not that humans can sometimes determine halakhah—for they assume that to be the case—but rather that the Jewish ethic un-

---

[34]Cf. Exodus 23:2.

derlying the halakhah is our submission to God's will. *That* is what is lacking from the *sugyot* that we commonly cite, *that* is what a historical approach to Jewish life can never passionately advocate, and *that* is what Conservative Judaism will have to begin to stress if it is to survive.

Where, then, do we go from here? If not history, what will be our unique construction of Jewish life? If not *tanur shel akhnai*, where in the rabbinic corpus will we find an effective *raison d'être*? If we begin to advocate halakhah as submission to God's will, what will be unique about the Conservative voice in the American Jewish chorus? Will we still have anything unique to say?

My sense is that we will have much to say. Our Movement's commitment to women's issues will set us apart from all other traditional voices for the foreseeable future. Similarly, our commitment to the critical study of sacred text cannot be confused with an Orthodox approach. But perhaps more important, we will now have the opportunity to make an argument for halakhah not on the basis of theology—which is, after all, what the "dox" in "Orthodoxy" means—but on the basis of what the halakhic experience actually does for the Jewish person who observes it. By downplaying theology[35] while at the same time insisting that halakhah remains vital, we may find our unique and passionate voices.

Such an orientation may mean giving up our mantra of *nizḥuni banai, nizḥuni banai*, but it does not keep us from finding important evidence in rabbinic sources to support our worldview. It we make this change in orientation and rhetoric, we will find our position supported by other, equally compelling texts. In the idiom of classic *sugyot*, we might call the necessary shift a move from *tanur shel akhnai* to *kafah aleihem et ha-har ke-gigit*.

In the famed *sugya* in which God suspends Mount Sinai over the heads of the Jews assembled around it,[36] the Gemara asserts that the original circumstances of the covenant at Sinai may well have been coercive, thus rendering the "contract" null and void. If that is the case, what authority does the Torah—and by implication, the entire halakhic system—have over us? Rava's celebrated response is crucial, not only for what it says, but for what it does not say and also for what it implies.

When R. Aḥa bar Ya'akov asserts that God's suspending the mountain over the Jews offers a legitimate reason to reject the halakhic contract (which could then have been accepted under duress), Rava responds that Sinai is not the enduring reason for the contract's validity. Rather, he asserts, the halakhic contract is still in force because in the days of Esther the Jews accepted the arrangement once again (*kiyymu ve-kibbelu*).[37] On the surface, Rava's[38] response simply asserts that although the circumstances of Sinai *may* have been coercive, Jews subsequently invested the tradition with authority when they accepted it "anew" at the

---

[35]Moving away from "theology" need not mean moving away from God. I use the word "theology" here in a very narrow sense to mean a clean, rational argument based on some conception of revelation that seeks to demonstrate the authority of halakhah. That *God* has to remain crucial to our discussions of halakhah is clear and is addressed below.

[36]B T. Shabbat 88a.

[37]Cf. Esther 9:27.

[38]The Tosafot raise some question as to whether the authority was Rava or Rabbah. But that question, while interesting in its own right, has no bearing here. The point deserves attention, regardless of who made it.

time of Ahaseurus. On that level alone, it is an interesting claim for the rabbinic tradition to make.

But Rava's prooftext is significant in additional ways which are easily over-looked, for what is most important is what he does not say. Within his response is the subtle claim that theological arguments for the authority of halakhah do not matter. What matters, he suggests, is the power of the tradition to make Jews Jewish—the unique power possessed only by halakhah to infuse the lives of Jews with Jewish resonance and passion. Although Rava does not use such language, the *sugya* contains a variety of subtle suggestions that this is the point he wishes to make.

The fact that the verse cited is from the book of Esther has profound impli-cations. Not only does Rava himself not inject the issue of God into his discus-sion of the authority of the tradition, he selects a prooftext from a biblical book well-known for its glaring omission of God's name. Could the implication be that God's authority in the creation of the covenant is secondary to the spiritual needs and desires of the people?

If we are willing to hazard an affirmative answer to that question, other is-sues arise immediately. Just what are those needs and desires? Would it be push-ing this *sugya* too far to remind ourselves that one of the central themes of the book of Esther is assimilation? The names of the two primary Jewish characters,[39] the fact that they hide their Jewishness,[40] and the fact that Esther "marries" a pa-gan king all attest to the centrality of this issue.

Could it therefore be that Rava was suggesting in part that the reason for our communal acceptance of the covenant must be not a theological argument, but the deep-seated sense that without a unique pattern of Jewish behavior we will ultimately blend into the larger culture that surrounds us? Could he similarly be arguing that Jewish life without a sense of partnership with God as expressed through command cannot arouse the *mesirut nefesh*—which we will here call de-votion—necessary for sustaining proud, committed Jewish life?[41] Is it possible that Rava chooses a book whose central theme is assimilation because he wants to argue that without halakhah at the core of its communal ethos, Judaism sim-ply cannot survive?

We will never know how far Rava would have been willing to "push" the significance of his choice for a prooftext. But even if that argument is not Rava's, it virtually beckons to the leadership of Conservative Judaism today. For it sug-gests that what effectively justifies the tradition and motivates our attachment to

---

[39]The names of the two primary Hebrew characters are taken from the names of pagan Babylonian gods. Mordecai, "is the hebraized form of *marduk,* whose theophorous element is Marduk" (Carey A. Moore, *Esther: Introduction, Translation and Notes,* The Anchor Bible, General Editors William Foxwell Albright and David Noel Freedman, p. 19). Similarly, Esther's name is commonly considered to be related to Ishtar, a Babylonian goddess of love (ibid., p. 20). That Jews would take the names of pagan gods is a clear sign, in the mind of the biblical author, of serious assimilationist tendencies.

[40]The text is explicit in relating that Esther and Mordecai sought to keep their Jewishness a secret. Verse 2:20 relates that even after being selected for a second inspection by the King, "Es-ther still did not reveal her kindred or her people, as Mordecai had instructed her."

[41]The continuation of the *sugya,* in a beautiful midrash on Genesis 1:31 attributed to Resh Lakish, actually raises the possibility that without a devotion to law, life itself could not continue. The implications of that notion are astonishing but deserve a separate treatment.

it is not "authority" in the sense that we have traditionally used the term, but "power" in the sense of the mystery, joy, and belonging that halakhic living adds to our lives. Ultimately, when we set aside *nizḥuni banai* for *kafa aleihem et ha-har ke-gigit*, we move our arguments for halakhic commitment from claims of legitimacy to claims of relevance. It is a shift, in other words, from historico-theological arguments to personal, spiritual claims about the religious power of a traditional Jewish way of life and the unique ability of that way of life to perpetuate Judaism as we know it.

Such a shift would enable many of us as rabbis to be more personal about our own paths of Jewish growth, and most important, it would speak to people we desperately want to touch. We now have the opportunity to make an argument for halakhah that is more important in our modern societal setting than anything that "pure" theology can say. Our commitment to traditional Jewish observance can effectively convey to our laity that participation in the Jewish people means making commitments. It means being willing to say to oneself and to others, in no uncertain terms, that there are certain elements of our lives that are simply non-negotiable. If we happen to be in the Bahamas on Friday night, then it means that somehow or other we need to make sure that we have a Kiddush cup, wine, challah, and a place to be until sundown Saturday night. If we plan to eat a meal outside our home, then halakhah suggests that what we eat at that meal makes no less difference than what we eat at any other time inside our house. If we care about the survival of our people,[42] halakhah suggests, then the decision of whom to marry is not entirely a personal one. Ultimately, halakhic Judaism conveys the sense that it is not antithetical to a religious, moral way of life to make demands.[43]

To many American Jews, schooled in the social and political traditions of individual choice and autonomy, the idea of a religious tradition that can make non-negotiable demands is strange at best, anathema at worst. To many, the concept of "law" in religion seems out of place, even inappropriate. But perhaps it is the word *law* that is the problem. Perhaps, as is suggested above, the issue ought to be defined not as the *authority* of the legal word, but as the *power* of our tradition's spiritual discipline.

While we rabbis are often uncomfortable being in the position of urging serious attention to the legal dimension of Jewish life, there is no reason for that discomfort. Our congregants surely take both spirituality and discipline seriously. Indeed, they recognize that those persons and causes in their lives to whom they are seriously committed *do* exert upon them non-negotiable demands. Who would expect a marriage to last without some non-negotiable commitments

---

[42]Though we commonly assume the importance of the survival of the Jewish people in our teaching and our writing, this is a matter of concern and confusion for many laypeople. Without recourse to certain theological arguments that both we and they find not entirely satisfactory, the question "why should Judaism survive" is a profoundly difficult one to answer. While an exploration of that issue is clearly beyond the scope of this paper, it is a question to which our Movement ought to devote considerable energies.

[43]I have explored this issue in greater depth in two popular pieces. A discussion of "non-negotiability" as a fundamental element of halakhah is found in "Jewish Love, Jewish Law: Can Liberal Judaism Weather the Intermarriage Crisis," *The Jewish Spectator* (Winter 1992). The link between commandedness and Jewish continuity is explored in "The End of Survivalist Judaism? American Jews in Search of Direction," *Sh'ma*, 24/466 (January 21, 1994).

which two partners struggle to maintain? Children add to our lives yet another layer of commitment which (in functioning parental relationships) are never violated, no matter what. But our congregants do not resent the demands of marriage or of children, because those are relationships that they take seriously and that they often find extraordinarily nurturing.

But here we confront the "chicken and the egg" syndrome. Relationships with parents, spouse, and children are naturally committed ones *precisely because* they pervade every fiber of our being. In many cases, they provide warmth, comfort, nurturing, and a sense of context for our lives because there is little that goes on in our lives that does not revolve around them. We need to stress to our congregants that the genius of a halakhah that encompasses the way we dress, where we live, what we study, how we interact with our spouse and our children, our sexual behavior and our other moral commitments is that it creates a "relationship" with a God and a people which also pervades every fiber of our being.

To the extent that our congregants have experienced Jewish life as less spiritually fulfilling than they might have, we need to help them assign responsibility for that disappointment not to the Jewish tradition, but to themselves, and to us, their rabbis. They need to appreciate that their own consumer attitude to religious satisfaction—their sense that religious fulfillment can be had by "purchasing" a membership or a child's religious education without making the long-term palpable investments of time and emotion that any other satisfying dimension of life requires—is the root cause of the Jewish alienation for which they often blame us or their tradition. We need to teach and to reiterate that key to our Conservative sense of Jewish power and spirituality—and key to Rava's argument, I believe—is the sense that a necessary component of Jewish life is submission to God's command[44] or submission to the will and the tradition of a community.[45]

But we cannot lay all the blame at the feet of our congregants and students. We, too, need to recognize that we have been much too reticent to call these shortcomings to their attention. Our tradition suggests that prophecy, because it required the prophet to assume challenging and often unpopular positions, was never easy. There is no reason to assume that serious religious leadership today should be any easier.

To our credit, we have often tried to fill that prophetic role. For decades we have championed the view that even sophisticated, secularly educated and reli-

---

[44]This certainly need not be blind submission. The genius of Conservative Judaism will remain our commitment to examining halakhah in partnership with the best that our moral senses can offer. Nor does this emphasis on command imply a repudiation of *ta 'amei ha-mitzvot* along the lines of what one finds in the work of Yeshayahu Leibowitz. It is simply to suggest that one cannot claim to be part of the tradition of the Garden of Eden, the story of Noah (and God's command after the flood), Sinai, and the rabbinic tradition without taking submission to command, *qua* command, very seriously.

[45]Here one might raise the legitimate question of why, in the absence of basic theological claims, one particular form of covenantal behavior should be chosen over other possibilities. The question deserves serious attention, but in this brief space it *is* important to point out that for ritual to have true power, it needs to be communal. In our age, it is highly unlikely that any new ritual could win a sufficient number of adherents to make it reflect the power of what we now call Jewish tradition. For that reason alone (and there are many others), we should be very suspect of claims that we can produce a new halakhah, some modern and innovative code of Jewish covenantal behavior.

giously skeptical Jews can take the halakhic system seriously. But by using history in our rhetoric, we have made the wrong arguments. The vocabulary of the theoretical authority of the halakhic tradition has not spoken to the people whose religious lives we hope to enrich. What *will* speak to our community is the tradition's power.

In the final analysis, *this* must be our theological claim. Conservative laypeople who commit themselves to halakhah will do so because they understand halakhah's capacity to touch them, to change them, and to invest their Jewish experience with meaning and with consequence. They will respond positively to Jewish observance when they begin to see it as our Jewish means of "hearing the music" in human life, of creating a sense of intimacy with the cosmic. For them to hear that message, however, we need to convey it regularly and unequivocally. We need to begin with the experiential, not the cerebral; we need to assure ourselves that the *experience* of Jewish life has the capacity to tell us that there is something divine about the mitzvot.

From Power to Passion

A Conservative message thus reformulated would permit the emergence of the passion in our collective message that is all too often missing. It has often been noted that in the American Jewish community it is Orthodoxy that by and large speaks with passion, and Conservative Judaism that "hems and haws." That appraisal is probably more true than we would like to believe,[46] but it is also understandable. Our theological arguments for the authority of halakhah, based as they are on talmudic selections such as those mentioned above, are subtle, elusive, and centrist positions. And it is notoriously difficult to argue passionately for centrist positions. This is true in politics, and it is true with religious claims.

But passion is exactly what much of our populace desperately seeks as they search to provide more cosmic meaning—read "spirituality" for some—for themselves and their children. Until the Conservative Movement refashions the vocabulary of its claims, thus vitiating the "plagu[e] of self-doubt, disquiet and gloom" of which Shapiro speaks and replacing it with passion, we will concede much of the battle to the Orthodox establishment. That is not to suggest that Orthodoxy does not deserve some of these "victories"; it is only to suggest that if we are to remain in the fray, we need to recognize that we are losing badly; some strategy needs to change.

The change must impact the very way we think about ourselves, and maybe even the way we speak about ourselves. Following the lead of our Israeli colleagues, it is time to think of ourselves as representatives not necessarily of "Conservative Judaism," but of "Traditional Judaism." Rabbi Schorsch is correct that the appellation "Conservative Judaism" is an unfortunate one, but "Historical Judaism" is surely not the answer. We need to move from "tradition and change" to "in the face of all the change—tradition." Our language needs to advocate not the notion of a changing tradition (though we will still be the group that represents

---

[46]One key target of this accusation has, of course, been *Emet Ve-emunah*, whose critics contend that it seeks to reflect such a wide variety of positions that it fails to speak with passion about any of them. Whether such critiques are fair would require much more space than we have here.

that worldview), but the notion of tradition as the source of the energy and meaning of Jewish life. We need to become the representatives of America's "traditional Judaism" without the baggage of so-called traditional theologies that our laypeople will not find plausible. This new vocabulary would reflect our most longstanding and deepest passions, and regardless of what our laypeople want, it is surely what they *need*.

Whether or not we are willing to refashion our most fundamental vocabulary will be the ultimate test of whether we are serious about playing a pivotal role in American Jewish life, or whether we will abdicate that role to other groups, many of whom predicted long ago that we were not a viable form of Jewish tradition.

My sense is that though we are deeply troubled, we are not so despondent as to give up trying. Because our task is so sacred, my prayer is that this appraisal is not unjustifiably optimistic.[47]

---

[47]I would like to thank my teachers and colleagues who participated in the Annual Conference of the Pacific Southwest Region of the Rabbinical Assembly in January 1994, when this material was first presented. This paper has been vastly enriched by their questions and critiques, and I am deeply in their debt. My thanks as well to Rabbi Bradley Shavit Artson for his review of an earlier draft of this paper, and to Shawn and Tom Fields-Meyer for their valuable suggestions. Of course, responsibility for the abiding limitations of this paper rests exclusively with me.

PART THREE

The Practice of Judaism in Contemporary North America

23 Introduction

When we turn to the practice of Judaism in contemporary North America, we continue our study of Judaism in modern times. Two further questions left open by *The Way of Torah* are dealt with here. First, how did Judaism change through its encounter with the conditions of American life and thought, and second, how does Judaism fit within the framework of religion in the United States? The accounts provided here have to be brought into comparison and contrast with the picture of matters I give in *The Way of Torah*. From these broad social issues we move on to examine the inner world of Jewry and Judaism in the United States and Canada. In that context, three issues stand out.

The first is the advent of feminist Judaism, here represented by a sustained discussion of the feminization of the rabbinate and what it has meant. We begin with a contribution of a feminist theologian in Judaism to the discussion of the *halakhah*. Rachel Adler, whom we have already met, not only calls for rethinking *halakhah* with women's participation in mind but here shows how such a process of renewal will yield solid results. The most important single development of feminism in Judaism has opened the rabbinate and scholarship to women; Reform, Reconstructionist, and Conservative Judaisms in the United States, and their counterparts overseas, all find ample place for women in leadership roles within Judaism. To discuss this development, I am proud to include an essay from a quarter-century ago by a student of mine, Laura Geller, who first introduced me to the possibility that a woman might enter the rabbinate. I recall that she asked me, when she was an undergraduate at the college where I then taught, whether I thought she would be a good rabbi. I said to her, "But I didn't know that they were accepting women in rabbinical schools." She said, "Yes, they are," to which I replied, "So why not? Of course." That, at any rate, is how I remember matters. Over the next decade I recruited one or two women a year for the rabbinical calling. I stopped my efforts when I thought they were no longer required. Women were no longer a novelty in the center of Judaic authority, the Rabbinate. Here a review of Chapter 11 on the doctrine of women in Rabbinic Judaism will underscore ways in which a religion generally described as patriarchal finds solutions to longstanding problems of framing for women a role appropriate to the presence and importance of one half or more of all the Jews in the world and of all those who practice Judaism as well.

The second issue is the formation in the United States and Canada of New Age Judaisms, unconventional Judaisms, Judaisms of profound spirituality but slight connection with the classical sources of the Torah, Judaisms outside the framework of Reform, Orthodox, and Conservative Judaisms—the explosion within the community of Jews of Judaic religious life in quite unanticipated forms. Whether these New Age Judaisms will make a permanent mark, as has Reform or integregationist Orthodoxy, or will not survive even for another edition of this book, no one can now say. But at this moment, anyone who wants to come to a full and balanced picture of the practice of Judaism(s) in contemporary North America needs to find out what is happening in that intensely spiritual, but only episodically Judaic, world of experimentation and (the players maintain) religious renewal.

Three essays from a journal that devoted an issue to the "new spirituality" speak in the authentic voice of an acutely contemporary quest for God within the framework of holy Israel and in dialogue with the received liturgy and Torah. Here students will want to draw on their knowledge of other New Age religions, and they may find interesting things to say about what makes a religion Jewish— is it something only Jews do? something connected to a Judaism?—and whether they regard as data for the study of Judaism the new Jewish spirituality described in the articles given here. They may also want to ask whether an ethnic Jewish religiosity belongs within the framework of a religious Judaic system, as defined in these pages. In these questions we move well beyond the limits of the ideal types that have made the work possible at the outset but that now get in the way of our learning about how religions really work.

At the other end of the Judaic spectrum, Orthodoxy in diverse definitions— some integrating the life of the faith into the culture of modern times, some seeking total segregation from modern and contemporary cultural life—have enjoyed a renaissance as well. In intensity of participation, numbers, and diversity, the Orthodox Judaisms, both segregationist and integrationist, sustain a religious discourse at least as vivid and full of energy as the New Age Judaisms. To give a taste of how Orthodox Judaic debate is carried forward, I present an address to a gathering of so-called Modern Orthodox Jews—I call them integrationist Orthodox—who find themselves under pressure from segregationist Orthodoxy. These Modern, or integrationist, Orthodox Jews are trying to find a balance between the claims of the Torah, which they affirm as God's will and word for holy Israel, and the demands of contemporary science and circumstance: How to keep the law in a world that knows nothing of the Torah? We have already seen how Samson Raphael Hirsch in the nineteenth century and Emanuel Rackman in our own time respond to that question.

In many ways, integrationist Orthodoxy struggles with the questions that confronted Reform, Orthodox, and Conservative Judaisms in their initial century, but frames those questions in a considerably more sophisticated way than its nineteenth-century predecessors were able to do. Class discussion here may find interesting the comparison of the complexity of Orthodox Judaism and the diversity of Catholic Christianity—Anglican, Roman, and Orthodox—and, within (Roman) Catholic Christianity, the ways in which "being a Catholic" prove diverse and complex. People imagine that they have defined Catholic (or Roman Catholic) when they have invoked the papacy, or that they have defined Orthodox Judaism when they have introduced the notion that the Torah is God's word, in a literal sense. Now that we hear how Orthodox Judaic thinkers lay out the complexities and conflicts that confront them (and here another glance at the account of Judaism in the state of Israel will enrich the discussion), matters prove more subtle and complex than we originally supposed.

From the readings before us, let us turn to some more general considerations. Reform, Orthodox, and Conservative Judaisms all built their systems upon the received Torah set forth by Rabbinic Judaism; the issues over which they struggled derived from that Torah. Most, though not all, Judaisms in North America, and in particular the new systems that have begun to take shape at the turn of the twenty-first century, begin elsewhere than in the Torah, which serves merely as a resource but not as the dominant definition of matters. The practice of Judaism in today's North America encompasses both the received Judaisms of the nineteenth century—Orthodox, Reform, and Conservative Judaisms—as well as other Judaisms altogether, different in their very foundation from those that continued Rabbinic Judaism, that is, the Judaism of the dual Torah. These encompass Zionism, the American Judaism of Holocaust and Redemption (familiar from the pages of *The Way of Torah*), feminist and New Age Judaisms, and the renaissance of Orthodox Judaism in the United States and Canada. Let us place into context these current events in the history of Judaism.

To begin with, the contrast between the nineteenth- and twentieth-century systems, not only in Europe but also in the United States, should be drawn. The Judaisms of the nineteenth century retained close and nurturing ties to the Judaism of the dual Torah. All three confronted its issues, drew heavily on its symbolic system, cited its texts as proof texts, eagerly referred to its sources in justification for the new formations. All of them looked backward and assumed responsibility toward that long past of the Judaism of the dual Torah, acknowledging its authority, accepting its program of thought, acceding to its way of life—if only by way of explicit rejection. While the nineteenth-century Judaisms made constant reference to the received system of the dual Torah and its writings, values, requirements, viewpoints, and way of life, the twentieth-century Judaisms did not. True, each Judaism born in the nineteenth century faced the task of validating change. But all of the new Judaisms of the nineteenth century articulated a principle of change guiding relationships within the received system, which continued to define the agenda of law and theology alike. All the Judaisms of that age recognized themselves as answerable to something they deemed the tradition.

We cannot point to a similar relationship between the received Judaism of the dual Torah and the new Judaisms of the twentieth century—but not Reform, Orthodox, and Conservative Judaisms as these continued to flourish in the twentieth century. For none of the new Judaisms made much use of the intellectual resources of that system, found important issues deemed urgent within that system, or even regarded itself as answerable to the Judaism of the dual Torah. Between the new and old Judaisms lay a century of time. That made part of the difference. But the real explanation for the character of the Judaisms of the twentieth century derives from what happened in that worst of all centuries in the history of humanity, the age of total death. Confronting the urgent and inescapable questions of the twentieth century, the system makers of Judaisms came up with no self-evident answers. There was none. There could have been none. What is there to say in the face of "extermination"—that is, of the murder of human beings because they were Jews? And what system could have answered the urgent question of life?

Three Judaisms were born in the twentieth century, two in 1897 and one in 1967. The first was Jewish Socialism and Yiddishism, the second, Zionism, and the third, three generations later, the American Judaic system of Holocaust and Redemption. Jewish Socialism took shape in the Bund, a Jewish union organized in Poland in 1897. Zionism was founded in the World Zionist Organization, created in Basel in 1897. American Judaism of Holocaust and Redemption came to powerful expression in the aftermath of the 1967 war in the Middle East. All three Judaic systems answered profoundly political questions; their agenda attended to the status of the Jews as a group (Zionism, American Judaism) and the definition of the Jews in the context of larger political and social change (Jewish Socialism, Zionism). It follows that the urgent questions addressed by the twentieth-century Judaisms differed in kind from those found acute in the nineteenth century. In the twentieth century, powerful forces for social and economic change took political form in movements meant to shape government to the interests of particular classes or groups—the working classes or racial or ethnic entities, for instance. The Judaic systems of the century responded in kind.

Jewish Socialism presented a Judaic system geared to the political task of economic reform through state action. The Jews would form unions and engage in mass activity of an economic, and ultimately political, character. That topic is not treated here because it falls outside the framework of religion; Judaic Socialism was a secular movement in politics and culture in many ways strongly opposed to the religion Judaism. No account of modern and contemporary Judaism need take account of secular Jewish ideologies and institutions, even though a history or sociology of the Jews as a distinctive group will pay close attention to such a mass movement as Jewish Socialism. But since no one can conceive of divorcing the religion Judaism from the affairs of the ethnic group the Jews, Jewish Socialism is also not to be ignored even in this account of Judaism.

In that same century the definition of citizenship, encompassing ethnic and genealogical traits, presented the Jews with the problem of how they were to find a place in a nation-state that understood itself in an exclusionary and exclusive, racist way—whether Nazi Germany or nationalist Poland or Hungary or Rumania or revanchist and irredentist France. The movement called Zionism declared the Jews "a people, one people," and proposed as its purpose the creation of the Jewish state. Zionism does fit into an account of modern and contemporary Judaism, for two reasons.

First, Zionism appealed to the received symbolism and myth of the Torah, defining its program in the terms of the Messianic doctrine that at the end of time the "exiles" would "return" to the Land of Israel. Zionism found in the Hebrew Scriptures the foundation for its claim that the Jews constitute a people, one people, and that the Jews should regain that political definition of themselves as a nation-state that they lost in ancient times. Even though Zionism is not a Judaism, then, it makes extensive use of the heritage of Judaism. Zionism represents a special way of reading the Torah, one with enormous consequences for contemporary Judaic religious affairs.

Second, though Jewish Socialism had no impact upon any Judaism (except, in a complex way, Reform Judaism), Zionism exercised definitive influence upon many Judaisms. Some defined themselves by their opposition to Zionism—Reform Judaism in Germany and the United States in the nineteenth and earlier twentieth centuries being the best instance—but certain segregationist-Orthodox Judaisms providing good ones as well. Other Judaisms defined themselves around and within Zionism, including the influential Orthodox Judaism that formed a Zionist political party and that, in the recent past, affirmed the right of Jews to settle throughout the Greater Land of Israel. Because of its success in creating the

Jewish state, Zionism would define the conditions under which various Judaisms would take shape for the long future.

Later on, shifting currents in American politics and a renewed ethnicism and emphasis on intrinsic traits of birth rather than extrinsic ones of ability called into question Jews' identification with the democratic system of America as that system defined permissible difference. A Jewish ethnicism, counterpart to the search for roots among diverse ethnic groups, responded with a tale of Jewish "uniqueness"—unique suffering—and unique Jewish ethnic salvation, redemption in the Jewish state—far away, to be sure.

So three powerful and attractive movements—Jewish Socialism, Zionism, and American Judaism—presented answers to critical issues confronting groups of Jews. All of these movements addressed political questions and responded with essentially political programs. Zionism wanted to create a Jewish state, American Judaism wanted the Jews to form an active political community on their own, and Jewish Socialism in its day framed the Jews into political as much as economic organizations, seeing the two as one, a single and inseparable mode of defining economic activity and public policy.

In arguing that the several systems constitute Judaisms, of course, we cannot imagine that these Judaisms are like the ones that came to formation in the nineteenth century, for two reasons. First, on the surface the three Judaic systems of the twentieth century took up political, social, and economic but not theological questions. That fact is self-evident. Second, though the nineteenth-century Judaisms addressed issues particular to Jews, the matters of public policy that the twentieth-century Judaic systems emphasized concerned everyone, not only Jews. So none of the Judaisms of the twentieth century proves congruent in each detail of structure to the continuator Judaisms of the nineteenth. All of the new Judaisms intersected with comparable systems—like in character, unlike in content—among other Europeans and Americans. Socialism, then, is the genus, Jewish Socialism the species; American ethnic assertion the genus, American Judaism the species.

Accordingly, we move from a set of Judaisms that form species of a single genus—the Judaism of the dual Torah—to examine, in the context of Judaism in the United States and Canada, some Judaisms that take up a new set of problems. Specifically, the reconsideration of the theory of American society, produced, alongside the total homogenization of American life, renewed interest in ethnic origins and also in American Judaism. So, as is clear, the point of origin of the nineteenth-century Judaisms locates perspective from the dual Torah; Jews in the twentieth century had other things on their minds.

The nineteenth-century Judaisms made constant reference to the received system of the dual Torah, the twentieth-century Judaisms did not. True, each Judaism born in the nineteenth century faced the task of validating change that all the borning Judaisms in one way or another affirmed. But all these new Judaisms articulated a principle of change guiding relationships with the received system, which continued to define the agenda of law and theology alike, and to which—in diverse ways, to be sure—all the Judaisms recognized themselves as answerable. We cannot point to a similar relationship between the new Judaisms of the twentieth century and the received Judaism of the dual Torah. For none of them made much use of the intellectual resources of that system, found important issues deemed urgent within that system, or even regarded itself as answerable to the Judaism of the dual Torah.

For the twentieth-century systems, as we now realize, birth came about within another matrix altogether—the larger world of socialism and linguistic nationalism for Jewish Socialism and Yiddishism; the realm of the nationalisms of the smaller peoples of Europe, rejecting the government of the international empires of Central and Eastern Europe, for Zionism; the reframing, in American culture, of the policy governing social and ethnic difference for American Judaism. None of these Judaic systems of believing and behaving drew extensively on the received Judaic system of the dual Torah, and all of them for a time vastly overshadowed, in acceptance among Jews, the Judaisms that did. So the passage of time, from the eighteenth to the twentieth century, produced a radical attenuation of the bonds that joined the Jews to Rabbinic or Classical Judaism with its appeal to the dual Torah.

The difference between the twentieth-century Judaisms and the nineteenth-century ones was much more than a century. It was the difference between the civilization of the West in its Christian form and that same civilization as it took new forms altogether. What pertinence did the Judaism form in response to Christianity, with its interest in Scripture, Messiah, the long trends of history and salvation? The new world imposed its own categories: class and class struggle, the nation-state composed of homogeneous cultural and ethnic units (the lowest common denominator of bonding for a society), the search, among diverse and rootless people, for ethnic identity. These issues characterized a world that had cast loose the moorings that had long held things firm and whole.

The two traits common to the twentieth-century Judaisms contradict each other. First is the power to persuade by a logic deemed self-evident, and second, the incapacity to last for very long. The half-life of a Judaism in this century appears to encompass not much more than a generation. What accounts for the impermanence of these Judaic systems of the twentieth century? The ideological Judaisms addressed transient moments and treated as particular and unique what are structural, permanent problems. As a result, none of the Judaisms before us exhibits stability, all of them presently appearing to serve, for a generation or two, as the explanation in cosmic terms of rather humble circumstances.

For not more than three generations, Zionism thrived as an ideal for life and a solution to urgent problems. It essentially solved the meager "Jewish problem," left by the catastrophe to the Jewish people that took place in World War II, with the creation of the state of Israel, passed on into institutional continuations bereft of all ideological interest. Socialism and Yiddishism turn out to have expressed the ideals of exactly that sector of Jewry to which they spoke, the Yiddish-speaking workers. When the vast Yiddish-speaking populations were murdered between 1941 and 1945, Yiddishism lost its natural constituency.

Jewish Socialism in the United States thrived for that one generation, the immigrant one, that worked in factories; the Jewish unions then folded into the larger amalgam of unionism and lost their distinctive ethnic character; the Jewish voters, originally socialist or radical, found a comfortable home in New Deal Democracy in America. The Jewish Communists of Poland and the USSR in Stalin's time survived their revolution's success only with difficulty. Disqualified by perfect faith in what they were doing, most lost out to the bureaucrats that made the new order permanent. In all, then, the Judaic systems of the morning of this century, eager in the light of day to exhibit their promise of a renewed Judaic worldview and way of life, one to bring a rebirth to "all humanity, not just the Jews," turned into desiccated faces and tottering gait in the harsh light of afternoon. Not without reason do Israeli teenagers say, "When we get old, we'll talk in Yiddish."

Of the American Judaism of Holocaust and Redemption we may scarcely speak; it is the birth of a single generation. Its power to mediate between a generation out of touch with its roots and a society willing to affirm ethnic difference—on carefully defined and limited bases, to be sure—remains to be tested. For the moment we may only affirm that this system presently functions like a Judaism and presents a structure in conformity with the systemic requirements of a Judaism. Whether or not it will turn out to form more than an effect of a sociological shift and a political ripple only time will tell. Ours is not a task of predicting currents in public opinion, or even of measuring them, but only of trying to discern the inner workings of the ideas that coalesce to generate opinion and justify it for groups of like-minded Jews and phalanxes of generations.

The several Judaisms share enormously emotional appeals to the experiences of history, what is happening today. Each framed a grievance for itself, a doctrine of resentment—for Zionism, statelessness; for Jewish Socialism and Yiddishism, economic deprivation; for American Judaism, a sense of alienation expressed that grievance, bringing to words the underlying feeling of resentment. Instead of transforming feeling into sensibility and sentiment into an intellectual explanation of the world, the ideologies of the twentieth-century Judaisms came after the fact of experience and emotion and explained them. The systems in common derive from a visceral response to intolerable experience near at hand. Unemployment and starvation made entirely credible the worldview and explanation of Jewish Socialism and made compelling the program of activity, the way of life, it demanded. Zionism formed the experiences of remarkably diverse people living in widely separated places into a single whole, showing that all those experiences formed a single fact, the experience of a single sort—exclusion, victimization, anti-Semitism—that Zionism could confront. American Judaism linked to an inchoate past the aspirations of a third and fourth generation of Jews who wanted desperately to be Jewish but in their own experience and intellectual resources could find slight access to this identity.

Emotion—the emotion of resentment in particular—formed the road within for all: strong feeling about suffering and redemption, for American Judaism; powerful appeal to concrete deed in the here and now by people who thought themselves helpless, for Zionism; outlet for the rage of the dispossessed, for the suffering workers of Czarist Russia and turn of the century America alike, for Jewish Socialism. The power and appeal of the three ideological systems, all enjoying self-evidence for those for whom they answered basic questions, proved not only uniform, but also apt. For the problems they proposed to solve—political, cultural, social, economic—raised the everyday and the factitious into issues for deep reflection. What, after all, preoccupied Jews in the twentieth century? Politics, economics, the crumbling of connection to a thousand-year-old Yiddish culture and a fifteen-hundred-year-old way of life and worldview, the Judaism of the dual Torah. These were pressing issues the most sanguine person could not ignore.

What distinguishes the Judaic system of the dual Torah from its continuators and competition in the nineteenth and twentieth centuries is a simple trait. The Judaism of the dual Torah encompassed the whole of the existence of the Jews who found its truth self-evident, its definition of life ineluctable. In that system's way of life a Jew was not always a Jew, he or she was *only* a Jew. The other Judaisms acknowledged the former fact: Jews never stopped being Jews; the world would not let them, even if they wanted to. But the Judaism of the dual Torah made slight provision for Jews to be anything but Jews: the holy people had no other vocation, no alternative, to its holiness. Its history as a people different in kind from other peoples, its destiny at the end of time—these matched its distinctive holy way of life in the here and now. So Israel was always Israel and only Israel. But in modern times Israel became one of several things that Jews would be: also Americans, also workers, also Israelis, among the twentieth-century Judaisms, but never *only* Israel, God's people. And that theory of Israel matches the conception of the individual person in social terms as well. For in the received Torah, Israel, the Jew, lived out life in the rhythm of sanctification of the here and now, realizing in concrete deeds the Torah's words. It was not a romance, it was a marriage.

The conception of Israel once more presents us with the key to interpreting a Judaic system. From antiquity forward, the Judaism of the dual Torah saw Israel as solely that. But from the eighteenth century onward, Judaic systems took shape that saw Israel as that and more. They differed on the question: What more? They took issue, further, on the range of permissible difference, on issues of segregation versus integration. But all concurred that, in some ways, Jews would integrate. That concurrence by itself distinguished all modern Judaic systems from the received system of the dual Torah. In the nineteenth-century systems of continuation, for instance, the Jew was a citizen as well as a Jew. That meant that being a Jew required reframing: a new theory of Israel, demanding also a fresh conception of the way of life of that Israel, and, it would follow, also a new worldview to explain that way of life and situate it among the received texts.

The mythic Judaisms of the twentieth century, for their part, accepted as given the multiple dimensions that took the measure of the Jew: individual, member of diverse groups, among them, a Jewish one. So the Jewish Socialist was a Socialist, too, and between Zionism and Jews' other worlds, or between American Judaism and Jewish Americans' other concerns, competition for commitment could scarcely come to resolution. For in modern and contemporary times, the Jews concerned themselves with many things, even though, from the world's viewpoint, a Jew might be only that.

What this meant in practice we see in both the nineteenth- and the twentieth-century systems: a redefinition not only of the range of difference, but also of the degree of commitment. A Jew in Eastern Europe, within the received system, wore Jewish clothes and talked a Jewish language, and in it said thoughts he or she took for granted were uniquely Jewish. Jews in Germany, Britain, and America did not. Zionism in its Israeli realization produced Jews whose commitment to profession—state building, army building, institution building—in no way demanded particularly Judaic (in context: Zionist) action and activity. True, the state builders would say that everything they did was by definition Zionist action, and so it was. But in other contexts, as we have repeatedly noticed, others did the same action, and, by definition, they were not Zionists. Now, as the nineteenth century drew to its close, the divisions within a human existence, setting apart the Jewish from the not-Jewish, yielded two curious modes of Judaic existence. For a small minority, on whom we shall concentrate, "being Jewish" in the partial definitions of available systems left dissatisfaction.

This small minority determined to find a mode of "being Jewish"—in our terms, a Judaic system—that would encompass not part but the whole of life. They wished not a protracted romance but a marriage: something permanent, whole, enduring, and complete. For larger numbers, typified in our survey by the devotees of American Judaism, "being Jewish" represented a kind of ongoing romantic attachment: episodic but intense. American Judaism, as we have noted, left Jews free to be many things, some of them Jewish (or, in our terms, Judaic), others not. That fluidity represented its appeal. No permanent and encompassing commitment required American Jews to be only or mainly Jewish (that is, in our language, devotees of the American Judaic system). But the romantic attachment, did mean that, when these Jewish Americans chose to "be Jewish," they entered into an intense and exhausting encounter. (And, when they did not so choose, they did not). The emotional appeal of this Judaism of Holocaust and Redemption should not be missed: it allowed ready access to deep feelings and direct encounter with transcendental experience.

But this Judaism did not demand, or even make provision for, protracted feelings and a lasting encounter with that transcendent moment of redemption. In carrying out the critical act, within the American Judaic way of life, of visiting the state of Israel, American Judaists ended up not as pilgrims, come to celebrate and stay, but as tourists. They went home and reentered those other dimensions of human experience that they shared with others in the same time and place as undifferentiated Americans. The diverse Judaic systems of the modern age have had in common a certain transient intensity: Deep, enduring commitment for about fifteen minutes was what people were prepared to give.

Our picture of the practice of Judaism in contemporary North America covers four topics: (1) how Judaism has changed in its encounter with life in the United States and Canada, explained by Joseph L. Blau and set into context by Jack Wertheimer; (2) the advent of women in a central position in the life of most Judaisms, the single most consequential fact of the final quarter of the twentieth century, by entering the rabbinate, from which they had been excluded for the entire history of Rabbinic Judaism; (3) three vignettes concerning the "new spirituality," or New Age Judaisms, providing some insight into the developments on the margins; and, finally, (4) the renaissance of Orthodoxy as illustrated by an important debate within Orthodoxy in the United States, showing what has been happening within the integrationist Orthodoxy that began with Samson Raphael Hirsch. For that purpose an important address by William Helmreich lays out the issues.

24 *The Americanization of American Judaism*

JOSEPH L. BLAU

1. Why is this reading important?

When we consider what happens to a European, African, or Asian ethnic group or religious community in the encounter with American life, we learn something more about America and its capacities to change and be changed by new people. When it comes to religion, matters prove complicated. That is because America accepts difference in religious form, so that people expect diverse religions to believe different things and engage in different practices. But America also insists that immigrants must find a place in the mainstream of language and culture; it affords little opportunity for isolated communities, though it tolerates them, as the Amish and the Hasidim have found. Integrationist Judaisms—and among the Judaic religious systems that flourish here as well as among secular and ethnic Jews, probably 98 percent of the Jewish population can be classified as integrationist—then have to find the limits of permissible difference. The Jews want and expect to be different, but not so different that they cannot find a place within the American consensus. They also want that consensus to be so defined as to make a place for them. The impact that this dual aspiration makes upon the shape of Judaisms in the United States defines a major chapter in the history of Judaism in the twentieth century.

2. What should you notice as you proceed?

First, Blau correctly speaks about the situation of the Jews as an ethnic group, not as a religious community—hence the image of "the Jew" in American culture. Then he turns to the institutional and organizational arrangements that together constitute the "organized Jewish community." So he treats the Jews as a group, not concentrating on personal preference (lifestyles) and individual tastes. That is necessary when we study a religion that, by definition, is collective and social, something that people do together that can be studied and analyzed, not merely something subjective and personal that can merely be recorded and reported on, like a private vision. In Blau's fine chapter, look for attention to religion in its own terms, not merely as a detail of an ethnic culture. It is hard to distinguish the ethnic from the religious. When Blau turns to the "protestantization" of American Judaism, he comes to more particularly religious concerns. But here, too, his definition of issues remains essentially secular.

3. How should you frame a question for class discussion in response to what you have read?

If you were composing an essay on the Americanization of Judaism in the United States, what issues would you introduce that Blau treats only briefly, if at all? What questions would you ask, what data would you collect, and what sort of comparisons and contrasts would you undertake? It is possible to establish a grid, with vertical and horizontal lines, one covering the continuity of Judaism, the other the intersection with Americanism. The definition of "Judaism" at the moment of entry into the American commonwealth will dictate the vertical lines, the characteristics of American politics and culture; the definition of what we in this country mean by religion and accept as religion will determine the horizontals. An interesting discussion may then go forward on three separate but related topics: (1) how such a grid would govern the collection of data, (2) the sorts of questions we would frame, and (3) the way in which, as a result of the work, we should better understand religion in general, religion in America, and the potentialities of Judaism through time and change. Keep in mind that when we study religion, a new and young academic field, we define the work even while we do it. Religious studies has no long tradition of learning as a freestanding field within the humanities (as distinct from the long tradition of the theological study by various religions, respectively, of their own religion and others). So here we have the opportunity to design research into an accessible religious world, that of Judaism in the United States, and into the social order, America itself, that sustains that religion and all others, dictating the terms of their existence. Here again, Judaism ought to serve, as every other religion ought, as a case through which to examine a principle.

American Roots for the Uprooted

The question that has most often been asked by scholars is how the Jews living in the United States of America have become more and more like the other residents; that is, how the Jews of America have become Americanized. Other students have examined the Jewish community in the United States and questioned whether it has not become a variety of American community rather than a continued example of what the earlier European Jewish communities were like. Still others have been concerned with the psychological transition from identifying oneself as a Jew living in America to self-identification as an American Jew, and, in a second step, from American Jew to Jewish American. Only incidentally, in discussions of these matters, has the question central to this essay been touched upon. The primary concern here has been to determine how, and how extensively, the patterns of religious practice and belief of the Jews of the United States and the institutions through which these practices and beliefs are expressed have been modified by the cultural, and especially the religious, environment surrounding Judaism in America.

Heinz Politzer, a student of comic strips, wrote an essay some years ago under the title "From Little Nemo to Li'l Abner," that expressed very lucidly, in terms of the popular culture medium of his study, a theme that is most helpful to the understanding of the popular culture medium of religion:

> It is here that Abie the Agent comes in. Abie Kabibble is as Jewish as the Katzenjammers are German: in him the ethnic minority enriches the American scene by the peculiarity of its speech, mentality, and group character. Abie is a *schlemiel* and a realist, outrageously sentimental and stubbornly matter-of-fact, the wandering Jew taking a short rest in the suburbs of the world. But the suburbs are those of pre–World War I America. Abie shows neither complacency nor self-hatred; his flat feet have plodded into reality and there he has settled down. He is the general underdog, proclaiming the philosophy of the socially underprivileged. He, too, is the last, the best of all the game. In his mouth, to be sure, this assurance has a faintly ironic ring.

Parenthetically, in the light of this paragraph, it is easy to understand that it is not altogether accidental that it was a Jew, Arthur Miller, who wrote *Death of a Salesman*, although Willy Loman is not presented as a Jewish character. To continue with Heinz Politzer:

> *Abie the Agent* is the explicit contribution of American Jewry to the comic strip. Elsewhere, Jews function more as a leaven and a seasoning. Such artists as Rube Goldberg season the general trends with their wit rather than reflect themselves. And with Alfred Gerald Caplin who is Al Capp, American Jewry demonstrates its advanced position in American society. Al Capp has only to express in his strip his own desires, drives and anxieties—like, say, Saul Steinberg in his cartoons—in order to answer the desires, drives, and anxieties of all his contemporaries, regardless of variety of origin or creed. By their very name, Abie and Li'l Abner show the stages in the path American Jews have followed in integrating themselves in the context of American civilization.[1]

The point of Politzer's keen analysis is that, between the years before World War I and the present, the image of the Jew and of his role in American society changed from that of the outsider, "taking a short rest in the suburbs of the world," to that of the paradigm of American sensitivities. Within the past three-quarters of a century, approximately, Jews began to feel comfortable and at home in the United States of America and therefore to express and reflect current forms of American "consciousness." Implied, too, in what Politzer says about Al Capp is the conclusion that a large part of the non-Jewish population of the United States has begun to feel more comfortable with its Jewish neighbors, and therefore to accept this reflection of its own consciousness.

---

[1]Heinz Politzer, "From Little Nemo to Li'l Abner," in *The Funnies: An American Idiom*, ed. David Manning White and Robert H. Abel (Glencoe, Illinois, 1963), p. 48.

Politzer's fascinating text contains a large measure of truth, particularly with respect to the post-1881 Jewish immigration from Eastern Europe. More important, the text suggests a way of describing, if not defining, the meaning of the difficult term "Americanization." The usual method of conceptualizing this term has been to make efforts to discover objective and preferably quantifiable data by means of which to create a device for measuring Americanization. Some of the questions asked had to do with official attitudes: Were there laws written into the statutes of the nation or any subdivision of the nation that limited or restricted the full participation of Jews in any aspect of life? Could Jewish worship and Jewish religious education be carried on openly, according to the law? Was there legal discrimination against those who observed the Jewish holidays? On such matters the United States showed up fairly well from the earliest days of independence until quite recent times. Perhaps the major ground for complaint was the vigorous enforcement, in some sections of the country, of Sunday-closing laws. Such enforcement created a significant discrimination against all those who observed the Sabbath on Saturday, a class that included the Jews, though a larger part of the membership of the class was made up of Saturday-observing Christian sectarians, like Seventh-Day Adventists and Seventh-Day Baptists.

The virtual absence of discriminatory legislation does not, of course, entail the virtual absence of discrimination. Unofficial exclusions and limitations came into the picture, notoriously in the form of so-called "gentlemen's agreements." These are more difficult to pin down and to measure than are instances of official discrimination unless they are written down, as restrictive covenants, and thus brought into a public context where they are subject to legal prosecution. Unofficial discrimination of this sort has appeared frequently in the United States and is still a prevalent feature of American life, by no means always directed against the Jews or Judaism. *Numerus clausus* in the strict sense has not been official in the United States, prior to some recent administrative edicts of the federal Department of Health. Education, and Welfare, in which "benign" quotas are introduced under the name of "affirmative action goals." In a loose, nonofficial sense, *numerus clausus* has been common in the professions, in some forms of corporate business, in private education, and, in greatest measure, in social life.

In spite of the increase in unofficial anti-Jewish discrimination in some areas of American life and the suspicion of some increase in official discrimination, the Americanization of the Jews and of Judaism has proceeded apace, even among those who were most victimized by whatever discrimination did exist. The measure of Americanization cannot be entirely objective. Indeed, in many ways, the objective factors are secondary and derivative from a subjective factor that Politzer's analysis of comic strips makes clear. Abie the Agent, the incarnation of the Wandering Jew, was temporarily resting in America but subjectively felt himself to be a stranger and a visitor. Abie the Agent could never be alienated, because in his own mind, his own subjectivity, he was an alien; Al Capp, given the appropriate conditions, might feel alienated because his subjectivity is American. A stranger cannot be estranged; only one who feels himself a native can be estranged. Only a person who feels rooted can possibly be uprooted.

That this sense of at-homeness, of a comfortable rooted belonging, should have developed among the Jews of the United States of America is certainly not a unique emergent in Jewish experience. A similar rooting has taken place many times in earlier Jewish history. So recurrent has been the experience that one is tempted to speak of a Jewish talent for naturalization in a host environment, and of the Jewish experience in America as one more instance of the operation of this talent. Moreover, previous Jewish history teaches that naturalization does not preclude later deracination and estrangement. That the Jews feel comfortable in a host culture does not mean that the majorities that carry that culture will necessarily feel comfortable with, or about, their Jewish coresidents, nor that, if they do at any time, they will continue to do so. For that matter, there is no certainty that the same group will continue to be the chief carriers; and, if the carriers change, the culture will not remain the same. The lesson of Jewish history is that the wise guest, however much he is made to feel at home, may unpack his bags but should always keep them close at hand for instant repacking.

Whenever and wherever in the past a rooting comparable to that in the United States has taken place, there has been some degree of mutual religious influence between Judaism and the religions of the host culture. In such situations, Judaism itself (regardless of its internal variations) becomes an alternative religious interpretation of the fundamental spiritual qualities of living in that time and place. Innovations are introduced into Judaism to express the sanctification of the new mode of life. Some of these novelties become enshrined in Judaism and thus become part of the tradition of Judaism, considered as if they had been handed down to Moses at Mount Sinai. Innovations that successfully express a living religious need persist; if the need disappears or the innovation is inadequate, or if it is merely a temporary expedient, the novelty is forgotten. So the question how the Americanization experience has modified Judaism in America is both interesting in itself and a possible indication of some of the practices or beliefs or institutional arrangements that will survive into the Judaisms of the remote future.

Judaism in America—"Kosher Style"

In the sense in which, until the end of the eighteenth century, European (and, earlier, Asian) Jewry had a communal structure, the Jews of the United States have never been organized as communities. The older form of community was a device for governing Jewish life as a unified whole, without separating religious, ethnic, economic, and other aspects. In America, the various aspects of Jewish life have developed largely in independence of each other, because in the earliest times there were few Jews, and those few adopted the organizational patterns of their Protestant hosts and coresidents, and perhaps also because of the Marrano background of the earliest arrivals. There was no superstructure to hold together and rationalize the separate parts of the infrastructure.

Instead, there was a specialization of functions on an irrational basis. American Jewish life developed an institutional division of labor between, for example, synagogues and hospitals, synagogues and orphan asylums, synagogues and cemeteries, synagogues and an ordered system for maintaining and guaranteeing proper slaughtering of meats—even, at times, between synagogues and religious education. All these various institutional expressions of the three old religious requirements of Judaism—study (*Torah*), worship (*Abodah*), and philanthropy (*Gemilut Hasadim*)—developed in competition with each other for funding and for the time and personal services of individual Jews. All the structures of Jewish life in America were parts of a free-enterprise system, as were the institutions of Protestant Christianity. As a result, in contemporary American Judaism there may be institutional marriages of convenience, but there is no centralized control and therefore no common discipline or coercive force. Even such extreme traditional instruments of control as *herem*, the ban, roughly equivalent to excommunication, have no significance whatsoever in American Judaism.

A second consequence of the absence of community structure has been that, especially in the twentieth century, many synagogues have been transformed into "synagogue centers," which more accurately might be called "community centers." They provide opportunities for organized social activities on many age levels from play schools to senior citizens' clubs, and for special interest groups that cross age lines. The synagogue-center is a busy place; it needs an administrator who is a good traffic manager and who is also, sometimes, the rabbi. In larger and wealthier synagogues the administrative and spiritual leadership positions are separate. The need to provide space for all these activities has led to new tendencies in synagogue architecture. Just as the comparable variety of activities in the Protestant churches has led to a sharp reduction in the amount of "sacred space"—space that would seem to most people improperly used if it housed secular groups and their activities—so the "sanctuary" in newer urban synagogue buildings has been cut down to size, with various devices for occasional enlargement. Suburban synagogues that are not faced by limitations of available building space are not under the same pressures.

In the third place, as the community in the older sense fell into desuetude, the rabbi, or, in a populous area, the several rabbis who would earlier have constituted the court of Jewish law found their activities increasingly restricted to administrative and pastoral functions. The training of rabbis continues to rest heavily on the study of the codes. Rabbinical scholarship, where it exists, is still mainly legal scholarship. But many rabbis can go through a whole career in the service of American synagogues without having occasion to answer questions on religious law. Although little change has been made in rabbinical training programs, the role of the rabbi has changed significantly; once he was professionally an interpreter of the laws, a legist, whereas now he is professionally a minister. Like his Protestant counterparts, the rabbi of an American Jewish congregation visits the sick; comforts the bereaved; provides an intermediate level of counseling between the family conclave and the psychotherapist; represents his congregation in the broader community by serving on the boards of local hospitals, schools, philanthropies, and civil rights organizations, and in the Jewish world by his activity with "defense" or Zionist organizations; attends the meetings of American service societies, like Rotary and Kiwanis, and comparable Jewish groups; supervises the religious education carried on by his synagogue; participates with his reader and music director in the planning and conduct of services; and preaches. The modern American rabbi leads an extremely busy and useful life, but it is not the life of the rabbi of old.

Fourth, as Judaism moved first from Asia into Europe and then from Europe to America, it moved from host cultures in which women were socially secluded and religious practice principally a masculine prerogative (as, indeed, it was in classical forms of Judaism) into a cultural setting where women, though still by no means considered as important as men, were thought to have souls to be saved, to have religious rights and obligations. It has been said that were it not for the unsung part played by women in the male-dominated churches of Europe and the United States, Christianity would not have survived into the twentieth century. Whether this is true or an exaggeration with regard to Christianity, the story of the synagogues of the United States gives clear testimony that the survival of Judaism has been enormously helped, perhaps even made possible, by the dedication, the devotion, the directed energy of American Jewish women. Only very recently has their contribution been acknowledged. The recognition is, as yet, by no means adequate; too often it is grudgingly given. At the liberal end of the Jewish spectrum, a beginning has been made by the ordination of women and their election to important offices in denominational organizations.

A fifth illustration of ways in which the Judaisms of the United States have changed or are changing has to do with the religious regulations regarding food, the whole system of *Kashrut*. Let it not be said that this is a trivial matter in a religious context; for the committed member of many religions religious scruples about food are more frequently and more critically in the forefront of his mind than theology or creed. As Kallen has noted, "Among the items God diversely insures is, of course, the procurement and preparation of food. The gods participate both centrally and tangently in how we provide, prepare, and consume what we eat and drink. And eating and drinking, no less than being born and dying, mating and fighting and building, are, in every society, formations of the struggle to live and to grow in which the gods are held to play powerful roles."[2] Here we need not be concerned to account historically for the complex and incoherent system presented in the Old Testament and amplified, made more complex, and somewhat more coherent in the rabbinical codes. The only concern here is that *kashrut* is one of the central elements of practice in traditional Jewish religious life. It is an element that in many ways tended to enforce the social separation between Jew and non-Jew, for it is the very mark of friendship to share with another one's meat and drink.

In the early years of Judaism in America, the synagogues assumed responsibility for maintaining the supply of meat properly slaughtered, according to the rules laid down in the rabbinic literature. Finding a qualified and trustworthy slaughterer (*shohet*) was a major preoccupation of the authorities of the eighteenth-century synagogues. In the nineteenth century, however, as the number of synagogues and of ordained rabbis increased, ritual slaughtering became part of a laissez-faire system. Individual butchers and their wholesale suppliers made private contracts with rabbis to supervise their slaughtering practices. Stores, restaurants, and, later, catering establishments displayed in their windows or on their walls certificates from this rabbi or that attesting to his having "supervised" the *kashrut* of the establishment. The old Roman question cried out to

---

[2]Horace Kallen, *Cultural Pluralism*, p. 30. See also Marshall Sklare, *America's Jews:* "The dietary laws are a striking illustration of Judaism's sacramental tradition. They invest the routine and mundane act of eating with sacred significance and they provide the believer with recurring opportunities to show his obedience to God's will. . . . Furthermore, their observance affects the individual in the most profound ways. Observance of the laws may influence choice of friends, neighborhood, occupation, and spouse. Finally, they give the home an indisputably Jewish character" (p. 113).

be answered. "Quis custodiet ipse custodes?" Who was to supervise the supervisor, to keep watch over the watchman? In the absence of a communal structure nothing could be done. Except in major centers of Jewish population, where a voluntary consociation of rabbis tried (and still tries) to protect the Jewish consumer from fraudulent attestations, there was no real provision for protection. There was no guarantee that the consumer was getting the service for which he was being systematically overcharged.[3] Only where an official agency of state or municipal government protected the Jewish consumer as part of its general mandate to protect all consumers from false claims was there a totally responsible agency supervising slaughtering practice.

Recognition by members of the Jewish public that they had no way of validating the claims made in shop windows or on restaurant walls may have helped break down adherence to the rules of *kashrut*. One form taken by this breakdown, short of the total rejection of dietary laws in the Reform movement, is the retention of some of the dietary laws in the home, as a symbol of distinctiveness, while the whole question is disregarded when one is eating away from home. A more moderate form retains, even when "eating out," the ban on certain well-known prohibited foods, such as the flesh of the pig or shellfish, while other prohibited foods that are not known to be prohibited by those with whom one is likely to eat are consumed without hesitation.[4] There is no question that adherence to *kashrut* is rapidly losing its character as an enforcer of social separation while still retaining some force as a mode of self-identification.[5]

What has salvaged the notion of "Jewish" food as a mode of self-identification, the light at the end of the tunnel, is that it has been taken over by the American food-processing industry, as have "Italian," "Chinese" and "Black" foods. Symbolizing the change are such advertising slogans as "You don't have to be Jewish to love Levy's Jewish Rye bread." Many non-Jews in the United States have learned to like the taste of some Jewish food specialities, as many Jews have learned to enjoy the food specialties of other ethnic groups. To meet the demands of both Jews and non-Jews, a sub-branch of the "convenience foods" industry has

---

[3]Charles S. Liebman, in "Orthodoxy in American Jewish Life," wrote: "The issue which most severely damaged the image" of the member rabbis of the Union of Orthodox Rabbis of the United States and Canada "was *kashrut* supervision. Rightly or wrongly, an image persisted of the communal rabbi who, pressured by butchers, food processors, and slaughterers to ease *kashrut* requirements, and plagued by the indifference of Jewish consumers, lowered his standards of supervision" (p. 33). See also Harold O. Gastwirt, *Fraud, Corruption, and Holiness: The Controversy over the Supervision of Dietary Practice in New York City* (Port Washington, N.Y., 1972).

[4]Marshall Sklare, in *Conservative Judaism*, quotes one respondent to the question of the role of dietary laws among Conservative Jews: "I enjoy [eating] everything out that I don't have in my house, which is strictly Orthodox" (p. 204).

[5]Sklare, *Conservative Judaism*, also points out that the "really significant facts are that (1) the *isolating* function of the dietary laws no longer operates as far as most of Conservative Jewry is concerned; (2) nevertheless the role of *kashruth* as an axis of *Jewishness* is still manifest" (p. 203; italics in the original). Arthur Hertzberg, "The American Jew and His Religion," in *The American Jew: A Reappraisal*, ed. Oscar I. Janowsky (Philadelphia, 1964), writing ten years after Sklare, notes that "Obedience to the dietary laws, which are mandatory among both the Orthodox and the Conservative, has declined disastrously. A study of the most committed element of the Conservative laity, the members of the boards of congregations, has demonstrated that even in such circles no more than one in three keep completely *kosher* homes. American Orthodoxy is substantially more obedient in this area, but even among this element one-third does not observe *kashrut*" (p. 102).

grown up to produce and to market, through supermarkets across the nation, what are called "Kosher-style" foods. A homogenized version of a particular taste has become a commercial substitute for the following of a complicated set of rules. Many people who do not eat kosher, do eat kosher-style. Nostalgia as well as a sense of ethnic solidarity can be satisfied out of a can or jar.

Perhaps many Jewish Americans in all denominations have substituted a "kosher-style" Judaism, based on a combination of ethnicity and nostalgia, for the "kosher" Judaism of their ancestors.

25 *American Orthodoxy— Retrospect and Prospect*

EMANUEL RACKMAN

1. Why is this reading important?

Here is another perspective on Judaism in America, one that focuses upon questions of religious interest. Two features lend special importance to Rackman's essay. First, he takes a long perspective on Orthodox Judaism in the American context, which allows us to contrast his view of Orthodoxy with Orthodoxy in its larger Judaic context. Second, Rackman was writing nearly a half-century ago, before Orthodox Judaism in the United States had found the articulate and self-confident voice through which it speaks today. At the end of this unit, devoted to New Age Judaisms, we hear another Orthodox voice, one that speaks to Orthodox Judaism at the turn of the twenty-first century. The contrast between Rackman's perspective at the beginning of the great age of Orthodox renewal and Helmreich's at the apex of Orthodox success teaches us much about how religions change their views of themselves in response to historical developments and social and political forces. Rackman tries to justify and defend Orthodoxy, which he sees as weak and unappreciated. In doing so, however, he points to important facts that reveal the traits of Orthodox Judaism: its power to win loyalty, its capacity to persuade the faithful to accept the authority of the Torah even over that of the common culture of America. The real point of interest in this classic essay lies in Rackman's accounting of Orthodox achievements, which, seen in contemporary perspective, turn out to explain Orthodoxy's remarkable success later on.

2. What should you notice as you proceed?

How does Rackman identify the special achievements and contributions of Orthodox Judaism? The essay is carefully organized to amass facts in support of a proposition. Rackman concedes the errors of Orthodoxy, its failure to persuade the vast majority of immigrants and their children to remain loyal to the Torah in its classical formulation. But he points to the sources of Orthodox renewal: the uncompromising quality of the commitment of Orthodox Jews to the way of life and worldview of the

Torah, and to the Torah's definition of Israel not merely as an ethnic group or a nation-state but as the holy people of God. So Orthodoxy had to challenge the givenness of Christianity as the normative religion, on which basis people could sustain a different way of life from the normal one. Orthodoxy had to establish the institutions of religious life— synagogues, ritual baths, yeshivot (schools for Torah study), parochial schools, and the like. Reform and Conservative Jews could suffice with a partial range of institutions, but Orthodoxy had to have them all. Notice how Rackman points to the mere beginning fifty years ago of what is now a massive parochial school system established by Orthodox Judaism. He describes success in publishing and other ways in which Orthodoxy speaks beyond its own circle. And he outlines the areas in which Orthodoxy would have to take up unsolved problems of organizational life and the institutionalization of the faith. The key statement is: "Orthodox Judaism is endeavoring to recapture the loyalty of American Jews. However, it cannot 'adjust' to the American scene." Therein we discern the pathos and the power of Orthodox Judaism: its very capacity to stand firm attracts the religious virtuosi but repels those less ready to make an entire commitment.

3. How should you frame a question for class discussion in response to what you have read?

What makes Orthodox Judaism distinctive among Judaisms is its insistence upon the public and communal character of the practice of the faith. A person cannot keep the Sabbath all alone but requires a community—and is needed by the community. Reform Judaism speaks to the individual, his or her conscience and capacity to assent. So the two great Judaisms of modern times—Reform and Orthodox—differ upon absolutely fundamental definitions: of the individual conscience, of the collective consciousness, of the right of the individual to form an independent judgment, of the obligation of the community to transcend individual taste and judgment in the name of the revealed truth of the Torah. And that difference opens the way to a discussion of the rights of the individual and the obligations of the community, the duties of the individual and the demands of the tradition.

Catholics differ on important questions but recite the Creed, and so do the Reformation churches. But people leave one church in favor of another, or abandon Christianity altogether, by reason of conviction (or lack of the same). Many Christianities find entirely acceptable the imposition of public criteria of faith, just as Orthodox Judaism sets limits. But many other Christianities make a place for people of diverse beliefs or none, and some Judaisms do the same. Here we reach an issue that everyone can understand: To what extent do religions form public and communal statements to which individuals subordinate themselves, and to what extent is the believer's conscience the court of last judgment when it comes to religious truth? How do various religions define what is required and what is optional, and in what ways do they accommodate both the individual and dissent within the community and consensus? And how should they do so? Think of Luther, nailing his Ninety-Five Theses to the cathedral door in Wittenburg, and ask whether the Holy Catholic Church, one and united, could have addressed his dissent more wisely than it did when he said: "Here I stand, I can not do otherwise." The contrasting choices made by Orthodox and Reform Judaisms embody profound issues in the social order established by religious faith in community.

The earliest Jewish settlers on American soil brought with them the only Judaism they knew—Orthodox Judaism. Two centuries later Reform Judaism took root and still fifty years thereafter Conservative Judaism was born. Under the circumstances, one would have expected that Orthodox Judaism would be the first to meet the challenge of the American scene, ideologically and institutionally. In fact, it was the last to do so. Paradoxically enough, it is only in the last few decades that Orthodoxy seriously came to grips with the problem of its own future.

For too long a time Orthodoxy relied upon the fact that the preponderant number of American Jews professed to be its adherents. Majorities supporting the status quo in many social situations often rely upon the force of their numbers and their inertia, while well organized and dedicated minorities make gains for change. The Orthodox Jewish community once was such a majority. It was slow to realize the extent to which it was losing its numerical advantage. Second, the ranks of American Orthodoxy were ever replenished with thousands of immigrants from abroad. The new arrivals more than compensated for the defections to other groups. Now the loss of the European reservoir of Jews has caused American Orthodoxy to become concerned. It must find the way to command the loyalty of American born Jews. Third, Orthodoxy by its very nature compromises less easily with new environments and new philosophies, so that it could not avail itself of that flexibility which aided the growth of the Reform and Conservative movements. The challenge of the American scene had to be met differently and the solution was later in its formulation and implementation. Nonetheless, significant and many were the contributions of Orthodoxy to our dual heritage as Americans and as Jews.

It fell to the lot of Orthodoxy to establish the legal status of Jews and Judaism in American democracy. To the everlasting credit of our pioneering forbears it must be said that they were not content with second-class citizenship in the United States. George Washington confirmed this attitude in his now famous letter to the Orthodox congregation in Newport, Rhode Island. However, the false dictum that America is a "Christian state" must be challenged again and again, even in the twentieth century, and while the battle is now waged by all Jews, and especially the defense agencies, it is usually one Orthodox Jew or another who creates the issue. The right of Sabbath observers to special consideration where "Blue Sunday" laws are in effect; their right to special treatment in the armed forces; their right to unemployment insurance benefits when they decline employment because of religious scruples—these are typical of many problems that Orthodox Jews raise in the hope that their resolution will insure maximum expansion of the American concept of equality before the law. In many instances, bearded Orthodox Jews who retain their eastern European dress are also a challenge to the sincerity of most Americans who boast that their way of life spells respect for differences. The resistance of many of our co-religionists to the leveling character of American mores, and its inevitable discouragement of diversity, is a healthy contribution to our understanding and practice of democracy. Altogether too often American Jews require the reminder even more than American Christians.

In the same spirit it was American Orthodoxy that bore, and still bears, the lion's share of the resistance to world-wide calendar reform. Though all Jewish groups have cooperated, it is Orthodoxy alone that regards any tampering with the inviolability of the Sabbath day fixed at Creation as a mortal blow to Judaism and in the name of the religious freedom of minorities it seeks to alert the American conscience to desist from prejudicial action.

It was, however, in the establishment and construction of thousands of synagogues throughout the country that Orthodox Jews made manifest not only their loyalty to their ancestral heritage but their appreciation of their grand opportunity in this blessed land of freedom. How truly pauperized immigrants managed, in cities large and small, to rear beautiful edifices for worship is a saga worthy of more attention than it has heretofore received. What is particularly noteworthy is that no central agency guided or financed the movement. In every case it was individual Jews who banded together and performed the feat, a remarkable tribute to the effectiveness of our tradition in inducing in individual Jews the capacity to act on their own initiative for the greater glory of God. Even today no central body guides or directs the establishment of Orthodox synagogues. Orthodoxy's synagogue organization—the Union of Orthodox Jewish Congregations of America—is still totally ineffective in this kind of work. The initiative must always come from Jews who desire an Orthodox synagogue, and not from any resourceful, missionary, national or international body. In part, this is also one of the weaknesses of Orthodox Judaism which its leaders want to correct on the threshold of its fourth century on the American scene. However, it remains to be seen whether it will be the Union of Orthodox Jewish Congregations or Yeshiva University that will blaze the new path.

The extent to which Orthodox Jews gave of their worldly goods for the establishment and construction of synagogues was exceeded only by their willingness to sacrifice for the cause of Jewish education. Their first venture in this direction, even before the era of the public school, was a Jewish all-day school under the auspices of Congregation Shearit Israel in New York. The more usual approach to the problem, however, was via the Talmud Torah, the afternoon school in which children spent from five to ten hours weekly. In some instances the Talmud Torahs were successful, and many distinguished American Rabbis and scholars received their earliest instruction in Judaica in such schools. Yet altogether too often because of incompetent instructors, bizarre methods, and inadequate facilities, the Talmud Torahs failed to induce either a love or an understanding of Judaism. In the twentieth century, therefore, Orthodox Judaism countered with the Yeshiva movement. This movement has enjoyed a phenomenal growth. In the ranks of Conservative Judaism, too, it is receiving sympathetic attention and support, and even among Liberal Jews one occasionally hears it suggested that the all-day school is the most effective answer to Jewish illiteracy.

Three organizations of Orthodox Jewry now propagate the Yeshiva program and supervise the establishment of new schools. The Vaad Hachinuch Hacharedi of the Mizrachi Organization of America also deals with Talmud Torahs, while Torah Umesorah whose program and goal were conceived by the saintly Rabbi Faivel Mendelowitz, is concerned with Yeshivoth alone. The Lubavitscher Hasidim have their own unit for identical work. The Vaad Hachinuch Hacharedi is more Zionist in its outlook than the latter two groups; the latter two groups even regard the knowledge of Yiddish as important for the survival of Torah. Together, however, they stress the importance of a thorough background in Bible and Talmud at the same time that secular studies more than meet the standards of the American public schools. With the increase in the number of schools on the elementary level, there came also an increase in the number of schools on the secondary level. Beyond the high school level there was also established a network of schools which ordain Rabbis. At one time the Rabbi Isaac Elchanan Theological Seminary in New York (still the largest) and the Hebrew Theological College, founded by the late Rabbi Saul Silber of Chicago, were the only two Orthodox seminaries in America. Now there are at least a dozen. Unfortunately, however, these schools are not even federated with each other; there is no joint action whatever. Even their graduates are not affiliated with one Rabbinic body, although the Rabbinical Council of America has the largest percentage of all the graduates, while the Rabbinical Alliance of America, and the oldest of all, the Union of Orthodox Rabbis of the United States and Canada, get a fair measure as well. These three Rabbinic groups have recently sought some areas for joint action but as yet the results are meagre. And this is perhaps the greatest weakness of Orthodox Jewry—its inability to consolidate, or even coordinate, its educational institutions and their alumni.

Nonetheless, the enrollment of about thirty thousand Jewish boys and girls in the all-day schools constitutes Orthodox Jewry's proud achievement at the close of the third century of American Jewish history [1954]. The financial burden has been indescribably great. And the financial problem will be insoluble in times of economic depression. For that reason many supporters of the Yeshiva movement hope for state support of parochial schools. Heretofore Jews have been quite unanimous in their support of the defense agencies' position on the complete separation of church and state in America. However, with most welfare funds denying aid to the Yeshivoth of their own communities, or at best making niggardly allocations, one can predict that in the not too distant future, the sponsors of the Yeshivoth will be desperate enough to join with representatives of the Roman Catholic Church in an effort to obtain state or federal aid. Such a move may make for a further cleavage between Orthodox and non-Orthodox Jews. But Orthodox Jews feel that they have more than vindicated the right of the Yeshiva movement to be hailed as a major contribution to the survival of Judaism in America and that the time has come for welfare funds to abandon their hostility to the cause. New York City's Federation of Jewish Philanthropies, for example, has already begun to see the light.

One interesting by-product of the Yeshiva movement has been the remarkable financial success that publishers have enjoyed in their republication of classics in Judaica. The Union of Orthodox Rabbis republished the Babylonian Talmud about thirty-five years ago. Thereafter business firms have done it profitably several times and they have added many other works. Orthodox Judaism does not yet adequately subsidize its scholars nor provide for the publication of their original contributions to scholarship. Yet enough of a demand for books has been stimulated to make many a reprinting financially worthwhile.

Another interesting by-product of the Yeshiva movement has been the effect of the presence of a Yeshiva in many a mid-western city upon the Orthodox group within that city itself. Within the Orthodox community, where only chaos and anarchy reigned before, the Yeshiva became the great cohesive force, and the Yeshiva leadership inspired greater control over kashrut supervision, the construction of better facilities required by Orthodox Jews for all ritualistic observances, and even more cooperation in fund-raising for local and overseas religious needs.

How the Yeshiva movement served more than the cause of Torah, narrowly conceived, can be gleaned from the fact that it was a Yeshiva, led by the brilliant and visionary Dr. Bernard Revel, that established on American soil the first Jewish college of arts and science; later it became America's first Jewish University. More recently it undertook the construction of a medical and dental school. Furthermore, that Orthodoxy in America was prepared to abandon its historic indifference to the education of women, was made manifest not only by the fact that a large percentage of the children enrolled in the Yeshivoth are girls, but that Yeshiva University headed by the resourceful and indefatigable Dr. Samuel Belkin, now has a secondary school and college for them.

In the area of overseas relief Orthodoxy was always impatient with the general agencies because of their neglect of religious institutions, and as a result during and after World War I the Central Jewish Relief Committee and Ezrath Torah Fund were organized to bring aid and succor to European Yeshivoth. The Union of Orthodox Rabbis deserves special commendation for this achievement. With regard to Palestine, too, Orthodoxy was preoccupied with religious development. Within the framework of the World Zionist Organization, American Orthodoxy advanced the program of the Mizrachi and Hapoel Hamizrachi parties. Rabbi Meyer Berlin (Bar-Ilan), who was also the founder of the Teachers' Institute which became affiliated with the Rabbi Isaac Elchanan Theological Seminary and later was one of the larger schools of Yeshiva University, was the ideological spokesman and administrative head of every phase of the work. With the new wave of immigration immediately prior to, and after World War II, the separatist Agudath Yisrael party gained an appreciable following in the American Jewish community and created a very marked cleavage between the traditionalists who hoped for some synthesis of western thought with our ancestral heritage and the traditionalists who hoped to reestablish on American soil replicas of Eastern European Jewish communities. The former are also more cooperative with non-Orthodox Jewish groups and participate in the work of the Synagogue Council of America even as they are represented in the Commission on Jewish Chaplaincy of the National Jewish Welfare Board and organizations like the New York Board of Rabbis. The profound ideological differences between the two groups came to the fore with respect to the issue of the conscription of women in Israel. However, the same lack of unity that has weakened Orthodoxy's achievement in the fields of synagogue and Yeshiva organization has also undermined the esteem in which Orthodoxy's significant achievements for Israel ought be held. Nonetheless, it is American Orthodoxy that has always borne the brunt of the responsibility for the preservation of almost all of Israel's religious life.

Orthodox Judaism has maximalist objectives not only for religious education in America and abroad but also with regard to religious observances. Unfortunately, in this area too it has failed to achieve any measure of unity or coordination. Kashrut supervision for example, is under the aegis of no central body, and even the cooperation of states that have laws on the subject has not eliminated the anarchy that prevails. The most progressive step forward was taken by the Union of Orthodox Jewish Congregations, in cooperation with the Rabbinical Council of America, when it registered its "U" as a guarantee of kashrut and made the label available to firms that meet the strictest requirements. This helped to popularize Kashrut and the Union not only advertised the products it endorsed but published brochures on the significance of the dietary laws generally. The ultimate hope is to divest individual Rabbis of the right to act on their own for personal gain. The resistance of members of the Union of Orthodox Rabbis is great and even the Rabbinical Council of America had to pass resolutions censuring its members who flout the policy and give *Hechsherim* as individuals. In the area of Sabbath observance there has been less success although the number of professional and business firms that observe the Sabbath has been increasing. The Young Israel movement has helped to find employment for Sabbath observers but as yet the future of the Sabbath depends principally upon the establishment of the five day week in the American economy. The Young Israel movement, on the whole, not only helped to dignify orthodox religious services, and create social and economic opportunities for observant youth, but also made a magnificent contribution to Jewish adult education all over the country. Modern Mikvehs are being built in many communities and though the laws pertaining to *Taharat Hamishpacha* have suffered the greatest neglect, Orthodox Judaism has sought to improve the situation by constructing more attractive and inviting facilities for their observance and by publishing literature on the subject in English.

In the area of English publications and public relations generally, Orthodox Judaism must meet new challenges. Its Halakhic and scholarly journals, such as *Talpioth,* of Yeshiva University, have a limited circle of readers while most American Jews have only the vaguest notions of the nature of Orthodoxy and its spiritual and intellectual vitality. True, within the ranks of Orthodox Judaism there are many to whom the modern scene and western thought constitute no challenge. These elements are to be found principally among the recent immigrants to the United States. And they often intimidate the more progressive Orthodox elements who recognize that Jewish law was always dynamic and that Judaism never required an ostrich-like indifference to currents of thought that prevailed in the world about. A sad illustration of the dangers of such intolerance was recently afforded Orthodox Jews when an Orthodox Rabbinic Journal—which was never noted for its progressive approach, and even delighted in attacking the younger Rabbis of the Rabbinical Council of America—found itself under attack by an even more "rightist" journal because it published an article suggesting that the redactors of the Babylonian Talmud did not see the Palestinian Talmud! The tendency to canonize each and every view of the past with absolutely no critical or historical evaluation is strong among these "rightists." Some of them even favor the social and economic isolation of Orthodox Jews. They propose the establishment of Orthodox Jewish communities with Sabbath observing vendors of the necessities of life, Sabbath observing professional and service personnel, etc.

The position of these "rightists," however, is not typical. Most American Orthodox Rabbis are not isolationists. They admit that for at least another generation or two most American Jews will not be observant. Nevertheless, they want these Jews to appreciate their moral obligation to support the totality of their ancestral heritage as Jews that it may be transmitted intact to later generations whose knowledge of Judaism and whose spiritual climate may be more conducive to the development of Judaism in consonance with its historic philosophy and pattern rather than as a compromise with Jewish illiteracy and the materialistic, "sensate" values of the present era. The prevailing values of our day are antithetical to most of the values of Judaism. They, therefore, believe that to adjust Judaism to the values of today is to forfeit the role of religion as a goal and aspiration for a more spiritual tomorrow. Our posterity should not be prejudiced by us and receive from us only truncated conceptions or patterns of Jewish thought and practice. With this approach, most Orthodox Rabbis are urging even the non-observant to identify themselves with Orthodox synagogues and send their children to Yeshivoth. Serious problems do arise when such children are confronted with the contrast between what they are taught in school and what they see at home. However, the leaders of the day-school movement are trying to solve these problems through their publications, their conferences with parents, and their day-to-day contact with the children.

Most Orthodox synagogues now have English-speaking Rabbis who preach in English. Prayer-books and copies of the Pentateuch with English translations are the rule, not the exception. Especially noteworthy among the English translations of the traditional prayer-book is Dr. David de Sola Pool's add, recently sponsored by the Rabbinical Council of America. Under the auspices of the Union of Orthodox Jewish Congregations, Dr. Leo Jung edited a number of excellent volumes on Jewish information. Several of the essays have become classical expositions of Orthodox Judaism. At least one, "Study as a Form of Worship," by Professor Nathan Isaacs of Harvard University, has gained a world-wide currency among Jews. Rabbi Herbert S. Goldstein translated selections from Rashi's commentary on the Pentateuch for family use on the Sabbath, and more recently a linear translation was made available by a commercial publisher.

Orthodox Judaism is endeavoring to recapture the loyalty of American Jews. However, it cannot "adjust" to the American scene. The term "adjust" too often implies man's right to trim religion to meet his personal desires. Such a right Orthodoxy denies any Jew, and notwithstanding even Dr. Kinsey, the sixth commandment of the Decalogue is binding no matter how high the percentage of spouses who flout it. Nonetheless, most American Orthodox Rabbis recognize that there has always been, and still are, different modes of Orthodox Jewish thought and practice, and that Orthodoxy has always admitted a great measure of innovation. The innovation, however, is always within the Halakhic process and pursuant to its revealed norms. The result, therefore, is organic development of God's will, not man's.

In order to communicate this point of view to American Jews Orthodoxy must have leaders who are not only articulate in English but also masters of western thought and its temper. That is why Yeshiva University and the Hebrew Theological College advocate the mastering of all western thought in order to create an ultimate synthesis with Jewish learning. This goal will be achieved as more of the graduates of these schools and other Yeshivoth become expert in the natural and social sciences.

There already exists a society of Orthodox Jewish scientists which is dedicating itself to the solution of problems created for Orthodoxy by modern technology. Many a Halakhic point of view is receiving support from the natural sciences, and what is more important, these scientists are demonstrating that there is no conflict between natural science—which has abandoned the notion that it can attain any absolute truths whatever—and religion which calls for faith in given absolutes. The greater challenges to Orthodoxy, however, come from the social sciences and an impressive group of Orthodox leaders, lay and Rabbinic, are coping with them.

Orthodoxy's position vis-à-vis the Higher Criticism of the Bible is one such area. While Orthodoxy is committed to no one conception of Revelation, all Orthodox Jews regard the Pentateuch as divinely revealed. Moses wrote it while in direct communion with God. Moreover, with Moses too, the Oral Law had its beginnings and its process was ordained by God. German Jewish Orthodoxy perhaps made more progress in its defense of this position than has American Jewish Orthodoxy to date. However, Orthodoxy relies heavily on the fact that modern archaeological research has bolstered the historicity of the Biblical narrative and Orthodoxy is confident that further progress in philology will precipitate the same kind of retreat from anti-Orthodox viewpoints that the Bible's erstwhile plastic surgeons have suffered. Rabbi Chayim Heller, at Yeshiva University, is stimulating both the confidence and the type of research necessary to sustain the Orthodox position. Moreover, many Orthodox thinkers believe that with a retreat from humanism generally, humanism will no longer be the vantage point from which the revealed Word of God will be arrogantly evaluated. Man will not be the measure of God.

The greatest challenge of all, however, lies in the realm of Halakhah; first, the importance of its study, and second, the importance of living by its prescriptions. Is the Halakhah viable in the modern age? Can it and does it enrich our spiritual existence? Is it relevant to our yearnings and aspirations and can it edify and fulfill them? Only a small percentage of even Orthodox Jews are content with the mandate, "The Law is the Law and must, therefore, be obeyed." Philosophical approaches to Halakhah and philosophical analyses of the Halakhic process must be articulated. The undisputed leader of the Orthodox Jewish community in this domain is Dr. Joseph B. Soloveichik, of Yeshiva University, who is now also Chairman of the Halakhah Commission of the Rabbinical Council of America. In addition to his brilliant resolution of many involved Halakhic problems of the modern age, and his equally masterful analyses of Talmudic texts, he is demonstrating the viability of the Halakha, the relevance of its insights to abundant and adventurous spiritual living, and the intellectual harvests to be reaped from preoccupation with its study. Most of the great Halakhic scholars who adorn the faculties of America's Yeshivoth, and most of the distinguished Orthodox Rabbis who founded and still lead the Union of Orthodox Rabbis of the United States and Canada, deserve credit for their benign influence upon the loyalty of thousands of American Jews to our ancestral heritage. But they have done little more than transplant the Orthodoxy of Eastern Europe on American soil. It is to Dr. Soloveichik, his co-workers and students, that American Orthodoxy looks for the ideological content, the techniques and the conclusions required to stem the tide of defections to other groups by making it abundantly clear that Halakhic Judaism is eternal and has naught to fear from the challenges of western thought, present and future.

First, however, it wants to stimulate a renascence of Torah learning on American soil. Orthodoxy feels that until Jews are learned they cannot be pious. It insists that it sustained its greatest set-back in America because of Am ha-Arazuth,

Torah illiteracy. For more than two and a half centuries America could not boast of a score of men learned in the Law. How could Orthodoxy then achieve here that synthesis that was once the glory of Spanish Judaism? The first task, therefore, is to spread the knowledge of Torah. As tens of thousands become masters of the Halakha, the Halakha will have a new birth in the new world.

Second, Orthodoxy does not believe that the modern contribution to progressive revelation can come until the modern age recaptures basic religious experience. The commitment of our age to material values has deadened our capacity for religious experience. Yet, there is evidence that as we face the atomic era in human history, there will be a resurgence of religious values and a reawakening of religious experience. In such atmosphere, Judaism will thrive. Particularly will Halakhic Judaism thrive as more and more Jews seek to apprehend God's will rather than merely indulging their own.

26 In Your Blood, Live: Re-Visions of a Theology of Purity

RACHEL ADLER

1. Why is this reading important?

If the rebirth of Orthodox Judaism represents the single most important—and least anticipated—event in American Judaism in the past
half-century, the second most important is the advent of feminist thinking within various Judaisms. A fair portion of that thinking has laid
stress on the feminist side of matters; it has simply stated the viewpoint
of militant feminism in the language of Judaism, the religion, or in the
context of Jewishness, the ethnicity. All we learn from writing of that
kind is how the feminist ideology adapts itself to its diverse audiences.
But some of the writings of Jewish feminists have aspired to set forth a
Judaic statement of feminism, a feminism infused with the convictions
of a Judaism, and some have realized that aspiration. In this way feminist Judaism, rather than the Judaic wing of a common feminism, has
produced an important body of religious thought and expression. Feminist Judaism cannot be treated as a cogent system comparable to Reform
or Orthodox or Conservative Judaisms; rather, within the established Judaisms feminist perspectives have taken shape and come to expression.
Feminist Reform Judaism addresses its own issues, as does feminist Orthodox Judaism, and these issues are quite different.

While certain convictions characterize all feminist Judaic thought,
any attempt to characterize a single Jewish feminism or feminist Judaism obscures matters. I have chosen Rachel Adler as our first feminist
voice because she is one of the more interesting and original figures. We
have already met her in considering Classical Judaism; there she asked
for a place, within the *halakhah,* for women and their concerns. That essay represents Adler's position in the early 1970s. Twenty years later, she
gave up the struggle within the halakhic world and identified herself as
a feminist Reform theologian. How she reframes the issues is now a
point of considerable interest.

2. What should you notice as you proceed?

Notice how carefully Adler explains her original proposals, which she
wishes to reconsider here. Her earlier goal was to justify the purity laws

of the Torah as set forth by Orthodox Judaism. These involve the prohibition of sexual relations during a woman's period and a rite of purification afterward, making possible the resumption of those relations. Adler's purpose was to normalize the woman and make the woman equal to the man. Pay careful attention to how Adler spells out the obstacles that she now perceives to block the path toward normalization and equalization of women. How does she explain her failure and consequent decision to give up the task of a feminist theology within the *halakhah* of the Torah that Orthodox Judaism espouses? Of special interest is Adler's account of the success of her original article—and the embarrassment she feels when she meets women who are persuaded by her own ideas now that she has rejected them.

3. How should you frame a question for class discussion in response to what you have read?

First, what general, universal convictions of feminism do you find in the particular language that Adler uses? These givens of feminism govern this important and honest statement of hers throughout. Second, within these givens, are all religions in their received form equally able to respond to the challenge of contemporary feminism? Each religion works out its issues in response to its own rules—some intellectual in creeds, others political in institutional arrangements. Not all religions may find it possible, or even plausible, to accommodate the aspirations of contemporary feminism. What are the choices facing Catholic women who aspire to the priestly vocation? Muslim women who want to live by the faith but also function in Western society? Orthodox-Judaic women who take Adler's position of 1973 and reject the one outlined here? Academic scholars ordinarily take for granted the priority of feminist values and aspirations such as Adler defines here, but people in important parts of Islam, Christianity, and Judaism place a higher priority on other matters. How would you construct an argument, within the bounds of civility, between those two conflicting positions? What contribution do you think academic study has to make in the formation of civil discourse upon deeply divisive and therefore critical questions? Here is an opportunity to try to argue about something that counts.

Twenty years ago, as a young Orthodox woman, I began what became an influential essay with the words "All things die and are reborn continually." I was wrong. Sometimes we cannot repeat ourselves. We can only transform ourselves. Yet our moral responsibility for that earlier self and its acts lives on. Twenty years later, as a feminist Reform theologian I continue to be faced with an essay I wrote, an essay that continues to be quoted, cited, and reproduced, promulgating opinions and prescribing actions that I now cannot in good conscience endorse.

My essay, which was published both in the first *Jewish Catalogue* and in the first Jewish feminist anthology, *The Jewish Woman,* was called "Tum'ah and Taharah: Ends and Beginnings." It dealt with the ancient laws of purity whose major surviving form is the powerfully valenced body of law and custom concerning women's menstruation. Because this legislation governs sexual and social behavior and attitudes so pervasively, it can be said that menstrual impurity is constitutive of the religious selfhood of women in Orthodox Judaism. I undertook to justify this legislation by constructing around it a feminist theology of purity.

Confronting my essay, I have had to ask myself what is the responsibility of a theologian when she no longer believes what she taught to others as Torah? Merely to recant is insufficient, because theologians are not just theorists. They exemplify ways to live out Jewish commitments with integrity. What I owe to those who read and were persuaded by my theology of purity is not merely to outline abstractly my revised conclusions but to tell a richly detailed story about a particular process of rupture and transformation in a specific time and place.

My task is complicated by the fact that the earlier essay itself represents a kind of transformation—a reframing. Even the title of that project is eloquent: "Tum'ah and Taharah: Ends and Beginnings." It signals that I had defined my topic as a theological understanding of the entire ancient category, and not just the part of it pertaining to women. The title evades the words woman sex, *niddah* [menstrual impurity], menstruation, and mikveh [the ritual immersion by which purity is achieved]. It also eschews the common euphemism *taharat ha-mishpacha* [the purity of the family], in which women are reduced to a nameless function whereby families are produced and maintained in purity.

In the essay I attempted to reframe the meaning of women's menstrual impurity [*niddah*] by reintegrating it with the other purity regulations stipulated in the book of Leviticus rather than focusing upon it as a unique phenomenon. I interpreted all these regulations as ritual expressions of a single theology of purity equally relevant to women and men. I see clearly now how this generalized reframing reflected my awareness of and hopefulness about egalitarianism as a value in secular society. Probably, it was the discrepancy between my sense of self-worth and entitlement as a participant in secular and in traditional Jewish contexts that heightened my experience of *niddah* as a source of gender stigma. Egalitarianism seeks to normalize women by stressing their similarity to men. That is how I sought to neutralize the stigma of *niddah:* by emphasizing its kinship with the purity laws applicable to men. I maintained that all impurity ritual enacted a common set of meanings. Implicitly, this was a denial that any special "women's meaning" distinguished menstrual impurity from impurities contractable by men. The strategy I chose has been used extensively by secular jurisprudence to neutralize discrimination: Obscure or ignore the differences on which discrimination was predicated and stress instead the commonalties all are presumed to share. That the laws of pollution had once applied to men was therefore indispensible to my argument, even though men had not observed them for many hundreds of years.

It is important to understand that my concerns were as much theological as social. Existing theological justifications of menstrual impurity did not help me to make sense of myself as a God-created creature. They treated me, to use Kantian terminology, as a means to someone else's end, rather than as an end in myself. To have the observance of *niddah* and mikveh justified to me as the instrumentality whereby my husband was entitled lawfully to cohabit was both inadequate and insulting.

Indeed, the otherness and the instrumentality of women were foundational presumptions of the men who wrote about these laws. What was significant about menstruation for them was that it made women uniquely capable of causing men to sin by transmitting pollution to them. They never asked themselves how it would feel to be someone to whom such a capacity had been assigned, or whether menstruation might have other meanings to those who menstruated. Their one educational goal was to persuade or terrify women to keep their pollution to themselves.

Some sources threatened nonobservers with death in childbirth or deformed children.[1] Others promised observers a honeymoon every month in compensation for the estrangement of *niddah,* on the dubious assumption that sex is most satisfying when the participants are unfamiliar.[2] The only rationale the sources did not offer was the rationale that motivates all sincere piety, the one held out to men: that observing the commandments would make one holier and bring one closer to God.

I required an explanation which acknowledged my personhood as intrinsically important and affirmed my capacity for spiritual growth. Even more urgently, I needed to understand how a body that menstruates, a body that pollutes, could be a holy body. The male writers were concerned about how women were to comport themselves in their impurity. I wanted to know what it might mean to be pure.

Intuitively, I sensed that the classical texts by themselves would yield no answers. The topic had not interested their creators because women as spiritual subjects had not interested them.[3] I took my questions into fields of secular learning: anthropology, literary criticism, comparative religion. These areas provided perspectives to focus upon the Jewish texts. They offered forms of discourse in which I could view myself as a subject and participant rather than as an object to be passively defined. The classic anthropological work of Mary Douglas taught me a new way to understand the categories of purity and pollution. Douglas argues that the body may be viewed both as a symbol and as a mirror of society. Upon it are inscribed the categories that make sense of the universe. Protecting the demarcation lines of those categories protects us from chaos or meaninglessness. Pollution is the punishment for violating those boundaries, and thus endangering the coherent world. Supplementing Douglas' theory of pollution with a literary reading of the texts in Leviticus, I theorized that the boundary crossed by all those who incurred impurity was the boundary between life and death. I maintained that all of the forms of impurity were regarded as encounters with death and were associated with conditions imaged as death-like or life-diminishing, such as the erosive skin diseases the Bible calls "leprosy" [*tsara'at*], menstruation, and seminal emission, or from nexus situations that bridge the passage between life and death, such as childbirth and the purification ritual for corpse-impurity.

---

[1] A traditional source for this view is *B. Shabbath* 31b–32a.

[2] A traditional source for this view is *B. Niddah* 31b. Its most noted modern promulgator is Norman Lamm, *A Hedge of Roses,* 4th ed. (New York: Philip Feldheim, 1972).

[3] I discuss this point more extensively in, "I've Had Nothing Yet, So I Can't Take More" *Moment 8* (Sept. 1983), 22–26.

The comparative religion scholarship of Mircea Eliade provided me with an understanding of water as an ancient and universal symbol of regeneration and renewal and of cycles as markers of sacred time and affirmations of return and restoration. Using his formulation, I depicted the mikveh as the womb or the watery chaos from which Creation is elaborated, a life-giving fluidity in which forms can be repeatedly dissolved and made new.

Drawing on these sources, I formulated a theology of purity in which menstrual impurity and mikveh were relocated within a universal cyclical process in which all creation endlessly rehearses its death and rebirth. In the context of this theology, menstruation was not only normalized, it acquired powerful spiritual significance. While the theology justified the laws of menstrual impurity and supported their observance, it sought to reframe their meaning, to remove their stigma and to discover their spiritual value.

The sources I brought to my theology of purity, however, built their arguments upon assumptions very different from my own. In fact, some of the implications of these assumptions were incompatible with Orthodoxy: that diverse religions have comparable or analogous symbols, myths, and practices; that valuations such as pure and impure are socially constructed and not divinely proclaimed; that religious meanings are derived not merely from texts, but from how the words of the texts are lived out in communities. Rabbis who viewed my work as merely an effective apologia for getting educated women to use the mikveh had no interest in pursuing these disturbing implications. They regarded secular sources much the way they regarded women, as instruments, rather than as ends in themselves. But the more I came to understand the scholarly sources I had utilized, the deeper and more troubling were their implicit challenges to the work into which I had incorporated them.

What did it mean to formulate a theology of purity that was blind to gender difference and silent about gender stigma, when the only kind of impurity with behavioral consequences in Orthodox communities is gender specific—menstrual impurity? What did it mean to claim that the theological meaning of *niddah* had to do with symbolisms of life and death, when its impact on women's lives was obviously and concretely sexual? What did it mean to describe *niddah* as part of a cycle when, in the public life of the communities in which it was observed, women were always treated as if they were impure?

The social facts about impurity in living communities are about the impurity of women. Sexual relations with a *niddah* are forbidden. Also forbidden are physical contacts and expressions of affection, on the grounds that they could lead to sexual relations.[4] In all but the most left-wing Orthodox circles, the general presumption of *niddah* status is a reason for excluding women from conventional social courtesies like shaking hands, and for denying them access to the Torah.[5] In contrast, men experience themselves socially as pure. Although they may meet the qualifications for biblical impurity (having had a seminal emission, for in-

---

[4]Maimonides, *Misnneh Torah, Hilchot 'Isure Bi'ah* 12:18.

[5]Exclusion of menstruants from access to sancta is a matter of folk piety rather than law. See Shaye J. D. Cohen, "Purity and Piety: The Separation of Menstruants from the Sancta," *Daughters of the King: Women and the Synagogue,* edited by Susan Grossman and Rivka Haut. (Philadelphia: Jewish Publication Society, 1991).

stance, or contact with a corpse), there is no behavioral consequence. The only men who have to contend with impurity laws at all are *kohanim*, descendants of the priestly clan, who may not expose themselves to corpse impurity. *Kohanim* who obey these laws, although they probably bear some second hand impurity from polluted others, experience themselves as utterly pure. Socially, then, purity and impurity do not constitute a cycle through which all members of the society pass, as I argued in my essay. Instead, purity and impurity define a class system in which the most impure people are women.

Even a more rigorous literary analysis would have called into question my reading of Biblical purity law. The word *niddah* describes a state which is neither socially nor morally neutral. *Niddah*, from the root NDD, connotes abhorrence and repulsion. In a recurring prophetic motif, it is associated with adultery, idolatry, and murder.[6] The icon for sinful Israel wallowing in its corruption is not the corpse-handler or the leper but the exposed *niddah*, her skirts stained with menstrual blood, shunned by passersby.[7]

I explained that imagery away, interpreting it as an expression of prophetic despair and loathing at societal impurity that refuses to be cleansed. *Tum'ah* [impurity] is a stigma, I argued, only when it is divorced from the purification cycle. At some earlier time in Israel's history, I believed, there had been a Golden Age when the cycle had revolved smoothly and blamelessly for both women and men, and gender had not been a source of stigma. This belief informed my reading of the purity texts of Leviticus. But this belief is untenable.

In his cross-cultural anthropological study, *The Savage in Judaism*, Howard Eilberg-Schwartz argues convincingly that the stigma upon menstrual blood enables ancient Israelite religion to draw a crucial distinction between men's and women's capacities for holiness. The uncontrolled blood flowing from women's genitals is blood which has the power to contaminate. Its antithesis is the blood of circumcision deliberately drawn from men's genitals, which has the power to create covenant. Eilberg-Schwartz emphasizes that the symbolism of the body and its fluids as embedded in categories and rules does not merely reflect but is constitutive of the social structure within which it applies. The Israelite purity symbolism which associates masculinity with fertility and control and femininity with death and disorder constructs a culture in which men dominate women. This polarization of the symbolic meaning of gender is intensified by developments in rabbinic and post-rabbinic Judaism, in which purity laws affecting men become atrophied, while those affecting women are elaborated and made more stringent.

My theology claimed that impurity was universal. The social reality, since the rabbinic period at least, was that impurity was feminine. My theology claimed that impurity was normal and morally neutral. Literary and anthropological evidence, as well as that of contemporary social reality, identify impurity as deviant and a source of stigma and exclusion. In particular, all the meanings of menstrual impurity asserted by my theology are explicitly disconfirmed by historical precedent, by literary analysis, by linguistic usage and by communal practice. And yet women embraced this theology with great fervor and felt transformed by it.

---

[6]Lam. 1:8, 17; Ezek. 7:19, 36:17–18; Zac. 13:1; Ez. 7:19–20, 9:11; II Ch. 29:5.

[7]Lam. 1:8, 17.

What I had succeeded in creating was a theology for the despised, reminiscent of certain strains of early Christianity, where worldly power went unchecked, the slave remained a slave, the poor stayed poor, the woman subject to her husband, but the meaning of indignity was inverted and transfigured: humiliation was triumph, rejection was salvation, and death, eternal life. My theology upheld the rules and practices that sustained women's impurity by holding out to the impure a never-before experienced sense of purity. For women who were touched by this theology, mikveh became not merely the water that made one sexually accessible once more, but water that cleansed the soul.

It became acutely painful to me to meet these women at lectures and conferences and have them thank me for a theology I had come to believe both intellectually and morally unjustifiable. It seemed inadequate to tell them I had changed my mind, now that my teaching had been so strongly integrated into their spiritual praxis. I did not know how to be accountable to the people who learned from me. I had never heard a theologian say that he or she had been wrong. In addition, I was left with questions of faith and practice, some of which are still unresolved for me. Is the mikveh usable for women's ritual? Should we ritually acknowledge our menstruation? Can we continue to regard the Holiness Code of Leviticus as sacred text? What does it mean to be pure?

When Jewish women who were not Orthodox appropriated my reframing of immersion in the mikveh to mark occurrences for which no ritual expression had existed, they taught me an important lesson about the possibility of salvage. They began using the mikveh to purify themselves of events that had threatened their lives or left them feeling wounded or bereft or sullied as sexual beings: ovarian tumors, hysterectomies, mastectomies, miscarriages, incest, rape. In waters whose meaning they had transformed and made their own, they blessed God for renewed life. The makers have imbued these rituals with a different understanding of what purity means.

They appear to agree with the writers of the ancient texts that impurity afflicts the embodied human self; it is not a malaise of disembodied soul. But for the feminist Jew, impurity seems to mean the violation of physical or sexual integrity, death by invasion. If purity is the mirroring of God's oneness in human wholeness, it is no less fragile and transitory than humankind itself. Our flesh is gnawed by disease, eroded by age, menaced by human violence and natural disasters. Our minds and our souls are subject to intrusions, exploitations, indignities. We keep breaking or being breached. We keep knitting ourselves together, restoring ourselves, so we can once again reflect God's completeness in our female or male humanity.

When I was Orthodox, I thought that God's Torah was as complete as God: inerrant, invulnerable, invariable truth. I thought that I, the erring, bleeding, mutable creature, had to bend myself to this truth. Whatever I was or saw that did not fit had to be cut off, had to be blocked out. The eye—or the I—was alone at fault. I tried to make a theology to uphold this truth, and as hard as I tried to make it truthful, it unfolded itself to me as a theology of lies.

I do not believe the laws of purity will ever be reinstated, nor should they be. The worlds reflected in such rules are not worlds we inhabit. Neither should we seek to replicate such worlds. They are unjust.

In the mind of God, according to a midrash, is a Torah of black fire written on white fire. In the hands of Jews is a Torah written in gall on the skins of dead animals. And the miracle is that the fire of God's Torah flickers through our scroll. I continue to learn the purity texts, hoping for some yet unglimpsed spark, but that is not enough. I must learn what purity can mean in my own world and in the most human world I can envision. For if ours is a Torah of and for human beings, it may be perfected only in the way that we perfect ourselves. We do not become more God-like by becoming less human, but by becoming more deeply, more broadly, more comprehensively human.

We must keep asking the Torah to speak to us in human, this crude jargon studded with constraints and distortions, silences and brutalities, that is our only vessel for holiness and truth and peace. We must keep teaching each other, we and our study partner the Torah, all that it means to be human. Human is not whole. Human is full of holes. Human bleeds. Human births its worlds in agonies of blood and bellyaches. Human owns no perfect, timeless texts because human inhabits no perfect, timeless contexts. Human knows that what it weds need not be perfect to be infinitely dear.

Sacred need not mean inerrant; it is enough for the sacred to be inexhaustible. In the depths of Your Torah, I seek You out, *Eheyeh,* creator of a world of blood. I tear Your Torah verse from verse, until it is broken and bleeding just like me. Over and over I find You in the bloody fragments. Beneath even the woman-hating words of Ezekiel I hear You breathing, "In your blood, live."

27 *From Equality to Transformation: The Challenge of Women's Rabbinic Leadership*

LAURA GELLER

1. Why is this reading important?

To realize its goal of equality and normality for women, feminism requires not only theology but actualization: women in positions of authority and leadership, women as models of virtue and piety. What is important in Rabbi Geller's account is her description of the actualities faced by the first women to be ordained as rabbis, all of them in Reform Judaism. What she stresses is that when one thing changes in a religious system, everything changes. People think that a woman as rabbi represents the Torah in the same way that a man as rabbi does. That conception hits wide of the mark. What registers here is how broad and deep a range of changes come about in consequence of the opening of the rabbinate to women. To show how deep, we need only reflect on Geller's statement, "The very presence of women rabbis has forced many congregants to confront God in different ways." So, too, she points to new rites within the faith or the revision of received ones. A great deal has gone right, and the promise of feminist Judaism within Reform Judaism is being kept.

2. What should you notice as you proceed?

If everything is all right, then what has gone wrong? Notice how, having spelled out the gains, Rabbi Geller catalogues the pains. What has gone wrong is that women's rabbinical careers do not run parallel to men's. Geller tries to spell out what that means and why it is so. First, women define the careers to which they aspire in terms different from those important to men. That illustrates the basic thesis offered here: in a well-constructed system, if one thing changes everything else changes, too. Second, the opportunities set before women do not match those set before men. Geller spells out the rabbinical counterpart to the "glass ceiling" in large corporations: Women are paid less than men; they are not given the same opportunities to serve large and important temples or synagogues. Third, women are mothers, and their careers follow a different rhythm by reason of that fact. Maternity leave represents a transient solution to a lasting condition: commitments that simply transcend career considerations. Finally, Geller points to the failure of women to make their way into positions of power and authority as professors in rabbinical schools and leaders of organizations.

3. How should you frame a question for class discussion in response to what you have read?

Rabbi Geller defines the issue for class discussion when she says, "The impact of women rabbis on Judaism begins with the revolutionary idea that women's experience ought to be acknowledged and valued." To paraphrase her language in the setting of other religions: "What would Catholic institutions look like if they were shaped in response to the values that seem to be shared by so many women—balance, intimacy, and empowerment?" Now frame the same question for Islam. Try to imagine how matters would unfold were women to exercise equal and proportionate influence even in those religions that welcome them as rabbis or ministers or other religious virtuosi. So far, feminism has accomplished the easy goals, the formalities; the hard ones, the matters of substance, have yet to come to definition, let alone accomplishment. Feminism forms one result of the movement to end the caste system affecting African Americans in the United States, a secondary articulation of a basic aspiration. In many ways you can make the case that just as the end of segregation marked the easy stage, the attainment of full equality has yet to come about; the ordination of women into the rabbinate (and the counterpart clergy of other religions) marks only the beginning. But what, then, do you demand of the future, and what cost do you conceive will be exacted in the realization of that demand? Here are questions for which no easy answers seem available. They mark the border between the theoretical and the actual, where learning becomes relevant.

Twenty years ago some people thought we had come to the end of a journey, that we had reached the promised land of equality for Jewish men and women. After all, a revolution had occurred in Jewish life. Women could be rabbis.

Twenty years ago I was a rabbinic student at Hebrew Union College–Jewish Institute of Religion (HUC-JIR) in New York. I studied in the old building on West 68th Street, which was around the corner from where Sally Priesand was serving as the first woman rabbi. I was the only woman in my class, one of only two women rabbinic students in the New York school. My classmates were supportive and friendly; generally my teachers, all of whom were men, were rooting for my success. Most of them believed that because there were women rabbis and women rabbinic students, we had already succeeded in reaching equality and equal opportunity.

Few of them understood the particular pressures and the unique challenges that I experienced in my years at the College. Only other women understood the pain of patriarchal texts, the confusion of finding myself absent in the stories that shape our tradition, the desperate need to re-envision a Judaism that includes the experience of all Jews. Only other women understood the pressure of being a pioneer, of wanting to be considered as capable as the men without being forced to give up my own sense of balance, of wanting a life where work is a blessing within the context of other blessings—family, commitments, friends.

Although these were problems only women understood twenty years ago, there were hardly any other women with whom to share these feelings. I felt as though I was wandering in the wilderness, lonely for the dancing of Miriam and the women.

What a difference two decades make! As of this June 1993 there were 219 women ordained as Reform rabbis, and women now comprise almost half the students at HUC-JIR. Also by June 1993, there were 52 women rabbis ordained by the Reconstructionist Rabbinical College and 50 from the Jewish Theological Seminary. Our lives as women who are rabbis are full of blessings: work that challenges and stimulates us; colleagues, both women and men, to share our struggles and our successes; partners, children, friends, community. We have much to celebrate.

Women rabbis have changed the face of Judaism. At the simplest level, the change is obvious. As Rabbi Ellen Lewis wrote a few years ago: "When I first assumed my present pulpit, I tried to do everything just like my predecessor did. I had great respect for his work in the congregation and was not looking to be revolutionary. I just wanted to be the rabbi. What I found was that, even if I did the same things he did, when I did it it looked and sounded different." At her first Bat Mitzvah as a student rabbi, the young thirteen-year-old girl looked up at Rabbi Lewis as they practiced on the pulpit and asked: "At my Bat Mitzvah do you think we can wear matching dresses?"

Other similar stories abound. Rabbi Deborah Prinz tells the story of her first Shabbat on the pulpit of Central Synagogue. Rabbi Sheldon Zimmerman had for years been changing the language of the prayerbook to make it gender neutral. Rabbi Prinz read the prayerbook the same way. But at the end of the service a congregant came up to Rabbi Zimmerman to complain: "See, you hire a woman and the first thing she does is change the prayerbook!"

At the conclusion of my first High Holy Days services as the rabbi at the University of Southern California, two congregates rushed up to me. The first, a middle-age woman, blurted out:

> Rabbi, I can't tell you how different I felt about services because you are a woman. I found myself feeling that if you can be a rabbi maybe I can be a rabbi too. For the first time in my life I felt as if I could learn those prayers, I could study Torah, I could lead this service, I could do anything you could do. Knowing that made me feel much more involved in the service, much more involved with Judaism! Also the service made me think about God in a different way, I'm not sure why.

The second congregant had something very similar to say, but with a slightly different emphasis. He was a man in his late twenties.

> Rabbi, I realized that if you could be a rabbi then *certainly* I could be a rabbi. Knowing that made the service somehow more accessible for me. I didn't need you to do it for me. I could do it, be involved with Jewish tradition, without depending on you.

In each of these anecdotes, and there are hundreds more, the theme is the same: people experience women rabbis differently from the way they experience male rabbis. And that difference changes everything: the way they experience prayer, their connection to the tradition, and even their image of divinity.

When women function as clergy, the traditional American division between clergy and lay person begins to break down. A woman who is an Episcopal priest told me that when she offers the Eucharist, people take it from her differently from the way they would take it from a male priest, even though she follows the identical ritual. People are used to being fed by women, and so the experience is more natural, and hence less mysterious.

People don't attribute to women the power and prestige often attributed to men. Therefore when women become rabbis, or clergy of any kind, there is often less social distance between the congregant and the clergy. The lessening of social distance and the reduction of the attribution of power and status leads to the breakdown of hierarchy within a religious institution. "If you can be a rabbi, then certainly I can be a rabbi!" "Can we wear matching dresses?"

Women rabbis have had a profound impact on the way many Jews experience divinity. Although most of the systematic work in the area of Jewish feminist theology has been done by women scholars who are not themselves rabbis, the very presence of women rabbis has forced many congregants to confront God in different ways. For some Jews, there is an unconscious transference that they make between their rabbi and God. As long as their rabbi is male, they are not even aware that they associate him in some way with a male divinity. But when the rabbi is female, they can't make that unconscious transference. And so they begin to confront directly their images of God and perhaps even open themselves to ask "who is the God I experience and how can I speak toward God in prayer?" Here too, although much of the most creative work in prayer and liturgy is being written by feminists who are not themselves rabbis, it is often women rabbis who are on the front line when it comes to liturgy.

Rabbis are on the front line of ritual work as well. Congregants come to rabbis for help in negotiating the transitions of their lives—the joys and the losses. Women rabbis have created ceremonies and rituals to meet the real-life experience of the Jews they serve, and many of those rituals are for women. Covenant ceremonies for daughters, b'not mitzvah, weddings, divorces, ceremonies of healing from loss, miscarriage, abortion, infertility, adult survivors of childhood incest, becoming fifty, and sixty, children leaving home . . . are all actual transitions in the lives of Jews that have led women rabbis to create ritual. Along with other feminists—scholars, educators, cantors, lay people—women rabbis have been part of the transformation of Judaism. After twenty years, we do have much to celebrate.

What would Jewish institutions look like if they were shaped in response to the values that seem to be shared by so many women—balance, intimacy, and empowerment? Already the impact of women has been felt by the men who have been their classmates and colleagues. Rabbi Sher told me that, in his view, women rabbis have "humanized" male rabbis, that women have taught men about balance. He argues that the definition of success is starting to change as men as well as women are choosing more often to stay in middle-size congregations, preferring continuity and intimacy and the pleasures of organic growth to the more traditional rewards of prestige and power. These kinds of changes may well change

the shape of synagogues and raise new kinds of questions. What would a synagogue look like if success were defined not as climbing to the top of a hierarchy,
but rather as being at the center of a web of connections? What will careers in the
rabbinate look like when maleness is no longer assumed to be the norm, when
rabbis are partners rather than seniors and associates, when job sharing is a real
possibility, when parental leave is equally accessible to men as to women? What
will salaries be like when men as well as women choose to trade some money for
more flexible schedules? What will Jewish communities be like when rabbis stop
being surrogate Jews and instead enable their communities to take responsibility
for their Jewish lives? What will Jewish institutions be like when we make room
for the many different kinds of Jews we know there are: Jews in different kinds
of families, Jews searching for community and spirituality? And what will the
rabbinate be like when we value the diversity among us rabbis: women and men;
married and single; lesbian, gay, and heterosexual; parents and non-parents;
scholars and activists; rabbis who serve in congregations and Hillels and organizations and hospitals and schools—and the list goes on.

These questions of transformation are the most important questions posed
by women's rabbinic leadership after twenty years. These are the questions that
will shape the next twenty years of our journey. And these are the questions that
will lead us out of the wilderness to a Judaism that truly embraces both women
and men.

28 The New Spirituality

DEBRA CASH

1. Why is this reading important?

The third important development in American Judaism, besides the resurgence of Orthodoxy and the advent of feminism, is the formation of what may be called "New Age Judaism"—that range of personal lifestyles and public, communal organizations that lay stress upon spirituality; direct encounter with God; the formulation of rites responsive to types of Jews formerly ignored by or excluded from public life altogether, such as gays and lesbians; as well as experimentation, within the framework of an organized Judaism, with forms of worship familiar in other religions, such as meditation. Joseph Blau's discussion of the Americanization of Judaism should have led us to anticipate the development of just such Judaic modes of a common American religious trend. The following reading, as well as the two selections afterward, comes from a special issue of *Hadassah Magazine*, November 1996, devoted to the "new spirituality." It is a brief, well-focused, and sprightly essay that treats the topic in a sympathetic way. To be sure, like the two readings that follow, it leaves the hard questions for others to ask.

2. What should you notice as you proceed?

Since the given of New Age Judaism is its novelty, we have to ask ourselves how new it really is. To find answers to that question in Cash's essay, ignore the critique of conventional Jewish community institutions and pay close attention to the language of the advocates themselves. Cash points to spiritual practice. What practices do you find that you should deem genuinely fresh and surprising? How would the Hasidic masters about whom you read in Buber's presentation have responded, and what would they have wished to teach? Second, notice the stress on the personal and the individual and see whether you can frame an enduring Judaism out of New Age ideals. Rabbi Rachel Cowan, a foundation director, speaks of such questions as "What is my responsibility in this world?" Would a standard Reform rabbi have found that question fresh and surprising? In other words, when Cash says, "You don't have to be Jewish to pose such questions," you might find evidence in her essay to support the premise that you have to adopt the language of the New Age in place of that of the Torah to ask the same questions.

3. How should you frame a question for class discussion in response to what you have read?

The first question is this: Is this a New Age religion with a Jewish accent, or is it a Judaism's response to New Age religiosity? And a deeper question, pertinent to the study of religion in general, lies in the background. Some people maintain that all religions say much the same thing. A subset of that conviction is that at a given time and place, in diverse ways, various religious communities work through the same problems, each making in its own way a statement to which all may assent. A discussion of New Age Judaism provides a chance to reflect in more general terms on where and how religions really do differ, and where and how they converge. The discussion may focus on the religious condition of the United States in particular, where a powerful and pervasive culture takes over and reshapes religions to conform to a single pattern. Then we must wonder whether the American way of dealing with difference—celebrate what is trivial and suppress what really matters—has shaped the religiosity of American religions. President Eisenhower was reputed to have said, "It doesn't matter what you believe, as long as you're a good man." In that context, homogenization takes the form of defining the single contents of diverse packages, wrapped in different paper. To put it simply, what is Judaic about New Age Judaism, and would a Catholic or a Baptist of the New Age persuasion find much, apart from petty detail, to reject?

Why then have so many found themselves alienated, detached, starved for meaning in their Jewish lives? Blame downsizing jitters, the graying of the baby boomers or a consumer culture that has not delivered on its shiny promises. Point to a traumatized, post-Holocaust Jewish community that has often been better at teaching how Jews were destroyed than at describing how Jews lived. Note that an exclusive focus on Israel puts American Jews in the position of outsiders looking in: proud, but acting out of vicarious connection.

Whatever the explanation, a shift is being felt across the country. Radiating out from Philadelphia and Albuquerque, Berkeley and Los Angeles, and growing in less visible places including Montpelier, Vermont, and Madison, Wisconsin, Jewish communities and individuals are developing a new—or perhaps merely a refreshed—spiritual practice. It ranges from deeply private efforts focusing on ritual, liturgy and personal healing to those that embrace the public and political spheres in areas such as *tzedaka* and the inclusion of gays and lesbians in Jewish communal life.

Some are led by charismatic rabbis and teachers such as Zalman Schachter-Shalomi of ALEPH (previously P'nai Or) in Philadelphia, Lynn Gottlieb of Congregation Nahalat Shalom in Albuquerque and the late Shlomo Carlebach, who founded the House of Love and Prayer in San Francisco and established communities of followers in the United States and Israel. Such leaders' creative influence often extends far beyond the communities where they work. Others are led by lay people, shifting annually, and even seasonally, in response to personalities, skills and needs.

What these efforts have in common is a commitment to creating Jewish lives that express contemporary beliefs and values. "People are returning to the ultimate spiritual questions," says Rabbi Peter Knobel of Evanston, Illinois. "What is the meaning of my life and how can Judaism help me live better, make sense of my tragedies, doubts and fears?"

Adds Rabbi Rachel Cowan, who directs the Jewish Life Program of the Nathan Cummings Foundation in New York, "The Jewish tradition is how you live out those questions: What is my responsibility in this world? How do I maintain optimism, keep from lapsing into cynicism? How do I nourish my capacity for hope, for lovingkindness?"

You don't have to be Jewish to pose such questions. But increasingly American Jews are recognizing that it helps to have a Jewish base from which to explore.

The new Jewish spirituality in America flows from many cultural streams: neo-Hasidism to Buddhist meditation, feminist to left-liberal understanding of the requirement for *tikkun olam*, repair of the world through acts of social justice. For many, this emerging practice offers an alternative to a religious identity based on Orthodox norms, and one open to the values they carry over from other commitments such as feminism, ecology, multiculturalism.

The way Rabbi Arthur Waskow explains it, a "holistic" contemporary Jewish spirituality calls for "new ways of imaging and addressing God and new ways of acting in our down-to-earth lives. New sexual ethics, new eco-*kashrut* (not just about food but also about all the other things we consume: coal, oil, paper, wood, plastics); new outlooks on communal ethics and on the relationship to the Land of Israel; new kinds of prayer that involve the whole body, not just words, and chant and meditation; and new ways of incorporating, supporting and even celebrating a cultural pluralism that includes the presence of gays and lesbians, alternate families and the intermarried. It is a heady undertaking, one that calls for a high tolerance of experimentation and for living with contradiction.

The roots of this movement—if it can be called a movement at all—lie in the independent *havurot* founded in the late 60's, the experimentation in feminist *midrash* that flowered in the 70's and 80's and the commitments of numerous Conservative, Reform, Reconstructionist and even a few Modern Orthodox congregational rabbis to re-examine life-cycle and prayer activities. This steady, experienced core of activists, visionaries, educators and members of *havurot* who spent the last two decades on the fringes of Jewish communal life are now finding their experiments being adopted by far more mainstream institutions, sometimes with unanticipated results.

For previously unaffiliated Jews, these new practices offer access without, for the most part, demanding much Jewish education. Rabbi Moshe Waldoks, who often speaks and teaches at New Age centers and has been deeply involved in Jewish-Buddhist dialogue, notes that such Jews "are shocked to hear that one can be Jewish and nonjudgmental about other traditions. Many of them have never gotten beyond their rejection of the sterile Judaism of their childhoods, and finding options—other, adult, ways of expressing Jewish identity—comes as a revelation."

Another group is the Jews who had found homes, perhaps temporarily, in other spiritual-cultural traditions such as Buddhism. Although many find his opinion controversial, Rabbi Jeff Roth, who cofounded Elat Chayyim, a Jewish renewal retreat center in upper New York State, argues that the presence of Jews in these communities is no tragedy; instead, he sees opportunity. These Jews-by-birth "have mined the other traditions and gotten those vitamins and minerals we need for healing our own community," Roth says. As he invites them to participate in his workshops, he argues that "we can take advantage of what they've harvested."

A third, perhaps less visible group, is Jews who have been synagogue members, donors to federations or Jewishly educated. Although by most lights they were never outside the circle of Jewish commitments, they too, are challenging their communities to find new, more personally relevant modes of expression and behavior. Thus did Hadassah respond to the findings of a study by The National Commission on American Jewish Women that women want more spirituality in their lives by including for the first time an adult bat mitzva program in its national convention this past summer. "It was an opportunity for 123 women to grow Jewishly and enhance their spirituality," says Barbara Spack, chair of Hadassah's National Jewish Education Department. "For those with little Jewish knowledge, it changed their lives. For others, it was a terrific eye-opener."

Last year in addition to Jewish study becoming part of every program slot at the annual General Assembly of the Council of Jewish Federations, a significant component of the Continuity Institute included intensified text study and more openly spiritual expression. At one point everyone joined hands and swayed, transported by the music of singer Debbie Friedman. In announcing an emphasis on a full Sabbath celebration to culminate this year's GA, the cochairs stated that "The strongest message we received from last year's participants was the renewed interest in spirituality."

But in this arena, notes Cowan, there is always the danger of opportunism. "We have to change and enhance the quality of institutional life, not just decorate it."

Yet the activities spurred by the new spirituality seem destined to have far-reaching implications. "We have needed unique rituals for moments that haven't been ritualized," Knobel says, "rituals in connection with infertility, with divorce, with a new job, with retirement." The development of healing centers and healing liturgy is part and parcel of that effort. Penina Adelman, whose 1986 book, *Miriam's Well: Rituals for Jewish Women Around the Year,* has been the Bible of the Rosh Hodesh movement, points out that a monthly gathering of women to celebrate the new moon offers "Judaism 101" for previously unaffiliated women, while it deepens the practice and sense of leadership even among women in the observant community.

New contexts for Jewish study are emerging as well. In Beverly Hills, Rabbi Laura Geller passes out classical Jewish texts at board of directors' meetings, so that financial spreadsheets and the text of resolutions can be discussed alongside sources of Jewish tradition. At Temple Beth Emet in Evanston, one evening was set aside for Jews-by-choice to talk frankly about their spiritual journeys. "Ultimately what we have to deal with is the openness to the presence of God in our lives," Geller says. "People experience that very differently. I have to bear in mind that what might be evocative for me might be a closed door to someone else."

"In some communities, and even in part of our own tradition, the spiritual path deals with going away from the world, *lekh lekha,* leave your home," says Rabbi Julie Greenberg, who leads the Jewish Renewal Center in Philadelphia. "Judaism includes that, but it also teaches the opposite: What is most intimate and inward can also be a path."

"We've done extraordinary things with prayer, *midrash*, the arts, music and going down into our *kishkes* to have a direct encounter with Torah, to take it seriously," says Waskow, her Philadelphia neighbor. "But we are only just beginning to deal with money, work." Some simply have to do with recognizing the spiritual component in daily life for what it is. "For a lot of people raising kids is the passionate, life-changing experience they may not have articulated but it is where their spiritual growth is happening," says Greenberg, whose children are 8, 6 and 4.

Others have to do with changing the focus of certain activities. Jeffrey Dekro, who heads the Shefa Fund, which promotes and supports social responsibility, is passionate as he argues that how we deal with money and our beliefs about community building must be integrated into our spiritual practice. He points to the tradition of passing the *pushke* at the conclusion of a prayer service as a visible embodiment of the command to love your neighbor as yourself. "Having made our wealth in cities, the American Jewish community has an obligation to rebuild those cities," he says. To that end, the Shefa Fund has made as its centerpiece a commitment to help Jewish institutions—federations, synagogues and community relations organizations—invest in the economic development of low-income communities. The spiritual challenge, he says, is "to draw a straight line between our values and our experiences."

The new Jewish spirituality flowers from the challenges of living at the end of the twentieth century, but it echoes the ancient words of Scripture: "For this commandment is not too hard for you, neither is it far off . . . but the word is very close to you, in your mouth and in your heart so that you may do it . . . therefore, choose life."

29 *Rabbis at the Frontier: Beyond the Fringe*

JUDITH FEIN

1. Why is this reading important?

Religious specialists shape the religious systems that recognize them. That generalization emerges from feminist theories on the rabbinate that we have now examined. How does that same generalization apply to rabbis in the New Age sector of American Judaism? Here we have an acutely contemporary account of how rabbis redefine themselves in response to the Judaic system they espouse. *The Way of Torah* contains ample information on the definition of the rabbi in the classical writings, and we have noted how Reform, Orthodox, and Conservative rabbis defined the ideas of their Judaisms. So far as the Judaism of the dual Torah and its continuators in modern times are concerned, a rabbi qualifies for his or her position by studying the Torah. The leadership of a rabbi rests on the premise that he or she is defined by the Torah and therefore embodies its teachings. What, then, does the word *rabbi* signify when holders of that title lay no claim to learning at all, but rather point to their gifts of the spirit? "To be a vessel of God's creativity and love" in Classical Judaism meant to master the teachings of the Torah and to exemplify them. But a different, freehand meaning, in no way modified by the teachings of the Torah, applies to New Age rabbis—by their own word.

2. What should you notice as you proceed?

Notice the definition of the rabbi's qualifications and profession that are put forth in this article. Where do the rabbis come from, and what models do they have in their mind for their own rabbinate? When these rabbis use the word *Judaism*, what do they understand by that word? Would Reformers such as Abraham Geiger, or Hasidic rabbis such as the Besht, have understood them as rabbis in the model they adopted for themselves? In this account, you may find it difficult to distinguish between the ethnic and the religious, the Jewish and the Judaic, with the result that traits in other religions deemed secular here are given religious significance. What you know about the Judaism of the dual Torah has already told you the character of religious encounter—the meeting with God—that that Judaism brings about. It is through God's words in the Torah, through prayer in the holy community, through acts of loving-kindness, and through repentance that holy Israel meets God. And these activities take place in public, in a community of the faithful. All of these represent very particular, in combination unique, ways to God. Is the religious encounter to which New Age rabbis afford access equivalently public and communal, and is it particular, item by item or in combination, to any Judaism as defined by Chapter 1?

3. How should you frame a question for class discussion in response to what you have read?

In a traditional religion, what place do you assign to "creativity?" And what are the materials that "creative" religious leaders utilize in their creation? If you believe in the possibility of religion in general, of a religiosity that may be shared by people of diverse origins, then you will assign no limits to what is subject to religious creativity, whether flower arranging, dancing, or long silences. But if you maintain that religion exists, in this world, only in the form of specific religions, then you will compose a fairly short list of the media of piety available in any given religion. For example, in some contemporary Islamic systems, piety may come to expression in bomb throwing, and in the name of Islam the novelist Salman Rushdie was condemned to death for writing about the Prophet in a manner deemed offensive by many Muslims. In some moments in the history of Christianity piety required martyrdom, and at others piety consisted in burning apostates or heretics to death. Scripture records that for ancient Israel, wiping out every Canaanite man, woman, and child served God's purpose. These cases illustrate the proposition that a religious system also defines the limits of piety. In that context, consider the piety of "creativity" put forth in New Age Judaism. One point of discussion may focus upon how original and innovative, how authentically creative, that "creativity" is. Another may address the issue of whether or not the conventional synagogues or temples, whether Orthodox or Reform, ought to learn from some of the rites invented in the New Age. A third question returns to Rabbi Petuchowski's inquiry into the limits of liberal Judaism: Will any prior Judaism concur with Rabbi Winkler's insistence on the sacred status of the earth, when the prophets, beginning with Moses, condemned the celebration of trees and mountains and the proliferation of nature gods?

When Rabbi Nachum Ward-Lev of Santa Fe answers questions, he closes his eyes, tuning in to an inner voice. "People are drawn to New Mexico because it is holy," he says. "It has been held as sacred by Native Americans, Hispanic peoples, artists and the more recent arrivals. I feel the effect of the land, the light and the sky. I find it spiritually uplifting and feel challenged to live at a certain spiritual level, to be a vessel of God's creativity and love."

"When you are really present," he says, "then things start to happen."

For Ward-Lev, who had a Reform background, things have been happening since he began looking for a spiritual connection. He experimented with Eastern religions—Zen centers, retreats, meditations and aikido. The summer he was a counselor at the Brandeis Camp Institute, he wandered over to hear guest speakers at a nearby college camp and his life changed. They danced, drew, reconnected the Jewish heart and soul. "I began to feel the living juice of Judaism."

Swept up in the politics of the late 60's Ward-Lev grew disenchanted with "the morality of American society" and began to see Judaism as a culture that centered around justice and compassion. When he saw beatnik poet Allen Ginsberg performing in San Francisco swaying in a lotus position, the audience chanting with him as he prayed, "It hit me. Ginsberg was a Jew, Judaism was my spiritual path."

Today Ward-Lev is rabbi of Temple Beth Shalom. He leads services that are almost entirely sung. "Music opens and lifts the heart," he says. Ward-Lev has excised all responsive readings because "they are controlled and prayer involves a certain kind of surrender." He includes an extensive period of silence for meditation and believes in the power of prayer as medicine. The congregants call out the names of people who are in need of healing and then pray for them. "It's all about *kavana* [intent and concentration]."

"New Mexico is a center for creative expression, which is central in religious life, prayer, Torah study, holiday celebration," Ward-Lev explains. He encourages people to be at the creative center of their own Jewish lives. For example, in reciting the *Shema* he invites them to evoke images of God's Oneness from inside themselves. "What images come up? What body sensations, smells, pictures, yearnings? What are the questions, the doubts?"

In the drama workshops Ward-Lev conducts around the country, participants explore Bible stories through writing, movement and acting and create their own *midrashim*. In workshops on Jewish meditative writing, a Torah portion is read and people are encouraged to note their own associations and responses.

Creativity is also central to Rabbi Lynn Gottlieb of Albuquerque. A descendent of German Jews, Gottlieb hails from eastern Pennsylvania where her ancestors founded a Reform synagogue. At 14 she knew she wanted to be a rabbi. The civil rights movement influenced her deeply and studies in Israel led to understanding Judaism "as a multicultural and diverse religious tradition."

When she studied with writer Elie Wiesel, "it reinforced my belief that storytelling . . . allowed the tradition to flourish." And then, Jewish feminism opened the door to the question: How can we tell the traditional stories from women's perspectives?

Gottlieb leads an often itinerant congregation that includes over 40 artists. She is committed to a deinstitutionalized, grass-roots Judaism based on the extended family and describes her approach as "theatrical or folk art." On Yom Kippur, for example, she draws on the custom of filling the entire synagogue with *yahrzeit* candles. "People are literally surrounded by light," she says. Many deliver sermons and everyone blows the *shofar*, a Sefardic tradition.

Amid New Mexico's cultures with active ceremonial lives, "Jewish people feel more at home with their tribal roots," Gottlieb explains. She uses the spiritually charged environment as settings for ceremonies. The entire congregation uses Jemez Springs as a *mikve* several times a year. Since 1976, Gottlieb has been traveling around the world telling stories to renew the spirit of Judaism. She employs sign language, drumming and dance. For Passover, she dons a crone mask and embodies Serah who, like Elijah, never died.

Women play a central role in Gottlieb's thinking. Her recent book, *She Who Dwells Within* (Harper-SanFrancisco), includes guided meditations, prayers and rituals for a nonsexist Judaism. "The *Shekhina* . . . is the feminine aspect of God in exile Who has to wait for the spiritual efforts of pious men to release Her. We have to redeem the image of woman as helpless victim; she must be an active participant in her own redemption." Female equality, she says, "[is now] about creativity because that is a source of spiritual liberation. Women have to gain po-litical power. We look at issues like violence with the self-confidence that we can contribute our resources in public life and make a difference."

Gottlieb's rabbinate is active, provocative and joyous—"Judaism is a cele-bratory religion, and it's a *mitzva* to come before the Spirit of Life in joy," she says.

If anything, Rabbi Gershon Winkler is even more itinerant, his personal jour-ney radical and remarkable. Born in Copenhagen, the son and grandson of rab-bis, he came to the United States at seven. He received an Orthodox ordination in Jerusalem. "I was a nice *frum* rabbi," he says. In New York he was involved in Orthodox outreach and "as I [taught] I became less Orthodox and more flexidox," he recalls. His students were wrestling with injunctions against such contempo-rary mores as premarital sex and living together. "I began to feel the party line didn't fit where people were at."

This led him to examine Judaism's ancient sources and he found the farther back he went the more lenient were the teachings. He began to teach divergent opinions and got fired from the yeshiva where he was teaching. "Something be-gan to free up inside of me," he says of that seminal period.

Needing a drastic change he drove to California to meditate in solitude. "I began to get clarity about the direction I was going in. I also realized that living in the boonies was me." The proximity to nature inspired in him "a whole dif-ferent experience of being Jewish." He's remained there ever since. Author of *The Place Where You Are Standing Is Holy* (Jason Aronson), Winkler lives in the moun-tains of the San Pedro wilderness. "If you want to find me, go to the Navajo reser-vation and for $1.50 they'll send me a smoke signal," he jokingly says.

Winkler lives about two hours from the communities he serves: Farmington, New Mexico, and Durango, Colorado. He laughingly refers to himself as a "circuit-ridin' *rebbe*," but his quick, stand-up comic wit and verbal dexterity be-lie his seriousness of purpose: "to reconnect with the relationship our people had with the land in ancient times and up to about 1,800 years ago."

To Winkler the earth is sacred and God is revealed through the natural world. Whenever possible, Winkler holds services outdoors. "We stand with the trees," he says. "We conduct our service as though we were *davening* with grasses and trees. We include them in our *minyan*."

Although Winkler is geographically and philosophically distant from main-stream Judaism, his beliefs are based on Torah. "One finds that all the major festivals and a significant bulk of the commandments are rooted in the cycles of nature and the gifts of the earth," he says. Isaac went out and meditated in the fields. Abraham, the son of Maimonides, taught that ancient teachers and prophets always found their inspiration in meditative solitude and nature.

Like Ward and Gottlieb, Winkler makes lavish use of music. "When we pray all the psalms say 'sing, sing, sing.' And we read this in synagogue. It becomes a narration about singing rather than the experience of singing." To Winkler music is a form of praying "with all of who you are." And then, with the buoyant humor that characterizes his rabbinate, he adds, "When you sing your *kishkes* are praying."

Rabbi Carol Carp of Taos also tries to involve the *kishkes*. She was fortunate to have caring and influential Conservative teachers. When at her bat mitzva the rabbi kissed her on the to of her head, something spiritually transformative happened. It was at that moment that Carp's life as a Jew began. When she became a substitute teacher at the Hebrew school where her mother was a principal, she was off and running.

Carp looks anew at the traditions and rituals and imagines "if we were all living in tents communally, what would we be doing?"

On Rosh Hashana she places an aspen pole in the middle of the service with 40 strings hanging from it. Each person takes a string and knots it around the pole while saying aloud what his or her intentions are to the community. "A fellow congregant holds the pole, thereby making both the pole and the congregant witnesses, as when God wrote the Ten Commandments and the two tablets were witnesses," Carp explains.

While studying the *Azazel* portion of the Torah, Carp asked her congregants to break into pairs. Each person had to place his sins on the head of his partner and then receive his partner's sins on his own head. "And they had to live with this for the day . . . or perhaps for a year, until they were clean." In this way the congregation experienced how their lives are intertwined and how deep an impact one makes on another.

Carp speaks with the depth and feeling of a woman who is always growing and learning. Her Shabbat women's group has embarked on a 10-month experiential journey. Each month they focus on one commandment in a daily meditative mantra. "We have even called each other up, identified ourselves and said, 'I am the Lord your God, Who brought you out of Egypt, out of the house of bondage,' and then hung up," Carp says. "It's a reminder . . . that teaches you to let go and it freed the women from the tensions of their everyday lives." They learned that through their relationship with God they didn't have to carry the burdens all by themselves.

New Mexico is also blessed with a guitar-strumming, angelic-voiced *hazzan*, Mark Malachi. "I was an atheist as a teenager and I had a spiritual awakening when I was 20 where God made His/Her presence known to me," recalls Malachi, who was raised in a Reform home. "In a flash, I went from being a complete nonbeliever to being a believer. I began to search out God in every church and house of worship I could find." After a while he felt a strong calling to go back to Judaism. When he discovered Kabbala, he found that in it he could integrate all the wisdom he had learned.

Malachi began composing liturgical melodies. His inspired songs exhort listeners to give praise and thanks and revel in the munificent Divine spirit.

"Sound and music have the power to heal," says Malachi. "When you create the vibration of joy through music you are stimulating other people to vibrate to the frequency of love. I'm a sound healer and I know the physics of healing with sound. When I'm singing I'm consciously creating healing vibrations." Through song Malachi seeks to connect to God's presence to permit the uninterrupted flow of energy necessary for healing.

For Malachi, who studies and teaches Kabbala in Santa Fe and around the country, "Kabbala is the art and science of revelation." It is about how to link one's inner being to the Source so that one may receive direct spiritual inspiration. "Kabbala . . . for me is pure mystical experience," says Malachi. "If you're not experiencing God's presence through your studies, then what's the point?"

Hasidic teacher Yehudiss Fishman is another inspired presence in Santa Fe. Raised in a nonobservant home, Fishman became serious about Judaism as a teen. She was drawn to Hasidic and mystical literature and was impressed by the Lubavitcher *Rebbe*. "I also met people who were studying Torah and I found them to be . . . the kind of people I wanted to be."

As Fishman began to study, she became spiritually connected to her grandfather, a Hasidic *rebbe* she'd never met but whom she is named after. Her destiny seems to be to teach Torah and share her passion and inspiration. Her weekly classes in Torah and *hasidut* (Hasidic teachings) are dynamic outpourings of knowledge, love and joy, drawing Jews and non-Jews. The atmosphere is highly interactive. Fishman invites her students to "bring in anything from any other religion" and she'll find the equivalent in Judaism.

"My goal is to bring as many people as I can a little bit closer to Torah and Judaism," she says. "If people were more open God in a total way, their lives would be better and they would relate to each other in a more loving and trusting manner because of their trust in God. Nothing happens that wasn't meant to happen and since God is good, it's all for the best."

At a recent Lubavitch celebration the community honored Fishman's birthday. After she was toasted, Fishman told several Hasidic tales, captivating the children and adults. "Stories are a major teaching device," says Fishman, who is writing a book about the feminine as drawn from Hasidic teachings. "Telling a story about a righteous person connects the teller and the listener to the soul of that righteous person."

Suddenly, her voice lowers and she confides, "Sometimes the words I am saying are teaching me. . . . They seem to come from a higher source than my conscious being."

For a small state with a sparse population, New Mexico just might be the national cutting edge of Jewish spiritual renewal.

30 *Dissing Their Way Back Home*

JUDITH FEIN

1. Why is this reading important?

Here we turn to the everyday life of a community of Judaism formed by reversioners—people who by their own word have returned to a Judaism they once abandoned or simply ignored to begin with. So we move from the theoretical to the practical side of New Age Judaism. Just as we examined the definition of *rabbi* in that Judaism, now we consider the definition of *congregation* or *community*. What the group does when it convenes, therefore, forms a statement of its own Judaism just as much as what the group affirms together and to God. In the same place, New Mexico, where the New Age Judaism flourishes, synagogues of Reform Judaism embody another competing Judaism. Clearly, the practitioners of New Age Judaism do not adopt as their models the pattern of Reform temples, and the Reform Jews do not wish to practice the Judaism of the New Age. Consequently, we have the opportunity to consider the question: Why do the New Age communities do the things they do, and why do they not do the things that they do not do?

2. What should you notice as you proceed?

See whether you could reduce the activities described here to an agenda: How often does the group assemble? On what occasions, and for what purposes? Since we define a religious system as a way of life, a worldview, and a theory of the social entity, we have here important data about one component, its way of life. Pick out the details that permit comparison and contrast with a conventional Reform temple's agenda for itself: regular weekly services on the Sabbath as against a monthly gathering; a generally cool entry as against hugging and kissing; a stable community—the same faces, pretty much, from week to week—as against newcomers and dropouts and returnees. At the Reform temple prayer is the focus of the gathering, a snack afterward an additional treat. Here the main activity is the meal. No dietary laws are described, but vegetarianism often rules in New Age settings. Words are said, and these count. What words are acceptable, and what is their source? How does the act of prayer take place? Clearly, a group experience is contemplated, so see what definition of suitable, and unsuitable, experiences for the group governs. To what do the participants wish to say a loud no? Why do you think Hanukka is rejected but Nonukka is accepted?

3. How should you frame a question for class discussion in response to what you have read?

"The whisperers wanted non-rote, non-prescribed, non-crappola Judaism." A point of worthwhile contention is this: Why do the people want to call their gathering "Jewish," and why do they want what they do to be called a "Judaism"? Class discussion can examine the further proposition that when members of an ethnic group abandon the universal religion that ethnic group espoused, they still not only retain ethnic affiliation but also wish to retain a connection to the universal religion. Otherwise, why assemble with other Jews? The gathering itself attests to the desire to retain the ethnic connection. Other Jews who give up Judaism in any organized form may remain active in the organized Jewish community but make no pretense at Judaic commitment. Still others abandon Judaism and adopt some other religion and its social world, as the Southern Baptists hope all the Jews will do. Such Jews would not join a New Age group with other Jews, though some would happily find a place in a nonsectarian New Age setting. And yet others accept a Christianity and do so in company with other Jews and attempt a Jewish idiom for their Christianity, as in the case of the Jews for Jesus. It is in that context that the particular decisions of the New Age Jews take on specificity and meaning. The task of a class meeting is to sort out the confusion of ethnicity and religiosity that characterizes American society and is also embodied by American Jews.

We're pretty famous here in Santa Fe. We are the Disaffected Jews. Disenchanted Jews. Or Disappointed, Disillusioned, Dismayed, Disgruntled. We are Jews who dropped out of synagogue life many years ago because institutional Judaism didn't meet our spiritual needs. But no matter how far we human apples fell from the Jewish tree of life, in our cores we consider ourselves Jewish—without knowing what that means. We are as diverse in age, appearance, profession, religious upbringing, interests and personality as any group can be. But we come together with open hearts and a desire to see if there is something in Judaism to nourish our souls. And, yes, we are alive and well here in the middle of the southwestern desert.

Our monthly gatherings always start the same way. There are funny signs posted on the front door so the arrival is warm and personal. People greet and hug each other. There are always newcomers, dropouts, dropouts who come back—so the arrivals are a surprise. We never know who or how many are going to show up. Everyone brings food for a potluck and there is no organization whatsoever about the menu. Sometimes it's a cornucopia of delights, other times it's a slapdash affair with people grousing they are hungry. We eat and schmooze and catch up on each others' news. Whoops—there was one exception. The time when we ate in total silence, a hard thing for Jews to do. We tried to eat attentively, to watch what we were eating and think about where food comes from and how it got to our plates. We got to think about how trivial much social chatter is. Maybe some of us were composing shopping lists in our heads as we shoveled in the grub. And while we ate different members got up and read sacred texts they had written. They spoke about personal crises and hopes, about God, the world, universal order, pain and whatever else shimmered with sacred truth in their hearts. The idea was that we were not going to look in prayer books or anywhere outside ourselves for sacred words. We were going to speak them for ourselves and thus, hopefully, connect to them in a deep and personal way.

After the meal there are announcements and this is where pandemonium begins. Our meetings have been described as a Jewish family dinner, where everyone cuts everyone else off, the humor is hilarious and it's hard to hear above the din. It's as if we need to get this out of our systems, to fulfill our cultural destinies of being bright and funny. And then, the more substantive part begins.

Each month we have a group experience. At the moment, I seem to be the funnel for these ideas. My secret is that I do nothing. Once a month I am sitting in the dentist's chair or opening my mail or turning on my computer and I hear words being whispered in my ear. The words tell me what event to propose for the next month. Who is whispering in my ear? I wouldn't presume to answer.

The first experience was a "whisper." We turned off all the lights, lit candles and got down on our bellies to be close to Momma Earth. It took a lot of time to get going because there were kvetches from the group—"My back hurts when I get down." "Could you whisper a little louder?" "Could you please move over, you're pinching my shirt!"

Once we had settled down, we had to answer the question, "What do I want from this group?" The hushed answers were moving. People expressed a need to have an extended family and to be cared about by other members of a community. Others felt they were "different" from the mainstream and wanted to be accepted fully for who they were. Some wanted to see if there was anything at all for them in Judaism or to have a direct, spiritual connection to the religion they were born into. One wanted to be around funny, verbal Jews. Another wanted an opportunity to explore being Jewish in a non-synagogue setting. The whispers seemed to come straight from the heart. The whisperers wanted non-rote, non-prescribed, non-crappola Judaism. They wanted to have meaning in their lives. They also wanted the comfort of being around other people with a similar cultural background.

In retrospect it is possible that this whisper, which took place almost a year ago, set the tone for the group. We set about trying to create a community. We took absolutely NOTHING for granted about Judaism. Hanukka was coming up? We wouldn't do anything that wasn't heartfelt. We wouldn't celebrate it because we were supposed to celebrate it. As a matter of fact, maybe we wouldn't celebrate it at all, but we would commit to exploring it.

I think I was cleaning the sink when I heard the whisper in my ear. "Call it Nonukka," said the voice. "And because there was a miracle on Hanukka, let everyone talk about one miracle in his or her life." Okay, Nonukka it would be. One man volunteered to bring a *menora* and do some research on Hanukka and why it is celebrated. "Boy, my parents wouldn't believe I am doing this!" he said with a grin.

So Nonukka arrived and one woman showed up early and gave latke-making lessons. Then the *menora* volunteer lit the candles and talked about the holiday. He questioned if it was a miracle or a military campaign. People joined in with wisdom and wisecracks, information, skepticism and gratitude. Yes, gratitude. They thanked the man for taking the time to prepare his presentation.

We then sat in a large circle, as always, and people told their miracles. One man tells of how his grandparents, through happenstance and cleverness, fled Germany. A woman *schlepps* out an *American Heritage Dictionary* and defines miracle as "An event that appears inexplicable by nature . . . incites awe . . . an act of God." A man confesses that he doesn't believe in miracles. He talks about drinking water when he is thirsty, getting a good night's sleep, seeing an old friend who had dropped out of his life or being angry and then encountering a quadriplegic. He says, "I am in a miraculous state all the time—and I didn't even realize it."

A woman tells of working for an animal shelter and, at the eleventh hour, finding homes for two un-cute, ostensibly undesirable animals just as their earthly time was running out. Another woman tells of being lost and terrified on a mountain hike, when an old man leading a blind woman materialized, "like a miracle." Then the woman turns to the group and asks us for a miracle, to please pray for her brother, who may have cancer. (This was the beginning of people asking for prayers from the group.)

A man tells of being in a supermarket with an atheist friend who accidentally knocked over a book called *How To Pray.* The man suddenly realized that he didn't know how to pray and bought the book. While reading a section about praying for other people, he began to think about his own self-centeredness. When he was hosting his radio show the next week he asked, on air, if anyone out there knew of a prayer group to pray for other people.

A blonde German woman follows. She tells us how she grew up in Germany, horrified by what her people did to Jews. And then when she was living in America many years later she saw a Holocaust article in the paper. When she read it she realized there was a profile of her German village and even a picture of her house. To her amazement, the German words scrawled on the door indicated that *Juden,* Jews, lived inside. After much probing she found out her ancestors on both sides were Jewish and it had all been hidden and buried. She tells how interconnected we all are. We are all Jews, all Germans, all related and bound inextricably.

The last man to speak informs us that until this night he has rarely shared his story. He was close to his father and before his death they made a pact about contact beyond the grave. Five months after his father's demise, he was in school and he saw a bright "light" coming down the stairs toward him. "I dropped my books, I freaked, I thought I would die," he says. He didn't tell anyone about it for a year. He realized it was a miraculous occurrence and it gave him perspective on the "minor, stupid things" people choose to focus on. He decided to work with death and the dying, and it has given meaning to his life.

After the miracle stories, there is a long pause. No one says anything but I suspect we are all feeling moved, reflective, extremely grateful to share these intimate stories. And then we have a grab bag. We all start laughing and joking again. When one man leaves he says, "This is the most healing experience I have had in years. I laughed, I felt, it was amazing."

Sometimes a newcomer asks how we got started. I think back to the beginning, when I met Rabbi Nahum Ward-Lev and he asked why I don't come to synagogue.

I laughed and said, "If you really wanted to know the answer to that one, you'd have an evening at the synagogue for people like me to find out what we really thought." Amazingly, Ward-Lev did just that. With a few small announcements in the local papers, about 70 people showed up. They poured out their stories of pain, anger, frustration and alienation. The women related how they were ignored as women and deprived of any meaningful initiation into the religion.

They expressed dismay at the emphasis on money and having to pay to go to services. They spoke about parents who didn't raise them as Jews or parents who raised them "too Jewish," without any choice or respect for their questions. They spoke about bourgeois conformity, prayers and prayer books that meant nothing to them, co-congregationists who never called or visited when they were sick or in distress. They talked of how traumatic learning about the Holocaust was and how no one helped them deal with that trauma. They spoke of being excluded and their dislike of excluding others or considering Jews as apart and superior. They confided that they had been ashamed of being Jewish, of how uncool it was to be observant. They spoke of religion, spiritual longings—and how they were unmet. We all spoke and listened, without judgment. There we were, sitting in a holy place, a synagogue, speaking our truths for the first time.

At the end of that first synagogue encounter, we set up another meeting in the synagogue. Another 60 or 70 came. Each story was a gem. At the end of the second session we decided to meet once a month outside the synagogue, in a home. We would try to right the wrongs, ferret out the meanings, form a community based on truth and openness.

Soon our anniversary will be coming up. Each monthly meeting is a surprise, a fresh awakening or reawakening. More new people come and some people disappear and we gradually take them off our calling sheet. The group self-selects. As one man wisely put it, "Whoever is meant to come, comes." And they just keep on coming.

31 Modern Orthodoxy in the New Age

WILLIAM HELMREICH

1. Why is this reading important?

In this account of New Age Judaisms, why end with Professor Helmreich's keynote address to the Orthodox Union's annual meeting in 1996? It would be difficult to point to a more mainstream, less sectarian setting than that. But Helmreich points to traits in Orthodoxy we are more used to seeing in the setting of New Age Judaisms. What characterizes those Judaisms is marginality, unconventionality, and distance from, and indifference to, the large majority of Judaic faithful organized in Orthodox, Reform, and Conservative Judaisms. To be "mainstream" is to want to argue with everybody and persuade all Jews that a given Judaism demands their assent. Geiger, Hirsch, Ginzberg, not to mention Rackman, Borowitz, and Gordis—both the historic and the contemporary voices of mainstream Judaisms face outward, wanting to find a language that all Judaic audiences understand, to frame an argument to which all Judaic participants will respond. But Helmreich points to (an) Orthodox Judaism that "has failed on the open market," and so turned inward. He refers to the Orthodox Judaism associated with the world of study centers, or yeshivot, in which the participants wear distinctive clothing, practice only some few careers or professions or businesses, eat food they alone deem "kosher" and reject the food that other observant Orthodox Jews accept, and in many other ways isolate themselves from the rest of Orthodoxy, not to mention all other Judaisms and Jews. The kind of Orthodox sectarianism that Helmreich describes exhibits the same social characteristics as the New Age Judaism of New Mexico: highly selective about who gets in and disdainful of everybody else. Helmreich's article shows a mirror image of New Age Judaism.

2. What should you notice as you proceed?

Helmreich's complaint concerns not the yeshiva Orthodox or the Hasidic Orthodox, or the other self-segregationist Orthodox Judaisms. It addresses the integrationist Orthodoxy founded by Samson Raphael Hirsch and represented in the twentieth century by figures such as Emanuel Rackman (and Helmreich himself). Notice the trends to which he points in the self-sectarianization of Modern Orthodoxy. Out of his list of changes compose a list of opposites, and you will emerge with a systematic definition of a mainstream Judaism, whether Orthodox or Reform: openness to outsiders, concerned for the state of Israel, respect for the place and role of women, and the like. Pay close attention to the reasons that Helmreich gives for the shift in the character of Modern Orthodoxy, and for his arguments against those changes. Finally, what arguments does Helmreich adduce in favor of a different policy from the self-segregationist one that presently appeals to Orthodoxy? Do you think the other side will be persuaded by these arguments, and what do you suppose they might present as counterarguments? Finally, where do you think arguments based on theology—not politics, sociology, or cultural policy—are relevant?

3. How should you frame a question for class discussion in response to what you have read?

Here is the chance to speculate about the reasons for change in the character of a given religious community or system. Helmreich documents changes over a few decades in a single, small, coherent religious world. He explains those changes by appeal to reasons particular to that Judaic system and its community. But to test his account, you may want to translate into a general theory of religious change the particular reasons that he gives—"the Right Wing had charismatic leadership," "the Right Wing rejected the rest of the world." Certainly other religious worlds and the systems encompassed by them have changed in remarkable ways. Why do you think that is so? How do you explain the alteration of long-established patterns of belief and behavior in ongoing, enduring religious worlds? One aspect of the discussion might take up the theory that massive, historical events make all the difference, or no difference at all, to religion. For Judaism the Holocaust serves as a good case in point. For some theologians, such as David R. Blumenthal, the Holocaust defines the context in which all Judaic theological thought must be carried on. For others, the Holocaust marks the end of Judaism as it was known. The newcomers to the United States to whom Helmreich makes reference were mostly survivors of the death factories that Germany built and ran from 1933 through 1945. They did not lose the faith; they affirmed it in its strictest formulation. In *The Way of Torah* you have learned to see the formation of Rabbinic Judaism from its initial document, the Mishnah, forward as a large-scale response to the crisis brought about by the destruction of the Temple in 70 C.E. by the Romans and the cessation of the sacrificial service decreed by the Torah. Many viewpoints on the basis for religious change have to be sorted out and evaluated, and an interesting class discussion can begin that work.

Orthodox Jewish leadership often congratulates itself on what it has accomplished. To all appearances, it has reason to. The increased visibility of black hats, the charisma of today's yeshiva rebbes and the dynamic growth of Orthodox institutions give rise to a sense of religious renewal. Watching young Orthodox men and women flood the Upper-West side on Simchat Torah is to behold the very face of religious revival.

Or, perhaps more appropriately, the mask. Beneath the surface, in fact, the spirit we display safely in the confines of our own ghettos serves only to blind us with the illusion of vitality, and to hide from us an uncomfortable truth: Orthodox Judaism has failed on the open market. Beneath the fervor, religious Jewish outreach has, for the most part, reached only inward, and is losing the larger battle for the soul of the Jewish community.

Comprising only five percent of the larger Jewish population, Orthodoxy is also drifting farther away from that population. The eminent historian Jack Wertheimer has conducted a study of American Jewry that includes the following data: About 36% of Conservative Jews and 49% of Reform Jews who are not synagogue members are intermarried; nearly four times as many Conservative Jews, 107,000, have left the faith as have entered it. This is not success by any standards.

At the frontlines of this uphill battle is the Modern Orthodox movement, not because it is taking an active role—quite the opposite—but because it bears the most responsibility for Jewish outreach. As a movement encouraging the embrace of the best of both the religious and modern worlds, with the tools to resist the dangers of both, Modern Orthodoxy has the potential to attract a broad and enlightened following. But it has, instead, gone in the opposite direction. It can be shown that Modern Orthodoxy has helped bring about the narrowing of the Orthodox mindset. The movement's failure to express itself in the Jewish ideological spectrum stems directly from its failure to assert itself, forcefully, within Orthodoxy itself. And the results, quite simply, have been devastating.

There is no question that Orthodoxy has moved substantially to the Right. There are many practices and customs along those lines today that simply didn't exist twenty years ago: separate seating at concerts and weddings; no watching of television at all. We have today a situation where a principal of one of the Yeshiva University High Schools is reported to have said that he doesn't approve of Yeshiva University's stated motto of *Torah Umaddah* (Torah & Science).

In my own town of Great Neck, which is still a Modern Orthodox community, parents wanted to enroll their two year old child in the local yeshiva's toddler class. But when they found out that the teacher was not planning to discuss the weekly portion of the Torah reading with the class as part of the curriculum, they refused to enroll her. And how does one teach the Torah portion in a meaningful way to a two year old?

I know of a principal in a Modern Orthodox day school who did not allow seventh grade male team members of the school's basketball team to wear sleeveless uniforms because it wasn't "modest attire." This same individual refused to permit a nine year old girl to dress up as a Hasid on Purim. The question isn't so much what the law is, but rather why there is such an emphasis on these things today?

Telling a third grader in a yeshiva that her relative got cancer because she watched too much television—Is that appropriate? Or that if you travel in an automobile on the Sabbath, God will personally punish you. Is this how you bring people closer to Judaism?

One of the problems in the community is this notion that every Jewish young man is entitled to spend years of his adulthood studying all day in a yeshiva, regardless of whether they're really capable of successfully studying at such an intense level. Call it the "proletarianization" of the *Kollel* (post-college institution). Naturally, this causes economic dislocation. Thus, one man living in Boro Park observed that people in his circles cannot retire on their pensions because if they do, their grandchildren will starve.

Now let's look at the "year in an Israeli yeshiva" programs. When they first began they were moderate; but as the years went on they became more and more Right Wing. One of the heads of these yeshivas for boys addressed a group of girls in a high school with his eyes shut because he did not want to look at them.

Some of the yeshivas, while purporting to be Modern Orthodox, refuse to say the *Hallel* service on Israel Independence Day, "We're not anti-Zionists," they say, "just neutral." Others mimic the Right Wing yeshivas by allowing very little study of Prophets or Jewish law, insisting that 90% of all course work be in Talmud. It's certainly legitimate, but it does indicate a different approach than was previously the case in such schools. It's one which I respect, but I have to ask those of you in the audience if it's the one you want.

The yeshivas also invite *Haredi* speakers to lecture the students. As more and more young men who arrived in knitted-yarmulkes, return sporting black hats and criticizing their Orthodox parents for being, in their eyes, insufficiently observant, it has gradually begun to dawn on the parents that these schools may be practicing indoctrination rather than providing an education and a love for the State of Israel. Again, this is fine if that's what you want.

There are still quite a few yeshivas who espouse more moderate views in the same path as that followed by the Modern Orthodox high schools in America, but they have a lot of competition. Not surprisingly, some schools here report a bit of a backlash in terms of sending children to study in Israel, as parents become apprehensive about what their loved ones are really being taught.

And then we have the sad story, as told by Rabbi Jacob J. Schachter in the 1990 issue of *The Torah U-Madda Journal,* about the book produced by Artscroll Publishers, *My Uncle, the Netziv.* The book was an English translation of a volume writing by the Netziv's (Rabbi Naftali Zvi Yehudah Berlin) nephew, Rabbi Boruch Halevi Epstein. The book contained the following points among others: The Netziv read secular newspapers, even on the Sabbath; he discussed current events at the Sabbath table; the Netziv had secular books in his library; and secular studies were, in fact, taught for a short time at his famed Volozhin Yeshiva, albeit under duress.

When these revelations became known in the Right Wing yeshiva world, the book was immediately withdrawn from circulation. Those who run that world were simply unable to admit that the Netziv, a revered Rosh Yeshiva, had such enlightened views. Refunds were offered for returned books, but there were reportedly few takers. After all, the yeshiva world's "banned in Boston" book was now an underground best seller.

But if the yeshiva world engages in censorship, today's Modern Orthodox do not seem far behind, looking constantly, it seems, over their Right shoulder. You can follow Agudah if you want. But if you do you will always be a paler shade of black, lacking real passion and conviction. This is no way to build a movement.

Why was there a move to the Right? For the following reasons:

1. The Right Wing had charismatic leadership.
2. Its members had a higher birth rate.

3. The immigrant post World War Two generation was more Right Wing in its orientation.

4. They had better political organization.

5. The Right Wing saw the rest of the world and said, in effect, "Look at what's going on out there. What we have is far better." The moral laxness in society at large made the Orthodox feel insecure. And in that kind of situation people need to find new restrictions (*"chumrahs"*) to prove how religious they are. The older generation didn't have this need. *Kolisha,* listening to a woman sing a song, is now treated by many in the Orthodox community as the same as not eating kosher food, a view that has entered many Modern Orthodox circles.

    (This despite the well-known fact that listening to a woman sing an opera was fully permitted by the great Rabbi Joseph B. Soloveitchik. And, I might add, he also favored co-education, which was the case at the Maimonides School in Boston, which he founded.)

6. *Ba'alei teshuvah* [returnees to religious observance] especially, need constant reassurance that they are truly doing God's will and chumrahs provide that reassurance.

7. The influence of the Hasidim, the "Hasidization" of Orthodoxy, as it were, has also moved Orthodoxy to the Right.

8. The volume and complexity of minutiae regarding Orthodox observance give greater respect and authority to the rabbis because it is they who decide what the new ones are and how they are to be observed. The more chumrahs and the more widely observed they are, the more important the role of the rabbis.

9. Significantly too, the Modern Orthodox are victims of their own success. After all, the Modern Orthodox were told by their leaders—"Go to college, you can be a doctor, lawyer, whatever, and still be fully Ortho-dox." So, they went into the professions. They did not, by and large, enter Jewish education. Thus, it was left to the Right Wing yeshiva graduates to become rebbes, or teachers. And so their ideology prevails more and more in the curriculum being taught to children of Modern Orthodox parents. And the Modern Orthodox viewpoint is being lost. You can't have it both ways.

One of my colleagues remarked that Modern Orthodoxy made a deal with the Right Wing: We accept some chumrahs as Modern Orthodox Jews—covering the hair, etc. and you accept the validity of getting a college degree and being loyal to the State of Israel.

The problem is that's not what happened. Less than 5 percent of the students at the Lakewood, N.J.'s, Beth Medrash Govoha Yeshiva have gone to college. And many of the students from Right Wing yeshivas who do study for a B.A. degree enroll in schools where they never set foot inside an actual college. And when they do get degrees, they tend to be in "religiously safe" areas like accounting or computer science. Nothing wrong with that either, if you believe in the primacy of Torah study, but it's not the same as seriously studying philosophy, psychol-ogy, or political theory.

Other scholars of the Jewish Orthodox scene point out that Yeshiva University and its rebbes are increasingly accepted in Right Wing yeshiva circles. True, but this is because YU has become a much more Right Wing school in the last twenty years. Look at the tepid response, or non-response of the Right Wing yeshivas when Rabbi Soloveitchik passed away several years ago. He was given no eulogy whatsoever in their media organs.

In fact, YU, embodies the inconsistencies that characterize Modern Orthodoxy today. While academically a fine school—it was recently ranked 45th nationally among universities—its religious direction is curiously ambiguous. Rabbi Norman Lamm, its President, is definitely Modern Orthodox, but he is under constant attack from his Right Wing rebbes. On the one hand, these rebbes inveigh against kol isha, while at the same time the Women's Organization sponsors evenings at the opera for alumni.

One of Modern Orthodoxy's greatest problems is its lack of leadership. Very few rabbis in the community have been willing to publicly express views that reflect the ideologically progressive philosophy of Modern Orthodoxy, as exemplified by past greats such as Rabbis Azriel Hildescheimer, Samson Raphael Hirsch, and Rabbi Yechiel Weinberg. And I think that part of it is because they're afraid. And I don't blame them. Who wants to be drummed out of a community? Who wants to lose his job?

Those few rabbis who have spoken out, such as Norman Lamm, Maurice Lamm, Saul Berman, Avi Weiss, Yitz Greenberg, and Ronald Price, all men of courage and principle, have been either attacked, or worse, marginalized. Such treatment has silenced others and unless it stops, the future of Modern Orthodoxy is very much in doubt.

Meanwhile, the besieged rabbis of Modern Orthodoxy are drifting farther from their congregants. The life and worldview of a rabbi fighting for legitimacy from the Right is fundamentally different from that of a modern Orthodox congregant looking for leadership. We must find a way to bridge this widening gap.

The central point of my remarks is that if we would present an approach to nonobservant Jews that synthesizes secular and religious knowledge, one that encourages the study of science and philosophy and literature while at the same time stressing the beauty and meaningfulness of a religious life, then Orthodoxy could attract *hundreds of thousands of Jews*, not just thousands. This is because most Jews out there are not willing to retreat into a closed off world. It's not worth it to them. But many of them are dying spiritually. If an Orthodoxy that doesn't bury its head in the sand can be presented to them, then perhaps they can be reached. The fact is, one can be a full participant in the larger society and be a completely observant Jew. That is the essence of Modern Orthodoxy.

Notwithstanding these criticisms, there are some very positive things happening. The picture is not all that bleak. Orthodoxy has been accepted by both the larger Jewish community and by America in general. In part, this is due to the popularity of cultural pluralism but it is also because many American Jews are losing their children to assimilation, while anti-Semitism, the memory of the Holocaust, and Israel, are receding as focal points of Jewish identity.

As a result, religion and spirituality are becoming more important and in this context Orthodox Judaism is a very viable option. American Jews have a sufficient degree of loyalty to their roots to want their children to remain Jews even if this means that they'll be quite observant.

The greater emphasis on kashruth, for which the OU deserves much credit has greatly strengthened Orthodoxy. The fact that so many products have kosher labels serves as a constant reminder to people that identifying and living as a Jew is "in." This is critical because Jews, as a threatened group have always craved acceptance and any group that can provide it has cache. Many Jews have always felt vaguely guilty about playing down their Jewishness. They know it's wrong.

When a Noach Dear walks out of a City Council meeting wearing his yarmulke, what do nonobservant Jews think, they who opted for the tradeoff of blending in to gain a place at the American table? Those of you who still get HBO could have seen an entire segment last week on the popular "Larry Sanders Show" devoted to a ba'al teshuvah who said he's going to wear his *kippah* while on his job at the television studio (the show's setting).

Take Murray Laulicht, the president of New Jersey's Metro West Federation. Most of his community is not Orthodox and Laulicht is, but it's simply not an issue. The same is true for many other Federations and major Jewish organizations where Orthodox Jews are in positions of influence.

The fact is that Orthodoxy today has a voice. People from the OU, like Mendy Ganchrow, others in the Agudah and the Young Israel, have become articulate spokesmen, expressing the community's position on a host of issues such as affirmative action, abortion, race relations, and separation of church and state.

There are problems in all segments of the Orthodox community, right and left—rising divorce rates, spouse abuse, cheating on welfare, financial scandals, etc., you name it. Nonetheless, on the whole, they're probably doing a lot better than the rest of the Jewish world and that should be stressed too.

There are some very good programs also that are sponsored by the Orthodox. For example, Touro College has announced plans to open a four year American-accredited university in Israel that will be open to both observant and nonobservant students from the United States. There is no such school in Israel today and its creation would be an important step in promoting Jewish identity for its youth, who, after all, represent the future of the community. Similarly, the OU's NCSY Programs, provided they remain tolerant in their approach, can do much good.

If it wants to save itself, Modern Orthodoxy should renew its commitment to its principles, which go all the way back to Maimonides. *Extremism represents the outer margins of our fears and insecurities.* Don't give in to it. Show yourselves and your children that you can do both.

I conclude with the words of Rachel Wohlgelernter, a graduate of Yeshiva University's Los Angeles High School, who wrote a very thoughtful piece that appears in the current issue of the OU's publication, *Jewish Action.* Currently a student at Michlallah, a one year yeshiva program in Israel, she plans to enter Yale University next year.

> Clearly even in the finest of secular colleges the existing social realities mirror the decadence of our culture. Am I prepared, I wonder, to immerse myself in such an unwholesome environment and still retain an unwavering commitment to *Yiddishkeit?* . . .
>
> As *frum* [rigorously observant] teens, we dare not solely pay heed to the untempered voice of our reason or intuition. Additionally, we need to recognize that the immutable Torah ethic, as opposed to subjective societal ethics, is the rule by which modern man should live. . . .

In Jewish high schools today, learning *Tanach* [Bible and Prophets] with commentaries is insufficient preparation for the challenges we will face. We must emerge from high school with a lucid understanding of our responsibility to embody the ideals of *Torah im derech eretz*. As Rav Samson Raphael Hirsch explained, this concept mandates the realization of the Torah in harmonious unity with all the conditions under which its laws will have to be observed amidst the developments of changing times. . . .

The Torah does not demand the withdrawal of the Jew from the world. Nor does it view such a retreat as an ideal. Accordingly, instead of dissuading students from attending secular colleges, the Judaic teachers at yeshiva high schools might undertake the weighty responsibility of demonstrating that the Torah contains the answer to every social and spiritual question which concerns modern man and that every subject is within the purview of the Torah. . . .

Sending students to face the world with faith as their only weapon, is like sending 20th century soldiers to combat with only bows and arrows. To prevent ourselves from faltering, we, the young American Jews, now more than ever, need to avail ourselves of every resource in order to bolster our absolute convictions and place our trust in the timeless and invaluable handbook that is our Torah.

PART FOUR

Zionism and Judaism in the State of Israel

Any account of Judaism in modern times must include Zionism among Judaisms and the state of Israel among the most important locations, along with Europe and North and Latin America, where Judaisms are practiced. Begun outside the framework of any Judaism, Zionism was put forth by a secular Jew, Theodor Herzl, as a solution to a secular political problem—anti-Semitism in the form of political parties advocating a public policy of exclusion and, ultimately, mass murder of the Jews. But Zionism proved a complex body of thought and activity, involving reformulations of some Judaisms within the framework of Orthodox, and responses to Zionism on the part of several Judaisms formed a principal chapter in the history of Judaism in the twentieth century.

We start with Zionism, which created the state of Israel. The picture given in *The Way of Torah* of the role of the state of Israel in contemporary Judaic life leaves the unbalanced view that the state of Israel forms part of the Jews' response to the Holocaust and that the importance of the state of Israel within Judaism derives from its place in the aftermath of that catastrophe. Before the advent of the state of Israel in 1948, however, as an approach to the formation of the social order of Jews quite different from the Judaic-religious one, Zionism had long labored not only to bring the Jewish state into being, but also to present a theory of what the Jews were as a social group, an account of the way of life that that group ought to live, and a worldview that explained the one and lent meaning to the other.

Zionism defined a Judaism in structure, but not a conventional Judaism in content, lacking as it did a religious dimension for its worldview and taking a secular position on principal matters. The Jews were to constitute a people, one people, and make of themselves a political entity, so aiming at the creation of the Jewish state as a secular solution to a this-worldly political crisis. Zionism is omitted from *The Way of Torah*, but any effort to round out the picture, both for Judaism in modern times in general and also for Judaism in North America in particular, requires attention to that powerful Jewish (if not Judaic) system.

Zionism is included in the setting of the practice of Judaism in contemporary North America because of its importance to North American Jewry, past and present. In *The Way of Torah* I construct an ideal type for the analysis of Judaism, in which I carefully differentiate between secular Jewishness and religious Judaism. Zionism here is set forth as an essentially secular system; yet we quickly see that in its structure it corresponds to the shape of any Judaic religious system. And more to the point, there are important ways in which Judaism and Zionism flow together, each shaping the direction of the other.

Next we take up the practice of Judaism in that other center where the faith lives and evolves, the state of Israel. The state of Israel competes with the United

States in the variety and vitality of the Judaisms that flourish in its midst. Most, though not all, of the Judaic religious systems that flourish in the state of Israel fall into the classification of "Orthodox," affirming the Oral and Written Torah as the literal record of God's verbatim revelation at Sinai. While nearly wholly falling within the classification of Orthodox Judaism because of important shared convictions about the origin and divine authority of the Torah, the Judaisms of the state of Israel divide on much else. The dividing lines are many. First comes Zionism. Some of the Orthodox Judaisms of the state of Israel deny that Zionism is a legitimate theory of Jewish existence and reject the notion that there can be a Jewish state, a state of Israel. They hold that only God through the Messiah can found the state of Israel. Other Orthodox Judaisms affirm the state of Israel as legitimate within Judaism, that is, by the law of the Torah. Still others regard the state of Israel as the beginning of the advent of the age of redemption and maintain that possessing the whole of the Land of Israel of which the Torah speaks as Israel's heritage represents the principal task of the present generation.

Another point of division is set by modern learning and culture. Some Orthodox Judaisms in the state of Israel affirm the union of science and religion and integrate secular and sacred subjects. That is by reason of conviction as well as necessity. Other Orthodox Judaisms maintain that one may master secular subjects only so far as these are needed for practical reasons, that is, for making a living. Still others reject altogether all contact with modern culture, including learning.

Reform and Conservative Judaisms in the state of Israel also have their own communities and convictions. These other-than-Orthodox Judaisms form a very small proportion of the practitioners of a Judaism in the state of Israel and exercise remarkably slight influence. A vast population of secular Jews, who practice no religion at all but define "being Jewish" in national terms within the framework of Israeli nationalism and its culture, completes the Jewish population of the country.

A systematic account of matters is presented by Israeli social scientist Shlomo Deshen, who stresses the social foundations of Judaisms. What makes Deshen's essay deserving of attention long after its original publication is his stress on two points. First, Deshen recognizes the diversity of Judaisms and does not propose a single uniform picture. Second, he underscores that no one Judaism may claim to constitute the natural outgrowth of "tradition" and deems all equally other than traditional; in this way he avoids making theological judgments about matters of social description. Rather, he identifies patterns of religiosity. Deshen's essay has the further merit of deepening our understanding of the social foundations of the various Judaisms in modern times in Europe and its diaspora as well. He enriches our grasp of the ecology of Judaism in the nineteenth and twentieth centuries, identifying the major trends that characterize Jews' response to the challenges of social and political change in the modern age.

When we take up the topics of Zionism and the practice of Judaism in the state of Israel, we cross that frontier between religion and ethnicity that the Jews straddle. Here, therefore, is a suitable occasion for a systematic account of the interplay of religion and ethnicity in Judaism, both in the United States and in the state of Israel, the two important locations for the practice of Judaism.

What we have read to this point about New Age Judaism has alerted us to the distinction between "feeling Jewish," an ethnic sentiment that may or may not encompass religious attitudes, and practicing Judaism, a religious conviction that overspreads ethnic identification. And Zionism, like counterpart Judaisms, finds itself on both sides of that same frontier, with a religious formulation of Zionism in contemporary Reform, Conservative, and Orthodox Judaisms and a secular, political formulation addressed to ethnic Jews as well.

How are we to form a perspective on the confusion of categories ordinarily kept distinct? Certainly no confusion of the ethnic with the religious presents more anomalies than the mixture of ethnic Jewishness and religious Judaism that American Jews have concocted for themselves. But the brew is fresh, not vintage. For nearly the entire history of the Jews, to be a Jew meant to practice the religion set forth in the Torah revealed by God to Moses at Sinai, which the world knows as "Judaism." A Jew who gave up Judaism adopted some other religion and ceased to identify himself or herself with the Jews as a group. The religion, Judaism, defined the group at both the entry and the exit points.

For the entire history of Judaism, and for most of the history of the Jews, the definition of the Jewish group invoked purely theological categories. In that religion the Jews are called "Israel," meaning the Israel of which Scriptures speak, the holy social entity ("people," "nation") that God called into being through the saints beginning with Abraham and Sarah. Belonging to imposes divine requirements: (1) belief in the one God who created Heaven and earth and made himself known to Abraham, Isaac, and Jacob, then to Moses at Sinai and to prophets thereafter, (2) commandments that define the holy way of life that marks Israel as God's people. So "Israel" in Judaism corresponds to the religious social entity Christianity calls "Church" or "mystical body of Christ." "Only you have I known of all the families of man, therefore I will visit on you all your iniquities," "all Israelites have a portion in the world to come [when the dead are resurrected] except for . . ."—these formed the center of the identification of the "Israel" of Judaism. Give up the Judaism (which calls itself "the Torah") and although the Torah continues to regard you as an Israelite (a sinning Israelite), you would probably not have wanted to stay around.

In that context of faith, historical and classical, "Israel" not only does not correspond to the state of Israel today or to the particular Holy Land, it also has no relationship to the "Jewish People" (the *P* stands for a particular type of group) or the "Jewish community" or any of the other secular formulations of what it means to be a Jew and to belong to the Jewish ethnic group. Above all, no imperative attaches itself to the continuation of the Jewish people, and "Jewish survival" bears no urgency in its own terms. One of the Ten Commandments is to honor father and mother, another is to keep the Sabbath, a third is not to steal. None of the Ten Commandments maintains that God regards as an end in itself the maintenance of the Jews as a distinct social entity.

To show in a simple way what the distinction between the Israel of the Torah and the various secular and cultural definitions of who is a Jew and what the Jewish group is ("People") is easy: until the seventeenth-century philosopher of Jewish origin, Benedict Spinoza, no single instance in which a Jew gave up the religion of the Torah ("Judaism") and remained Jewish—adopting no other religion, affiliating with no other social entity—in some other sense or meaning can be located. That is, from Abraham to Spinoza, to be Israel meant to practice Judaism, and, more to the point, to cease to practice Judaism marked the end of belonging to Israel. (If, for Spinoza, one could be a Jew without practicing Judaism, he did not leave the model of how long secular Jewishness might persist.) That is why historians point to Spinoza as the first secular or "modern" Jew.

But until the middle of the nineteenth century, Spinoza remained a singular figure. So it was taken as the norm that someone who ceased to practice the religion Judaism also abandoned the Jewish group and presumably entered some other religion and its community. When, in the aftermath of the Enlightenment, Jews thought they were gaining entry into the civil society of Western civilization in Germany, France, Britain, and the United States, some, continuing to see themselves as Israelites in the religious meaning of the word, reformed Judaism to fit the new circumstance. Defining Emancipation on the terms of the Torah, others reaffirmed the received meaning of Israel as a people dwelling apart, in God's eternal presence. They framed what they learned to call Orthodox Judaism, integrationist politically and in neutral dimensions of culture, separate religiously, in the many aspects of culture subject to the Torah's commandments. A few remained Jewish without practicing Judaism (yielding the counterpart to religious Judaism in secular Jewishness). But a great many opted out. They are represented by the composer Felix Mendelsohn's father, Karl Marx's father, and Benjamin Disraeli's father, among the many Jews who purchased Christianity as their ticket to Western civilization. During an age in which Jews labored to gain civil rights (calling the movement "Emancipation"), Jews in the West who ceased to practice Judaism commonly adopted the Christianity that ruled in the country of their citizenship (just as, after the massacres of World War II, numerous Jews cut off all ties to not only Judaism but the Jewish group). Until well into the twentieth century, to be a Jew meant to practice Judaism, and to cease to practice Judaism meant to stop being a Jew. If Spinoza really was the first secular Jew, it took a long time to produce a second.

Only toward the end of the nineteenth century did large numbers of European Jews drop Judaism but remain Jewish. Many of these lived in those ethnic mosaics of Central and Eastern Europe where large populations of diverse tradition lived side by side but interacted only as foreigners. There to be a Jew meant to speak Yiddish, to dress in Jewish clothing, to make a living in callings deemed distinctly Jewish, and above all to define the world in a system particular to the Jewish group. To be a Pole or a Ukrainian or a Latvian or a Romanian or a Hungarian bore the same social meanings. In a given city, natives might speak several languages, depending on origin, and points of encounter outside the circle of faith and culture were severely circumscribed. As far to the West as Britain, people took for granted one could be either English by birth or marriage or Jewish, but not both. In the United States today we should call such a definition of culture ethnic tribalization, but in Canada by public policy ethnicity as a medium of social differentiation is subsidized.

It was in that context that Jews who lost the faith sought to frame for themselves a secular definition of who is a Jew and what is "Judaism" or "Jewishness." A Pole of the Jewish persuasion, or an authentic German of the Mosaic persuasion, so far as other Poles or Germans were concerned, was no more plausible than a flying cow or a book-writing horse. Nor did Jews themselves believe it, though in Germany, France, Britain, and the United States, many tried. That left the secular option Jewishness—and, in response to the anti-religious propaganda of the Enlightenment joined to the militant secularism of Socialism, communism, and some formulations of Liberalism, large numbers of Jews exercised that option. But, as we saw in the reports of New Age Judaism in New Mexico, these rigid divisions no longer apply.

For some, the Jewish group would be recast as "a people, one people," which should, and ultimately did, attain a political definition for itself as a nation. Specifically, Zionists thought up and realized the state of Israel. For others, the Jews would form a language community, with Yiddish and renewed Hebrew competing. For Jewish Socialists (as distinct from Jews who left the Jewish world and became socialists or communists), the Jews would form a division in the united army of the international workers of the world; these formed Yiddish-speaking unions of enormous influence. Zionism and the Jewish Works Union, or Bund, took shape in the same year, 1897, and in Eastern Europe the latter became, after the religion Judaism in its classical forms, the single most influential way of "being Jewish." And for some few in Europe, but a great many, a century later in the United States, the Jewish group would form a cultural entity, redefining the religious practices as cultural forms, turning commandments of God into customs and ceremonies.

33 Zionism

JACOB NEUSNER

1. Why is this reading important?

The importance of Zionism in its own framework cannot be overstated. It is a singularly successful political ideology and movement, one that in fifty years from its founding accomplished all of its principal goals. But why study Zionism in the context of Judaism? The reason is that Zionism is the only secular ideology that made an impact upon Judaisms of the twentieth century—not only upon the Jews as an ethnic group, but upon Judaic religious systems across the board. It is important to approach Zionism in its own terms, not only in relationship to the religion, Judaism, and to examine it as a system comparable to a Judaic religious system: its way of life, worldview, and theory of the social entity constituted by its "Israel." Still, if Zionism intersects with several Judaic systems, it also finds its place in the category of national movements of liberation, coming at the end of a century of nation building and at the start of the breakup of the multiethnic empires of Central and Eastern Europe and their replacement with nation-states more or less coextensive with ethnic groups, such as Ukraine, the Czech Republic, Poland, Lithuania, and the like. But Zionism also is not exactly a secular and ethnic political movement. Finally, Zionism is important because after a century of optimism, when Jews in general thought political emancipation a good thing, Zionism took seriously the rise of political anti-Semitism and is the only movement among Jews that could account for the disaster that actually took place in the twentieth century. After the Holocaust, Zionism offered an explanation and a program, and that is why it succeeded in such a remarkable way.

2. What should you notice as you proceed?

The interplay of religion and politics characterizes religions in most of the world, certainly in the state of Israel for Judaism and in all Muslim nations for Islam; and the established position of Christianity in most, though not all, Western democracies is a fact as well. So we want to pay close attention to the Zionist theory of the Jewish state: Is it to be secular or is it meant to realize Judaism, and, if so, which Judaism? But the interplay of religion and public policy—in this case, Judaism and

Socialism—should also capture our attention, for Zionism was joined not only with Judaism by part of Orthodoxy, it also was formulated as a Socialism by Jewish Socialists in Europe and the United States. Finally, Zionism formed the contents of a secular Jewish culture, meant to succeed the religious Judaic culture put forth by (mostly Orthodox) Judaism. It represented the formation of a new tradition for the Jews, one that made use of the received religious tradition to form an essentially secular cultural statement. Above all, pay attention to what is new and fresh in Zionism, which is its theory of who and what "Israel" is. Judaisms spoke of "Israel" in a way comparable to Muslim and Christian understandings of the social order built upon those religions. It was a holy community of the faithful. But Zionism declared the Jews to constitute not a holy community but a political entity, a people in quest of its own nation-state, a people to be empowered. That conviction is Zionism's main contribution, what makes Zionism original and challenging.

3. How should you frame a question for class discussion in response to what you have read?

How to explain the success of Zionism? Models of explanation should be explored here, since that question fits well with the larger issue in the study of any religion: Why does it work when it works, and why does it not work when it does not work? In this reading a strong case is made for the explanation that appeals to relevance. Zionism answered a question that people found urgent. The answer of Zionism to the question of anti-Semitism—the Gentiles hate us, so we have to get out of Europe and found our own state somewhere else—made no sense in 1897 but a great deal of sense in 1937 and attained the status of dogma in 1947, when the United Nations voted to create a Jewish and an Arab state in what was then Palestine. So, to generalize, a religion works when it works because it answers an urgent question with an answer people find self-evidently valid. And it does not work when it fails because, however logical its system of thought, however profound its reshaping of everyday life, the religion answers questions people are not asking. But that theory ignores considerations of plausibility and even demonstrations of truth. A class discussion may well begin with the remarkable success of Christianity in the fourth century C.E., when Constantine legitimated and then adopted the persecuted faith, and the equally amazing success of Islam in the seventh century C.E., when the new religion swept regions that had been Christian for many centuries, the Middle East and North Africa in particular. That opens the further question: Why does a religion collapse when it fails, as Christianity did in the face of Islam and so lost Spain, North Africa from west to east, and most of the Roman (Byzantine) Middle East as well. The same explanation that accounts for the rise of Christianity under Constantine—before a minority cult, afterward the state religion—ought to explain its collapse. Students who have studied Islam in modern times will also want to contribute their knowledge of why Islam failed for so long to meet the challenge of the West, and why it has now become an aggressive force against Christianity within the West itself. Why do religions change over time, and what are the factors that account for the types of change that they exhibit? These questions of theory, shading over into concrete fact, ought to make for an interesting class discussion.

Zionism constituted the Jews' movement of self-emancipation, responding to the failure of the nations'—German, French—promises of Jewish emancipation. So Zionism responded to a political crisis—the failure, by the end of the nineteenth century, of expectations of political improvement in the Jews' status and condition. Zionism called to the Jews to emancipate themselves by facing the fact that Gentiles in the main hated Jews and founding a Jewish state where Jews could free themselves of anti-Semitism and build their own destiny. The Zionist system of Judaism declared that the Jews form one people and should transform themselves into a political entity and build a Jewish state.

Zionism came into existence with the founding of the Zionist Organization in 1897 and reached its fulfilment, and dissolution in its original form, with the founding of the state of Israel in May, 1948. Zionism defined, first of all, its theory of Israel: a people, one people, in a secular sense. Jews all over the world now formed a single entity not alone (or at all) in God's view, but in humanity's. Then came the worldview, which composed of the diverse histories of Jews a single history of the Jewish nation leading from the Land of Israel through exile back to the Land of Israel, a recapitulation of the biblical narrative derived not from a religious but from a nationalist perspective. The elitist's or activist's way of life required participation in meetings, organizing within the local community, attendance at national and international conferences—a focus of life's energy on the movement. Later, as settlement in Israel itself became possible, Zionism defined migration to the Land as the most noble way of living life and, for the Socialist wing of Zionism, building a collective community (kibbutz). In this way Zionism presented a complete and fully articulated Judaism, and, in its day, one of the most powerful and effective of them all.

Since Zionism carried out a political program, its relevance to the study of Judaisms born in modern times requires explanation. Not everything Jews did constituted a Judaism, but Zionism did. In fact, among the Judaic systems of the twentieth century, Zionism took second place only to Jewish Socialism (joined to the affirmation of the Yiddish language as the medium of Jewish identity, hence: Yiddishism) in its attraction to large numbers of Jews. And after World War II, Zionism offered the sole explanation for what had happened and what people then should do: a way of life and a worldview meeting the ineluctable crisis assigned to it by history. Like Jewish Socialism joined with Yiddishism, therefore, Zionism supplied a sizable part of the Jews of Europe and America with a comprehensive account of themselves and what they should do with their lives. And that account involved deeply mythic Judaic truths, as we will presently see.

True, Zionism forms part of a larger idiom of international and modern life, just as much as Socialism does. Zionism takes shape against "the general background of European and Jewish history since the French Revolution . . . and the spread of modern anti-Semitism."[1] Not only so, but Zionism also arose "within the milieu of European nationalism."[2] But Zionism bears traits all its own, as Hertzberg points out in his classic account:

> All of the other nineteenth-century nationalisms based their struggle for political sovereignty on an already existing national land or language. . . . Zionism alone proposed to acquire both of these usual preconditions of national identity by the élan of its nationalist will.[3]

Our interest in Zionism, of course, requires a different focus altogether. Our interest, we recall, is in the analysis of Judaic systems and in the comparison of one system to another.[4]

The word *Zionism* in modern times became into use in the 1890s, with the sense of a political movement of "Jewish self-emancipation." The word "emancipation" had earlier stood for the Jews' receiving political rights as citizens in various nations. So "self-emancipation" turned on its head the entire political program of nineteenth-century Jewry. That shift alerts us to the relationship between Zionism and the earlier political changes of which, at the start of the century, Reform Judaism had made so much. Clearly the history of the Jews, then as earlier, would contribute the main themes for the Judaisms that would emerge; no surprise there. But the particular themes of the Zionist system derived from rather specific events. What had happened in the course of the nineteenth century to shift discourse from emancipation to self-emancipation?

First were the disappointments with the persistence of anti-Semitism in the West. Second were the disheartening failures to attain political rights in the East. Jews concluded that they would have to attain emancipation on their own terms and through their own efforts. The stress on Zionism as a political movement, however, came specifically from Theodor Herzl, a Viennese journalist who, in response to the resurgence of anti-Semitism he witnessed in Paris, discovered the Jewish problem and proposed its solution. To be sure, Herzl had earlier given thought to the problem of anti-Semitism, and the public anti-Semitism that accompanied the degradation of Dreyfus, a Jewish officer falsely accused of treason, marked merely another stage in the development of his ideas. What Herzl contributed, in the beginning, was the notion that the Jews all lived in a single situation, wherever they were located. They should then live in a single country, in their own state (wherever it might be located). Anti-Semitism formed the antithesis of Zionism, and anti-Semites, growing in strength in European politics, would assist the Jews in building their state and thereby also solve their "Jewish problem."

The solution entailed the founding of a Jewish state, and that formed a wholly new conception with a specific worldview, and concrete, detailed program for the

---

[1]Walter Laqueur, *A History of Zionism* (New York: Holt, Rinehart and Winston, 1972), xiii.

[2]Arthur Hertzberg, *The Zionist Idea. A Historical Analysis and Reader* (N.Y., 1959: Doubleday and Co., Inc. and Herzl Press), p. 15.

[3]Ibid., p. 15.

[4]Again, the program of Max Weber.

conduct of life. For the Jews were now to become something that they had not been for that "two thousand years" of which Zionism persistently spoke: a political entity. The Judaism of the dual Torah made no provision for a this-worldly politics, and no political tradition had sustained itself during the long period in which that Judaism had absorbed within itself and transformed all other views and modes of life. In founding the Zionist Organization in Basel in 1897, Herzl said that he had founded the Jewish state, and that, in a half century, the world would know it, as indeed the world did.

Three main streams of theory flowed abundantly and side by side in the formative decades. One, represented by Ahad HaAm, laid stress on Zion as a spiritual center, to unite all parts of the Jewish people. Ahad HaAm and his associates laid emphasis on spiritual preparation, ideological and cultural activities, and the long-term intellectual issues of persuading the Jews of the Zionist premises.[5]

Another stream, the political one, maintained from the beginning that the Jews should provide for the emigration of the masses of their nation from Eastern Europe, then entering a protracted state of political disintegration and already long suffering from economic dislocation, to the land of Israel—or somewhere, anywhere. Herzl in particular placed the requirement for legal recognition of a Jewish state over the location of the state and, in doing so, set forth the policy that the practical salvation of the Jews through political means would form the definition of Zionism. Herzl stressed that the Jewish state would come into existence in the forum of international politics.[6] The instruments of state—a political forum, a bank, a mode of national allegiance, a press, a central body and leader—came into being in the aftermath of the first Zionist congress in Basel. Herzl spent the rest of his life—less than a decade—seeking an international charter and recognition of the Jews' state.

A third stream derived from Socialism and expressed a Zionist vision of Socialism or a Socialist vision of Zionism. The Jewish state was to be socialist—as indeed, for its first three decades, it was. Socialist Zionism in its earlier theoretical formulation (before its near-total bureaucratization) emphasized that a proletarian Zionism would define the arena for the class struggle within the Jewish people to be realized. Ber Borochov, ideologist for this Zionism, explained:

> Jewish immigration is slowly tending to divert itself to a country where petty Jewish capital and labor may be utilized in such forms of production as will serve as a transition from an urban to an agricultural economy and from the production of consumers' goods to more basic forms of industry. . . . This land will be the only one available to the Jews. . . . It will be a country of low cultural and political development. Big capital will hardly find use for itself there, while Jewish petty and middle capital will find a market for its products. . . . The land of spontaneously concentrated Jewish immigration will be Palestine. . . . Political territorial autonomy in Palestine is the ultimate aim of Zionism. For proletarian Zionists, this is also a step toward socialism.[7]

---

[5]S. Ettinger, "Hibbat Zion," in "Zionism," *Encyclopaedia Judaica* 16:1031–1178.

[6]Arthur Hertzberg, "Ideological Evolution," in "Zionism," *Encyclopaedia Judaica* 16:1044–1045.

[7]Cited in Arthur Hertzberg, ed., *The Zionist Idea. A Historical Analysis and Reader* (New York: Doubleday and Herzl Press, 1959): pp. 365–366.

The Socialist Zionists predominated in the settlement of the Land of Israel and controlled the political institutions for three quarters of a century. They founded the labor unions, the large-scale industries, the health institutions and organizations. They controlled the national institutions that were taking shape. They created the press, the nascent army—the nation. No wonder that for the first quarter-century after independence, the Socialist Zionists made all the decisions and controlled everything.

They formed a distinctive way of life, finding their ideal in collective settlements in farming, and they expressed a worldview entirely their own: the building of an ideal society by Israel, the Jewish nation, on its own land, in agriculture. The Socialist Zionists accepted the Socialist critique of the Jews as a people made up of parasites, not productive workers. They held that the Jews should create a productive society of their own, so that they could enter the arena of the class struggle, which would result in due course in the creation of a classless society. It is a somewhat complicated notion. Socialist Zionism maintained that the Jews had first to constitute an appropriately divided society of classes, and this they would accomplish only when they formed their own nation. They had further to enter productive economies and build an economy of their own. Then the Jews would work out the class struggle in terms appropriate to their nation and produce the classless society. The creation of a Jewish national economy took on importance as the mode of establishing a healthy class struggle; above all, physical labor and the development of rootedness in the soil would accomplish that goal. That thesis carried within itself the prescription of the way of life that would lead to the founding of collective farms and the building of a Jewish agricultural life in the land of Israel.

Zionism as a political movement enjoys its own audience. For our purpose, it is the Zionism that functioned as a Judaism that draws our attention to the movement. In this regard Ahad HaAm made the explicit claim that Zionism would succeed Judaism, as Hertzberg says:

> The function that revealed religion had performed in talmudic and medieval Judaism, that of guaranteeing the survival of the Jews as a separate entity because of their belief in the divinely ordained importance of the Jewish religion and people, it was no longer performing and could not be expected to perform. The crucial task facing Jews in the modern era was to devise new structures to contain the separate individual of the Jews and to keep them loyal to their own tradition. This analysis of the situation implied . . . a view of Jewish history which Ahad HaAm produced as undoubted . . . that the Jews in all ages were essentially a nation and that all other factors profoundly important to the life of this people, even religion, were mainly instrumental values.[8]

Hertzberg contrasts that statement with one made a thousand years earlier by Saadiah, in the tenth century: "The Jewish people is a people only for the sake of its Torah." That statement of the Judaism of the dual Torah contrasts with that of Zionism and allows us to set the one against the other as Judaisms. For, as is clear, each proposed to answer the same type of questions, and the answers provided

---

[8]Hertzberg, "Ideological Evolution," col. 1046.

by each enjoyed the status of not mere truth but fact—and not merely fact but just and right and appropriate fact.

Herzl's thesis, in contrast to Ahad HaAm's, laid stress on the power of anti-Semitism to keep the Jews together, and that was the problem he proposed to solve. So Ahad HaAm's conception serves more adequately than Herzl's to express a worldview within Zionism comparable to the worldview of a Judaism. Hertzberg points out that Ahad HaAm described the Jews' "national spirit as an authoritative guide and standard to which he attributed a majesty comparable to that which the religious had once ascribed to the God of revelation." That conception competed with another, which laid stress on the re-creation of the Jews in a natural and this-worldly sense, "a bold and earthy people, whose hands would not be tied by the rules of the rabbis or even the self-doubts of the prophets."[9]

Debates within Zionism focused on the differences between the narrowly political Zionists, who wished to stress work in the Diaspora, and the cultural Zionists. By World War I, Zionist progress in European Jewry proved considerable, and with the British conquest of Palestine, the Balfour Declaration, a statement issued on November 2, 1917, supplied that charter that Herzl had sought in his lifetime: the British government declared itself to favor a Jewish national home in Palestine, provided that the civil and religious rights of non-Jews in the country were protected. That same declaration won the endorsement of other countries, and Zionism began to move from the realm of the system formation to the work of nation building. Its three principal theoretical statements had come to expression.

Let us then turn to the analysis of Zionism as a Judaic system. For one thing, Zionism enunciated a powerful doctrine of Israel. The Jews form a people, one people. Given the Jews' diversity, people could more easily concede the supernatural reading of Judaic existence than the national construction given to it. For, scattered across the European countries as well as in the Moslem world, Jews did not speak a single language, follow a single way of life, or adhere in common to a single code of belief and behavior. What made them a people, one people and further validated their claim and right to a state, of their own, constituted the central theme of the Zionist worldview. No facts of perceived society validated that view. In no way, except for a common fate, did the Jews form a people, one people. True, in Judaic systems they commonly did. But the Judaic system of the dual Torah and its continuators imputed to Israel, the Jewish people, a supernatural status, a mission, a calling, a purpose. Zionism did not: a people, one people—that is all.

What makes Zionism especially interesting as a theory that imputes to Judaism a single, linear and incremental history? It is that Zionist theory, more than Yiddishism and Socialism, sought roots for its principal ideas in the documents of the received Judaism of the dual Torah. Zionist theory had the task of explaining how the Jews formed a people, one people, and in the study of "Jewish history," read as a single and unitary story, Zionist theory solved that problem. The Jews all came from one place, traveled together, and were going back to that same one place as one people. Zionist theory therefore derived strength from the

---

[9]Ibid., col. 1047.

study of history, much as had Reform Judaism, and in time generated a great renaissance of Judaic studies as the scholarly community of the nascent Jewish state took up the task at hand. The sort of history that emerged took the form of factual and descriptive narrative. But its selection of facts, its recognition of problems requiring explanation, its choice of what mattered and what did not—all of these definitive questions found answers in the larger program of nationalist ideology. So the form was secular and descriptive, but the substance ideological in the extreme.

At the same time, Zionist theory explicitly rejected the precedent formed by that Torah, selecting as its history not the history of the faith, but the history of the nation Israel construed as a secular entity. Zionism defined episodes as history, linear history, Jewish history, and appealed to those strung-together events as vindication for its program of action. So we find a distinctive worldview that explains a very particular way of life and defines for itself that Israel to which it wishes to speak. True, like Reform Judaism, Zionism found the Written Torah more interesting than the Oral. And in its search for a usable past, it turned to documents formerly neglected or treated as not authoritative such as the book of Maccabees. As we shall see, Zionism went in search of heroes unlike those of the present—warriors, political figures, and others who might provide a model for the movement's future, and for the projected state beyond. Instead of rabbis or sages, Zionism chose figures such as David the warrior king, Judah Maccabee, who had led the revolt against the Syrian Hellenists, or Samson the powerful fighter. These figures provided the appropriate heroes for a Zionism that proposed to redefine Jewish consciousness, to turn storekeepers into soldiers, lawyers into farmers, corner grocers into builders and administrators of great institutions of state and government. The Judaism of the dual Torah treated David as a rabbi. The Zionist system of Judaism saw David as a hero in a more worldly sense: a courageous nation builder.

In its eagerness to appropriate a usable past, Zionism, and Israeli nationalism its successor, dug for roots in the sands of history. In pre-state times and after the creation of the state of Israel in 1948, Zionist scholars and institutions devoted great effort to digging up the ancient monuments of the Land of Israel, finding in archaeological work the link to the past that the people, one people, so desperately sought. Archaeology uncovered the Jews' roots in the Land of Israel and became a principal instrument of national expression, much as, for contemporary believers in Scripture, archaeology would prove the truths of the biblical narrative. It was not surprising, therefore, that in the Israeli War of Independence in 1948–1949, and in later times as well, Israeli generals explained to the world that by following the biblical record of the nation they had found hidden roads, appropriate strategies—in all, the key to victory.

So Zionism framed its worldview by inventing—or selecting—a past for itself. Its appeal for legitimation invoked the precedent of history, or, rather, Jewish history, much as did Reform. Orthodoxy, in its (quite natural) appeal to the past as the record of its valid conduct in the present, also produced an argument of the same sort. None of the exemplary figures Zionism chose for itself, of course, served as did their counterpart components in Reform, Orthodox, and Conservative Judaisms, to link the new movement to the received Torah. As we saw, Zionism sought a new kind of hero as a model for the new kind of Jew it proposed to call into being. Like Socialism and Yiddishism, Zionism in its appeal to history represented a deliberate act of rejection of the received Torah and construction of a new system altogether. But Zionism found far richer and more serviceable than Socialism and Yiddishism the inherited writings and made more ample use of them. Its particular stress, as time went on, focused upon the biblical portrait of Israel's possession of the Land of Israel.

We should not find surprising, therefore, the power of Zionism to appropriate those components of the received writings that it found pertinent and to reshape them into a powerful claim upon continuity, indeed in behalf of the self-evidence of the Zionist position: the Jews form a people, one people, and should have the land back and build a state on it. Calling the new Jewish city Tel Aviv, for example, invoked the memory of Ezekiel's reference to a Tel Aviv, and that only symbolizes much else. No wonder, then, that professors at the Hebrew University of Jerusalem in later times would confuse their own scholarly authority with Isaiah's promise that Torah would go forth from Zion and the word of God from Jerusalem. It was a perfectly natural identification of past and present, an appeal not for authority alone to a historical precedent, but rather a reentry into a perfect world of mythic being, an eternal present. Zionism would reconstitute the age of the Return to Zion in the time of Ezra and Nehemiah, so carrying out the prophetic promises. The mode of thought, again, is entirely reminiscent of that of Reform Judaism—which, to be sure, selected a different perfect world of mythic being, a golden age other than the one that to Zionism glistened so brightly.

Yet the continuity should not be overstated. For alongside the search of Scripture, Zionism articulated a very clear perception of what it wished to find there. And what Zionism did not find, it deposited on its own: celebration of the nation as a secular, not a supernatural category, imposition of the nation and its heroism in place of the heroic works of the supernatural God. A classic shift took the verse of Psalms, "Who will retell the great deeds of God," producing "Who will retell the great deeds of Israel," and that only typifies the profound revisioning of Israel's history accomplished by Zionism. Israel in its dual Torah formed a supernatural entity, a social unit unlike any other on the face of the earth. All humanity divided into two parts, Israel and the (undifferentiated) nations. The doctrine of Israel in the Judaism given literary expression in Constantine's day, moreover, maintained that the one thing Israel should not do is arrogant deeds. That meant waiting on God to save Israel, assigning to Israel the task of patience, loyalty, humility, obedience, all in preparation for God's intervention. The earliest pronouncements of a Zionist movement, received in the Jewish heartland of Eastern Europe like the ram's horn blown for the coming Messiah, for that same reason impressed the sages of the dual Torah as blasphemy. God will do it—or it will not be done. Considerable time would elapse before the avatars of the dual Torah could make their peace with Zionism, and some of them never did.

The doctrine of Israel joined together with well-considered doctrines, competing with those of Socialism, on how to solve what was then called the "Jewish problem." That same doctrine told Jews what they should do, which, as in the Socialist case, entailed a great deal of organizing and politicking. The worldview, centered on Israel's (potential) nationhood, absorbed much of the idealism of liberal nationalism in the nineteenth century and imparted to it a distinctively Judaic character. Claiming that in its formative decades Zionism constituted a Judaism—a way of life, a worldview, addressed to a social group and lived out by that group—certainly accords with the facts of the matter.

When it reached fulfilment, Zionism described the way of life it prescribed in a simple way: living in the Land of Israel, and, still, later, building the state of Israel. The worldview of Zionism in contemporary times came to coincide with the policies and programs of the government of the state of Israel. In the beginning, however, when Zionism fairly laid claim to compete with Socialism and Yiddishism, on one side, and the continuator Judaisms of Reform and Orthodoxy, on the other, matters were different. Then Zionism formed a distinctive way of life, to be lived out in daily life by its adherents, and further taught a particular worldview, very much its own.

Zionism comprised a movement led by intellectuals—not scholars, but also not workers. Its earliest members thought about action, debated with pleasure, and laid their hopes in ideas. Speaking of the Zionist labor movement in what was then Palestine, Anita Shapira characterizes a large sector of the movement:

> The labor movement was response to the written word, to education, to dialog. . . . Its faith in the power of words was an integral part of its belief that society could be changed by educating mankind and raising their social consciousness.[10]

If there is a single activity characteristic of the several Judaisms of the twentieth century, it is the capacity to sit long and talk intensely at meetings. Zionism found its way of life in organizational activity, much as did the other political and mass movements put forth by Judaisms of the twentieth century. In terms of concrete activity, nothing differentiated the Jewish Socialist from the Zionist in Warsaw or New York—except *which* meeting he went to. We should not miss the power of this kind of activity, its ritual quality, its capacity to express in rather mundane and undistinguished gesture a very deep commitment.

Accordingly, Zionism is to be compared to Jewish Socialism and to Yiddishism. As to the former, its way of life encompassed a Socialism of its own, as we have already noted, and the Zionist Socialists built a most attractive and distinctive way of life in the kibbutz communities, collective farms, which captured the imagination of world Socialism and of Jewry as well. Zionism in its Socialist version furthermore concurred with Socialism that conflict derived from class struggle. National conflicts derived from social tensions, and fraternity between the workers of the peoples will resolve them.[11] The brotherhood of peoples will resolve the Zionist-Arab national conflict, so the Zionist Socialist maintained.

In its competition with Yiddishism, Zionism adopted the renewed Hebrew language and made a principal indicator of Zionist loyalty the study of the Hebrew language, which, of course, later became the national language of the Jews of the state of Israel. So in these two ways, Zionism offered its counterpart to the ways of life posited by the competing movements, the one with its picture of class struggle and regeneration, the other with its doctrine of the language as bearer of values. But Zionism bore within itself traits to which the other movements lacked all counterpart, and that explains its enduring power to capture the imagination of the Jewish people.

---

[10]Anita Shapira, *Berl: The Biography of a Socialist Zionist. Berl Katznelson 1887–1944* (Cambridge: Cambridge University Press, 1974), p. 137.

[11]Ibid., p. 167.

The Zionist worldview explicitly competed with the religious one. The formidable statement by Jacob Klatzkin (1882–1948) provides the solid basis for comparison:

> In the past there have been two criteria of Judaism: the criterion of religion, according to which Judaism is a system of positive and negative commandments, and the criterion of the spirit, which saw Judaism as a complex of ideas, like monotheism, messianism, absolute justice, etc. According to both these criteria, therefore, Judaism rests on a subjective basis, on the acceptance of a creed . . . a religious denomination . . . or a community of individuals who share in a *Weltanschauung.* . . . In opposition to these two criteria, which make of Judaism a matter of creed, a third has now arisen, the criterion of a consistent nationalism. According to it, Judaism rests on an objective basis: to be a Jew means the acceptance of neither a religious nor an ethical creed. We are neither a denomination or a school of thought, but members of one family, bearers of a common history. . . . The national definition too requires an act of will. It defines our nationalism by two criteria: partnership in the past and the conscious desire to continue such partnership in the future. There are, therefore, two bases for Jewish nationalism—the compulsion of history and a will expressed in that history.[12]

Klatzkin's stress on "a will expressed in history" of course carries us back to the appeals of Reform and Conservative theologians to facts of history as precedents for faith. Zionists would find it necessary to reread the whole of the histories of Jews and compose of them Jewish History, a single and linear system leading inexorably to the point which, to the Zionist historians, seemed inexorable: the formation of the Jewish state on the other end of time.

Klatzkin defined being a Jew not as something subjective but something objective: "on land and language. These are the basic categories of national being."[13] That definition, of course, would lead directly to the signal of calling the Jewish state "the state of Israel," so making a clear statement of the doctrine formed by Zionism of who is Israel. In contributing, as Klatzkin said, the "territorial-political definition of Jewish nationalism," Zionism offered a genuinely fresh worldview:

> Either the Jewish people shall redeem the land and thereby continue to live, even if the spiritual content of Judaism changes radically, or we shall remain in exile and rot away, even if the spiritual tradition continues to exist.[14]

It goes without saying that, like Christianity at its original encounter with the task of making sense of history, so Zionism posited that a new era began with its formation: "not only for the purpose of making an end to the Diaspora but also in order to establish a new definition of Jewish identity—a secular definition."[15] In this way Zionism clearly stated the intention of providing a worldview instead of that of the received Judaism of the dual Torah and in competition with all efforts of the continuators of that Judaism.

---

[12]Cited in Hertzberg, "Ideological Evolution," p. 317.

[13]Cited in ibid., p. 318.

[14]Cited in ibid., p. 319.

[15]Klatzkin, cited in ibid., p. 319.

Zionism offered not merely a political program, solving secular problems of anti-Semitism and political disabilities. It gave its adherents a vision of a new heaven and a new earth, a salvific way of life and worldview, that drew the system closer in overall structure to the more conventionally religious Judaic systems of the nineteenth century. The vision of the new Jerusalem, promised in Isaiah 65:17–19 and 66:22, can help us to understand people who have yearned for, and then beheld, the new Jerusalem. Any account of Zionism in the context of the new Judaisms of the modern times will require a grasp of the mental world of the Zionists who lived out the experience of salvation. For when we speak of a transition from self-evidence to self-consciousness to a new age of self-evidence, Zionism rises to the head of the agenda.

The creators of the state of Israel, brilliantly described by Amos Elon,[16] formed a cadre of romantic messianists who realized their dream and attained their eschaton. Elon's account of the founders is pertinent to American Jewry, for the same Jews who created the state of Israel also created the American Jewish community as we now know it. They were the emigrants from the heartland of world Jewry, the East European shtetls in Poland, Lithuania, the old Austro-Hungarian empire, White Russia, Rumania, and the Ukraine.[17] Those emigrants, whether to Palestine or to America, endowed their movement with more than this-worldly, rational meaning. They fled not starvation but hell, and their goal was not a better life, but the Promised Land.

We deal with generations of figures who fall into the classification of heroes and saints, not ordinary men and women. For the founders lived for a cause. They had little in the way of private lives. Theirs was a public task, a public arena, as Elon tells us: "Few had hobbies; hardly anyone pursued a sport . . . they pursued and served the idea of Zion Revived. Socialists and Zionists, they were secular rabbis of a new faith of redemption." One cannot improve on Elon's description of these seekers for the new earth and the new heaven: "Resolute and resourceful abroad, at home they often fought one another with a ferocity that seems to characterize the infighting of most revolutions. In their lifetime historical processes normally much longer had shortened sensationally. They had lived their Utopias in their own lives." What was this Utopia? It was the Jewish state, no less. What reasonable man in nineteenth-century Poland could take seriously such a notion, such an aspiration? The condition of the country was pitiful. Why bother?

The answer was, because it is time to bother. As Elon says: "Zionism profoundly affected the lives of men. It gave people, thus far powerless and disenfranchised, a measure of power to decide their own fate." And it gave them something to do—a sense that their private lives might be spent in a great, public, and meaningful cause. It further lent to the otherwise inconsequential affairs of small people a grand, even transcendental, significance. Zionism means more than messianism; it transformed the worldly and natural to whatever modern, secular man may perceive as the other-other-worldly and supernatural. That is what makes Zionism one of the more interesting movements in the history of religions in the postarchaic epoch.

---

[16]In *The Israelis: Founders and Sons* (New York: Holt, Rinehart, and Winston, 1971).

[17]In this connection I recommend Raphael Mahler, *A History of Modern Jewry, 1780–1815* (New York: Schocken, 1971), an extraordinarily rich account of the various communities of European Jewry, especially in the east, during the modern formative period.

What has characterized the postarchaic epoch, if not faith in the twin myths of secularity and democracy? The latter would open society to all people, the former would make the open society worthwhile. But as Elon writes:

> The crucial experience which lies at the origin of Israel as a modern state was the persecution generated by the failure of emancipation and democracy in Europe. Its myth of mission was the creation of a new and just society. This new society was to be another Eden, a Utopia never before seen on sea or land. The pioneers looked forward to the creation of a "new man." A national renaissance, they felt, was meaningless without a structural renewal of society.[18]

Zionism therefore represents the rejection of modernity, of the confidence of modern man in democracy and—because of Zionism's espousal of a "myth of mission" and a renaissance of society—in secularity. For there is nothing wholly secular about Zionism, and there never was. It is not modern, but, as some say, the first of the postmodern religious movements.

The Zionists, so devoted to that dream, did not take seriously their dependence, in the realization of that dream, on others who spent their lives in "real" world. Seeing only visions, they did not perceive their time to dream was paid for by more practical people, who also wanted a dream, one to be lived by others to be sure, and who were willing to pay for the right to a fantasy. Elon portrays Baron Edmond de Rothschild (1848–1934) as resenting "his colonists' European clothes and wanted them to wear the local Arab dress; he insisted they observe meticulously the Jewish Sabbath, dietary, and other laws of orthodox Jewish religion, which he himself . . . ignored." Rothschild was the model for American Jewry later on: "We shall pay a ransom for the absent soul. In exchange, give us pride, purpose, a trace of color and excitement for unheroic lives. We shall pay you to be the new and courageous Jew—to keep the Sabbath on a dangerous hill, to wear *tefillin* in a tank." Rothschild, too, was one of the founders; he too lives on. Elon calls the founders "beggars with dreams," but they were honest brokers of dreams. And what they promised they delivered. In time they invested world Jewry with new purpose, gave meaning to its endurance, promised hope in its darkest hour.

Throughout Elon's account one discovers the evidences of a new rite, a new cult, along with the new myth. He stresses, for example, that the changing of names was not mere routine:

> The Zionist mania for renaming was too widespread to be dismissed as a mere bagatelle. The new names they chose were too suggestive to be ignored as elements in the complicated jigsaw that represents the transient sensibility of an epoch. Names are elementary symbols of identity. They are seldom the heart of the matter, but they often shed a sharp light on where the heart can be found. . . . A Zionist settler, in changing his name from Rachmilewitz to Onn ("Vigor"), was not only Hebraicizing a foreign sound. He was in fact re-enacting a piece of primitive magic, reminiscent of the initiation rites of certain Australian tribes, in which boys receive new names at puberty and are then considered reborn as men and the reincarnation of ancestors.[19]

---

[18]Elon, *Israelis,* p. 13.

[19]Ibid., p. 13.

Likewise the communities they founded were represented in the minds of some as religious communes:

> David Horowitz . . . compared Bittania to a "monastic order without God." It was no simple matter to be accepted as a member; candidates passed a trial period, a kind of novitiate. Horowitz likened Bittania to a "religious sect . . . with its own charismatic leader and set of symbols, an a ritual of confessions in public reminiscent of efforts by religious mystics to exorcise God and Satan at one and the same time."[20]

No wonder, then, that the impact of Zionism is to be measured not merely in this-worldly matters.

Zionism did more than create a state, a country, a government. It regenerated a whole people. That the day of Zionism, in the form of which I speak, is past does not mean that the movement is dead. But for the second and third and later generations, the myth, evocative symbols, cult and rites of Zionism had to be revised and reworked. For the initial power of the movement to present a set of self-evident truths leading to necessary and legitimate actions worked itself out in its complete success. That very success explains why we have to speak of Zionism, as a Judaism, in the past tense. It yielded Israeli nationalism, a different composition altogether, and, it can be argued, not a Judaism at all. But in its day, from 1897 to 1948, Zionism emerged as a powerful movement of salvation and affected women's and men's lives in a more profound way than—if truth be told—Reform, Orthodoxy, and Conservative Judaisms taken together.

The extraordinary success of this Judaism requires explanation. For, as we have seen, the three continuators of the received system of the dual Torah worked out, mainly for intellectuals, certain problems of conflict between doctrine and contemporary academic dogma. But Zionism changed lives and accomplished its salvific goals. No wonder, then, that it enjoyed the status of self-evident truth to the true believers of the movement—which came, in time, to encompass nearly the whole of the contemporary Jewish world and to affect all the Judaisms of the day. It was, in other words, the single most successful Judaism since the formation, fifteen hundred years earlier, of the Judaism of the dual Torah. The reason for the success of Zionism derives from that very source to which, to begin with, Zionism appealed: history, Jewish History. In a way no one would have wanted to imagine, what happened to Jews—Jewish History—validated the ideology of Zionism, its worldview, and, furthermore, vindicated its way of life. When the surviving Jews of Europe straggled out of the death camps in 1945, Zionism came forth with an explanation of what had happened and a program to effect salvation for the remnant.

Until the massacre of the Jews of Europe, between 1933 and 1945 and the founding of the state of Israel three years later, Zionism remained very much a minority movement in Jewry. Jewish Socialism and Yiddishism, in the new nations of Eastern Europe, and the New Deal in American Democratic politics, attracted a far larger part of Jewry, and the former, though not the latter, formed a competing Judaic system in particular. Before 1948, the Jewish population of the Land of Israel/Palestine had scarcely reached half a million, a small portion of

---

[20]Ibid., p. 125, 141.

the Jews of the world. In the United States and in Western Europe, Zionist sentiment did not predominate, even though a certain romantic appeal attached to the
pioneers in the Land. Down, indeed, to 1967, Zionism constituted one choice
among many for Jews throughout the world. Since at the present time Jewry
nearly unanimously attaches the status of the Jewish state to the state of Israel;
affirms that the Jews form a people, one people; concedes all of the principal
propositions of Zionism; and places the achievement of the Zionist program as
the highest priority for Jewry throughout the world, we may say that today at
least Zionism forms a system bearing self-evident truth for vast numbers of Jews.

And the truth endured. Since we have already outlined the reasons for classifying Zionism as a Judaism, it must follow, on the surface at least, that Zionism
constitutes a Judaism of self-evidence. Its truths are received as facts, its system—
its way of life, involving emphasis on building the land or at least raising money
for it through an absorbing round of meetings and activities, and its worldview,
placing the state at the center of Judaic existence—strikes vast numbers of Jews
as self-evidently true, an obvious and ineluctable next step in the history of the
Jews, and, in that sense at least, an inevitable increment in the history of Judaism
as well. Zionism therefore inaugurated a long history for itself in a way in which
its competing systems did not: There was a second and a third generation. In
America, as Ruth Wisse points out, Yiddishism served a single generation only,
and Yiddish served as a language not of systemic consequence ("ideology") but
of nostalgia. Why did Zionism persuade a second and a third and a fourth generations of Jews, while Socialism and Yiddishism constituted movements of an
essentially transient character? And why did Zionism gain the support—as a set
of self-evident truths—of the bulk of Jews in the world? Because Zionism, alone
of the Judaisms of the nineteenth and twentieth centuries, possessed the potential of accurately assessing the power of anti-Semitism and its ultimate destiny.
Zionism turns out to have selected the right problem and given the right solution
(at least, so it now seems) to that problem.

The cheerful prognostications of world brotherhood, characteristic of Reform
Judaism and of Socialism alike, perished, and the Reform Judaism of the nineteenth century lost its hold even on the heirs of the movement. But Zionism faced
reality and explained it and offered a program, inclusive of a worldview and a
way of life, that worked. The power of the Zionist theory of the Jews' existence
came to expression not only at the end of World War II, when Zionism offered
world Jewry the sole meaningful explanation of how to endure. It led at least
some Zionists to realize as early as 1940 what Hitler's Germany was going to do.
At a meeting in December 1940, Berl Katznelson, an architect of Socialist Zionism in the Jewish community of Palestine before the creation of the state of Israel,
announced that European Jewry was finished:

> The essence of Zionist awareness must be that what existed in Vienna will never
> return, what existed in Berlin will never return, nor in Prague, and what we had
> in Warsaw and Lodz is finished, and we must realize this! . . . Why don't we un-
> derstand that what Hitler has done, and this war is a kind of Rubicon, an outer
> limit, and what existed before will never exist again. . . . And I declare that the
> fate of European Jewry is sealed.[21]

---

[21]Shapira, *Berl*, p. 290.

Zionism, in the person of Katznelson, even before the systematic mass murder got underway, grasped that, after World War II Jews would not wish to return to Europe, certainly not to those places in which they had flourished for a thousand years, and Zionism offered the alternative: the building, outside Europe, of the Jewish state.

Zionism, then, took a position of prophecy and found its prophesy fulfilled. Its fundamental dogma about the character of the Diaspora as Exile found verification in the destruction of European Jewry. And Zionism's further claim to point the way forward proved to be Israel's salvation in the formation of the state of Israel on the other side of the Holocaust. So Katznelson maintained: "If Zionism wanted to be the future force of the Jewish people, it must prepare to solve the Jewish question in all its scope." The secret of the power of Zionism lay in its power to make sense of the world and to propose a program to solve the problems of the age. In its context, brief though it turned out to be, Zionism formed the counterpart, as to power and success and self-evidence, to the Judaism of the dual Torah of the fourth through nineteenth centuries.

34 Contemporary Zionism Speaks: In Defense of Perpetual Zionist Revolt

YOSEF GORNY

1. Why is this reading important?

A leading historian of Zionism, Yosef Gorny examines what he calls "Jewish public thought," meaning how Jews debate the issues of their shared life as an ethnic entity (the United States and Europe) or a political entity (the state of Israel). The reason his assessment of Zionism is important is simple. Gorny takes Zionism seriously, and he understands by Zionism not merely the "nationalism of the state of Israel," but rather, an international and transnational movement of the Jewish people. Gorny does not concede that because Zionism accomplished its initial goal—to form of the Jews "a people, one people," and to empower that people in a state of its own—Zionism therefore has run its course. He argues that Zionism, in its own terms, has important tasks to perform, and any account of Zionism in the setting of the study of Judaism has to hear this acutely contemporary voice. The focus of his essay is this: How much is Zionism predetermined by circumstance—anti-Semitism, the rise of anti-Semitic political parties culminating in the German National Socialist Workers Party ("Nazis") and the Holocaust—and how much is Zionism the result of free choice? That same question faces us when we consider any powerful body of ideas, whether political or religious. Though the topic is distinctive to Judaism, the issue is one of general intelligibility.

2. What should you notice as you proceed?

Gorny is a sophisticated thinker, and some of his language will require close reading. But he asks a very interesting question: To what extent is this movement the outcome of necessity, and how much is it the product of free ideological choice? To understand that question and how he answers it, watch for the evidence that Gorny assembles to show that Zionism then and now is not the result of impersonal, historical forces about which people can do nothing. He wants to demonstrate that people make and carry out choices. How does he do this? More to the point, once he concludes that people do make choices, what are the things he wants Jews to do?

3. How should you frame a question for class discussion in response to what you have read?

Note how Gorny redefines the state of Israel into something considerably different from other nation-states: "the state as guarantor and preserver of Jewish values, as an 'open refuge,' as the guardian of historical tradition, bolstering the unity of the people and demonstrating the change in the status of the Jews." In this context, class discussion might well address the status of overseas Chinese; Muslims in France, Britain, and Germany; Christians in China; Tibetans in India; and other cases in which members of religious or ethnic-cultural communities find themselves minorities in nations dominated by religions other than theirs or other ethnic-cultural traits than those that characterize them. Gorny wants Americans of Jewish origin, for instance, to relate to the state of Israel in a way different from the way they relate to any other country in the world, and he also wants to explain how and why they should do so. Can you frame an equivalent argument for Americans of Irish or Italian origin in respect to Ireland and Italy? Americans of Roman Catholic faith in respect to the Catholic Church throughout the world, or of Episcopalian faith in respect to the Anglican Church?

Here the ambiguity of Zionism—a political movement that has made a deep impact upon the religion Judaism—comes to the surface: a transnational nationalism meant to form of diverse persons a single people. Can a political movement in the end serve such a purpose, without creating contradictions in the political loyalties of the proposed members of that movement? When Zionism first began, rabbis in Europe objected that only the Messiah could bring holy Israel back to the Land of Israel, and Jewish citizens of Western countries objected that they were citizens of their countries of birth and residence and did not need any other citizenship. So far as the Jews constitute a religious community, by contrast, the dilemmas of Zionism pass from the scene. But, on the other hand, the Jews form an ethnic group, part of which practices Judaism. Jews who do not practice Judaism but who do wish to retain a place within the Jewish world ("Jewish People") will find implausible the religious answer to the question of transnational connections and communities. To the ambiguities of the social world comprised by the Jews, no easy answers present themselves. That is why the Jews' favorite indoor sport is to argue about who is a Jew. In that argument, Gorny excels: He has thought clearly and deeply and has much to say.

Never in modern times have Jews in the West been more committed to Jewish peoplehood. And most of them see Israel as its chief embodiment.

Michael Meyer, JEWISH IDENTITY IN THE MODERN WORLD

The full reckoning is not yet over.

Y. H. Brenner, FROM HERE TO THERE

Zionism today is in a state of profound crisis. The Zionist Organization appears to be powerless, and its way of thinking seems outdated. This sorry situation stems not only from the fact that the movement lacks authoritative and influential leaders, and its institutions are perceived as ineffectual, but because it has not succeeded in capturing the imagination of contemporary Jews by offering a central ideal, suited to the new realities in which they live.

Like every long-lived social movement, Zionism, in its century of existence, has undergone so many crises that its history can be classified accordingly. The Hibbat Zion era ended in a crisis of leadership, which began in the early 1890s. Pinsker died in 1891, disillusioned with the prospects for Jewish settlement in Palestine; the waning of the second wave of immigration in that same year (because of restrictions imposed by the Ottoman authorities) seemed to confirm his pessimism. Herzl's inspiring debut in 1897 ended in bitter polemics on the question of settlement in Uganda, and he died after only seven years of activity within the Zionist movement. The days of glory of Weizmannite Zionism—from the Balfour Declaration in 1917 to the establishment of the Jewish Agency in 1929—also terminated in a profound political crisis with the British Government and in a dispute within the Zionist movement, which led eventually to the reluctant resignation of Weizmann from presidency of the movement. The *sturm und drang* days of the 1930s, when immigration flowed into Palestine and settlements sprang up all over the country, ended in the partition controversy which threatened to split the Zionist movement, and in the 1939 White Paper, aimed at repudiating Great Britain's commitment to the Zionist movement by establishing a Palestinian state. The mass mobilization of US Jewry for the political struggle for statehood and their financial aid to immigrant absorption came to an end in a spirit of mutual recrimination and estrangement between Israel and the Diaspora, which lasted from the mid-fifties to the Six Day War.

The four decades of statehood have also been marked by periodic crises, but there is a fundamental difference between pre- and post-state crises. The former resulted from the weakness of the Zionist movement and political circumstances, which it was powerless to change; the latter were caused, paradoxically enough, by its achievements. Moreover, the crises stem from the dual achievements of Zionism and of Diaspora Jewry. In the past two generations, a period in which Zionism became the greatest collective achievement of the Jewish people throughout their history, the Jews of the free world have won individual achievements, on a scale unparalleled in Diaspora history. These two developments are not necessarily at odds, but in certain historic situations, there is a basic conflict between them. Thus, the collective achievement of establishing a state and the guaranteeing of its survival in this troubled region places a heavy burden on the individual. The revolution wrought by mass immigration, which, for the first time in Jewish history, brought together Jews from east and west at the core of Jewish historical action, led to the cultural transformation of that society. The new reality, reflected in lifestyle and quality of life, is of great concern to many of those who have achieved personal success in the West and in Israel. When Jews in search of individual success and prosperity prefer to emigrate to the United States instead of to Israel, Zionism's prestige is dimmed and the reputation of the state suffers. But this is so because the Zionist state reflects the collective will of the people by observing the Law of Return. And finally, the fact that Zionism has succeeded in restoring to the Jewish people their ancient political and spiritual center, arouses in successful Jews abroad great expectations, which, because of their intensity, can be transformed swiftly into deep disillusionment.

This disillusionment, still confined to a minority of Diaspora Jews, is expressed in the tendency to question the very principle of the centrality of Israel in Jewish life. It is altering the focus of the Jewish collective effort, which was once directed towards Israel and on Israel's behalf, towards the development of other Jewish centers coexisting with Israel and of equal standing. These ideas, although still held by a minority of Jews, should not be dismissed lightly, because they enfold a threat.

At the present state, these ideas seem to confirm Dubnow's views on the proliferation of Jewish centers and the shift from place to place throughout history. Yet, in a world in which Jews are integrated and involved in the culture of their countries of residence, this neo-Dubnowianism could develop into a kind of neo-Bundism, and to gradual erosion of acceptance of the existence of one Jewish people throughout the world. In other words: this trend will not lead to the flowering of Jewish cultural autonomy in the countries where Jews live, as Dubnow or the Bund leaders believed, but will cause the total assimilation of Jewish ethnic groups into the pluralistic societies of their countries of residence, and the loss of their national common denominator. This trend, essentially anti-Zionist, is confined, ideologically, to an intellectual minority, but is latent and subconscious, in the social sense, among the Jewish masses in the Diaspora and in Israel.

In light of this trend, is Zionist ideology still necessary? This query leads us to one of the central issues for understanding of the roots and ideology of the Zionist movement. It is worth pondering to what extent this movement is the outcome of necessity and how much it is the product of free ideological choice. In other words: which ephemeral historical elements and which metahistorical elements exist and operate within it?

Zionism was undoubtedly born out of the political and economic predicament of the Jews of Eastern Europe, and was greatly influenced by the national and social ideologies prevailing in nineteenth-century Europe. But it was not only necessity or cultural milieu which determined its essence and its destiny: it is a fact that want and persecution led the masses of Jewish emigrés from Eastern Europe to the United States and not to Eretz Israel. The awakening of nationalist feeling in Europe aroused other forms of Jewish nationalism apart from Zionism. Jewish territorialism sought to establish a Jewish state in a more congenial territory than Palestine. Autonomism, the brainchild of Dubnow, advocated the establishment of Jewish cultural autonomy in Jewish centers in the Diaspora, and even the Bund had its own socialist-national outlook. Zionism was distinctive among these ideologies in that it offered an absolute alternative, based on freedom of choice.

The basic principles of this choice were: return to the historic homeland in the Land of Israel, settlement on the land and control of all economic spheres, creation of a Jewish majority in the country, and revival of the Hebrew language as the national tongue of the people. All these goals were contradictory to the processes developing objectively throughout the world, namely the flow of migration from the agricultural nations to the industrial ones. Elsewhere, the masses were moving from village to city, and among the Jews the trend was to increasing socio-cultural integration in their countries of residence or places of migration. From this we may learn that Zionism, in essence, is not only the fruit of reality, but also the personification of a rebellion against reality. This revolt was expressed in ideas and in actions.

The "rebels" were the naive settlers of the First Aliyah, who chose the difficult path of founding colonies and rejected the easier path of urban life in the older Jewish urban communities. They were followed by the young activists of the Second Aliyah, who launched a struggle on behalf of "Hebrew labor" in defiance of economic logic. With their inspiration and guidance, the Third Aliyah settlers implemented the idea of "constructive socialism," both by founding the General Federation of Labor, which differed from any other labor federation in the world, and by establishing the cooperative settlement movement. By these actions they rebelled against reality in the name of utopia and created a model of realistic utopianism, which became a driving and constructive social force, which eventually also made a decisive contribution to the establishment of the state. These Zionist rebels included the teachers who revived the Hebrew language, through protracted efforts, as well as the leaders of the Zionist movement who succeeded, by unconventional means, in transforming objective weakness into subjective political force.

This "rebellious" trait of Zionism highlights an additional paradox inherent in the movement. This movement, which restored the Jewish people to its history, did so by means of its will and by measures which were, to a large extent, superhistorical: thus, it is not the changes wrought by time and place which will determine its fate, but the will and aspirations of the Jews. This statement does not answer the cardinal question: Is Zionism necessary to Jews in their present situation? I believe that we can answer this question only after clarifying the basic ideological essence of Zionism.

From the outset—the Hibbat Zion era—Zionism was a pluralistic movement, which succeeded in concentrating within it, on the basis of a possible consensus, conflicting ideological currents and political groups: religious and secular, political and practical, socialist and middle-class, liberal and totalitarian. The basis for compromise, agreed upon by most of those participating in the movement, were the principles of the Zionist revolt, as follows: the return to Eretz Israel, the historic homeland of the Jewish people; creation of a Jewish majority in Eretz Israel, as the expression and guarantee of change in the historic status of the people; creation of a normal Jewish economy, as the condition for independence of the national society; and the revival of the Hebrew language as the supreme stage in cultural renaissance. Beyond these basic tenets, opinions were divided on all ideological and political issues. Even on the question of attitudes towards the *golah*, there was no single viewpoint. Ostensibly, Zionism, which aimed at establishing a society which would be the antithesis of the Diaspora, should have negated it absolutely. But this was not the case. Zionism negated the Diaspora in the sense that it denied its ability to survive in the long term by its own powers, as an entity with Jewish identity, but in practice there was no consensus as to its fate, namely that it was destined to disappear.

On this point, Ahad ha-Am and Herzl differed from the outset. Ahad ha-Am sought a way of preserving the Jewish character of the *golah*, because he did not anticipate its physical disappearance; while Herzl, who despaired of the idea of Jewish integration in European society, advocated the exodus of the majority of European Jews. Paradoxically enough, therefore, although Herzlian Zionism became the predominant trend in the pre-State Zionist movement, it was Ahad ha-Am's views on the future of the Diaspora that prevailed. In other words: the various trends in Zionism, from the moderate to the activist and radical, perceived immigration to Eretz Israel as a practical solution only for part of the Jewish people.

Furthermore: the demand for territorial concentration in Palestine, and the creation of a Jewish majority, was not perceived as dependent on the immigration of the large part of the Jewish people. Zionism always took a selective view of the Diaspora, related primarily to the predicament of Eastern European Jewry. The Jews of Western Europe, and particularly the United States, were not considered candidates for immigration; and the Jews of Asia and Africa did not constitute a problem at that time. In the 1930s, when the plight of Europe's Jews worsened, Weizmann and Greenbaum anticipated the immigration of one to two million Jews from that continent. Shortly before his death, in 1940, Jabotinsky envisioned a Jewish state of five million Jewish citizens and two million Arabs. After the 1942 Biltmore Conference, Ben-Gurion spoke of the immediate immigration of two million Jewish refugees to the future Jewish state. But, by the fifties he was no longer confident that the vision of the ingathering of the exiles would be realized where U.S. Jews were concerned.

At the same time, inherent in Zionism was a qualitative "negation of the *golah*" which stemmed from the fundamental Zionist view of Diaspora life and the alternative which Zionism hoped to offer. Ahad ha-Am negated cultural assimilation, or what he denoted "slavery within freedom," the condition of the Jews of the free Western countries. Chaim Weizmann condemned the lack of aesthetic sense among Eastern European Jews in the widest meaning of the term. Jabotinsky abhorred *galut* life, as lacking dignity and self-pride. The labor movement rejected the parasitic element in Jewish life in the Diaspora, the total and undignified dependence of the Jews on their surroundings. In short, "negation of the *golah*" in Zionism, with the exclusion of Herzl, was relative, and linked to time and place. This being so, one cannot accept the reverse of "negation of *golah*," namely "negation of Zionism" which is based on the argument that in the light of the fact that the Diaspora did not wane after the establishment of Israel, Zionist ideology is no longer valid. This view of confrontation between the Zionist and Diaspora ideologies emphasizes their mutual negation. It should be stressed that this view does not imply opposition to the state or even its depreciation. The reverse is true. The very connection with the state becomes the argument against Zionism.

Since Israel came into being, its ties with Diaspora Jews have strengthened, despite problems and upheavals. Israel is today the central public interest of Diaspora Jews, a kind of "religion," common to secular and religious Jews. But, together with this profound identification, there is a natural tendency to distinguish between the value of the state and the value of Zionism in the context of Jewish interests. Whereas the distinction between the sovereign State of Israel and the Zionist Organization, whose members are citizens of other countries, is essential for political reasons, the distinction between the Jewish state and Zionist ideology is artificial and spurious.

The Zionist-Jewish combination is built into the essence of the state and finds expression in its everyday life. It constitutes the territorial-national framework, guaranteeing the continuum of Jewish life, with its religious and secular aspects. As an open refuge for all Jews in trouble, it maintains in practice the value of mutual responsibility. The centrality of the state in the consciousness of Jews, reflected both in their concern for it and their quarrels with it, their support for it and their reservations, reinforces Jewish unity and identity, which is the basis of Zionism, as laid down by Herzl. Thus, when the Jews of the Diaspora define their devotion to the state as a form of Zionism, this view should neither be belittled nor dismissed as hypocritical and self-indulgent.

Ostensibly, it is the almost unconditional support of Diaspora Jews for Israel which demonstrates the validity of Zionist ideology for our times as well. One could interpret this identification, against the general background and the objective developments of today, as an inner need. There is an element of truth in this, but it is not the whole truth. This need stems from the unique lives of Western Jewry, who are preoccupied with the question of their own freedom, but it lacks the elements of the conscious rebellion, which was once the symbol of Zionism. In other words, the Jews of the West are living in a society which not only allots respected status to the Jewish religion, but also sanctions ethnicity. Ethnic pluralism is the cultural-psychological norm in the free countries. And as such, it offers a new and different path to assimilation in non-Jewish society. Henceforth, in order to become part of general society, there is no longer any need to convert to Christianity or to deny Jewish culture. On the contrary: to maintain a degree of ethnic distinctiveness is the respected and accepted way to total assimilation.

The significance of this trend is that, in the final analysis, the traditional-Jewish character, which on principle, was separate and distinct, will be forfeited. One might say that the ethnic trend among Jews is an expression of objective processes occurring within the general society. These processes may cause the Jewish sense of unity to deviate from the idea of the center in Israel, towards the Dubnowian theory and thence to the Bundist ideology. Anyone who rejects this possibility must choose Zionism instead.

Because of the need for Zionism, for the preservation of universal Judaism, it is incumbent on us to clarify its suitability for this task, by examining the essence of the Zionist praxis as a movement operating within history. Let it be stated at once: Zionism was never a religious faith or an ideological doctrine, though such elements existed in many of the ideological groups which composed it. In general, however, Zionism was always the reverse of doctrinarian. Its power lay in the ability to adapt its ideals to changing conditions and to select the right means and instruments for their implementation: all this without losing sight of the main goal. Therefore, over three generations—from Hibbat Zion to statehood—it changed its priorities and shifted its trends without deviating from its path. First, political Zionism replaced Hibbat Zion; then constructive Zionism, headed by Weizmann and implemented by the socialist labor movement, dominated it in the 1920s; from the mid-thirties, in the period of national emergency, the main concern was the struggle for the survival of the Yishuv, which developed into the fight for statehood; after the state was established, it became a movement whose overt and proclaimed aim had been achieved and Jewish sovereignty became its main concern. Each period was characterized by its unique mood.

The Hibbat Zion period was colored by the romanticism of intellectuals who "saw the light"; political Zionism—by the aspiration for normalization; constructive Zionism—by social utopianism; in the time of national emergency, the mood was one of readiness for combat; and in the era of statehood—the desire to consolidate the patterns of life of an independent society. I believe that we are now on the threshold of a new movement—post-sovereignty.

As we approach the year 2000, Jewish life is characterized worldwide by two conflicting features. On the one hand world Jewry has never been so united in the political sense, and on the other Judaism has never before been so divided culturally. Political unity is fostered by concern for Israel, concern for Soviet Jewry, a vigilant stand against neo-Fascist tendencies, etc. But all these are issues which, by their very nature, are transient. The cultural dimension, on the other hand, is durable and profound. In effect, Judaism is split up in a number of ways: the religious and secular camps, the former divided into a number of trends, which are increasingly divided on questions of conversion, mixed marriages and the Law of Return; Jews who are an integral part of their countries of residence and those who are citizens of their own sovereign state; Jewish communities speaking different languages, who not only enjoy the culture of their countries but contribute to it as well.

The present balance between political unity and cultural division may be disrupted some day because of the changing character of the former and the durability and increasing intensity of the latter. In face of these trends, those Jews who wish to preserve their Jewish identity as a people with its own distinctive character, require an ideology of revolt against objective reality. Of all the trends and movements which have struggled in the past to preserve Jewish distinctiveness and continue to do so, Zionism is the most comprehensive. Extreme orthodoxy represents only a small part of the people, and the more fanatic this minority becomes, the more it promotes division. The modern religious trend, Reform and Conservative, have attracted only a part of the Jewish people. Secular Jews are left without guiding ideology apart from their political support for Israel. Zionism as a pluralistic movement succeeded in the past and can do so in the present, in embracing various conflicting trends on the basis of a common denominator. But in order to do so it needs to place at the core of Jewish consciousness an idea which has been deeply repressed until now.

In its century of existence, Zionist thought and action has emphasized the trend to national normalization. This was true of the idea of the return to the historic homeland, the return to physical labor and productivization of the masses, as well as the establishment of a socialist society, the political struggle for the right to self-determination, the desire to achieve sovereignty for the Yishuv, etc. The distinctive anomalous element was reflected mainly in the measures adopted in order to implement these trends. Thus the return to nature became an ideal, and physical labor became a value ("the religion of labor"), the class struggle was transformed into constructive socialism, the national commitment of the labor movement took the form of effort to achieve a cooperative utopia, and the migration movement aspired to become an "ingathering of the exiles." The anomalous means maintained normal tendencies and without them the goals could not have been achieved. Without agricultural settlement, "Hebrew labor," the kibbutz movement and the ideology of ingathering of the exiles, the state could not have come into being and could not have survived. But in the course of history, the anomality of the means has been overwhelmed by the normality of the tendencies, and society in the Jewish state increasingly resembles other societies. Now, in light of the prevailing situation, the time has come to reverse the order of things. The Jewish people should face the challenge of anomalous trends which should be achieved through normal deeds.

For those Diaspora Jews who wish it, the consolidation of the sense of distinctiveness in a society which is becoming increasingly uniform entails elevating ethnic consciousness to the sphere of overall national consciousness. Such consciousness will constitute a kind of declaration that the Jewish people is one, although Jews, for the most part, are not concentrated in their national territory; are not, for the most part, religious; speak many languages and live in diverse cultures; and this being so, the Jewish people does not intend to submit to objective developments. Just as their forefathers fought in the name of religious injunctions, they now rebel in the name of national principles. Such a revolt demands intensified awareness of *galut*.

Golah, in the political and economic sense, disappeared when the Jews were given a choice between immigrating to their national home or remaining in their countries of birth. For those who chose the Diaspora—the sense of *galut* is the condition for their Judaism—*galut* not in the overall social meaning, namely a place where injustice prevails, nor in the traditional-religious sense of exile of the Divine Presence (*Shekhina*) and anticipation of the messianic era, but *galut* as the historic experience of an extraordinary people, who are a minority wherever they live and struggle for collective survival. This sense of *galut* is not universal, but distinctively national.

The rebellious desire of the Jews to maintain their national unity, leads, by internal logic, to acknowledgment of the State of Israel as their center; a scattered people, without a cultural and territorial framework, needs a focus where its parts can come together. No diaspora can substitute for Israel's historic function. But, according to that same principle of unity, just as the Jews of the Diaspora must promote the center, Israel must encourage autonomous, cultural and ideological trends in the Diaspora. This will create the abnormal balance between mutual dependence and independence.

Acknowledgment of the centrality of Israel requires that a distinction be drawn between the state as an etatist organization with vital normal functions and natural weaknesses, stemming from the very fact of its activity within history, and the state as guarantor and preserver of Jewish values, as an "open refuge," as the guardian of historical tradition, bolstering the unity of the people and demonstrating the change in the status of the Jews.

The special connection of Diaspora Jews to the state demands of them that they recognize immigration to Israel as the most important act of bonding and the supreme expression of the revolt against reality. Immigration, even when limited in scope (and perhaps precisely because of its restricted nature), should be the jewel in the crown of "rebellious Jewry." In addition, study of the Hebrew language should play a central role. The effort invested in study of a language which is neither fashionable nor useful, is the most important popular expression of the communal will to survive.

And finally, the last "abnormal" principle, binding together all the others, is the equal right to mutual intervention. On all the distinctive issues, namely, the standing of religion in society, Jewish education, natural increase, immigration and migration and the guaranteeing of the Jewish character of the state, the Jewish people in the Diaspora and in Israel have the right to intervene. But fertile thought on these matters can develop and exert influence only within the framework of an all-Jewish movement.

35 Israeli Judaism

SHLOMO DESHEN

1. Why is this reading important?

The practice of Judaism in the state of Israel differs in no important
ways from the practice of Judaism in the diaspora or Exile (as Classical
Judaism and also Zionism call the place where the Jews live who do not
live in the Land of Israel). The same holidays impose rhythm upon the
year, the same Torah is declaimed in the synagogue and studied in the
school, the same Sabbath defines the goal of the week, the same worldview and way of life shape the definition of the same holy Israel of
which the faith speaks everywhere. But the conditions under which Judaism is practiced so differ from those that pertain outside the state of
Israel that everything in the practiced faith is redefined and takes on
new meaning. The Torah presupposes that Jews form "Israel," which is
a political entity that is also a kingdom of priests and a holy people.
Moses not only set down the laws and teachings of the Torah but he
also governed the everyday affairs of Israel. When the sages of the Oral
Torah completed the picture, they too took for granted that Israel forms
a political entity, living on its own terms and under its own laws that
holy life that God wanted them to realize. When the Jews lost their political autonomy with the destruction of the Temple in 70 C.E., the conditions under which the Torah would define the life of holy Israel changed
radically. The state of Israel presents the first occasion since 70 C.E. in
which the religion Judaism is embodied by Jews living under their own
government, forming their own autonomous and normative culture, and
shaping their own future. How the Judaic religious systems, particularly
the ones put forth by the Judaism of the dual Torah, respond to so radical a change in the political foundations of the religious life forms a critical chapter in the contemporary history of Judaism.

2. What should you notice as you proceed?

Deshen has the merit of recognizing and proposing to explain the religious diversity characteristic of all of the Orthodox Judaic religious systems that flourish in the state of Israel. He does not try to homogenize
but prefers to differentiate. Moreover, he looks for categories that will
accommodate the diverse patterns of religious observance characteristic

of various sectors of the Jewish population of the state of Israel. In this way he wants to describe the religiosity of that population. He faces the task—as do all scholars of religions—of explaining why this, not that? Why do Reform and Conservative Judaisms predominate in the United States—nearly 90 percent of all Jews who practice a Judaism in North America choose one or the other—but make slight impact on religiosity in the state of Israel? And, conversely, why do segregationist Orthodox Judaisms enjoy so much influence in the state of Israel that they are major players in the political life of the country, while overseas they gain only negligible numbers of adherents? Notice, also, how Deshen differentiates Israeli Judaism(s) by reference to the diverse cultural origins of the practitioners, seeing those from Muslim countries as fundamentally unlike those from Christian ones. He finds four sectors of Israeli Judaism (we would call them, roughly speaking, four Judaisms, meaning four social groupings each with its own way of life and worldview): nationalist, neo-Orthodox, Orthodox, and Oriental. Clearly, these "groupings" are not really comparable, for they do not differ on a common agenda but define themselves each in terms of traits that have no counterpart in the other. So how he explains and defines these Judaisms ought to capture your attention. This is the longest single essay in this anthology, notable for its systematic and orderly exposition of the facts of how Judaism is practiced in the unique setting of the Jewish state.

3. How should you frame a question for class discussion in response to what you have read?

What Deshen shows us is that Judaism is to the state of Israel what Christianity is to the United States: the source of norms, the definitive faith of the country at large. Therefore he discusses Judaism in the state of Israel in the same way we would discuss Christianity in the United States. He considers the entire population of the country, the relationship of the country's politics and culture to its religious groupings, the history of the country and its impact upon the history of its dominant religion. When we considered Judaism in the United States and other diaspora settings, we did not relate the religion, Judaism, to the history of the United States or Britain or Germany, only to what was happening to the Jews in those countries. The contrast between studying a religion held by the majority of a population and one held by a small minority provokes an interesting question: When we describe, analyze, and interpret a religious system, at what point do we begin the work, and why there, not somewhere else?

You may find it possible to make a powerful case that the first question to ask, when you want to describe a religion, is the political one: What is the political status of this religion in the setting in which this religion flourishes? To describe the social realities of Catholicism in Italy, one set of categories serves; to do the same for Catholicism in Britain or New Zealand will require a different set of questions. That is what the contrast between describing American Judaism—say, New Age Judaism in New Mexico—and Israeli Judaism shows us. In the former case, we hear from individuals and their attitudes and aspirations and personal judgments. In the latter, we learn about large public bodies, institutions and their politics, movements of faith and culture that are public and that shape the common life of entire communities. If to practice Catholicism in Italy or Mexico is to engage with public culture, then to be a Catholic in New Zealand or England is to conduct an essentially private, if never wholly personal, religious life. So a second question might be: Do the political and demographic facts make a difference when you study a religion, and if so, what difference do you think they will make?

A third question is: If practicing Judaism in the United States is so profoundly different in all dimensions from doing so in the state of Israel, do common convictions and a common way of life suffice to permit us to speak of a single religious system, a Judaism? Or, in response to principal differences in the social orders in which two or more systems flourish, do we have to subdivide religious systems that exhibit numerous shared traits of worldview and way of life? And if we do, then how important are common traits of worldview and way of life? Can we speak of Catholicism one and universal, or only of Catholicisms here and there, and if the former, what makes the difference? For Judaism or Islam or other Christianities, where do we find the counterparts to the Catholic difference (which is, after all, the Pope)? Comparing religions is a task that can keep us occupied for a long time.

The Diaspora Background

Israel is mainly a society of immigrants. Discussing the religion of various social groups necessarily leads us to the recent past in their countries of origin where the present religious and cultural patterns emerged. A relevant categorization of Israeli Jews for the purposes of this discussion is that of immigrants from Christian countries and immigrants from Muslim countries. Numerically, the categories are more or less equal.[1] In terms of social status, however, immigrants from Christian countries predominate. The reason for this is that during the late nineteenth and early twentieth centuries immigration from Muslim countries lagged. A steady stream of immigrants from Europe kept coming to the country, whereas comparatively large numbers from the Orient immigrated only after 1948. Of the 70,000 immigrants who arrived during the first two decades of the twentieth century—crucially formative years for Israeli society—almost all were from Russian territories. This means that immigrants from Muslim countries, the Orientals as we shall now term them, came to a society whose institutions were already formed and were manned by immigrants of the earlier wave. Therefore, they had to adapt perforce, whether to a greater or to a lesser extent, to the institutions and

---

[1]This estimate is based on the findings of Peres (1976) who, on the basis of data from 1969, extrapolated the proportions of the population originating in Europe and in Muslim countries. According to his study, the respective figures are 51.7 percent and 48.3 percent. They include Israeli-born descendants of the immigrants.

norms they found in the new country. The crucial historical background of the society is thus that of the Europeans.

For many centuries, Jews had lived as corporate autonomous communities within Christian and Muslim societies.[2] The host societies were, of course, not mass societies of a democratic type, but societies in the line of contemporary premodern models. Living as Jews in these societies entailed many specific sociocultural features—such as making one's living along certain lines, having the choice of area of residence and friends delimited, the use of a particular language, having recourse to particular legal institutions, and many others. Thus, in addition to their own religious practices, Jews were engaged in many particular social and cultural practices, as were members of other strata of premodern society. Through the centuries, Jewish religion became intertwined with these practices, many of them gaining the legitimation and actual sanction of religion. Analytically, it is often very difficult to decide where in Judaism a religious practice ends and mere custom and social exigency begin.

This social situation has changed since the late eighteenth century. Premodern states evolved into mass societies whose tolerance for the legal and cultural autonomy of groups and strata was comparatively minimal.[3] In the course of these radical social changes, the status of members of Jewish communities has tended to be transformed from that of 'Jews' to that of 'citizens of the Jewish faith'. The transition implied the granting of universal rights while at the same time annulling ancient rights (such as autonomy in the dispensing of justice) pertaining to membership in the particular stratum of Jews. These ancient rights were, however, intertwined with the Jewish religion and Jewish social practices. To the Jews, the societies undergoing change posed acute and profound dilemmas. As ghetto walls began to crumble, Jews faced the predicament of reorganizing their lives in society at large. This process of political and social modernization of the Jews, or of 'the Emancipation' as it was called in the nineteenth century, started first in Western Europe in the late eighteenth century, gradually moved to Central Europe, and much later to some of the Muslim countries. The process did not develop consistently and radically, however, as later events, culminating in the German massacre of European Jewry, tragically attest. Powerful social forces from both sides of the old ghetto walls—the Jewish and the Gentile—operated to obstruct the total dismantling of partitions. But the social, cultural, and religious problems inherent in the terms of the Emancipation faced all Jews.

The various responses to these problems constitute the core of the internal Jewish conflicts of modern times. To understand the current Israeli religiocultural situation, we must follow the main trends of the clashing Diaspora responses that have been carried over into latter-day Israel. They all grapple with the root problem of outlining Jewish positions on the question of assimilation to Gentile society on the one hand, and the question of adherence to traditional Jewish life on the other. While the two are mutually exclusive, and some circles opted for a stand

---

[2]In the historical resume that follows, I am indebted to the works of Jacob Katz (1968, 1973) and his pupil Moshe Samet (1969, 1970).

[3]The vicissitudes of the modern Mennonites, even in the traditionally tolerant New World, are quite typical in this context.

on one side or the other, many chose to make for themselves an ideological and existential niche at some place along the continuum between the extremes. The varied responses, far from being abstract philosophical exercises, entailed grappling with acute personal problems concerning life-styles and practices. They were programs for mapping out one's existence on many levels, practical and ideological: in worship, in one's choice of occupation, in the company of strangers, and in one's kitchen. Some of these programs were carried over more or less intact by immigrants to the new society. Three major trends of Diaspora responses are notable: (1) nationalism, (2) neo-orthodoxy, and (3) orthodoxy.

The Jewish national movement, which in time came to be instrumental in the formation of the State of Israel, strove for the reconstitution of formal elements of national existence: primarily the return to the ancient homeland, the revival of the Hebrew language, and the creation of a stratum of farmers deemed essential for national existence. These aims became absolute values. The nationalists rejected the fundamental, traditional, G-d-centered, ideological rationale for Jewish existence. Their ideology was founded on the belief in a Jewish national genius that expressed itself through the ages in the craving for existence as a people. The precise nature of this genius and of Jewish identity generally were accepted as self-evident and consequently remained vague and confused.

On the plane of religious practice, nationalism, particularly that branch of the movement that came to dominate the Israeli scene after the early 1900s, combines radical antinomian tendencies with profound traditionalism. While the early nationalist pioneers who settled in Palestine were, in many ways, radically heterodox, they nevertheless transplanted many practices from their traditional Diaspora homes which they deemed compatible with their new roles and tasks as pioneers. Thus, the Jewish calendar with its cycle of festivals and Sabbath days continued, fundamentally, to regulate time. Traditional Jewish literary materials remained, albeit most selectively, the core of culture and schooling. Many religious practices, such as circumcision and food ritual (refraining from raising hogs and many similar matters) stayed in force. Through the use of the Hebrew language, numerous traditional symbols, sentiments, and association survived, though the symbols often underwent change and profanation. Even the essential utopian elements of traditional Messianism remained, and only the more unrealistic and supernatural beliefs were abandoned.[4]

Neo-orthodoxy, the second major Diaspora response to the nineteenth-century predicament, sought to divorce religious practices from other cultural elements of traditional Judaism. Religion was to be retained while many of the other elements, such as the restricted range of occupations, or the use of the Yiddish language, were to be discarded. Because of the age-old minimal differentiation of religion from other elements of culture, the task neo-orthodoxy set itself was highly problematic. The protagonists of neo-orthodoxy moved on the continuum, out of the ghetto toward modernity, as far as religion in the strictest sense of the word (barren of cultural appendages) permitted. They remained punctilious in their adherence to the practices of traditional religion as strictly defined. At the same time, the neo-orthodox accepted the dissolution of the an-

---

[4]For an insightful treatment of late nineteenth-century Jewish nationalism see Katz (1968).

cient institutions, such as the autonomous judicial, political, and educational organs of the corporate communities. Immigrating during the 1920s and 1930s, the neo-orthodox strove for and welcomed the nationalist state. As religious nationalists, they participated actively in the roles and tasks of society, all the while remaining loyal to traditional Jewish religion as strictly defined.

One innovation of neo-orthodoxy is particularly notable in the context of the argument that I develop in this paper. In traditional Judaism the study of Torah ('the divine teaching'), in the form of talmudic literature, was a major act of religious merit. At the same time, it was also a standard cultural and leisure activity, and this had important ramifications in the areas of occupation, education, and the social life of traditional Jewry. In neo-orthodoxy, the worth that came to be attached to advanced technical training and to non-Jewish culture generally led to a deemphasis of the study of Torah as an act of value in itself. People engaged less in Torah study and devoted time to other cultural activities. This shift has never attained clear religious legitimation in neo-orthodox thought and has therefore remained a source of religious malaise that we shall come across again in our discussion. Neo-orthodoxy as a way of life also entails many problems in religious practice. I cite one broad range of problems. Traditionally, Jews did not normally engage in certain occupations, notably army and police service, farming, heavy industry, and the maintenance of essential public services (e.g., the provisions of water and power). Inherent in all these activities are clashes with the norms of the traditional way of life and of religion specifically, as, for example, in matters of Sabbath observance. But religious nationalists, because of their commitment to the general society, do not want to shun these activities. Ways therefore are sought to adapt the practice of these occupations to religious norms, and rabbinical figures associated with the movement grapple with the problems. But many remain intractable (see Fishman 1957; Singer 1967).

In orthodoxy, the third major Diaspora response to nineteenth-century problems, the traditional way of life, gains value as a total system for its own sake. As distinct from neo-orthodoxy, orthodoxy does not seek to isolate the specifically religious elements in tradition. It is a conservative movement in the full sense of the word, and at the same time a novel phenomenon in Judaism. In the traditional past, Judaism had been characterized by a precarious balance between this-worldliness and other-worldliness. At the side of the basic orientation to spiritual life there was high value, albeit qualified and delimited, placed on achievement in material matters and on secular scholarship. By the late nineteenth century, as a result of two major Jewish religious movements in Eastern Europe, Hassidut and Musar, the balance tilted in favor of spirituality and other-worldliness.

One of the concrete expressions of the shift in the world view of orthodoxy was in the area of traditional learning. In the traditional past, East European learning in Torah had had a standing roughly analogous to that of classical humanistic learning—a requisite for a self-respecting Jew—and, because of its religious importance, it was universally practiced at various levels. There existed a two-stage degree system operated by senior scholars (in a fashion again analogous to contemporary university honors). Specific religious roles, such as community rabbis, were esteemed and called for ranking scholars.

In latter-day orthodoxy, however, learning in Torah attained a more elevated, quasi-mystical standing. The theme of learning for its own sake, without thought of degree or professional reward, not to mention actual ulterior material and social motives, was emphasized with unprecedented force. In the context of Eastern European Jewish society, where traditional bonds were wearing thin, learning in Torah among the orthodox came to be conceived of as insurance that secured Judaism against erosion. Adults proceeded with their studies, practically unsupported, while raising their growing families, and self-privation among the orthodox became a familiar feature. A new variant of the Jewish religious ideal character, in the form of the unworldly and ascetic Torah scholar, relatively oblivious to professional and realistic elements in his study, thus became more and more common during the nineteenth century. At the same time, among the neo-orthodox, because of their increasing involvement in the modern economy and in modern culture generally, the study of Torah actually declined.

The vicissitudes of the old ideal of learning in Torah among various sectors of nineteenth-century Jewry lead us to a point of major importance. Both nationalists and neo-orthodox were ambivalent, although in different ways and to different extents, about traditional Judaism. To a certain extent, they dissociated themselves from tradition, whereas orthodoxy, notwithstanding its own considerable innovations, professed to perpetuate tradition and formulated a conservative ideology. The orthodox claim that it constitutes the main-road continuation of traditional Judaism has never been consistently challenged by protagonists of other Jewish trends. The neo-orthodox, in view of their relative situation in matters of Torah learning and the attainment of the new religious ideal, have always been apologetic and on the defensive vis-à-vis orthodoxy. Even the nationalists, repudiating much of tradition themselves, by and large accepted the orthodox claim to historical continuity. This means, in effect, that whatever one's views on tradition, only those of orthodoxy have the weight of subjective legitimacy.

While recognizing that about half the Israeli population stems from Muslim or Oriental countries, I have thus far focused on the background of that half of the population which originated in Europe. There is justification in this up to a point, because the Orientals, mostly latecomers to the country, have not had a formative impact on most of the institutions of Israeli society. By and large, these immigrants came from traditional communities, such as in Iraq, Morocco, Iran, and Tunisia, which were only beginning to disintegrate socially and culturally at the time of emigration. Although the traditional Jewish background of communities from both Europe and the Muslim Orient is similar in many ways (see Katz 1960), there are salient differences between the immigrants of European and of Oriental origin. The reason for this lies primarily in the time lag between the occurrence of events, which in themselves were not entirely disparate, in Europe and in the Orient—the disintegration of traditional Jewry in the West started in the eighteenth century, while the same process in Muslim countries, specifically in Algeria and in Turkey, began over a century later. In many Muslim countries, traditional Jewry remained viable well into the present century and in some regions, such as the Yemen and parts of the Maghreb, it remained so right up to the time of emigration.

The European religiocultural movements that have concerned us—nationalism, neo-orthodoxy, and orthodoxy—are the organized and studied responses of people who experienced the crumbling of their societies gradually and while mostly still located in their old homes. Oriental immigrants, however, while abroad, hardly sensed the problems and constraints that aroused these particular movements.[5] Innovative Jewish religious movements were almost nonexistent in Muslim countries, where the Zionist movement emerged late and then only embryonically in a few communities that were beginning to disintegrate culturally, most characteristically in Iraq (see Cohen n.d.). Therefore most Oriental Jews, upon immigrating to Israel in the 1950s, were catapulted into a cultural situation much more secular, heterogeneous, and problematic than they had previously experienced. The religious reaction of Oriental immigrants to this situation is discussed in the final section of this paper.

The Israeli Background

On the current Israeli scene, nationalism, neo-orthodoxy, and orthodoxy are the three major contributions of European Jewry to Israeli Judaism. Oriental Jewry has contributed a fourth distinctive pattern. Each of the four patterns is adhered to by a whole range of groups distinguished by other detailed and subtle religious distinctions. These must, of course, be considered in a full treatment of Israeli religion. But from a broad cultural and historical perspective, the four patterns that I have isolated are crucially distinct, and for the present I deliberately eschew details that might blur the main outlines of the picture.

In Israel the names and labels of the various religious patterns change constantly, while the essential phenomena remain stable. A sociological understanding of current Israeli Judaism demands the elucidation of the characteristics of these religious patterns and of their mutual relationships. The three European movements emerged finally on the Israeli scene during the 1920s in the form of social movements cum political parties. The orthodox position was represented by the Agudat Yisrael party, the nationalist by the nationalist, so-called secular Zionist, parties, and the neo-orthodox by the Mafdal party. The neo-orthodox position, as organized in the Mafdal party, was also nationalist-Zionist. But it was a complex, hyphenated position—it was both nationalist and neo-orthodox. I choose to discuss the Mafdal position under the neo-orthodox label because that is where its distinctiveness lies, whereas the other nationalists are much more radically removed from tradition, and often consider themselves socialist Zionists. The Orientals have not consistently organized themselves for political action. During the prestate period, attempts of this nature were somewhat sustained. In recent decades, the attempts have become ephemeral, and the Orientals participate in the various political parties that have emerged from the European social and religious movements.

Numerically, the adherents of the various religious patterns are very disparate. One can obtain a very rough idea of their relative numbers from general election returns, keeping in mind the limitations of such a survey analysis. The Agudat Yisrael party usually wins about 5 percent of the general Jewish vote, a figure that more or less represents the actual percentage of the orthodox in the

---

[5]See Sharot (1974) for further considerations in support of the conception that Oriental immigrants constitute a disparate sociocultural category.

population; Mafdal usually gains about 10 percent, probably the optimal figure for Israeli neo-orthodoxy.[6] I estimate that the rest, the 85 percent returned by the nonreligious parties, is drawn more or less equally from the Oriental and the nationalist sectors. This places the Oriental and the nationalist figures each at around 40 percent of the population. The smallness of the orthodox and neo-orthodox figures should not lead us to underestimate the intrinsic importance of the religious patterns they represent. Orthodoxy is recognized as carrying the weight of legitimate Jewish tradition, and as will become clearer below, this gives the views of orthodox circles an importance disproportionate to their numbers.

In contrast with the immigrant background of the 'secular' and Mafdal parties, the core of Agudat Yisrael lies in the ancient traditional Jerusalem community that preceded the nationalist immigration. Both Agudat Yisrael and Mafdal were rather weak parties during the prestate period: Agudat Yisrael because of its lack of involvement and its self-insulation from the nationalist immigrant movements that exerted themselves in laying the foundations of the embryonic State; Mafdal because of its comparatively late appearance on the scene. The social life and culture of the country, owing to the revolutionary element in Zionism, had an antiorthodox and antitraditional atmosphere. Intolerance and impatience toward the observant, and particularly toward the Agudat Yisrael circles, were in the air. For their part, the Agudat Yisrael circles dissociated themselves from the nationalists and their political aims and institutions. They did not, for example, participate in the Jewish paramilitary defense force.

On the other hand, beginning in the late 1920s, a political partnership developed between Mafdal and most of the other major parties (the latter merging later to form the Labor party), all of which had a good deal in common as nationalist parties. The partnership was founded, *inter alia*, on a theological legitimization developed by Rabbi Kook, a spiritual figure of great stature who associated himself with Mafdal. The major parties were not averse to religion in the neo-orthodox form, and this had one particularly important ramification: the institutionalization of the Chief Rabbinate. During the state period, the Chief Rabbinate was to become an important institution. Yet in the 1920s and 1930s, although the newly created office was manned by as impressive a personality as Rabbi Kook, it was weak and ineffectual. One can hardly speak of the Chief Rabbinate of that period as an authority; it was accepted only by the small Mafdal circle then beginning to strike roots in the country, ignored by the secular circles, and vociferously opposed by the orthodox.[7]

The effective opposition of the orthodox to Rabbi Kook and the Mafdal circles is particularly notable on the following issue. Rabbi Kook and the Mafdal circles repeatedly tried to establish a seminary for the training of rabbis of modern outlook, as the neo-orthodox had done in the Diaspora. Their efforts were thwarted by Agudat Yisrael rabbis, who fought for the supremacy of their con-

---

[6]Mafdal draws a great deal of its support from the Oriental electorate, which represents a different religious pattern from that of the neo-orthodox. On the other hand, some neo-orthodox people support nonreligious parties. The latter are, however, much fewer than the Orientals who vote for Mafdal. Therefore the 10 percent figure I have given tends, if anything, to be exaggerated.

[7]For accounts of the Chief Rabbinate see Friedman (1972) and Morgenstern (1973).

ception of the rabbinical role, but the issue has remained alive. When later, in the 1950s, the religious Bar-Ilan University was founded by Mafdal circles, the orthodox again ensured that the university, paradoxically, would not establish a school of rabbinics. In contrast with Mafdal, Agudat Yisrael rabbis have crucial institutionalized powers as members of the party's Council of Torah Sages, which has the decisive voice in the party's general policy and concrete decisions. Not infrequently does the council figure as a rival to the Chief Rabbinate. The views and decisions of its rabbis also often echo in Mafdal circles, and, though not always accepted, they cause uneasiness and soul-searching.

Agudat Yisrael's greater influence is not rooted in any substantial socioeconomic or political power. To a small extent, it derives from the capability of the orthodox circles to rouse emotional demonstrations of various kinds (sometimes peppered with a little violence). More fundamentally, however, it lies in Mafdal's basic lack of self-confidence, or 'weakness of nerve,' derived from the problem of religious legitimacy. The Mafdal failure on the issue of rabbinical training has perpetuated the problem, and, until very recently, religious nationalist circles have by and large not trained their own leaders. More often than not, Mafdal-associated rabbis receive their training and religiosocial outlook from orthodox scholars in *talmudei torah, yeshivot,* and *kolelim,* rabbinical seminaries of varying levels oriented toward Agudat Yisrael circles. Some of the most senior of their scholars are members of the Council of Torah Sages. Naturally the graduates of the yeshivot often look back over their shoulders to their alma mater when deciding on controversial matters.

The social life of Mafdal people during the 1930s and the 1940s had a good deal in common with that of other nationalists. They intermingled as neighbors in many localities throughout the country, particularly in the growing towns and in the larger villages that were beginning to lose their rural character. Religious observance in these localities, insofar as it did not concern practice upon which everyone agreed, tended largely to be a matter for the individual. Mafdal circles as such were not very forceful in pressing—certainly not in pressing successfully—religious policies. In localities with large, concentrated orthodox communities, particularly in Jerusalem, it was different. Here the Agudat Yisrael circles struggled with the secular parties over the religious and cultural character of public life. Demonstrations, at times agitated and at times more restrained, over such issues as the desecration of the Sabbath in public, the opening of modern schools, and the enfranchisement of women, were endemic.

In the sphere of educational activities, there also were notable differences among the various social circles. The nationalist circles developed a modern schooling system in which biblical literature played an important, but far from major role. The schools sought to provide a broad, diversified curriculum, but in matters of religious practice, they inculcated indifference (and sometimes an actively antireligious attitude). While basically all nationalist schools were structured similarly, Mafdal circles created a network of schools that differed on two counts: traditional studies were quantitatively more prominent (but again not predominant), and religious practice was actively taught and encouraged. Agudat Yisrael circles, by and large, carried on and developed the traditional schools (the *talmud torah, yeshiva,* and *kolel*) with their paramount emphasis on talmudic studies. The rift between the educational patterns of the orthodox and the neo-orthodox is in many ways deeper than that between the educational patterns of the neo-orthodox and nationalists. This rift has profound religious ramifications.

Examining the Agudat Yisrael educational pattern in greater detail will lead us to an understanding of some of the crucial characteristics of orthodox and neo-orthodox religiosity.

The Orthodox Pattern

As Israeli secularism grew through nationalist immigration during the first decades of the century, the traditional schooling system became ideologically buttressed by a new conservative ideology, causing it to react to innovations. At a time when schools everywhere were becoming sensitive to the need for technical training, Agudat Yisrael educators were reluctant to introduce changes in the traditional curriculum. It is probably because of the social insulation of Agudat Yisrael circles that their youth accepted the limitations of the curriculum. Consequently, the Agudat Yisrael circles were quite successful in perpetuating themselves through their schooling system. Mafdal circles, on the other hand, apparently withstood secularism less successfully; during the 1930s and 1940s, many of their youth abandoned religious practices and joined the other nationalist circles. Since the mid-1940s, in the wake of two very dramatic events—the German massacre of European Jewry and the attainment of Israeli independence—much of that has changed. While the more profound effects of the European massacre on Jewish religion and spirituality still remain to be explored, the following crucial development is clear.

At the end of World War II, the major remnants of European Jewish orthodoxy were in eastern Hungary and in Romania. In the past, most of this region had constituted one Jewish culture area, a bastion of orthodoxy that had a history of acute conflict with other trends of modern Judaism (Katz 1974). Hungarian Jews, vociferously anti-Zionist, were now driven to migrate. Many came to Israel where they joined both the old Jerusalem community and new religious communities (such as the Tel Aviv suburb of Benei-Brak). Israeli orthodoxy thus came to include a new and aggressively conservative element, people whose conservatism was compounded by the experience of having seen their communities shattered and who now strove to reconstruct them in emulation of the past.

The events in Europe also prompted many of the surviving orthodox rabbis and talmudic scholars to move to Israel and to establish numerous yeshivot and kolelim, institutions of advanced talmudic learning, in various localities throughout the country, including the new towns founded by the nationalists. The combination of an immigrant rabbinical leadership of ranking stature and the Hungarian immigration elicited much religious vitality. The new yeshivot flourished quantitatively and qualitatively, attracting increasing numbers of students, so many that yeshivot now perforce sometimes reject applicants, contrary to all traditional practice.[8] The new Israeli yeshivot have become the world center of

---

[8]In 1973 some 15,600 male adults and boys were reported studying in orthodox yeshivot; of these 5,400, who presumably have their own dependent families, were in kolelim. See Ministry of Religious Affairs (1974) as a source for these, and other, data cited below.

traditional Jewish learning, taking over from the Lithuanian and Polish yeshivot which had filled this role before World War II. They are looked up to by observant Jews throughout the world and even attract students from communities—such as in New York—which are themselves major centers of traditional learning. The yeshivot are the core of orthodoxy, and their flourishing is one of the most crucial features of Israeli Judaism. Characteristically, the yeshivot, while maintaining high academic standards, practice talmudic scholarship in a completely traditional way, consciously shunning modern scholarship in the field.

The scholars of the yeshivot are concerned with religious problems in a manner that is a continuation of their nineteenth-century Lithuanian and Polish forebears. There are considerable productivity and publication in the discussion of problems of ritual, custom, and law, both in the abstract and in the context of present-day technological and social contingencies. The work of ranking yeshiva scholars has relevance for Israeli society generally because the rabbinical courts, which exercise religious law (*halakha*), have exclusive jurisdiction over marital affairs. The ultimate interpretation of religious law, while theoretically resting with the Mafdal-oriented Chief Rabbinate, in fact resides to a very considerable extent in the hands of eminent scholars of yeshiva circles. Members of the High Rabbinical Court pay attention to the informally expressed opinions of these scholars, despite their lack of formal authority. Though there are ancient historical precedents to this kind of mutual regard among rabbinical authorities, in Israel it is also nurtured by the disparity in legitimacy and self-assurance between orthodox and neo-orthodox interpreters of tradition.

The most recent development, within the last few years, is a tendency for yeshiva-oriented rabbis to gain dominant positions within the Chief Rabbinate itself. In this context it is notable that the yeshiva scholars have a tendency to interpret halakhic requirements, in many different areas, in increasingly strict and unequivocal terms.[9] Consistent with this tendency is the new, occasional practice of Israeli halakhic authorities to substantiate their rulings by declaring them to be authoritative *da'at Torah* (Torah Wisdom), along a pattern reminiscent of Catholic pontifical ex cathedra pronouncements. Traditionally, halakhic rulings, even when handed down by most eminent authorities, would always have been annotated with the rational explication of pertinent legal considerations and would consequently have been open for discussion.

Traditionally, abstract religious thought has not been consistently emphasized in Judaism; it is therefore not unusual that the productivity of yeshiva scholars in this area is comparatively poor. Given this background, the fair amount of productivity in the area of ethics is notable; a small number of new moralistic works appears constantly. The social scope of the works emanating from yeshiva circles is, however, largely restricted to orthodox circles. The halakhic tracts, insofar as they are not juridical or concretely textual, mainly discuss matters that are only of concern to strictly observant people. The ethical works are even more restricted. They mostly focus on the problems of the yeshiva student, not on the mundane problems of the observant after termination of his full-time studies.

---

[9]See Rabinowitz (1971) and M. Elon (1973: 22–28) for descriptions of this tendency through analyses of the mutations of legal opinion of particular scholars over particular issues.

Yeshiva circles constitute in many ways an enclosed, self-sufficient subcul-
ture. Terms such as 'religious order' and 'monasticism', while only grossly ap-
proximate, do denote some of the features of most Israeli yeshiva circles.
Characteristic is a feeling of corporateness and difference from other people and
a powerful sensation of superior religious status that sometimes expresses itself
in actual haughtiness. This feeling evolved from the shift, previously noted, in
nineteenth-century Eastern European Judaism toward other-worldly spirituality.
Yeshiva culture often nurtures the Yiddish language of traditional Europe. Although foreign to many students, they pick up the language in the course of their
studies, at least to the extent that they can follow lectures. But even the common
Hebrew speech of yeshiva students has many particular characteristics, both in
vocabulary and in pronunciation, making yeshiva Hebrew rather distinctive.
These peculiarities derive from the Yiddish language, frequently used in scholarly and daily discourse, and the Aramaic language of the talmudic texts. Yeshiva
students dress almost uniformly—dark suit and hat, and white shirt usually with
a dark tie. This kind of attire, immaculate and formal, considering Israeli culture
and the country's subtropical climate, renders yeshiva students a highly visible
and self-conscious group.

The distinctiveness of yeshiva life also reaches into the sphere of marital and
household activities. Owing to the consistent traditional segregation of the sexes
at all stages of socialization, marital bonds are formed through the traditional
mode of matchmaking. Ties are thus established not only between orthodox cou-
ples in Israel, but between people living in Israel and in orthodox communities
overseas as well. The strong hold of yeshiva life on the students also molds the
structure of the family. The wives very often are as keen as their husbands that
the latter continue their studies indefinitely. Consequently, a pattern has developed whereby the wife is the main breadwinner through such work as elementary school teaching. At the same time, little family planning is practised, so that
families grow very fast. Because of the wife's occupation, the husband is much
involved in child care, probably comparatively more than in the traditional Jewish family. The students receive only very small stipends, so that the general standard and style of life in yeshiva circles is modest, sometimes virtually ascetic.
Gradually, most of them are driven by financial need and domestic pressures to
terminate full-time, and eventually part-time, studies and to move into teaching,
commerce, or lower-grade clerical work. Socially and culturally, however, they
maintain many of their characteristics, and their lives continue to revolve around
the yeshivot and their spiritual leaders.

Agudat Yisrael circles also include a handful of people who, despite the draw-
back of not having received a higher secular education, have attained relatively
advanced positions in the economy. They have also attracted a trickle of American and Western immigrants of neo-orthodox background (some of them in advanced professional positions), who, with immigration, shifted their religious
orientation. Their numbers, however, are not very significant, and, more crucially,
these people submit to the religious authority of the yeshivot.

The relative insulation of yeshiva circles from broad social concerns and cultural trends is fostered by two major factors: exemption from army service and
the structure of yeshiva finances. Yeshiva students serve in the army only to a
very limited extent, or not at all. The yeshiva heads, supported by the religious

parties, have insisted on exemption for their students, their feeling being that military service would expose the students to cultural and social influences which might eventually lead them to move away from yeshiva life.[10] It can be assumed that the present flowering of yeshivot in Israel is linked to the military service exemption that yeshiva students can enjoy.[11]

The insulation of yeshiva circles is further reinforced by the structure of yeshiva financing. The main source of funds generally rests with the philanthropy of American and Western orthodoxy. Distance and the relative anonymity of the benefactors render the yeshivot rather independent in the management of their affairs; a fact that, most significantly, sponsors a sense of separation and self-sufficiency vis-à-vis the immediate Israeli environment. Although the Israeli government is in fact an important financial source of support, it does not have actual controlling power or even much influence over the yeshivot, as the case of exemption from military service shows. The government grants support only because of the political power of the religious parties that back the yeshivot, and its concessions probably do not stem from a conviction of the moral right of yeshiva circles to preferential treatment. As a result of this situation, yeshiva circles do not feel obligated to the government—at the most, perhaps, to the Mafdal party that sustains the concessions. Plagued by its fundamental lack of self-assurance, Mafdal, far from controlling the yeshivot, is, in fact, much under their influence. The peculiarities of yeshiva financing and the minimal civic participation of latter-day yeshiva circles cultivate in them a tendency to aloofness and lack of rapport with society. These characteristics are again rooted in the particular spiritualistic and other-worldly turn that Eastern European Jewish religiosity took in the nineteenth century.[12]

I have emphasized the importance of the new yeshiva circles in Israeli orthodoxy. They are distinctive in having been formed by recent immigrants who are involved in the mainstream of the nationalist economy. Characteristically, the new yeshiva circles are centered in the Tel Aviv area, the dynamic economic and social center of the population, and they are more consistently militant as conservatives than their older Jerusalem counterparts. Many features of the Israeli rabbinate that have been pointed out by both neo-orthodox and secular critics, particularly the limited concern with social and moral issues in contrast with the preoccupation with ritual and legal matters (see Singer 1967 and many others), can be traced to the rabbis' personal roots in yeshiva circles. The phenomena are only deceptively exotic; they lie on the main road of present-day Israeli Judaism.

---

[10]See Horowitz and Kimmerling (1974) for a discussion on the important function that Israeli military reserves service plays in social integration.

[11]This assumption is based on my impression that orthodox circles in Western countries, which otherwise have much in common with their Israeli counterparts, maintain comparatively few yeshivot and kolelim and provide for a much shorter yeshiva education. Their youth move quite soon either into commerce or to studying a profession.

[12]My very informal, comparative impressions of yeshiva circles in Israel and in Britain lead me to the conclusion that in Britain, where the yeshivot are in close rapport with their sources of munificence, relations with the community are generally much closer, and yeshiva circles are not as clearly delimited, culturally and socially, from other sectors of the community.

The Nationalist Pattern

In contrast with the relatively small orthodox and neo-orthodox circles, the 'secular' nationalist circles, the third major pattern of Israeli Judaism, form a much larger and more complex sector of the population. The particular religious pattern of this sector was formatively influenced by Ahad Ha'am, a turn-of-the-century Zionist ideologist, whose views were paramount in nationalist circles for many decades.

The ideology of Ahad Ha'am contains profoundly traditional elements such as the concept of national election, the ideal of a stern morality, and many other points of traditional belief and practice. But the traditional elements have been loosened from their old theological moorings: national election is no longer divine election, and morality lacks the religious rationale. Ahad Ha'am set forth new, atheistic anchors for the traditional elements, such as the concept of 'the national spirit', which stems from late nineteenth-century positivist thought. It is the Jewish 'national spirit' that generates the people's view of its unique, elected destiny, creates its lofty moral teachings, and nurtures the attachment to the historical homeland. Ahad Ha'am catalyzed the fusion of tradition and heterodoxy that has come to be characteristic of Zionism. The way was thus cleared for the development of secularism which, paradoxically, is couched in traditional symbols and language. The Bible is prominent in the culture and education of Zionist circles, but its standing is of a national historical–literary heritage, not of a divine testament. Messianism, to take another example, is present in Zionist ideology, but its restraining transcendental anchor has been removed. Hopes and ideals, such as the idea that the Jewish State should eventually become a social model for universal emulation, are vital; but the national destiny is not seen in traditional religious terms.

The combination of a traditional symbolic idiom with a secular nationalist ideology led to religiosymbolic innovations. The nationalists reinterpreted many traditional symbols by infusing them with an atheistic–nationalist content. I cite just one example. At an Independence Day parade in the early 1950s, the following slogan was unfurled across the parade route: 'Israel, Trust in the Army! It is the Help and Shield!' This is a parody of a biblical verse (Psalms 115:9) that figures in the liturgy, where the object of trust is, of course, G-d and not the army.[13] Nationalist circles engaged in symbolic innovations most consistently and creatively in the socialist *kibbutzim*. Here the traditional festivals were radically transformed. They were largely expurgated of their traditional religious content and became infused with new nationalist meaning, which is indeed present in tradition, but often in an understated idiom and always within a broader religious context. The relative importance of the festivals also changed in line with their potential for the expression of nationalist values. For instance, Hanuka, traditionally a festival of a markedly earthy nationalist character, attained increased and novel importance, whereas the Day of Atonement, traditionally the holiest of all days and the most transcendentally oriented, fell practically into desuetude.

---

[13]For further examples of profanation in the context of Ahad Ha'am's thought see Yaron (1975: 15–21).

The power to realize national aims now rests not in divine intervention, but exclusively in human action. The concrete needs of Nation and State have become the ultimate values. This equation is at the root of the symbolic innovations of nationalism where the nation now takes the place formerly held by Divinity. The equation of nationalism with ultimate values implies political and social ideas and policies, that, if consistently developed, lead to étatist conclusions typical of modern nationalist movements in general.[14]

Since the attainment of independence, secular nationalism as an ideological and symbolic system has been on the decline. The new festivals of the nationalist circles flowered for only a comparatively short period, during the 1930s and the 1940s. Since then, people have been losing interest and some of the customs, including most of the agricultural rites, have been abandoned. Lilker (1973) describes in detail some of the ceremonies of what he calls 'kibbutz Judaism', their decline and transformation. In addition, Israeli literature of the last two decades expresses a malaise and gropes for values. The innocent assurance that characterized the prestate generation of nationalists seems gone. A whole range of attitudes populates the cultural spectrum—from destructive, and sometimes vulgar, nihilism, to an introspective and sensitive ethic—all having in common a sense of disillusion with classical nationalism of the Ahad Ha'am type.[15]

On the other hand, we find among secular nationalists a new attraction to activities such as archaeological research in Israel, which are by all accounts expressive of the quest for new existential and ideological bearings (see A. Elon 1971: 279–289).[16] We also often have traditional content being reintroduced into various areas of life, both on the public and private planes. In kibbutz Judaism, traditional content now frequently fills the vacuum left by the agricultural rites that lost their resonance. For one kibbutz we have a graphic description of this development (Kressel 1974: 44): until 1964 the members of the kibbutz celebrated the feast of Shavuot with a wagon procession displaying agricultural produce. The celebration culminated in the ceremonial donation of the produce to a public national fund. In 1966 the kibbutz held only an agricultural exhibition, and people gathered for a picnic. In 1969 and 1970 just a picnic was held; and in 1971, for the first time, a traditional religious theme was introduced—a lecture on Shavuot as the traditional anniversary of the giving of the Torah on Mount Sinai.[17]

Tendencies of this kind are also noticeable in other sections of the secular nationalist circles, for example, in middle class suburbs. Here one gains the impression that people increasingly celebrate rites of passage in synagogues in the

---

[14]See A. Elon (1971) for a pertinent general characterization of the Israeli nationalist 'founding fathers' and of their views on relations between Arabs and Jews.

[15]See the work of the literary critic Kurzweil (1966), and, on a more popular plane, that of Leslie (1971: 72–89) and of A. Elon (1971: 256–279). See Reich (1972) for a detailed account of the vicissitudes of Passover celebrations in kibbutzim.

[16]Max Gluckman pointed out that the current popularity of archaeology seems to be a wider phenomenon, which is common to many countries besides Israel, such as Britain. The explanation of the particular Israeli case may have a wider applicability.

[17]But see Rosner and Ovnat (n.d.) who argue that the religious trend exemplified by such symbolic changes is characteristic of the moderate, rather than of the extreme Marxist, wing of the kibbutz movement. The kibbutz described by Kressel is of the former type.

traditional manner, which fewer would have done in the past. Many people tend to mill around synagogues, if not actually to attend services, on the Day of Atonement. Although completely disregarding religious norms in most contexts, they will revert to tradition in matters such as death and mourning. They will, more or less uncomplainingly, accept religious practice in various areas of life to the extent that it is required by Israeli law. Protest against the fusion of civil and halakhic law is limited to comparatively small groups, and is expressed inconsistently and in subdued form. At the same time, it is notable that modernistic religious movements, of such types as the American Jewish Conservative movement and Reform Judaism, have so far made little headway in Israel.[18] They have no more than a handful of congregations in the country (though more than existed before the State period). Quantitatively, there is no substantial trend toward acceptance of full orthodox or neo-orthodox patterns, although again, there have been individual cases in recent years.[19] Latter-day Israeli secular nationalism, as a form of Judaism, cannot be characterized unambiguously.

Also on the general societal level, ever since the formation of the State, we find nationalist ideologists and politicians turning to traditional religious sources, and traditional symbols now figure in various nationalist roles and activities. Thus, all State presidents since the presidential elections of 1952 have been conceived of as figures who, to an extent, exemplify Jewish tradition. The president's participation in synagogue worship and similar activities is well publicized.[20] and it would now be inconceivable for a president publicly to express atheistic views of the classical nationalist type. This would not, however, have been the case for Israeli leaders before independence, nor for Chaim Weizmann, the first president.[21]

These complex developments are still too fresh to afford us a complete assessment, but there are some overt explanatory factors. The successful attainment of the major Zionist aim with State independence fundamentally undermined the classical secular nationalist ideology, and the crisis was compounded with the disillusion and frustration inherent in any realized social vision. Another factor was the destruction of European Jewry during World War II. This catastrophe muted earlier Zionist criticism of the immediate past that was now irrevocably gone. Particularly the older generation, which remembers the fullness of prewar European Jewish life, has developed a new sentimental attachment to various bits and pieces of tradition.

---

[18]These movements are basically structured to answer the needs of essentially traditional minority communities struggling against assimilation in the midst of hospitable majorities in Western countries (see Sklare 1955, for a sociological analysis of their emergence). It is not surprising that these movements have not struck roots among Israelis whose backgrounds are radically different (see also Zenner 1965a), as comparatively few of them originate in Western countries. There is, of course, also the factor of the inimical attitude of the Israeli rabbinical establishment whose administrative power has consistently stymied the modernistic movements. In its sociological context, this factor should, however, be seen as only secondary.

[19]See again Rosner and Ovnat (n.d.) for a balanced view of the background of such kibbutz cases.

[20]This is true even for incumbent President Katzir, who, by temperament and background, is personally much further removed from religious observance than his predecessors.

[21]Liebman (1975), in a discussion of data of this kind from the aspect of general political integration, has suggested that there may be developing in Israel a civil religion' on the lines of Bellah's American counterpart. My analysis does not support that view.

The traditional ideas and folkways, moored in nineteenth-century positivism, which characterize nationalism of the classical Ahad Ha'am type, were now bolstered by unabashed sentimentalism. On the other hand, the practical exigencies of a vision that has essentially materialized have caused a mellowing and cutting to size of the messianic element in the ideology (see Decalo 1974). The nationalists' conception of statehood has been transformed into an instrumental goal whose ultimate aim is to provide a haven for all Jews. The decline of messianism in Israeli nationalism and the concomitant increasing realism have moral ramifications.[22] The destruction of European Jewry also sharpened the nationalists' awareness of their ties with Diaspora Jewry and of their need for moral and not only material support. The intensified consciousness of the Diaspora inevitably implies a heightened appreciation for traditional religion since it plays a central role in the existence of Diaspora Jewry.[23]

The eclipse of classical secular nationalism is contemporaneous with the reassertion of orthodoxy and with the Mafdal 'failure of nerve' that expressed itself in the Mafdal educational shift and in the phenomenon of the Young Mafdal. All these transformations occurred in the same environment and are fed by basically similar forces—primarily, the emotional upheaval stemming from the destruction of European Jewry; secondarily, the attainment of independence.

The Oriental Pattern

On the scene characterized by the three broad religious and cultural movements that I have described appeared the masses of Oriental immigrants who came in the 1950s, after the establishment of the state. In sharp contrast to the European immigrants, the Oriental newcomers, most of whom had escaped the trauma of German atrocities, did not experience in a searing personal way the situation that the Holocaust had brought about (despite, of course, their knowledge of the events). This is one of the crucial cultural factors that differentiates Oriental from European Israelis and is operative in the quite different courses subsequent religiocultural developments have taken among these two major sectors of the population.

Oriental immigrants have undergone a different but also very disturbing experience of their own, however, an experience rooted in their particular sociocultural situation: the abrupt, overnight transition from traditional life in backward Muslim societies to life in a confused, hectic, heterogeneous, and worldly new country. The immigrants had no ready solutions for the problems inherent in this situation. Worse, they were confronted with a range of solutions (outlined earlier) that European Jews had evolved long ago to cope with their own versions of those problems. The solutions, now in the form of specific socio-religio-political movements and patterns of living, were not tailored to the particular needs of the Oriental immigrants. The mere existence of these delimited solutions stultified the religious creativity of the Orientals which, given time,

---

[22]See Ben-Ezer (1974) for a collection of interviews, some of them very fascinating, on these themes and on secular nationalism in general; in particular see the interviews with Scholem and Alter. See also Har-Even (1970) and Rotenstreich (1965: 325–329); for a somewhat idealized profile of secular nationalist youth see Herman (1970: 165–177).

[23]See again A. Elon (1971: 198–215) for a description of present-day awareness of European World War II events.

might otherwise have expressed itself in the formulation of their own original responses to the situation.

Oriental immigrants compose a large, complex population. For the purpose of this discussion, however, I view them within the frame of a single religious pattern, because the distinguishing sociohistorical factors considered above are crucial. These factors are paramount in molding the religious response of Oriental immigrants to their new environment. While there are differences within the Oriental pattern, they are not sufficiently clear-cut to warrant discussion on the same plane as those of the major patterns. As we shall see, a religious distinction may possibly be emerging between the first and the second generations of Oriental immigrants, but we do not yet have enough empirical research to argue this definitively.

In Israel, many of the Oriental immigrants became fascinated by the socioeconomic superiority associated with Western culture and by its external, more spectacular and vulgar expressions, such as the trappings of material affluence. Their exposure to the influence of mass media eroded their own variants of traditional culture. Moreover, the confrontation of the Oriental immigrants with the existing religious movements had overt political expression. The various political parties that represent these movements vied among themselves to attract the new Oriental and other immigrants. Because their background was so different from that of the Europeans, Oriental immigrants often failed to understand the genuine religious and cultural forces at the root of the political bickering that went on about them. The fundamentally cultural and religious issues were frequently interpreted, or misinterpreted, as pure struggles for power, and the overt religious policies as slogans manipulated cynically for political ends.[24] Traditional religion, consequently, lost much of its appeal.

The gulf between the younger and the older generations of Oriental immigrants is now very deep. Generally speaking, the older generation retains very little prestige, and is often pathetically lacking even in self-respect. Sometimes the old religious leaders actually lose their flocks: new rabbis are elected and rabbis of the old generation move away to retire (Shokeid and Deshen 1977: Chap. 7). But in several studies of the religious life of first-generation Oriental immigrants, Moshe Shokeid and I have observed a series of assertive, creative activities that do constitute attempts to overcome the gulf between the old and the new. In the context of a religious pilgrimage, Shokeid describes the religious response of a group of Moroccan immigrants to a specific problem of reversal of status; and in a study on the emergence of mystical explanations for male barrenness he depicts the religious vitality that prompts people to interpret their new problems in religious terms (Deshen and Shokeid 1974: ch. 2, 4). In studies on memorial celebrations and synagogue ritual of Tunisian immigrants (*ibid:* ch. 3, 6, 7) and on publication activities of holy books (Deshen 1975), I have portrayed people's sensitivities to their new socioreligious creativity.

These religious responses, however, are a far cry from a real transmutation of tradition as represented by the religious movements of European Jewry, which

---

[24]See my accounts of electioneering among the Oriental electorate (Deshen 1970, 1972), and particularly Deshen and Shokeid (1974: ch. 5) and Deshen (1976), where I document religious responses to this situation.

evolved over several generations. Instead, they are altogether specific, serving to solve only the particular religious problems of the individuals and groups we describe. The rather tragic phenomenon of the first generation of traditional Oriental immigrants is transient because of the age factor. This is clearly visible. Oriental immigrants have established numerous synagogues throughout the country in which services were usually held twice daily. Over time, more and more synagogue communities find they cannot gather a quorum for weekday services because of the demise of old men, first-generation immigrants, who used to attend daily. Many of these synagogues now function only on the Sabbaths and during the festivals.

This brings us to the question of the religious character of second-generation Oriental immigrants. Very many younger Orientals attend synagogue services on the major festivals and at family festivities. Young people of Oriental origin are also prominent in religioethnic activities: Moroccans and Kurds in particular are active in revived pseudotraditional festivities peculiar to their traditions; Tunisians, Tripolitanians, and again Moroccans in pilgrimages; Tunisians and Yemenites in the publication of traditional religious texts and journals. These activities express religious vitality, but, as in the case of parallel activities of the older generation, we must caution against attributing too much significance to them. They are not very frequent and attract comparatively few people. At the same time, adherence to religious practice among second-generation Oriental immigrants is manifestly decreasing.[25] Religion does not even play a dominant role in the maintenance of the subethnic identities of immigrant groups. To the limited extent that Oriental immigrants act to sustain subethnic identities, they more commonly use nonreligious vehicles, such as supporting local football teams (particularly among the Yemenite younger generation) and engaging in local ethnic politics.[26]

Orientals do not generally participate in the new Mafdal educational and residential trends: ecological mobility is not toward particularly religious neighborhoods, and Orientals do not send their children to the new religious educational institutions in very significant numbers. The proportion of Mafdal adherents of European background who send their children to be trained in the new system is much larger. Those of Oriental background more often tend to educate their children in the regular religious high schools whose overall demands are far less rigorous than those of the new high school yeshivot. While these differentials are also related to general socioeconomic factors, they cannot be reduced only to these. The differentials express an actual religiocultural variety and a real weakness of Oriental traditionalism in the Israeli situation.

---

[25]This is also true for support on the part of Oriental immigrants for the religious parties. Etzioni-Halevy (1977, ch. 3) concludes, on the basis of survey materials, that 19 percent of the Orientals aged over 50 support religious parties in contrast with 4 percent and 7 percent of Israeli-born and European-born, respectively, in that age category. In the category of those 20 to 34 years old, however, the percentage of support for religious parties drops to about 6 percent among all subethnic categories.

[26]See Deschen (1974) for a discussion of the relationship between Israeli political ethnicity and religiocultural ethnicity, and Zenner (1967: 186) for a pertinent general evaluation. See Liebman (1977) for an approach to the phenomenon of Israeli football, also Klaus (1975).

This weakness can also be seen in the training of rabbis. The yeshivot, mostly founded by European scholars, foster the European variants of Jewish scholarship and religiosity. Oriental immigrants have established only very limited rabbinical training facilities. Consequently, the yeshivot produce many rabbis trained in the European tradition, and comparatively few rabbis in the Oriental tradition. Quite beside the dearth of Oriental-type training institutions, there is comparatively little demand among Oriental youth for advanced talmudic education. A fair number of students of Oriental background who are interested in rabbinical training, however, proceed to study in the more recently established yeshivot sponsored by Agudat Yisrael and Mafdal circles.[27] These students have become absorbed into the orthodox European yeshiva culture, sometimes to the extent of picking up the Yiddish language and even switching their particular ritual of prayer to the European ritual. In fact, they emerge from their studies more or less acculturated in European tradition. The opposite trend—European acculturation to Oriental religious traditions—does not exist. The present trend, while indicative of a potential avenue for the emergence of religious figures from among the Oriental immigrants, implies an adoption of European-style orthodox ways.

Parts of this evaluation of Oriental Judaism are supported by survey data.[28] Rakover, Yinon, and Arad (1971), in a study of religious observance among teenage girls attending religious high schools, found that girls of Oriental origin were less observant and less under the influence of their parents than were their European counterparts. Herman (1970: 122–125), basing himself on a comparatively large general sample of Israeli youth, reached the same conclusion. Earlier, Bachi and Matras (in Matras 1965: 103–108) in a general sample of maternity cases compared the religious observances of women with the religious observances of their mothers. Again, significantly, greater intergenerational differences were found among the Oriental than among European women. Moreover, Matras found that among Oriental women, failure to observe religious practices was positively correlated to increasing education. This finding is typical of people in the throes of a general breakdown of tradition—modern education acting as a catalytic agent in that direction. Among European women, however, there emerged the obverse correlation: religious defection was found to be negatively correlated to increasing education in religious high schools.[29] This finding is, again, understandable in the context of the orthodox and neo-orthodox trends of European Israelis. In these trends, in contrast with traditional Judaism, religiosity is rooted not in natural ongoing practice, but in considered rationalized decision. Therefore, modern religious education, in this context buttresses rather than under-

---

[27]See Herman (1970: 187–193) for a sketch of a young Yemenite acculturated to Mafdal yeshiva circles.

[28]In view of the reservations expressed earlier concerning survey analyses in the area of religion, a word of explanation is in order. Our historical overview has led us to perceive Oriental Israeli Jews as having particular cultural problems; therefore the variable 'Orientals', despite its inclusiveness, does have salience, in contrast with some of the other variables that figure in these surveys.

[29]It should, however, be noted that the findings of another survey (Arian 1973: 66–67) are less clear-cut on this point.

mines observance. In the traditional Oriental context, on the other hand, modern education, even when religious, tends to undermine observance since its inherent nontraditional components clash with custom.

The data concerning correlations of education and religious observance have ramifications for a prognosis of future developments. Formal educational standards are steadily improving in Israel. It is, therefore, to be expected that observance among Orientals will progressively decrease whereas among Europeans, exposed to more rigorous religious schooling, it will increase.

References

Antonovsky, A. (1963). Political-Social Attitudes in Israel. *Amot*, 6: 11–22. In Hebrew.

Antonovsky, A., and Arian, A. (1972). *Hopes and Fears of Israelis: Consensus in a New Society.* Jerusalem: Academic Press.

Arian, A. (1973). *The Choosing People: Voting Behavior in Israel.* Cleveland: Case Western Reserve University Press.

Aronoff, M. (1973). The Politics of Religion in a New Israeli Town. *Eastern Anthropologist*, 26: 145–171.

Ben-Ezer, E., ed. (1974). *Unease in Zion.* New York: Quadrangle Books.

Birnbaum, E. (1970). *The Politics of Compromise: State and Religion in Israel.* Cranbery, N.J.: Fairleigh Dickinson University Press.

Cohen, H. Y. (n.d.). *Zionist Activity in the Middle East.* Jerusalem: Zionist Organization. In Hebrew.

Decalo, S. (1974). Messianic Influences and Pragmatic Limitations in Israeli Foreign Policy. *International Problems*, 13: 373–382.

Deshen, S. (1970). *Immigrant Voters in Israel: Parties and Congregations in a Local Election Campaign.* Manchester: Manchester University Press.

Deshen, S. (1972). 'The Business of Ethnicity Is Finished!'? The Ethnic Factor in a Local Election Campaign, in A. Arian, ed., *The Elections in Israel 1969.* Jerusalem: Academic Press, pp. 278–304.

Deshen, S. (1974). Political Ethnicity and Cultural Ethnicity in Israel during the 1960s, in A. Cohen, ed., *Urban Ethnicity.* Association of Social Anthropologists monograph 12. London: Tavistock, pp. 281–309.

Deshen, S. (1975). Ritualization of Literacy: The Works of Tunisian Scholars in Israel. *American Ethnologist*, 2: 251–259.

Deshen, S. (1976). Of Signs and Symbols: The Transformation of Designations in Israeli Electioneering. *Political Anthropology*, 1: 83–100.

Deshen, S. and Shokeid, M. (1974). *The Predicament of Homecoming: Cultural and Social Life of North African Immigrants in Israel.* Ithaca, N.Y.: Cornell University Press.

Dittes, J. E. (1973). Beyond William James, in C. Y. Glock and P. E. Hammond, eds., *Beyond the Classics? Essays in the Scientific Study of Religion.* New York: Harper & Row, pp. 291–354.

Don-Yihye, E., and Liebman, C. (1972). The Separation of Religion and State: Slogan and Content. *Molad*, 5 (n.s.): 71–89. In Hebrew.

Eisenstadt, S. N. (1967). *Israeli Society.* New York: Basic Books.

Elon, A. (1971). *The Israelis: Founders and Sons.* London: Widenfeld and Nicholson.

Elon, M. (1973). *Halakhic Problems in Israeli State Law.* Jerusalem: Hebrew University Institute of Contemporary Jewry. In Hebrew.

Etzioni-Halevy, E. (1977). *Political Culture in Israel.* New York: Praeger.

Fishnam, A. (1957). *The Religious Kibbutz Movement: The Revival of the Jewish Religious Community.* Jerusalem: Zionist Organization.

Friedman, M. (1972). The Chief Rabbinate: An Insoluble Dilemma. *State and Government*, 1: 118–128. In Hebrew.

Friedman, M. (1975). Religious Zealotry in Israeli Society, in S. Poll and E. Krausz, eds., *On Ethnic and Religious Diversity in Israel.* Ramat Gan: Bar-Ilan University, pp. 91–111.

Goldman, E. (1964). *Religious Issues in Israel's Political Life.* Jerusalem: Jewish Agency.

Gutmann, E. (1972). Religion in Israeli Politics, in L. Landau, ed., *Man, State and Society in the Contemporary Middle East.* New York: Praeger, pp. 122–134.

Har-Even, S. (1970). A Secular Talk. *Ma'ariv, Aug. 8. In Hebrew. Also in M. Samet, ed., Religion and State.* Jerusalem: Hebrew University Faculty of Social Sciences, pp. 100–103. In Hebrew.

Herman, S. N. (1970). *Israelis and Jews: The Continuity of an Identity.* New York: Random House.

Horowitz, D. and Kimmerling, B. (1974). Some Implications of Military Service and the Reserve System in Israel. *Archives Européennes de Sociologie*, 15: 262–276.

Jacobsen, H. (1972). On the Social Structure of a Progressive Community in Israel. *Shalhevet*, 9: 4–6. In Hebrew.

Katz, E., and Gurevitch, M. (1973). *The Culture of Leisure in Israel: Patterns of Spending Time and Consuming Culture.* Tel Aviv: Am Oved. In Hebrew.

Katz, J. (1960). Traditional Society and Modern Society. *Megamot*, 10: 304–311. In Hebrew.

Katz, J. (1968). The Jewish National Movement: A Sociological Analysis. *Cahiers d'histoire mondiale*, 11: 267–283.

Katz, J. (1973). *Out of the Ghetto: The Social Background of Jewish Emancipation, 1770–1870.* Cambridge, Mass.: Harvard University Press.

Katz, J. (1977). The Uniqueness of Hungarian Jewry. *Forum* (Jerusalem). 2: 45–53.

Keshet, S. (1969). *An Arrow from Sylvy Keshet.* Jerusalem: Schocken. In Hebrew.

Klaus, A. (1975). Corruption and Violence in Israeli Sport. *Crime and Social Deviance*, 3: 35–48. In Hebrew.

Kressel, G. M. (1974). *'From Each According to His Ability . . . ': Stratification versus Equality in a Kibbutz.* Tel Aviv: Gome. In Hebrew.

Kurzweil, B. (1953). The New 'Canaanites' in Israel. *Judaism*, 2: 3–15.

Kurzweil, B. (1966). *Between Vision and the Absurd: Essays on our Twentieth-Century Literature.* Jerusalem: Schocken. In Hebrew.

Leslie, S. C. (1971). *The Rift in Israel: Religious Authority and Secular Democracy.* London: Routledge & Kegan Paul.

Liebman, C. (1975). Religion and Political Integration in Israel. *Jewish Journal of Sociology*, 17: 17–27.

Liebman, C. (1977). Toward the Study of Popular Religion in Israel. *Megamot*, 23: 95–109. In Hebrew.

Lilker, S. (1973). *Kibbutz Judaism: A New Tradition in the Making.* Ph.D. diss., Hebrew Union College, Jewish Institute of Religion, New York.

Matras, J. (1965). *Social Change in Israel.* Chicago: Aldine.

Ministry of Religious Affairs, Israel (1974). *Report of Activities, 1973.* Jerusalem: Government Printer. In Hebrew.

Morgenstern, A. (1973). *The Israeli Chief Rabbinate: The Foundation and Organization.* Jerusalem: Shorashim. In Hebrew.

Ocks, D. (1973). A Particular Yeshiva Pattern, in H. Urmian, ed., *Education in Israel.* Jerusalem: Ministry of Education, pp. 311–316. In Hebrew.

Peres, Y. (1976). *Ethnic Relations in Israel.* Tel Aviv: Sifríat Hapoalim. In Hebrew.

Petuchowski, J. J. (1971). The Shape of Israeli Judaism: Realities and Hopes. *Judaism,* 20: 141–152.

Rabinowitz, L. I. (1971). The New Trend in Halakha. *Tradition,* 11: 5–15.

Rakover, S., Y. Yinon, and R. Arad. (1971). Religious Observance among Girls. *Megamot,* 17: 166–177. In Hebrew.

Reich, A. (1972). *Changes and Developments in the Passover Haggadot of the Kibbutz Movement: 1935–1971.* Ph.D. diss. University of Texas, Austin.

Rim, Y. and Kurzweil, Z. E. (1965). A Note on Attitudes to Risk-Taking of Observant and Non-Observant Jews. *Jewish Journal of Sociology,* 8: 238–245.

Robertson, R. (1972). Religion, in P. Barker, ed., *A Sociological Portrait.* Penguin, pp. 151–162.

Rosner, M. and Ovnat, A. (n.d.). *Judaism and Zionism in the View of Kibbutz Youth.* Giv'at Haviva: The Institute for Research on Kibbutz Society. In Hebrew.

Rotenstreich, N. (1965). *The People and Its State.* Tel Aviv: Kibbutz Hameuhad. In Hebrew.

Rubinstein, A. (1967). Law and Religion in Israel. *Israel Law Review,* 3: 380–414.

Samet, M. S. (1969 and 1970). Orthodox Jewry in Modern Times. *Mahalkhim,* 1: 29–40; 2: 15–27. In Hebrew.

Shafran, N. (1973). The Red Rock: A Retrospective View. *Keshet,* 59: 5–22. In Hebrew.

Sharot, S. (1974). Minority Situation and Religious Acculturation: A Comparative Analysis of Jewish Communities. *Comparative Studies in Society and History,* 16: 329–354.

Shelah, L., Harlap, H., and Weiss, S. (1971). *The Social Structure of Israel.* Jerusalem: Hebrew University Institute of Contemporary Jewry.

Shokeid, M., and Deshen, S. (1977). *The Generation of Transition: First-Generation North African Immigrants in Israel.* Jerusalem: Ben-Zvi Institute. In Hebrew.

Singer, Z. (1967). Israel's Religious Establishment and Its Critics. *Midstream,* March: 50–56.

Sklare, M. (1955). *Conservative Judaism: An American Religious Movement.* Glencoe, Ill., Free Press.

Spiro, M. E. (1967). The Sabras and Zionism: A Study in Personality and Ideology. *Social Problems,* 5: 100–110.

Weiner, H. (1969). *9½ Mystics: The Kabbala Today.* New York: Collier.

Weller, L. (1974). *Sociology in Israel.* Westport, Conn.: Greenwood.

Weller, I. and Tabory, E. (1972). Religiosity of Nurses and Their Orientation to Patients. *Bar-Ilan University Annual,* 10: 97–110.

Werblowsky, R. Y. Z. (1960). Biblical Studies as a Religious Problem. *Molad,* 18: 162–168. In Hebrew.

Willner, D. (1965). Politics and Change in Israel: The Case of Land Settlement. *Human Organization*, 24: 65–72.

Yaron, Z. (1975). Religion in Israel. *American Jewish Yearbook:* 3–52.

Zenner, W. P. (1965*a*). The Israel Sephardim and Religion. *Alliance Review*, 39: 26–29.

Zenner, W. P. (1965*b*). Saints and Piecemeal Supernaturalism among the Jerusalem Sephardim. *Anthropological Quarterly*, 38: 201–217.

Zenner, W. P. (1967). Sephardic Communal Organizations in Israel. *Middle East Journal*, 21, 2: 175–186.

PART FIVE

What of the Future?

36 *Perspectives on the Future of Judaism*

Tracing their history back to Abraham and Sarah and counting a continuous life as a People for nearly 4,000 years, Jews dwell upon the uncertainty of their own future, deriving remarkably slight comfort from the record of the past. No picture of Judaism the religion can omit that dark corner of Jewish ethnic concern and Judaic religious consciousness as well: what of the future? That is why the future dictates where we conclude this dialogue with the voices of Judaism. In this way we hear how people express their deepest concerns and convictions, a music that pierces the silence of the age to come. Norms of behavior, norms of belief—these do not exhaust the record of the faith, for beyond we want to listen for the echoes of humanity: what do ordinary people, including extraordinary intellects, have to say for themselves in the privacy of their hearts?

True, the range of sounds startles, and we have already paid close attention to some of the most interesting and telling themes of the contemporary life of Judaism in the United States and in the state of Israel. Among them we cannot now say which will live and which perish. The traits of the new by definition always include transience. So whether the New Age or feminist or experimental Judaisms that presently attest to the religious vitality of holy Israel will make a permanent mark we cannot yet tell. But even now certain sounds pierce the silence, and, it is clear, certain themes out of the twentieth century will dominate in the twenty-first. The reason for certainty that these themes are going to persist comes to us out of the long past: These are the matters that have marked the imagination and intellect of Judaism for nearly the whole of recorded time. The first is a deep sense of the fragility of the life of Israel, the holy people; the second, a constant act of remembrance of the dreadful potentialities of time; the third, a perpetual encounter with God in worship and in contention as well, in the manner of Abraham and the Psalmist, and the fourth, an enduring trust in God. We may classify these enduring motifs as sociological, theological (for both the second and the third entries), and religious.

For our time, these lasting traits come to acutely contemporary expression. The sociological worry—will the Jews survive?—dominates the life of the organized Jewish community, ethnic and secular though it is. The theological dilemma, the meaning of Israel's suffering, takes over the cultural and intellectual life of Jewry in the acutely contemporary form of the Holocaust and its meaning. And the religious foundations of the life of holy Israel come to expression in the purity and certainty characteristic of a wise old man, who stands for eternal Israel.

Accordingly, these three dimensions of today's Judaic discourse about the future—the sociological, the theological, and the religious—take the measure of matters: the uneasiness that perpetually characterizes Jews when they peer over the horizon of time; the enduring, and probably eternal, reflection on the meaning, for the Jews and for Judaism, of the Holocaust, and—outweighing all else—the religious convictions of the faithful Jew who practices the religion, Judaism, as he understands the Torah.

We hear first from one of modern Judaism's most insightful intellectuals, Simon Rawidowitz, who reflects on the permanence of the sense of transience and ephemerality that, from the very beginning, has characterized Judaic consciousness. Scripture itself instills that sense, with its message that the existence of the people is not a given but a gift. Only if the conditions of the covenant with God are met will Israel, the holy people, endure.

The theological meaning of Auschwitz has reached full expression in the writing of nearly every postwar theologian of Judaism, but most powerfully and with the greatest influence in that of Emil L. Fackenheim. Here he answers the question, "What does the Voice of Auschwitz command?" But David R. Blumenthal wishes to reflect about not Auschwitz but God, not about the paralyzing problem of evil but the challenging question of holiness. He is important as a strong and self-confident voice that takes over the challenge of the Holocaust to theology and responds constructively and systematically with a way of religious thinking even about the unthinkable.

We close with the most important issue facing any religion: how to encounter God in prayer. Here the great issues become real, personal, and social. The great liturgist, Rabbi Jules Harlow, links prayer, Feminism, contemporary Judaism, and the heritage of two thousand years of worship—a fitting tribute to the future.

37 Israel the Ever-Dying People

SIMON RAWIDOWICZ

1. Why is this reading important?

Public debate within the religious communities of Judaism as well as in the larger secular Jewish world focuses upon problems of demography. Compared with the Chinese (as an ethnic community) or the Catholics or Muslims or Buddhists among religions, the Jews are not a numerous group. The readings you have now completed have shown you, further, that the Jews are not unified; we can speak about "the Jews" only from the perspective of the outsider, since up close they scarcely form a coherent group.

Moreover, since Classical Judaism takes the view that at the end of time the nations will give up idolatry and recognize the one true God when the Messiah comes, few Judaisms engage in trying to convert Gentiles (or even other Jews). Consequently the number of Jews increases, in the main, only through natural processes of procreation and effective nurture of children. The result is an ongoing concern that the Jews are dying out and with them Judaism in all its systems. The concern is well founded. In Britain since World War II, the Jewish community has diminished from nearly half a million in number to between a quarter of a million and 300,000. American Jewry, then 3.7 percent of the U.S. population, today is not much more than 2 percent.

And a further consideration preoccupies people when they think about the future. If Judaism is propagated in bed, then marriage of practicing Jews to one another takes on heightened consequence. When Jews marry outside the faith, the prospect of their raising children in the faith diminishes. While the rate of out-marriage of various other ethnic groups greatly exceeds the rate of the Jews, still the choice of mate of one out of every two Jews in the United States is an outsider to the faith. It is to this mentality—we are the last generation, I am the last Jew on earth—that the great social philosopher of Jewish culture Simon Rawidowicz addresses his profound remarks.

2. What should you notice as you proceed?

Rawidowicz wants to provide perspective on the mentality of Jews who face the future with foreboding. This he does by showing that from the very beginning of holy Israel as portrayed in Scripture, every generation thought of itself as the final one, the last link in a chain about to snap. Notice how he appeals to historical precedent, not to prove a point of sociology, but only to provide perspective and a source of confidence. It is true, he maintains, that the Jews have never competed in numbers with the Chinese or the Hindus, nor Judaism with Islam, let alone Christianity. But he also points to ancient empires best remembered today only by holy Israel in worship or by the Jews in their ethnic consciousness: Egypt, Assyria, Babylonia, and Persia, for example. The first outsider to refer to Israel in all of history declares that he has exterminated Israel, and chances are you never heard of him. Then why, defying the lessons of history, do Jews worry so much about the future? Rawidowicz thinks that that emotion of dread serves to motivate and energize. But that same emotion appeals to ego, giving a person a sense of self-importance and an individual calling. If people suppose that they decide the future, they are likely to make decisions and undertake action to shape the future that they want. If they think they make no difference, they will opt out. Judaism alerts the faithful to remember how few they are, and how important.

3. How should you frame a question for class discussion in response to what you have read?

The orientation toward the future that characterizes Judaism finds its counterpart in the worldview of other families of religious systems. In some instances, these focus upon individual life—for example, after death, promising reward in heaven or punishment in hell. In others they speak of the future of the entire community of the faithful. But it is hard to find a counterpart to the American Jews' special concern for their continuity as a distinctive group in American society (and in other democracies), and no parallel presents itself in Israeli thinking about the future. That Americans of diverse ethnic or religious origins intermarry surprises no one—half of Japanese Americans, more than half of all Catholics, nearly three-quarters of Italian Americans, 84 percent of Polish Americans, and so on. The majority of Jews who married after 1985 married non-Jews, and only a quarter of the children of those marriages are raised as Jews. But whether others declare a religious catastrophe, Jews call down heaven and earth in prognostications of gloom, counting the years to the last Jew in the United States, who will die in 2076. Not surprisingly, Israelis contemplate the future in national and political terms; they do not ask Judaism, the religion, to solve problems of political demography or to explain why people should carry forward the ethnic identification of "being Jewish" let alone the religious identity of forming "holy Israel."

From the Patriarch Abraham, who lamented that "I go hence childless, and he that shall be possessor of my house is Eliezer of Damascus" [Genesis 15:2], through the compilers of the *Mishnah* and the *Gemara*, and from Maimonides in the 12th century to [Joseph Hayyim] Brenner in the 20th, we encounter the same theme of *mi-she-met*, the last Jews! Rabbi Akiba was the last representative of Torah; Brenner and [Micah Joseph] Berdichevski, the last Jews.

When Brenner wrote about being the last, there were several million Jews in his country of origin, Russia, and another three millions or so in the other European lands. Now, after our great European tragedy—"tragedy" is too weak a word for this third great disaster in our history—the traditional dread of being the last naturally assumes dimensions of great magnitude in the minds of our European brethren—but not only with them. Every effort to revitalize Jewish life and learning is stamped—and handicapped—by the fear of being the last. Every Jewish teacher, community worker who toils for the sake of Israel, "for the sake of heaven in truthfulness," every Jewish scholar and thinker who dares to continue the great tradition of Jewish scholarship in the face of growing assimilation and adjustment to the outside world—each considers himself the last of his kind, and is so considered by those around him. They know he is the last—for they feel it in their very bones that they, too, are the last. How often do we feel—not only in the present-day diaspora—seeing a great creative Jew, watching a gathering of "good Jews" to preserve their identity by all means and whatever cost, that they are the last, that we all are the last; and how often are we full of doubt as to whether the future will give rise to further teachers, scholars and even plain ordinary Jews. Often it seems as if the overwhelming majority of our people go about driven by the panic of being the last. It hardly needs emphasizing that this sense of fear is naturally bound to exercise a most paralyzing effect on our conscious and subconscious life, on our emotions and thoughts.

When we analyze somewhat more deeply this constant dread of the end, we discover that one of its decisive psychological elements is the general, not particularly Jewish, sense of fear of losing ground, of being deprived of possessions and acquisitions—or, still deeper, the sense of fear which came over man when he first saw the sunset in the west, not knowing that every sunset is followed by a sunrise, as the *midrash* so beautifully described Adam's first great shock.

Is Israel alone a dying nation? Numerous civilizations have disappeared before there emerged the one in which we live so happily and unhappily at the same time. Each dying civilization was confident that earth and heaven would disappear with it. How often did man feel he was finished forever! When ancient Rome began to crumble, Romans and others felt sure that the end of the universe was at hand. St. Augustine thought that the "anti-Christ" would appear after the destruction of Rome and man would be called to his last day of judgment. In various aspects, this fear of being the last was also manifest in Christianity and Islam. In addition, the lamentation of *mi-she-met* has its psychological origin in man's great admiration for his living masters, in his fear lest the miracle will not occur again, lest there will be no second set of masters—as if genius rises only once, never again to re-appear.

Yet, making all allowances for the general motives in this dread of the end, it has nowhere been at home so incessantly, with such an acuteness and intensity, as in the House of Israel. The world may be constantly dying, but no nation was ever so incessantly dying as Israel.

Going deeper into the problem—and here I have to confine myself to a hint— I am often tempted to think that this fear of cessation in Israel was fundamentally a kind of protective individual and collective emotion. Israel has indulged so much in the fear of its end, that its constant vision of the end helped it to over-come every crisis, to emerge from every threatening end as a living unit, though much wounded and reduced. In anticipating the end, it became its master. Thus no catastrophe could ever take this end-fearing people by surprise, so as to put it off its balance, still less to obliterate it—as if Israel's incessant preparation for the end made this very end absolutely impossible.

Philosophers like Hegel and Schopenhauer have spoken of the guile of na-ture, of the guile of history. Is not this peculiar sense of the end also the guile of a nation *sui generis,* a nation that would use every device for its survival, even that of incessant anticipation of its disappearance, in order to rule it out forever? This aspect of national psychology deserves special attention.

As far as historical reality is concerned, we are confronted here with a phe-nomenon which has almost no parallel in mankind's story: a nation that has been disappearing constantly for the last two thousand years, exterminated in dozens of lands all over the globe, reduced to half or third of its population by tyrants ancient and modern—and yet it still exists, falls and rises, loses all its possessions and re-equips itself for a new start, a second, a third chance—always fearing the end, never afraid to make a new beginning, to snatch triumph from the jaws of defeat, whenever and wherever possible. There is no nation more dying than Is-rael, yet none better equipped to resist disaster, to fight alone, always alone.

As far as our foreign relations, if I may so call them, are concerned, there is much comfort in our thorny path in the world. The first ancient non-Jewish doc-ument which mentions Israel by name is, symbolically apt; a message of total an-nihilation. It is the monument—in possession of the British Museum—on which Merneptah, the thirteenth century B.C.E. Egyptian forerunner of Nasser, boasts of his great deeds and triumphs over nations, and, among other things, states suc-cinctly: "Israel is desolated; its seed is no more." Since 1215 B.C.E. how often did prophets at home and abroad prophesy Israel's desolation! How often did nations try to translate this prophecy into practice, and in the most cruel ways! About 3,150 years after that boastful Egyptian conqueror, there arose Satan in the heart of Europe and began to predict Israel's total annihilation—and to prepare the most modern technical devices to make his prophecy come true. And after it was given to him—to our greatest sorrow and the world's greatest shame—to reduce Israel by one-third, Israel is still alive—weakened, to be sure, robbed of its best resources for recuperation, of its reservoir, its fountains of life and learning, yet still standing on its feet, numbering four times as many souls as in the days of the French Revolution, rebuilding its national life in the State of Israel, in the face of so many obstacles! Though not perfect, its spiritual creativity continues. Filled with fear of its end, it seeks to make a new beginning in the diaspora and in the State of Israel.

If so, many will say, what is all the lamenting about? Many nations have suf-fered, and, if we suffered a little more, we should not exaggerate or carry on hys-terically. No need to worry, no need of superhuman efforts—wait and see—nothing will happen; and if it should happen—surely it has happened before. [. . .]

Such easy comfort, such exaggerated optimism is no less dangerous than the pessimism of Israel's end. Neither is justified, neither is helpful.

In the beginning, Israel's message was that of a universal optimism—salva-tion, happiness and perfection for all peoples. "The mountain of the Lord's house will be established in the top of the mountains" [Isaiah 2:2] means: the peoples of the world will also share alike, with Israel, in the blessing of the messianic age. Many well-known and understandable factors compelled post-exilic and medieval Messianism to become more one-sided and directed exclusively toward the redemption of Israel; optimistic toward Israel, pessimistic toward the world. In more recent times, most Jewish ideologies and political movements were dualistic inasmuch as they saw a world divided, Israel and world torn apart—nay, still more: Israel itself was to them no more. Thus, to give one illustration, Jewish Reform on both sides of the Rhine, 19th-century liberalism, was optimistic as far as the world's future was concerned, pessimistic for the survival of Israel as a nation with all national attributes. This same dualistic attitude was taken up by all kinds of assimilated Jewish revolutionaries in Eastern and Western Europe. Later, two Jewish ideologies fought each other in Europe: one was most optimistic for the remnant of Israel in Zion and pessimistic as far as the Jewish people in the diaspora was concerned, while the other reversed this dichotomy, maintaining that only diaspora Jewry had a future in some liberal or socialistic order.

Both made the fundamental mistake of dividing Israel into two parts. Israel must always be considered one and indivisible—*yisrael ehad*. As long as one part of Israel lives in a hell, the other cannot live in paradise.

I therefore say: we may not split up Israel into two spheres of reality. Israel is one. Neither may we approach the Jewish problem from an optimistic or pessimistic angle. Optimism and pessimism are only expressions or indications of our fears, doubts, hopes and desires. Hopes and desires we must have; fears and doubts we cannot escape. Yet, what we need most at present is a dynamic Jewish realism which will see our reality, the reality of the world, our problem, the problem of the world, in its entirety, without any dualism—hell-paradise or whatever.

Such a Jewish realism will also show us the real meaning of that fear of the end which is so inherent in us. A nation dying for thousands of years means a living nation. Our incessant dying means uninterrupted living, rising, standing up, beginning anew. We, the last Jews! Yes, in many respects it seems to us as if we are the last links in a particular chain of tradition and development. But if we are the last—let us be the last as our fathers and forefathers were. Let us prepare the ground for the last Jews who will come after us, and for the last Jews who will rise after them, and so on until the end of days.

If it has been decreed for Israel that it go on being a dying nation—let it be a nation that is constantly dying, which is to say: incessantly living and creating—one nation from Dan to Beersheba, from the sunny heights of Judea to the shadowy valleys of Europe and America.

To prepare the ground for this great oneness, for a Jewish realism built on it, is a task which requires the effort of Jewish scholarship and statesmanship alike. One nation, one in beginning and end, one in survival and extinction! May it be survival rather than extinction, a beginning rather than an ignominious end—one Israel, *yisrael ehad*.

38 The Voice of Auschwitz

EMIL L. FACKENHEIM

1. Why is this reading important?

The Holocaust—the Germans' systematic murder of Jews between 1933 and 1945—rightly dominates contemporary Judaic religious discourse. That is because monotheism, belief in one and only God, who is just, leaves no alternative. How in a world governed by God, made known to holy Israel in the Torah, such a thing can take place defines the urgent question confronting modern Judaic theologians. A religion of numerous gods finds many solutions to one problem; a religion of only one God presents one to many. Monotheism by nature explains many things in a single way. One God rules. Life is meant to be fair, and just rules are supposed to describe what is ordinary, all in the name of that one and only God. If one true God has done everything, then, since he is God all-powerful and omniscient, all things are credited to, and blamed on, him. In that case he can be either good or bad, just or unjust—but not both. The first and most important theologian writing in English to address this problem is Emil Fackenheim, who has tried to hear the message—"the commanding Voice"—of Auschwitz. Here he expands on his basic statement.

2. What should you notice as you proceed?

Fackenheim transforms events into lessons by identifying an exemplary moment and drawing a conclusion out of it. He stresses the importance of memory on one side, survival for survival's sake on the other. Notice how Fackenheim struggles with the distinction between religious and secularist in the Jewish world and appeals to the Holocaust as a means of obliterating that distinction. That accounts for the dialectic exposed in the fourth fragment: the religious Jew after Auschwitz must continue to wrestle with his God, the secular Jew may not use Auschwitz as a weapon to deny Him. Pay attention to how Fackenheim signals his own intellectual honesty, a brutal honesty that prevents him from retreating into slogans. He identifies the points of conflict in his several propositions. Finally, do not miss the use of language here, the resort to exceedingly provocative formulations, some might say, an excess of emotions. You may wonder whether the net effect of the writing overwhelms the message, so that the reasoned quality of philosophical-theological discourse is lost.

3. How should you frame a question for class discussion in response to what you have read?

As a work of theological apologetics, Fackenheim's essay raises a number of questions of broad, theoretical interest in the study of religion. We note at the outset that monotheism makes demands that other conceptions of God need not meet. If monotheism has to account for evil within the theory of a single, all-powerful God, then what are responses to evil that you can identify in the other monotheisms, Christianity and Islam. What choices have presented themselves in ancient Israel's Scriptures (the "Old Testament" of the Christian Bible), by Job, for example, or by Jeremiah? The Pentateuch, in both Leviticus and Deuteronomy, accounts for suffering in ways not considered by Fackenheim. An analytical discussion will compare and contrast other ways of formulating the message of the Holocaust, placing the way taken by Fackenheim into context.

That will lead to a second discussion, one that will place Fackenheim, a Reform rabbi, into the context of the history of the Judaism that he espouses: the religion of the dual Torah. Since Fackenheim has not taken the ways laid open by the traditions of the Torah, we not only have to compare his apologetics with the ones of the received traditions of monotheism. We also have to account for the particular character of his message, the need he evinces to deal with both secular and religious Jews. A wide-ranging discussion on the gains and pains of tailoring thought to one's audience can translate the case of Fackenheim into an example of choices thinkers make. In every line of this reading, you see what happens when a great thinker tries to persuade audiences that maintain contradictory premises.

Third, how long does memory matter? The long list of victims encompasses every age and land. African Americans, who came with the first European Americans but not by choice, Native Americans, dispossessed of holdings and heritage, Hispanic Americans, marginalized and disregarded, countless groups of aggrieved "minorities," encompassing even the majority, women—all clamor for priority. The Armenians preserve from World War I the memory of the massacre by the Turks of nearly half the Armenians in the world at that time. Understandably, Germans would like to forget and move on with their history. Their willing helpers elsewhere, the Swedes and Swiss who profited, the Lithuanians, Poles, Ukrainians, Rumanians, Hungarians, Slovakians, French and Dutch who joined in the slaughter and the expropriation of the victims—all counsel oblivion. A discussion within the framework of religion and memory (rather than religion and "history") will explore the uses and abuses of memory. Why does religion appeal to the past, and what authority does religion impute to history? Do you think that memory matters in all religions, or can you introduce religions that draw upon a different conception of time from the one that divides time by past, present, and future? Even an event unique in human history such as the Holocaust raises questions of general intelligibility. Here too, if we know this, what else do we know?

What Does the Voice of Auschwitz Command?

Jews are forbidden to hand Hitler posthumous victories. They are commanded to survive as Jews, lest the Jewish people perish. They are commanded to remember the victims of Auschwitz lest their memory perish. They are forbidden to despair of man and his world, and to escape into either cynicism or otherworldliness, lest they cooperate in delivering the world over to the forces of Auschwitz. Finally, they are forbidden to despair of the God of Israel, lest Judaism perish. A secularist Jew cannot make himself believe by a mere act of will, nor can he be commanded to do so. . . . And a religious Jew who has stayed with his God may be forced into new, possibly revolutionary relationships with Him. One possibility, however, is wholly unthinkable. A Jew may not respond to Hitler's attempt to destroy Judaism by himself cooperating in its destruction. In ancient times, the unthinkable Jewish sin was idolatry. Today, it is to respond to Hitler by doing his work.[1]

Elie Wiesel has compared the holocaust with Sinai in revelatory significance—and expressed the fear that we are not listening. We shrink from this daring comparison—but even more from not listening. We shrink from any claim to have heard—but even more from a false refuge, in an endless agnosticism, from a Voice speaking to us. I was able to make the above, fragmentary statement [. . .] only because it no more than articulates what is being heard by Jews the world over—rich and poor, learned and ignorant, believing and secularist. I cannot go beyond this earlier statement but only expand it.

1. The First Fragment

In the murder camps the unarmed, decimated, emaciated survivors often rallied their feeble remaining resources for a final, desperate attempt at revolt. The revolt was hopeless. There was no hope but one. One might escape. Why must one escape? To tell the tale. Why must the tale be told when evidence was already at hand that the world would not listen?[2] Because not to tell the tale, when it might be told, was unthinkable. The Nazis were not satisfied with mere murder. Before murdering Jews, they were trying to reduce them to numbers; after murdering them, they were dumping their corpses into nameless ditches or making them into soap. They were making as sure as was possible to wipe out every trace of memory. Millions would be as though they had never been. But to the pitiful and glorious desperadoes of Warsaw, Treblinka, and Auschwitz, who would soon themselves be as though they had never been, not to rescue for memory what could be rescued was unthinkable because it was sacrilege.[3]

---

[1]See E. Fackenheim, *Quest for Past and Future*, Bloomington and London, 1968, pp. 17–20.

[2]See especially Elie Wiesel, "A Plea for the Dead," *Legends of Our Time*, New York, 1968, pp. 174–97.

[3]See especially Yuri Suhl, *They Fought Back*, New York, 1967.

It will remain a sacrilege ever after. Today, suggestions come from every side to the effect that the past had best be forgotten, or at least remain unmentioned, or at least be coupled with the greatest and most thoughtless speed with other, but quite different, human tragedies. Sometimes these suggestions come from Jews rationalizing their flight from the Nazi holocaust. More often they come from non-Jews, who rationalize their own flight, or even maintain, affrontingly enough, that unless Jews universalize the holocaust, thus robbing the Jews of Auschwitz of their Jewish identity, they are guilty of disregard for humanity. But for a Jew hearing the commanding Voice of Auschwitz the duty to remember and to tell the tale, is not negotiable. It is holy. The religious Jew still possesses this word. The secularist Jew is commanded to restore it. A secular holiness, as it were, has forced itself into his vocabulary.

2. The Second Fragment

Jewish survival, were it even for no more than survival's sake, is a holy duty as well. The murderers of Auschwitz cut off Jews from humanity and denied them the right to existence; yet in being denied that right, Jews represented all humanity. Jews after Auschwitz represent all humanity when they affirm their Jewishness and deny the Nazi denial. They would fail if they affirmed the mere *right* to their Jewishness, participating, as it were, in an obscene debate between others who deny the right of Jews to exist and Jews who affirm it. Nor would they deny the Nazi denial if they affirmed merely their humanity-in-general, permitting an anti-Semitic split between their humanity and their Jewishness, or, worse, agreeing to vanish as Jews in one way, in response to Hitler's attempt to make them vanish in another. The commanding Voice of Auschwitz singles Jews out; Jewish survival is a commandment which brooks no compromise. It was this Voice which was heard by the Jews of Israel in May and June 1967 when they refused to lie down and be slaughtered.

Yet such is the extent of Hitler's posthumous victories that Jews, commanded to survive as Jews, are widely denied even the right. More precisely—for overt anti-Semitism is not popular in the post-holocaust world—they are granted the right only on certain conditions. Russians, Poles, Indians, and Arabs have a natural right to exist; Jews must earn that right. Other states must refrain from wars of aggression; the State of Israel is an "aggressor" even if it fights for its life. Peoples unscarred by Auschwitz ought to protest when any evil resembling Auschwitz is in sight, such as the black ghettoes or Vietnam. The Jewish survivors of Auschwitz have no right to survive unless they engage in such protests. Other peoples may include secularists and believers. Jews must be divided into bad secularists or Zionists, and good—albeit anachronistic—saints who stay on the cross.

The commanding Voice of Auschwitz bids Jews reject all such views as a monumental affront. It bids them reject as no longer tolerable every version— Christian or leftist, gentile or Jewish—of the view that the Jewish people is an anachronism, when it is the elements of the world perpetrating and permitting Auschwitz, not its survivors, that are anachronistic. A Jew is commanded to descend from the cross and, in so doing, not only to reiterate his ancient rejection of an ancient Christian view but also to suspend the time-honored Jewish exaltation of martyrdom. For after Auschwitz, Jewish life is more sacred than Jewish death, were it even for the sanctification of the divine Name. The left-wing secularist Israeli journalist Amos Kenan writes: "After the death camps, we are left only one supreme value: existence."[4]

3. The Third Fragment

But such as Kenan, being committed and unrepentant lovers of the downtrodden, accept other supreme values as well, and will suspend these only when Jewish existence itself is threatened or denied. Kenan has a universal vision of peace, justice, and brotherhood. He loves the poor of Cuba and hates death in Vietnam. In these and other commitments such left-wing secularists share the ancient Jewish religious, messianically inspired refusal to embrace either pagan cynicism (which despairs of the world and accepts the *status quo*) or Christian or pseudo-Christian otherworldiness (which despairs of the world and flees from it). The commanding Voice of Auschwitz bids Jews, religious and secularist, not to abandon the world to the forces of Auschwitz, but rather to continue to work and hope for it. Two possibilities are equally ruled out: to despair of the world on account of Auschwitz, abandoning the age-old Jewish identification with poor and persecuted humanity; and to abuse such identification as a means of flight from Jewish destiny. It is precisely *because* of the uniqueness of Auschwitz, and *in* his Jewish particularity, that a Jew must be at one with humanity. For it is precisely because Auschwitz has made the world a desperate place that a Jew is forbidden to despair of it. The hero of Wiesel's *The Gates of the Forest* asserts that it is too late for the Messiah—and that for exactly this reason we are commanded to hope.[5]

4. The Fourth Fragment

The Voice of Auschwitz commands the religious Jew after Auschwitz to continue to wrestle with his God in however revolutionary ways; and it forbids the secularist Jew (who has already, and on other grounds, lost Him) to use Auschwitz as an additional weapon wherewith to deny Him.

The ways of the religious Jew are revolutionary, for there is no previous Jewish protest against divine Power like his protest. Continuing to hear the Voice of Sinai as he hears the Voice of Auschwitz, his citing of God against God may have to assume extremes which dwarf those of Abraham, Jeremiah, Job, Rabbi Levi Yitzhak. (You have abandoned the covenant? We shall not abandon it! You no longer want Jews to survive? We shall survive, as better, more faithful, more pious Jews! You have destroyed all grounds for hope? We shall obey the commandment to hope which You Yourself have given!) Nor is there any previous Jewish compassion with divine powerlessness like the compassion required by such a powerlessness. (The fear of God is dead among the nations? We shall keep it alive and be its witnesses! The times are too late for the coming of the Messiah? We shall persist without hope and recreate hope—and, as it were, divine

---

[4]"A Letter to All Good People—To Fidel Castro, Sartre, Russell and All the Rest," *Midstream,* October 1968.

[5]P. 225.

Power—by our persistence!) For the religious Jew, who remains within the midrashic framework, the Voice of Auschwitz manifests a divine Presence which, as it were, is shorn of all except commanding Power. *This* Power, however, is inescapable.

No less inescapable is this Power for the secularist Jew who has all along been outside the midrashic framework and this despite the fact that the Voice of Auschwitz does not enable him to return into that framework. He cannot return; but neither may he turn the Voice of Auschwitz against that of Sinai. For he may not cut off his secular present from the religious past: the Voice of Auschwitz commands preservation of that past. Nor may he widen the chasm between himself and the religious Jew: the Voice of Auschwitz commands Jewish unity.

As religious and secularist Jews are united in kinship with all the victims of Auschwitz and against all the executioners, they face a many-sided mystery and find a simple certainty. As regards the minds and souls of the victims of Auschwitz, God's presence to them is a many-sided mystery which will never be exhausted either by subsequent committed believers or by subsequent committed unbelievers, and least of all by subsequent neutral theorists—psychological, sociological, philosophical, theological—who spin out their theories immune to love and hate, submission and rage, faith and despair. As regards the murderers of Auschwitz, however, there was no mystery, for they denied, mocked, murdered the God of Israel six million times—and together with Him four thousand years of Jewish faith. For a Jew after Auschwitz, only one thing is certain: he may not side with the murderers and do what they have left undone. The religious Jew who has heard the Voice of Sinai must continue to listen as he hears the commanding Voice of Auschwitz. And the secularist Jew, who has all along lost Sinai and now hears the Voice of Auschwitz, cannot abuse that Voice as a means to destroy four thousand years of Jewish believing testimony. The rabbis assert that the first Temple was destroyed because of idolatry. Jews may not destroy the Temple which is the tears of Auschwitz by doing, wittingly or unwittingly, Hitler's work.

5. The Clash Between the Fragments

Such is the commanding Voice of Auschwitz as it is increasingly being heard by Jews of this generation. But how can it be obeyed? Each of the four fragments described—and they are mere fragments, and the description has been poor and inadequate—is by itself overwhelming. Taken together, they seem unbearable. For there are clashes between them which tear us apart.

How can the religious Jew be faithful to both the faith of the past and the victims of the present? We have already asked this question, but are now further from an answer than before. For a reconciliation by means of willing martyrdom is ruled out by the duty to Jewish survival, and a reconciliation by means of refuge in otherworldly mysticism is ruled out by the duty to hold fast to the world and to continue to hope and work for it. God, world and Israel are in so total a conflict when they meet at Auschwitz as to seem to leave religious Jews confronting that conflict with nothing but a prayer addressed to God, yet spoken softly lest it be heard: in short, with madness.

But the conflict is no less unbearable for the secularist Jew. To be sure, the space once occupied by God is void for him or else occupied by a question mark.

Only three of the four fragments effectively remain. Yet the conflict which remains tears him asunder.

Søren Kierkegaard's "knight of faith" was obliged to retrace the road which led Abraham to Mount Moriah, where Isaac's sacrifice was to take place.[6] A Jew today is obliged to retrace the road which led his brethren to Auschwitz. It is a road of pain and mourning, of humiliation, guilt, and despair. To retrace it is living death. How suffer this death *and also* choose Jewish life which, like all life, must include joy, laughter, and childlike innocence? How reconcile *such* a remembrance with life itself? How dare a Jewish parent crush his child's innocence with the knowledge that his uncle or grandfather was denied life because of his Jewishness? And how dare he *not* burden him with this knowledge? The conflict is inescapable, for we may neither forget the past for the sake of present life, nor destroy present life by a mourning without relief—and there is no relief.

Nor is this all. The first two fragments above clash with each other: each clashes with the third as well. No Jewish secularist today may continue to hope and work for mankind as though Auschwitz had never happened, falling back on secularist beliefs of yesterday that man is good, progress real, and brotherhood inevitable. Yet neither may he, on account of Auschwitz, despair of human brotherhood and cease to hope and work for it. How face Auschwitz and not despair? How hope and work, and not act as though Auschwitz had never occurred? Yet to forget and to despair are both forbidden.

Perhaps reconciliation would be possible if the Jewish secularist of today, like the Trotskys and Rosa Luxemburgs of yesterday, could sacrifice Jewish existence on the altar of future humanity. (Is this in the minds of "progressive" Jews when they protest against war in Vietnam but refuse to protest against Polish anti-Semitism? Or in the minds of what Kenan calls the "good people" of the world when they demand that Israel hand over weapons to those sworn to destroy her?) This sacrifice, however, is forbidden, and the altar is false. The left-wing Israeli secularist Kenan may accept all sorts of advice from his progressive friends, but not that he allow himself to be shot for the good of humanity. Perhaps he has listened for a moment even to this advice, for he hates a gun in his hand. Perhaps he has even wished for a second he could accept it, feeling, like many of his pious ancestors, that it is better to be killed than to kill. Yet he firmly rejects such advice, for he is *commanded* to reject it; rather than be shot, he will shoot first when there is no third alternative. But he will shoot with tears in his eyes. He writes:

> Why weren't the June 4 borders peace borders on the fourth of June, but will only become so now? Why weren't the UN Partition Plan borders of 1947 peace borders then, but will become so now? Why should I return his gun to the bandit as a reward for having failed to kill me?
>
> I want peace peace peace peace, peace peace peace.
>
> I am ready to give everything back in exchange for peace. And I shall give nothing back without peace.
>
> I am ready to solve the refugee problem. I am ready to accept an independent Palestinian state. I am ready to sit and talk. About everything, all at the same time. Direct talks, indirect talks, all this is immaterial. But peace.

---

[6]See *Fear and Trembling*, New York, 1954.

Until you agree to have peace, I shall give back nothing. And if you force me to become a conqueror, I shall become a conqueror. And if you force me to become an oppressor, I shall become an oppressor. And if you force me into the same camp with all the forces of darkness in the world, there I shall be.[7]

Kenan's article ends:

... if I survive ... , without a god but without prophets either, my life will have no sense whatever. I shall have nothing else to do but walk on the banks of streams, or on the top of the rocks, watch the wonders of nature, and console myself with the words of Ecclesiastes, the wisest of men: "For the light is sweet, and it is good for the eyes to see the sun" [Ecclesiastes 11:7].[8]

The conclusion then, is inescapable. Secularist Jewish existence after Auschwitz is threatened with a madness no less extreme than that which produces a prayer addressed to God, yet spoken softly lest it be heard.

The Voice of Auschwitz commands Jews not to go mad. It commands them to accept their singled out condition, face up to its contradictions, and endure them. Moreover, it gives the power of endurance, the power of sanity. The Jew of today can *endure because he* must *endure, and he must endure because he is* commanded *to endure.*

We ask: whence has come our strength to endure even these twenty-five years—not to flee or disintegrate but rather to stay, however feebly, at our solitary post, to affirm, however weakly, our Jewishness, and to bear witness, if only by this affirmation, against the forces of hell itself? The question produces abiding wonder. It is at a commanding Voice without which we, like the Psalmist (Psalm 119:92), would have perished in our affliction.

---

[7]Amos Kenan, "A Letter to All Good People," p. 35.
[8]Ibid., p. 36.

39 *A Voice Beyond Auschwitz: Holiness*

DAVID R. BLUMENTHAL

1. Why is this reading important?

The theology of Judaism goes forward beyond the Holocaust. In a temporal sense all religious thinking within Judaism from 1945 onward has been, and always will be, post-Holocaust theology. But while the initial generation of Holocaust theologians framed matters in the pattern we see exemplified by Fackenheim—that is, deriving from the Holocaust its principal language and image—others chose a different path, including the Holocaust as an event within the received tradition of the Torah. If the Holocaust raised in acute form the problem of evil—how could an omnipotent and just God have permitted such things?—so did Job. If the Holocaust provoked the faithful to confront God with accusations, so did the Psalmists. If the Holocaust made urgent the issue of the meaning of holy Israel's history of suffering, Jeremiah and the author of Lamentations, Moses in Leviticus and Deuteronomy, explored the range of possible responses. The single greatest theologian of Judaism of the half-century after the Holocaust, Abraham Joshua Heschel, wrote a memorial essay, *"The Earth Is the Lords,"* and, not intimidated by that awful mystery, then undertook a massive program of constructive, nearly systematic theology out of the resources of the Torah.

But generations pass, and we now have the opportunity to see how the long-term legacy of the Holocaust—the statement of the problem of evil in its most acute form—finds its way to a new age. If Fackenheim is rightly classified as the premier Holocaust theologian, then, at half his age, David R. Blumenthal in his *Facing the Abusing God: A Theology of Protest* must be called the premier post-Holocaust theologian. Blumenthal frames the Holocaust within a field of vision that is defined, but not dominated, by this event. This he does in a fresh way in what is certainly the most original and compelling theological exercise in the immediately contemporary period.

2. What should you notice as you proceed?

This is not an easy essay. Blumenthal, like Heschel, wishes to evoke a religious response, to convey a direct encounter with God, through language. Notice the differences between Fackenheim's and Blumenthal's

"voices," their word choices, their selections of images, metaphors, simi-
les (keeping in mind that Blumenthal is a native speaker of American
English and Fackenheim is not). When Blumenthal writes about the
"holy," reckon with what is at stake for him. In the tradition of Heschel,
Blumenthal reaches into human experience to find metaphors for theological reality, then tries to expand the range of meaning ("one reaches
outward") and, passing through the range of the Torah's (that is, Judaism's) exemplifications of the holy, aims at a single target. He wants to
direct the reader to God himself, God as self-revealed in the Torah. Here
he joins private experience, feelings, attitudes, emotions, with the public
encounter of holy Israel with God. In so doing, he undertakes to transcend the difference between secular and religious that so shapes—and
paralyzes—Fackenheim's thought. Blumenthal advocates intentionality
(using the Hebrew word *kavvanah*) as the medium of transformation:
"the mode of consciousness by which one performs ordinary acts yet remains alert to the dimension of holiness concealed in them." That places
Blumenthal squarely into the center of the Torah's tradition, mediating,
as it does, the ordinary with the holy.

3. How should you frame a question for class discussion in response to what you have read?

Blumenthal is trying to find a way of evoking, then exploring, religious
experience in a book. That is not easy to do, but it is the principal
medium for recording, hence rendering accessible, the encounter with
God of prophets and sages, saints and martyrs, through the history of
Christian and Judaic religious life in the West. What are other media of
religious experience? Having seen how Blumenthal introduces the direct
encounter with holiness, you might consider other ways in which various religions afford the same experience—ways not limited to the liter-
ate, not defined by words. An interesting class discussion will survey
counterpart media of mysicism in Islam; media of aesthetics in Catholic
Christianity, with its powerful liturgical music; media of contemplation
and rules thereof, in some Protestant communions (the Quakers, for example); media of Temple rites in the Church of Jesus Christ of Latter-
Day Saints (the Mormons); not to mention dance and graphic and
plastic arts, activities of a sexual character, and on and on. Many times
in these pages you have read about how a system chooses a medium
that, on its own, conveys its message. Here is a chance to apply and test
those generalizations against concrete facts.

Holiness as an Attribute of God

HOLINESS IS A QUALITY. One senses it in objects, in moments, in texts, and in
certain people. It is not a feeling like joy or anger. It is not a commitment like love
or loyalty. It is not a state of mind like happiness or gloom. It is not a thought or
concept. It is an awareness of the sacred, a consciousness of the spiritual. It is an

experience of the *mysterium tremendum et fascinans*, a contact with the numinous. It is a perception of otherness, an intimation of the beyond.[1]

> The truly "mysterious" object is beyond our apprehension and comprehension, not only because our knowledge has certain irremovable limits, but because in it we come upon something inherently "wholly other," whose kind and character are incommensurable with our own, and before which we therefore recoil in a wonder that strikes us chill and numb.[2]

> [H]oliness is the abstract term taught man [*sic*] by God to mark God's difference and the nature of everything that comes to be included ... within his difference. . . . That which enters the class of things of which he is a member ("holiness") loses its provenance in nature and history at the moment it is restored to the precinct of divinity. . . . From the standpoint of human experience, therefore (the point of view of language), holy is not in the ordinary sense a predicate, a word that asserts something about a term, but the sign of withdrawal of all reference into its source, a determinator of the radical disablement of metaphor and the absolute preemption of the truth of discourse at the supremely privileged moment of reference to reality.[3]

The holy is encountered in many places and moments: in the grandeur of nature, in the still, small voice of conscience, in the silence of the soul, and in the rapture of beauty. It can be found in creativity of the mind, in gentleness of the heart, in the eye of a lover, and in the innocence of a child. The holy meets one in the depth of sacred texts, in moments of prayer, and in those rare moments when one truly meets an-other.

The holy approaches when one is weak or when one is strong. It draws near when one is least expecting it. The holy can be sought but it cannot be found. It breaks in upon awareness. It interrupts.

In the language of the tradition: "Holy, holy, holy is the Lord of hosts; the fullness of the universe is God's Glory. . . . And I said, 'Woe unto me; I am struck dumb, for I am a man of impure lips and I live among a people of impure lips, and now my eyes have seen the King, the Lord of hosts'" (Isa. 6:1–8). "You are holy, God Who dwells above the praises of Israel" (Ps. 22:4). "Holy are You and awesome is Your Name; there is nothing divine other than You. . . . Blessed are You, the holy King."[4]

---

[1]R. Otto, *The Idea of the Holy* (New York: Oxford University Press, 1958), chap. 27. Otto, following Schleiermacher, characterizes these moments as *Gefühle*, usually translated as "affections." However, the English translator, following the popular German usage, renders this as "feelings." "Feelings," as I see them, are more transient, while "awarenesses" or "moments of consciousness" are more intense and less the product of psychological stimuli. I also distinguish "feelings" from "dispositions" or "sustained emotional attitudes," the latter being more enduring and constituting virtues to be cultivated (see D. Saliers, *The Soul in Paraphrase: Prayer and the Religious Affections* [New York: Seabury Press, 1980] and p. 59 below).

[2]Otto, *Idea of the Holy*, p. 28.

[3]A. Grossman, "Holiness," in *Contemporary Jewish Religious Thought*, ed. A. Cohen and P. Mendes-Flohr (New York: Charles Scribner's Sons, 1987), pp. 389–390. See also A. Green, *Seek My Face, Speak My Name* (Northvale, N.J.: Jason Aronson, 1992; reviewed by me in *Modern Theology* 9:2 [April 1993] 223–225).

[4]The New Year liturgy, in *The Authorized Daily Prayer Book*, ed. J. Hertz (New York: Bloch Publishing, 1960), p. 850.

Words that Go in Circles

There are no words; or rather, the words go in circles. The holy is a quality *sui generis*. One knows it intuitively, as one knows beauty. It is irreducible. It can only be described by synonyms or by the traces it leaves. The holy is ineffable, yet it is identifiable. One can point to it and say, "This is holy," without being able to say what, or how, or why. One can identify the holy without being able to describe it, except by the word "holy" and its synonyms.

The circle of the holy superimposes itself on other circles as one tries to grasp the holy and to live within it. As one integrates the holy into life, one needs other words. One reaches outward: King, Lord, Name, justice, beauty, purity, Shabbat, Israel, You. One probes inward: awe, wonder, radical amazement, sublime, love, joy, bliss, bless, worship. One gropes for forms: holy day, temple, mitsva, liturgy, charity, study, Torah, acts of kindness, martyrdom. The failure of language is transformed into a rich vocabulary of response, always haunted by its own muteness. Silence overflows into words, an echo of an unfathomable depth.

The holy is intimately related to the beautiful, the personal, and the moral.

The holy need not be beautiful: "Here is Behemoth which I have made; in comparison with you . . ." (Job 40:15); Behemoth was ugly, yet holy as creature. However, the beautiful can be holy, and the holy can be beautiful: "Bow down to the Lord in the beauty of holiness" (Pss. 29:2; 96:9). And yet, the holy is more than the beautiful; it enfolds it.

The personal and the holy overlap: "You are my God; I search everywhere for You; my soul thirsts for You; my body yearns for You. . . . Indeed, I have visions of You in the holy place" (Ps. 63:2–3). "You are holy and Your Name is holy. . . . Blessed are You, the holy God."[5] But the holy is more than the personal; it envelops it.

The moral and the holy are coterminous: "The holy God is made holy by righteousness" (Isa. 5:16); "You shall be holy for I, the Lord your God, am holy" (Lev. 19:2). The holy cannot be immoral or amoral. Still, the holy is more than the moral; it encompasses it.

The holy, the beautiful, the moral, and the personal overlap and interact with one another. The beautiful may be holy but, if the beautiful is immoral or unnatural, it is not holy, no matter how beautiful it is. The personal can be holy but, if the personal is immoral or unnatural, it is not holy, no matter how intense it is. The moral must be holy but it need not be beautiful, perhaps not even personal.[6]

Kavvana and the Attribute of Holiness

How does one integrate the unintegratable? How does one live within that which is wholly other? These are two kinds of *kedusha* (holiness).[7]

---

[5]The daily liturgy, in *Authorized Daily Prayer Book,* ed. Hertz, p. 137.

[6]See pp. 33–43 below, where I have set forth these universes of discourse and their overlapping.

[7]The following discussion is based on M. Kadushin, *Worship and Ethics* (Chicago: Northwestern University Press, 1964), pp. 216–237. See also A. J. Heschel, *God in Search of Man* (New York: Meridian Books, 1951), part 3.

There is hierarchical *kedusha*. It is "a sensed mystical quality of certain objects, days, and persons."[8] The tradition ranks these in hierarchies; for example, the sequence of locations within the holy land, the set of sacrifices, the ranks of priesthood, and the degrees of impurity and purity.

There is also nonhierarchical *kedusha*. It is created by an individual act of will.[9] By it, one declares an object consecrated to God. Through it, one dedicates an act to God. It is a function of mitsva, of commanded act, and of the intention to fulfill that command. Holiness is generated by *kavvana*, by intent to holiness.

> Rather than just a mystical quality alone, *kedushah* is now something that must be achieved through effortful personal conduct. . . . The *kedushah* achieved through fulfilling the *mitzwot* is throughout, therefore nontheurgical. Instead, it is an experience in normal mysticism, an experience of a close relationship with God. . . . Such an experience of relationship can take place, of course, only when a *mizwah* is fulfilled with *kawwanah*. Indeed, *kawwanah* in this connection, we have noticed, itself implies an awareness of a relationship with God, a consciousness that a particular *mizwah* is a communication by God here and now. . . . During the process of performing a *mizwah* with *kawwanah*, a person has an experience of *kedushah*. It is a mystical experience and yet, being normal mysticism, it is in some degree describable.[10]

Holiness, then, is a matter of experience. It is an awareness that humans bring to the performance of the acts of daily living. Holiness is focused openness to holiness. It is numinous otherness within the mundane same; the ineffable within the effable.

Kavvana is the mode of consciousness by which one performs ordinary acts yet remains alert to the dimension of holiness concealed in them. *Kavvana* is the method by which one holds the presence of the holy in one's mind while doing everyday deeds: "I sleep but my heart waketh."[11] *Kavvana* is the process by which one opens one's consciousness to the multiple levels of reality that are implicit in any act, particularly to the sacred dimensions of action. *Kavvana* is the way one transforms routine acts into moments of awareness of the ineffable. *Kavvana* is the key to nonhierarchical holiness, to the holiness which does not greet one but which, rather, one must achieve.

"Normal mysticism" comes closest to describing the way one integrates the unintegratable. Everyday acts with everyday objects, when handled with an intent

---

[8]Kadushin, *Worship and Ethics*, p. 216.

[9]See also J. Neusner, *Judaism: The Evidence of the Mishnah* (Chicago: University of Chicago Press, 1981), pp. 270–281.

[10]Kadushin, *Worship and Ethics*, pp. 224–225, 232. I have not changed the spelling to conform to my own. Thus: *kedushah* = *kedusha*; *mizwah* = *mitsva*; and *kawwanah* = *kavvana*.

[11]The quotation is from Song of Songs 5:2 and is used by Maimonides in his *Guide of the Perplexed* III:51, trans. S. Pines (Chicago: University of Chicago Press, 1963), p. 623, to allude to the ongoingness of *kavvana*. For a fuller discussion of the levels of *kavvana*, see D. Blumenthal, *Understanding Jewish Mysticism* (New York: KTAV Publishing House, 1982), vol. 2, pp. 112–116, reprinted in idem, *God at the Center* (San Francisco: Harper & Row, 1989), pp. 186–190 (see also the index there) and in *News Notes* ([Fellowship of United Methodists in Worship, Music, and Other Arts, Atlanta] summer 1989), 3–5. When I wrote this passage, I was not yet sensitive to inclusive language but it should be read in that style and tone.

to be aware of the holy, yield a mysticism that is not ecstatic, not annihilative, and not theurgical, but "normal," habitual, usual. Life, which is composed of commonplace events, when approached with a willingness to be open to the sacredness of all existence, yields a spirituality that is customary, regular, familiar.[12]

The holy is, thus, encountered in the wholly other, at the edge of human existence. But the holy is also met in the confluence of the wholly other with the wholly mundane, at the center of normal existence. The holy is ec-static, standing outside; it is also famili-ar, standing within. God is holy person; humankind, created in God's image, is holy person.

Holiness, Fear, and Joy

Holiness overwhelms. It compels; it frightens. And holiness also comforts; it draws forth; it embraces. Holiness pervades existence and consciousness. There is no escape—neither from the *tremendum* nor from the intimate holiness of God's presence. The holy engenders fear, but the holy does not frighten God.

The human flees the holy. Moses pleads inexperience (Ex. 3:11–4:17). Isaiah pleads impurity (Isa. 6:5). Jeremiah pleads youth (Jer. 1:4–10). Ezekiel must be coerced (Ezek. 2:8–3.3). Jonah takes flight. The psalmist cries:

> Where can I go away from Your spirit and where can I flee from Your face? If I rise to heaven, You are there; if I plunge into the netherworld, You are there. If I travel on the wings of dawn or dwell at the end of the world, there too Your hand will rest upon me and Your right hand seize me. If I say, "Let darkness envelop me and let night be light for me," even darkness is not dark for You and night is as lit up as day; like darkness, like light. For You have possessed my insides; You encompassed me even in the womb of my mother. (Ps. 139:7–13)

Sin leads one away from the holy; it tempts. The forms of temptation are as many as the imagination: the tasks of daily living, sexual fantasy, ambition, despair. Purity and sin fluctuate; hope and despair alternate.

> Be generous to me, God, according to Your gracious love; in the abundance of Your compassionate love, wipe away my rebellion. . . . Truly, I know my rebellion; my sin is before me always. I have sinned before You alone and I have done evil in Your eyes. . . . Let me hear joy and gladness; let my bones which You have oppressed rejoice. . . . Hide Your Face from my sins and wipe away my iniquities. . . . Do not cast me away from before You, nor take Your holy presence away from me." (Ps. 51:3–14)

Holiness and sin are lovers; fear and flight are indissolubly linked to the call of holy presence. To know one is to know the other; to be attached to one is to cling to the other. Humankind struggles to incarnate the one and to resist the other, but they are a pair. God, too, struggles to let the one preponderate over the other: "May it be My will that My compassionate love predominate over My anger, overwhelming My other qualities, so that I comport Myself with the qual-

---

[12]M. Kadushin, *The Rabbinic Mind* (New York: Jewish Theological Seminary, 1952; reprint, New York: Bloch Publishing, 1977), esp. pp. 20–23.

ity of compassionate love toward My children, engaging them beyond the requirements of the law."[13]

Joy is not happiness.

Happiness comes from setting goals and achieving them. Happiness is social. It is a state of well-being derived from those around us. Not everyone is happy, and no one is happy all the time; yet we all know happiness from time to time.

Joy is an inner awareness, a moment of insight through our selves into that which is beyond. It is a connectedness between our inner being and that which transcends it.

Happiness requires contention, fighting for what one believes, compromise; joy is a moment of wholeness, and purity. Happiness is rooted in time and space; joy suspends us in a realm beyond ourselves.

Joy can strike us at any time. But it is more likely to come to us in moments of service, at times when we see ourselves within the larger meaning that embraces reality. Joy derives not from accomplishment but from centeredness within the greater whole.

> The rule is that, when a saint worships God, even the simple people have joy because the pious, by performing their mitsvot, bring blessing and joy to all the worlds. Thus, it happened that the people of the city of Shushan who were not Jews also had joy even though they did not know its cause, for Mordecai's stewardship brought blessing and joy on *all* the people, as it says, "the city of Shushan"—that is, its people, the non-Jews—"was cheerful and joyous" (Esther 8:15–16). But the Jews had special reason to be joyous because they had been saved from Haman. And the rule is that, when a person knows the reason why he or she is happy, then he or she experiences a joyous light, for reason enlightens them as to the purpose of things. Therefore, it also says, "and the Jews had light and joy" (ibid.)[14]

There are many kinds of joy.

There is the joy of knowing that God loves us, of knowing that we are objects of God's grace. And there is the joy of having served God, of having done a mitsva simply because it brings pleasure to the Creator.

> By the acts which people had to do—to plant and to sow, to raise cattle and to sacrifice—the Creator, blessed be He, caused the flow of blessing to descend upon them. . . . When Israel was in the desert, however, they were in the state that the Holy One, blessed be He, showered His blessing upon them because of His great grace as in the case of the manna and the well of water for, in these, there was no action of humans at all.[15]

---

[13]Talmud, Berakhot 7a, used in modified form in the High Holiday liturgy, in *Authorized Daily Prayer Book*, ed. Hertz, p. 882; see also below, pp. 263 and 290–291.

[14]See D. Blumenthal, *God at the Center*, p. 205. Levi Yitzhak was a nineteenth-century hasidic master beloved by all. He wrote a compilation of homilies entitled *Kedushat Levi*. This quotation is taken from that compilation. On Levi Yitzhak, see *God at the Center*, pp. xiv–xvi; and S. Dresner, *The World of a Hasidic Master* (New York: Shapolsky, 1986).

[15]Blumenthal, *God at the Center*, p. 75, quoting Levi Yitzhak's *Kedushat Levi*.

There is the joy of seeing the solution to a problem, and the joy of actually solving it.[16]

There are also the joys of worship:

> One should tremble and faint when standing to pray before the great King. And it is proper that one's limbs shake. Similarly, after praying, one should think, "How can I dare to bring out of my mouth useless words and enjoy them? Have I not just spoken before the great and awesome King? And will I not have to speak again before Him Whose Glory fills the universe?"[17]

> For when one meditates well on the greatest of the Creator, may He be blessed,— that He is the root and principle of all worlds, that He encompasses and fills all reality, that no thought can grasp Him at all, and that all the worlds, souls, and angels are all annihilated and as nothing and emptiness before Him—then one's soul is awakened to yearn and to be consumed in the flame of sweetness, bliss, and love. Then, one desires and has a passion to worship God at all times . . . one's heart is enflamed to worship God.[18]

Even God experiences joy.

> A person, in his or her worship of God, may He be blessed, through Torah and mistsvot, brings great joy above. And so, when a person wants to know if God, may He be blessed, had joy from this worship, the criterion is this: If one sees that one's heart burns like a fire and that one feels religious enthusiasm always to worship Him and that one has a passion and a will to worship the Creator, then it is certain that God, may He be blessed, has joy from that person's worship.[19]

The holy is joy-ful, even as it is fear-ful.

Second Thoughts

Does one have a right to speculate about God this way? Has the holocaust not intervened to force a distortion of categories, a rupture of language itself?

> On the march to work, limping in our large wooden shoes on the icy snow, we exchanged a few words, and I found out that Resnyk is Polish, he lived twenty years at Paris but speaks an incredible French. He is thirty, but like all of us, could be taken for seventeen or fifty. He told me his story, and today I have forgotten it, but it was certainly a sorrowful, cruel and moving story; because so are all our stories, hundreds of thousands of stories, all different and all full of a tragic disturbing necessity. We tell them to each other in the evening, and they take place in Norway, Italy, Algeria, the Ukraine, and are simple and incomprehensible like the stories in the Bible. But are they not themselves stories of a new Bible?
>
> Silence slowly prevails and then, from my bunk on the top row, I see and hear old Kuhn praying aloud, with his beret on his head, swaying backwards and

---

[16]Ibid., p. 197.

[17]Ibid., p. 37, quoting Levi Yitzhak's *Kedushat Levi.*

[18]Ibid., pp. 152, 148–150, 183–185, quoting Levi Yitzhak's *Kedushat Levi.*

[19]Ibid., p. 56, quoting Levi Yitzhak's *Kedushat Levi.* See also Heschel, *God in Search,* p. 199 (italics in the original: "The mystic experience is an ecstasy of humanity; revelation is *an ecstasy of God*").

forwards violently. Kuhn is thanking God because he has not been chosen.

Kuhn is out of his senses. Does he not see Beppo the Greek in the bunk next to him, Beppo who is twenty years old and is going to the gas chamber the day after tomorrow and knows it and lies there looking fixedly at the light without saying anything and without even thinking any more? Can Kuhn fail to realize that next time it will be his turn? Does Kuhn not understand that what has happened today is an abomination, which no propitiatory prayer, no pardon, no expiation by the guilty, which nothing at all in the power of man can ever clean again?

If I were God, I would spit at Kuhn's prayer.[20]

May one understand God as wholly other, as sacred, after Auschwitz? May one think of God as holy, if the holy cannot be immoral? Does one have a right to say that God is fair, addressable, possessed of power, loving, and choosing? Is not speaking of God's anger blasphemous in the context of the holocaust? Can one talk of God's essential attributes as holiness and personality after hearing the testimony of the distortion of personality and transcendence? Is any language adequate after the rupture of all human communication in the camps?[21]

And yet, can one not talk of God? Can one abandon God Who, for better or for worse, is the creator and judge? Can one cast even God into the abyss of silence? Can one deny one's own experience of God's holy otherness and of God's intimate personal presence?

And, can one close one's ears to the other testimony—the testimony of faith, the witness to the Jew's love of God? "Yea, though God slay me, I turn expectantly to God" (Job 13:15).[22]

The theology of image, a personalist theology, proposes, in humility and embarrassment, that there is no choice but to retrieve the hermeneutic of personal and of holy language; that one must speak, as best one can, always aware of the silence that haunts one's speech, of God and of humankind as holy person, in dialogue. The theology that understands God's essential attributes as personality and holiness teaches that there is no alternative to forming a vision of God and humankind that is rooted in personality and holiness; that one must do this, as clearly as possible, even as one must remain aware of the darkness that encompasses and threatens humanity.

---

[20]Primo Levi, *Survival in Auschwitz,* trans. S. Woolf (New York: Summit Books, 1960), pp. 65–66, 129–130.

[21]See pp. 8–9 in Blumenthal, *Facing the Abusing God,* for references to Shapiro and Langer on this.

[22]For stories of Jewish religious heroism, see M. Prager, *Sparks of Glory* (New York: Shengold Publishers, 1974). For Christian stories, see C. Ten Boom, *The Hiding Place* (Old Tappan, N.J.: Spire Books, 1971). There are other examples of this genre.

40 Women and Men Praying Together in Judaism

JULES HARLOW

1. Why is this reading important?

The capacity to respond to challenge marks a vital religious tradition, and by that criterion, contemporary Judaism in North America shows itself willing and well able to address the crisis of feminism, which has challenged the faith, Judaism, at its foundations. Before the earliest 1970s, women rarely found a place in the study of the Torah, in the conduct of public worship, or in the leadership of the Jewish community. Now, scarcely three decades later, the rabbinical seminaries of Reform, Conservative, and Reconstructionist Judaisms number large numbers of women, and over the same period women have come to form a principal part of the rabbinate. Orthodox Judaism has responded by forming for women yeshivot—academies for the sacred sciences, e.g., Talmud study—and other media for education and inclusion. Outside of Orthodoxy women are accorded an equal position in the conduct of the liturgy and in the provision of the rites and rituals of the faith. Within Orthodoxy—bound as it is by the requirements of the Torah for the separation of the sexes at prayer—provision for women to lead public worship has led to the formation of women's quorums for prayer. In these ways the religion, Judaism, has responded to the remarkable—and irreversible—movement in Christianity and in Judaism to secure for women equality in the realm of religion.

But the cutting edge of religion is prayer, where we speak to God and so embody in action the convictions of theology and piety that lead to public worship. And there, the language of the received, and for most Judaisms authoritative, liturgy presents a problem. How, at prayer, are the changes in consciousness and conviction about the equal status of women before God to register? Here is the test of the vitality of Judaism: can the newest generation of rabbis frame the received liturgy in a manner congruent with the convictions of praying Israel, the faithful of the synagogue, that women meet God as men do and conduct public worship in the name of all Israel? With this selection the readings on Judaism come to closure, because no single issue has so focused public Judaic discourse upon the critical issues of the Torah (a.k.a., Judaism)—

theological, liturgical, ethical, and even political—than the revolution brought about by feminism in Judaism. So far as Judaism is a living religion, this is where we see the life-blood flowing. It is with life that we conclude.

2. What should you notice as you proceed?

Rabbi Harlow is the leading liturgist in Judaism in the twentieth century, having translated the entire classical liturgy into American English and done so with art and aesthetic refinement. Not only so, but he embodies those myriads of holy Israel who, when they pray, speak to God in the language set forth by the sages of the Torah. To him and through him, in the prayerbooks he has put into affective American English, the poetry of faith transforms theology into the words of yearning and phrases of outreach upward. No one has struggled more courageously to address the feminist challenge. And none has more to say about it, with vast implications for the realm beyond synagogue prayer.

What to notice? How an exemplary rabbi, engaged by feminism, seeks the right way to translate so as to include women and men, and also to represent the received liturgy within its governing theology and its implicit convictions. Rabbi Harlow frames the matter as Conservative Judaism—centrist and balanced between Orthodox and Reform—has to see matters: to balance the heritage of the ages with the claims of the living generation. He therefore stands for the "integrity of the classic texts of Jewish prayer," and seeks to preserve the continuity between the language of the Bible and the language of the prayerbook: can Judaism remain authentic to its heritage and loyal to its commitment to fully inclusive theology and liturgy alike? God lives in the details, and that is where Rabbi Harlow's sane and balanced reading of matters is to be confronted.

3. How should you frame a question for class discussion in response to what you have read?

You can easily construct a debate between Rabbi Harlow and those with whom he takes issue, the writings of some of whom you have read in these very pages. He seeks a balance between tradition and change, a means of sustaining the authentic tradition within a new generation. How would you solve the problems of "God as she," "God as father," in the actual life of a community at prayer? What considerations do you think ought to register? In other words, answer Rabbi Harlow's question: "what now?"

... if each of us, in secret, were allowed to ask God one question, absolutely nobody would ask, "Are you a man or a woman?" or "What color's your skin?", proving that issues of gender and race are ultimately trivial. Most likely, we would inquire of God, "Any chance of getting out of here alive?" "Where'll I be when

I'm no longer around?" "Will I ever see so-and-so again?" "What's the punch line?" or "Cat got your tongue?"—questions we rarely ask one another because our intellectual betters consider them sophomoric and because we are privately convinced that any mortal, including clergy, can provide encouraging answers based upon more than circumstantial evidence.[1]

When we want to address to speak about God we are confronted by problems engendered by the limits of language. Language about God is a compromise between the impossibility of saying anything about the ineffable and the desire to express our praise and our gratitude, our pleas and our questions to and about the source of all creation. Religious traditions in their sacred scriptures provide a basic vocabulary which enables us to speak about God even though we are conscious of the limitations imposed by language.

That very vocabulary has given rise to a problem for many contemporaries, a problem based upon grammatical reality. Beginning with the Bible, references to God in monotheistic religions are expressed in the masculine gender.[2] The use of the pronouns "He," "Him," and "His," and the nouns "King," "Lord," and "Master," for example, is upsetting to those who believe that the use of such words leads people to form a male image of God. They contend that such an image of God is harmful since it implies that God is literally male or that only males, and not females, bear the image of God. This is damaging to women, they claim, because of the way it leads men to think of and treat women and in terms of a woman's limited self-image which may be formed. Other people contend that speaking of God in the masculine gender, which begins in the Bible, is simply a convention built into language, which can only be symbolic in referring to God. Therefore, nothing derogatory about females is implied. Furthermore, Jewish tradition has always taught that all people are in the image of God, following the verse from Genesis, "And God created man in His image, in the image of God created He him; male and female He created them."[3]

The grammatical gender of words used in referring to God has become a major topic in discussions about prayer in our time. The passage with which this essay begins is not a formal part of this discussion. It is, however, one example of thoughts which can place into proper perspective the not insignificant matter of gender language in religious texts. Concerns about gender language referring to the deity are real and abundant among women and men alike, both in discussions about liturgy and in the production of new books and new services of prayer. These concerns are trivial compared to ultimate questions about our life and death. The same could be said about almost any topic but we do care about language and about its use in religious settings.

---

[1]Tom Robbins, *Half Asleep in Frog Pajamas* (New York, Toronto: Bantam Books, 1995), pp. 220–221. This book was brought to my attention by Heather Zacker. Ilana Harlow's careful reading of this essay led to many improvements. I am grateful to Jon Levinson and to Edward Shapiro for their conversations and helpful suggestions. Final responsibility, of course, lodges with the author.

[2]This applies to Hebrew and to English, as well as to other languages with which I am familiar. I am told that Hungarian provides an exception to this rule.

[3]Genesis 1:27.

Since at least the 1960s a variety of books, essays and organizations have articulated a critique about the treatment and status of women in our time. They point to the basic contributions of women in all areas of life, and demand changes in the status and participation of women. Much of contemporary discussion about gender in religious language flows from a growing concern about the place and treatment of women in our society. Women have been and are being treated unfairly in the home and in the workplace. Daily newspapers tell the story, which includes unequal pay and unequal status for equal tasks in the marketplace as well as the physical and mental abuse of females by husbands, fathers, teachers and strangers. Fulfillment for a growing number of women lies not solely in their being homemakers, wives, mothers and daughters. The enactment of legislation designed to prevent discrimination against women testifies to the influence of those who have awakened society to the existence of social, economic and political prejudices against women which must be eliminated.

This general problem exists within the Jewish community as well. "The intellectual and leadership capacities of women have been largely ignored, downplayed, or discouraged in most Jewish cultures."[4] There are synagogue practices which exclude women from participation as full members, which is taken by many to imply that women do not share equality of status with men.

One example of this phenomenon has been presented strikingly by an Orthodox Jewish woman. She writes about a synagogue service she attends celebrating the annual completion and renewal of Reading the Torah, Simhat Torah. "Midway through the hakafah ceremonies, the decorum of the congregation is beginning to unravel." [She is referring to the extended part of the service when members of the congregation carry the Torah scrolls around the sanctuary in a series of seven processions.] Then, she tells us, ". . . the noise level reaches a new high. The rabbi pounds on the podium. 'Let us have silence here. We won't complete the service until every single person here has had a hakafah.' For a fleeting moment I find my husband's eyes across the partition. He smiles. He knows."[5] She felt excluded as a Jew (and as a person) by definition since in that congregation only men are allowed to carry a Torah scroll.

In some communities, changes have been accepted. To take one example, women in many congregations are offered the honor of being called for an *aliyah* to participate in the Torah service, and a young woman may commemorate becoming a bat mitzvah in a manner which parallels the ceremony at which a young man commemorates becoming a bar mitzvah.[6]

---

[4]Sylvia Barack Fishman, *A Breath of Life* (New York: The Free Press, A Division of Macmillan, Inc., 1993), p. 248.

[5]Blu Greenberg, *On Women and Judaism: A View from Tradition* (Philadelphia: The Jewish Publication Society of America, 1981), pp. 76–77.

[6]In some Orthodox synagogues, a young woman marks the occasion by presenting an appropriate lesson (*d'var Torah*) *after* the service and *outside* of the sanctuary. In others the young woman participates in services with a woman's minyan. A recent survey disclosed that in Conservative congregations, 49 percent of b'nei mitzvah and 51 percent of b'not mitzvah read part of the *sedrah* and chanted the Haftorah, and that 27 percent of b'nei mitzvah and 21 percent of b'not mitzvah read the entire *sedrah*. (Jack Wertheimer, editor, *Conservative Synagogues and Their Members: Highlights of the North American Survey of 1995–96*, New York: The Jewish Theological Seminary, 1996, p. 17.)

In a growing number of congregations, women as well as men read the Torah on Shabbat and on Festivals as well as on appropriate weekdays.[7] This includes young women who have celebrated their becoming b'not mitzvah by reading the Torah portion for the week on Shabbat morning. The Jewish community is richer for the participation of these women, young and old. In some congregations, including Orthodox congregations, women have a separate service in their own minyan.[8]

Women serve as presidents of congregations. The number of women serving as congregational officers is increasing, in Orthodox as well as in non-Orthodox congregations. This practice is accepted as routine in a growing number of communities, including those whose prayerbooks—non-Orthodox as well as Orthodox—contain a prayer which does not consider women to be members of the congregation. In this prayer, God is called upon ". . . to bless this entire holy congregation, along with all holy congregations, them *and their wives* and their sons and their daughters . . ." At a time when women were not officially members of congregations, it was appropriate to separate them this way since otherwise they would not have been mentioned in the prayer at all. Today, when women are members and officers of congregations, it is not appropriate.[9]

Many communities have instituted changes affecting women's participation in synagogue life. A significant number of people feel that justice for women in the synagogue demands something more—changing the language of liturgy. Among the advocates of this position there is no unanimity as to what specific course should be taken, what specific changes should be introduced into what is referred to as God language, although there is a clear consensus on the need for action. Many, both men and women, are adamant that change is required, and changes have been introduced into hard-bound new editions of prayerbooks as well as experimental booklets. In the English translation of Hebrew words referring to God, for example, these advocates avoid using the words "King," "Lord," and "Master," "He," "Him," and "His." Some of the advocates of change would

---

[7]The Conservative synagogue survey cited in footnote 6 points out that women may read from the Torah in over eighty percent of Conservative congregations. Since 1955 it has been permissible for women to have *aliyot* in Conservative congregations. (*Teshuvot* of the Committee on Jewish Law and Standards on this matter are found in *Proceedings of the Rabbinical Assembly,* 1955, pages 168–190.) The Talmud notes that a woman may receive an *aliyah* (*Megillah* 23b). [At that time people who received *aliyot* also read a portion from the Torah.] Nevertheless, the passage continues with the note that "the sages have stated that a woman shall not read in public because of the dignity of the congregation" (*k'vod ha-tzibbur*). Because of the changing involvements of women in society since that time, and the subsequent changing definitions of congregational dignity, I side with those who hold that this stricture may be abrogated in congregations where such action is not felt to be offensive.

[8]See Rabbi Avraham Weiss, *Women at Prayer* (Hoboken: KTAV Publishers, 1990). I would agree with Blu Greenberg's comment that a special minyan for women only is an interim solution at best. "A totally separatist solution is not what the covenantal community is all about. . . . A synagogue naturally is a place that strengthens family, not divides it." *On Women and Tradition* (Philadelphia: The Jewish Publication Society, 1981), pp. 95–96.

[9]Contemporary reality is reflected by a change in this particular non-canonical prayer in at least one prayerbook. Its text, in Hebrew and in English, asks God "to bless this entire congregation, together with all holy congregations: them, their sons and daughters . . ." See *Siddur Sim Shalom,* edited, with translations, by Rabbi Jules Harlow (New York: The Rabbinical Assembly and the United Synagogue of America, 1985), p. 415.

refer to God as She or as She/He, as Parent or as Mother. In the first blessing of the central prayer known as the *Sh'moneh Esreh* or as the Amidah, some have added the names of the matriarchs to the names of the patriarchs. (We shall be returning to these examples.) Often the leader of a service will introduce changes even though the printed text used by the congregation does not include them.

Those who are advocating and composing the changes do not articulate a desire to leave the framework of congregational life. Liturgy is obviously important to them, but they are uncomfortable with language currently used in most prayerbooks.[10] The proposals cannot be taken lightly since those proposing the changes are part of the community which cares deeply about liturgy and about the continuity of Jewish religious life. Rabbis and laypeople whom I admire and respect are among those who propose changes with which I disagree. The Reform[11] and the Reconstructionist[12] movements have published prayerbooks whose English translators insist that God not be referred to in the masculine gender. They prefer gender-neutral language as well as inclusive language; sometimes gender-specific female language is used. In the Conservative movement a preliminary version of a projected gender-sensitive edition of a prayerbook has been published.[13]

The Jewish prayerbook contains liturgy (fixed texts for formal, repeated public worship) and words of personal prayer. Each of us is entitled to formulate his or her personal prayers, or to apply our personal interpretations of the fixed texts when we pray by ourselves. In Hebrew, which is the language of Jewish prayer, a community of Jews in public prayer refers to itself in the first plural. Praying as part of a community which embraces all times and all places is one of the strengths of Jewish liturgical tradition. Unfortunately, advocates of what is identified as a feminist position introduce many changes that disrupt the integrity of Jewish liturgy which is so intimately connected to the language of the Hebrew Bible. (To cite but one example, the Hebrew Bible refers to God using the masculine gender, and the changes introduce language which is gender-neutral and sometimes even female gender-specific.) Such changes break the connection between the language of the Bible and the language of the prayerbook, a close connection which is a basic feature of Jewish liturgy. Large numbers of Jews are unable to participate fully in public prayer at congregations that include such changes. The use of gender-neutral God language, often referred to as "inclusive language," excludes many Jews.

Those who disagree with this position can, of course, argue that the *lack* of change is what reads *them* out of the community at public prayer. I do not believe that liturgical language should be used as a litmus test for Jewish piety. My concern is that changes based upon gender language referring to God disrupt the

---

[10]"Language" here, for the most part, refers to the English translation of the Hebrew original.

[11]*Gates of Prayer for Shabbat: A Gender Sensitive Prayerbook*, Chaim Stern, Editor (New York: Central Conference of American Rabbis, 1992).

[12]*Kol Haneshamah* (Wyncote, Pennsylvania: The Reconstructionist Press, 1995).

[13]Preliminary Edition of *Siddur Sim Shalom for Shabbat and Festivals* (New York: The Rabbinical Assembly and the United Synagogue of Conservative Judaism, 1995).

integrity of the classic texts of Jewish prayer, drive a wedge between the language of the Bible and the language of the prayerbook, and often misrepresent biblical and rabbinic tradition.

The Jewish community is not monolithic; even our religious movements are not monolithic. There are disagreements on significant issues within the Reform and the Conservative and the Orthodox movements respectively. Jews for centuries have been praying from prayerbooks whose texts differ from each other in a number of ways. Jewish religious movements and congregations within those movements do have more than one type of service. It is an unfortunate sign of disunity when a community intensifies and deepens its own differences by having services in which members of the same community or the same congregation must pray from different prayerbooks.[14]

It is upsetting to witness the splintering of those who care about prayer as a result of apparently irreconcilable differences on liturgical language referring to God in public prayer. Words, and commitment to what they represent, are vital to religious life. Classically, they have served to unite the Jewish community throughout time and throughout the world.

GENDER SPECIFICITY

An example of gender specificity is found in passages that refer to God as "He," "King," "Father," or "Lord." Many consider the use of these words in referring to God as undesirable in any context, not only in liturgy. Remedies abound, with "corrections" of innumerable texts from both the past and the present introduced in many publications, not only in prayerbooks.

Let us first consider some non-liturgical texts. The examples are representative and their lessons are applicable to liturgy as well. Our first example is taken from the most recent book that I read before first sitting down to write these words. *Journey of the Soul* presents the translation of seven traditional Hebrew texts on repentance in one volume.[15] In the first source presented in that book a classic author[16] cites a verse from the book of Job, a verse from a passage in one of Job's replies to his friend Eliphaz the Temanite. The standard contemporary Jewish translation of the Bible preserves the integrity of the Hebrew text with its masculine pronouns: "He is one, who can dissuade Him?"[17] (Some translations

---

[14]Disagreement on matters of gender language within the Reform movement is reflected by a Reform layman, Matthew Berke, in "God and Gender in Judaism" (*First Things,* June/July 1996, number 64). In the Orthodox community a source of disunity involves the State of Israel. Thus *The Complete ArtScroll Siddur* is now published in two editions. The original edition does not include a prayer for the State of Israel. Another edition (published for the Rabbinical Council of America) includes a prayer for the State of Israel.

[15]Leonard S. Kravitz and Kerry M. Olitzky (translators and editors), *The Journal of the Soul* (Northvale, New Jersey and London: Jason Aronson Inc., 1995). The editors are to be congratulated for their idea of producing such a volume.

[16]Isaac Aboav, in *Lamp of Light (Menorat Ha-maor).*

[17]*Tanakh, The Holy Scriptures* (Philadelphia, New York, Jerusalem: The Jewish Publication Society, 1988).

read ". . . who can turn to Him?") The translation of that verse by the editors of *Journey of the Soul* reads, "But God is at one with Godself, and who can turn to You" (Job 23:13).[18] The editors here prefer "God" to the gender specific third person masculine of the Hebrew *hu* (which means "He"). The word "You" at the end of the verse in their translation is another misleading representation of the Hebrew text, which refers to God in the third person—"Who can dissuade [or turn to] Him?" (*mi y'shivenu*) The verbal contortions that produced "Godself" apparently were also felt necessary to avoid the forbidden masculine "Himself." The editors explain the reasoning behind their English presentation of the verse from Job in their preface:

> . . . we have sought to make the texts as inclusive as possible, generally transcending the gender specificity of the text when the context allowed for such liberties.[19]

Poor Job did not suffer enough! He not only had to transcend the tragedy of his suffering. He now must have his use of gender specificity transcended. For the sake of their stated principle, would the editors also "correct" the entire text of Job to avoid the third person masculine pronoun in referring to God?[20] If they leave the Hebrew text of Job untouched, how important is their principle?

Many of those who change texts to conform with gender neutrality and inclusive language do much more than provide new translations. There are editors and authors who introduce their own words into texts that originated in other times, as well as texts by their contemporaries. In doing so, they attribute the revised text to the author of the original. An example of this is found in the most recent Reconstructionist book of prayer, *Kol Haneshamah*,[21] which adds "A Prayer for Peace" at the end of the Torah service.[22] The Hebrew prayer is "Attributed to Nahman of Bratzlav," who lived from 1772 to 1810 in the Ukraine. Apparently, he (or his disciple, Rabbi Nathan, who articulated the master's thoughts in these prayers) left out a significant word in an otherwise quotable prayer. The supposed lacuna is filled in by the editors, who have added *imoteinu* (our mothers) to *avoteinu* (our fathers) in the opening of the prayer. Notes at the back of the prayerbook give the Hebrew source.[23] Examination of that source reveals that the word *imoteinu* does not appear in the original. Many readers of the text as it is represented, perhaps unfamiliar with many aspects of eighteenth- and nineteenth-century Hasidism and its prayer formulations, could be misled

---

[18]Kravitz and Olitsky, op, cit., p. 5. In the Hebrew Bible this verse is preceded and followed by verses in which Job refers to God in the third person masculine. Verse 12: "I have not deviated from what His lips commanded; I have treasured His words more than my daily bread." Verse 14: "For He will bring my term to an end, but He has many more such at His disposal." If the editors were asked to translate the Book of Job, would they adjust the entire text (not only verse 13) in order to "transcend gender specificity"?

[19]Kravitz and Olitzky, idem., p. ix.

[20]See notes 18 and 19.

[21]Wyncote, Pennsylvania: The Reconstructionist Press, 1995.

[22]Ibid., p. 422.

[23]Ibid., p. 882. The source cited is *Likutey Tefilot*, part two, 53.

into the assumption that Rav Nahman foresaw the need for inclusive language as a leader ahead of his time.[24]

For an illustration of a non-liturgical text which avoids referring to God as Father at all costs, allow me to share a personal experience. An essay which I wrote was later anthologized. Imagine my surprise when I discovered that my original essay was misrepresented in the anthology. To present the matter as briefly as possible, I begin below by quoting from the original essay. The italicized words were changed for the anthology by its editor. The passage itself originally appeared as my own introduction to part of a prayer service in a volume which I edited. In that source, the selection begins with this sentence: "God's love for the people Israel is reflected in His gift of Torah." It then continues:

> Our love for *Him* is reflected in our acceptance of this gift with joy, and in our acceptance of *His* sovereignty which we declare by reciting the verse which follow, contained in that revelation. In an imperfect world, daily faced with choices, we must choose to show our love and our acceptance through the quality of our lives as together we bear witness to our *Father*, our *King*, and *King* of all humanity. Daily *He* renews creation; daily we must renew our allegiance to *Him*.[25]

Here is the text as it appears in the anthology, with the changes italicized:

> Our love for *the Holy One* is reflected in our acceptance of this gift with joy, and in our acceptance of *God's* sovereignty which we declare by reciting some of the verses contained in that revelation. In an imperfect world, where we are daily faced with choices, we must choose to show our love and acceptance through the quality of our lives as together we bear witness to our *Parent*, our *Ruler*, and *Ruler* of all humanity. Daily *God* renews creation; daily we must renew our allegiance to *God*.[26]

Although I gave permission to reprint the essay, I was never asked for permission to change any words of the text. The editor and publisher apparently believed that they were doing me a favor.[27] In contemporary publications the frequent replacement of the pronoun "He" with the word God, among other words, could place pronouns in the category of an endangered species. A dreary landscape spreads before us without them. Passages without pronouns become tedious with the constant repetition of the word "God" to replace "He," "His," and "Him" (as well as "Lord").

---

[24]The editors apparently saw no need to check the source at all, something that is revealed in another aspect of the text which they have printed, citing *Likutey Tefilot*, part two, 53. That source extends over slightly less than three full pages. The text in *Kol Haneshamah* consists of ten lines, set as poetry on less than one-half page. Curiously, the Hebrew they present (with the exception of the added word *imoteinu*) matches, word for word, a prayer for peace as it appears in *Siddur Sim Shalom* (New York: The Rabbinical Assembly and the United Synagogue of America, 1985), p. 416. Further, the last lines of the prayer as it appears in *Siddur Sim Shalom* (which notes that it is *adapted* from *Likutey Tefilot*) contains words from Amos chapter 5 and Isaiah chapter 11, words which do not appear in *Likutey Tefilot*. They appear in print at this point only in the adaptation by *Siddur Sim Shalom* (1985) and in the text presented by *Kol Haneshamah* (1995).

[25]Jules Harlow, editor, *The Bond of Life* (New York: The Rabbinical Assembly, 1975), p. 5.

[26]Alan D. Bennett, editor, *Journey through Judaism: The Best of* Keeping Posted (New York: UAHC Press, 1991), p. 114.

[27]I was told, "We do that for all of our authors." Subsequently, the publisher agreed to restore my original text in any reprints of the volume.

The use of the word "Parent" for "Father" is especially upsetting, for it eliminates the impact of an emotion-laden word. "Father" as an image for God works because it reflects the reality of a personal relationship in our lives in a way that the generic term "parent" does not. For example, what father or mother has ever heard a child crying out for help with, "Parent! My tummy hurts!"? In the words of Elizabeth Johnson, ". . . the father-child relationship is too basic a human datum and too important both for every human person and for men as generative persons to dispense with altogether and forever as a metaphor for God."[28]

We should be sensitive to matters of gender when referring to people in general discourse as well as in liturgy. One example is the word "man." Quite often it refers to human beings in general, not to males. But in many instances words such as "mortals" and "people" could be appropriate substitutes for "man."

Very often, however, the attempt to be egalitarian in matters of language when referring to people yields unfortunate results. The use of gender neutral language in at least one instance erases the category of joy for an entire group of women. Thus, at the end of Psalm 113[29] the Hebrew which celebrates *a childless woman* who has become *a happy mother* of children is translated into the neutral "turning *the childless household* into *a home rejoicing* with children."[30] The specific joy of once-childless women who become mothers, and all that this implies, are out of bounds for those who depend upon that particular translation of a verse from the Book of Psalms.

Another example of the unfortunate results of grappling with neutrality and inclusiveness is found in a recent edition of the Blessing After Meals.[31] The Hebrew of the first blessing here includes a reference to "Your covenant which You have sealed in our flesh" (*brit-kha sheh-hatamta biv'sareinu*). Well-intentioned but misleading sensitivity led the editors of this edition to offer a suggested alternate reading in both Hebrew and English: "Your covenant which You have sealed in our heart" (*brit-kha sheh-hatamta b'libeinu*). This is an example of egalitarianism gone astray, since the organ on which the covenant is sealed is not the heart. At a circumcision the concerns for the infant shown by female as well as male adults testify that it is indeed *our* flesh to which the text refers. The use of the word "flesh" in the blessing recalls the biblical verse which speaks of man and wife as "one flesh."[32]

GOD AS "SHE"

Some people consider the neutral "Parent" to be inadequate since they prefer to address God as "She." For example, Lynn Gottlieb, founder and Rabbi of Congregation Nahalat Shalom in Albuquerque, New Mexico, writes:

> Some people might question the need to rely on gender imagery in the service of prayer altogether. Many contemporary Jewish liturgists argue that God should

---

[28]Elizabeth A. Johnson, *She Who Is* (New York: Crossroads, 1992), p. 282.

[29]This is the first psalm in the liturgical compilation of psalms known as Hallel, recited on Festivals.

[30]*Kol Haneshamah*, op. cit., pp. 358–359.

[31]*Blessings After Meals* (Hoboken: KTAV Publishers, Inc., 1993).

[32]Genesis 1:24.

be addressed in neutral language. "He" is replaced with "You," King with Ruler or Creator, and Father, Parent. That way one can keep the traditional prayer structure with only minor alterations. However, these prayers still echo the hierarchical images embedded in the traditional phraseology in which God is He. Altering a noun or pronoun does not change the basic images of the maleness of God in prayer. In creating prayers for nonsexist Judaism, I want to be free to say God She.[33]

Among those who question the advisability of such freedom is Paula Reimers, Rabbi of Temple Emanuel in Burbank, California, who writes that "The use of God/She language, by conscious design or not, leads inevitably to the introduction of alien theological ideas into the heart of monotheistic religion."[34]

In the opinion of Rita Gross, Professor of Comparative Literature at the University of Wisconsin at Eau Claire, the inability to say "God-She" is the ultimate symbol of female degradation.

> Beginning to address God as "She" in addition to "He" is a powerful reflection and indication of the "becoming of women" in the Jewish context. The ultimate symbol of our degradation, of our essential non-Jewishness—which finds expression in all forms of Jewish life—is our *inability* to say "God-She" or to create female imagery of God. . . . "God-She" is not some new construct added onto the present resource of God language, but distinct and separate from it. Instead, "God-She" applies to all elements of Jewish God language. In other words, the familiar *ha-kadosh barukh hu* ("the Holy One, blessed be He") is also *ha-k'dosha barukha he* ("the Holy One, blessed be She") and *always has been*.[35]

The creators of normative Jewish liturgy, the ancient Rabbis who incorporated and extended the God language of the Hebrew Bible in the prayerbook, most likely would disagree.

Addressing God as Queen has also been suggested.[36] Among the responses to that suggestion are the words of Debra Cantor, formerly Rabbi of the Kane Street Synagogue in Brooklyn, New York, and now Director of Camp Ramah in New England.

> I really get nervous when I hear people praying to the "Queen of the Universe." I understand the motivation but to me it sounds like a slide down the slippery

---

[33]Lynn Gottlieb, *She Who Dwells Within* (New York: HarperCollins, 1995), p. 26.

[34]Paula Reimers, "Feminism, Judaism and God the Mother," in *Conservative Judaism*, Volume XLVI, Number 1 (Fall, 1993), p. 25. Rabbi Reimers continues: "Judaism and goddess religion represent two diametrically opposed world views, the essential characteristics of which develop from their respective mythologies of cosmic and human origins. The most common metaphor of origin in goddess religion represents the goddess giving birth to the universe and everything in it. This necessarily implies that everything in existence and all the processes of nature share in the divine essence, which is a pantheistic view. . . . Judaism's uncompromising monotheism, by contrast, is rooted in the creation metaphor of Genesis, in the conscious activity of God *upon* the natural world." (pp. 25–26).

[35](The emphasis is in the original.) Rita Gross, "Female God Language in a Jewish Context," in *Womanspirit Rising: A Feminist Reader in Religion*, edited by Carol P. Christ and Judith Plaskow (HarperSanFranciso, 1992), pp. 172–173.

[36]See, for example, Ellen Umansky, "(Re)Imaging the Divine," *Response* 13, 1–2 (Fall-Winter 1982).

slope toward paganism. "Queen of the Universe" reminds me of Diana, not of the God who created the world.[37]

Under certain conditions, we are informed, there is still some hope for retaining the father symbol: ". . . the father symbol can continue to be fruitful if used in the context of the model of God as mother, for then it will signify a caring parent rather than a domineering patriarch."[38] The writer apparently never heard of a domineering *matriarch*. Further, the news media overwhelm us with reports of mothers who abuse and murder their own children, and female teachers who abuse children left in their charge. Shall we say that such behavior makes it impossible to associate mothers with caring and compassion?

GOD AS FATHER

In the Bible, references to God as Father are not used to reinforce oppressive parental authority, for the image of the father conveys compassion. The verse "As a father has compassion for His children, so the Lord has compassion for those who fear Him,"[39] is but one example. It is a misleading cliché to confine the attribute of judgment to fathers and the attribute of compassion to mothers. The text of the Hebrew Bible makes no such distinctions. A source cited above declares that "gender specificity must be transcended." What really must be transcended is thinking about parental roles in gendered stereotypes! "The same God who directs also nurtures, the God who judges also has compassion."[40] Throughout the Bible, God, always spoken of in masculine gender, displays compassion as well as judgment. For example, in the words of the psalmist, God declares, "When he calls on Me, I will answer him; I will be with him in distress."[41]

It has been argued that the predominant use of Father is meaningless and insensitive to many women and men whose relation to their earthly father was or is traumatic or non-existent.

> Is disorder in human society to dictate what is normative in the selection of metaphors for God? The real change needed is one in human society—absent fathers, abusive fathers need to know that they are not normative. And what of those for whom father is a symbol of warmth, strength and security.[42]

---

[37]"Reclaiming Religious Tradition for Women's Perspectives," a lecture for the American Jewish Historical Society delivered in October of 1986. Cited in Sylvia Barack Fishman, op. cit., p. 238.

[38]Sallie McFague, *Models of God: Theology for an Ecological, Nuclear Age* (Fortress Press, 1987), p. 123.

[39]Psalms 103:13.

[40]See Tikva Frymer-Kensky, *In the Wake of the Goddesses* (New York: The Free Press, A Division of Macmillan Inc., 1992), p. 164.

[41]Psalms 91:15. "I will be with him in distress" is often cited in rabbinic literature to show God's compassionate empathy with a suffering people Israel. This is so even when the suffering has been caused by a divine punishment for the people's sins. For an example, see *Taanit* 16a, where Isaiah 63:9 is also cited: "In all their troubles He was troubled . . . In His love and pity He Himself redeemed them . . ."

[42]George T. Montague, "Freezing the Fire: The Death of Relational Language," in *America*, Volume 168, No. 9, March 13, 1993, pp. 5–7.

Still, if God is genderless, how can it matter if female imagery is used as well as male imagery? "If we do not mean that God is male when we use masculine pronouns and imagery, then why should there be any objections to using female imagery and pronouns as well?"[43]

One answer to this question has been presented by a translator of the New American Bible, Richard J. Clifford. He defends the use of inclusive language for human beings in Bible translation. Nevertheless, he declares: "Introducing feminine references to God in Bible translations for the sake of equality, e.g., 'father-mother' for 'father,' runs the risk of attributing gender to God and undoing the biblical portrait of God."[44] In calling God Mother or Mother/Father, "The sexist component in both terms is stressed, so that the non-sexist character of the father image is obscured."[45] Such changes make those who see them quite conscious of sexist categories. *"A change like this does not substitute inclusive for exclusive language; rather it replaces non-sexist metaphors with sexist metaphors."*[46] (Emphasis added.)

Why should there be any objections to using female imagery and pronouns? The question leads to a glaring gap in most discussions about gender language and Jewish liturgy. They discard the fact that the language of the Bible, the language of revelation, is Hebrew, and that the language of Jewish prayer is Hebrew (even though it is permissible halakhically to pray in other languages). Hebrew in its grammatical structure is gender specific, referring to God in masculine gender. Those who focus upon gender problems in English translations are ignoring the problems raised within their system for those who pray in Hebrew and study the Bible in Hebrew. If the change in English is a matter of principle, then the same principle should be reflected by changes in the Hebrew texts of the Bible and the prayerbook. If you avoid the use of gender specificity in referring to God in English, what do you do with the Hebrew text as a matter of conscience and justice? Forthright advocates of change in this particular area are not forthright in terms of the Hebrew text, which is the authentic language of Jewish liturgy, even for those Jews who advocate changes in English gender language referring to God. Why do they avoid inclusive language while praying, studying or teaching traditional Hebrew texts? They appear to be living a spiritual double life, maintaining the tradition of being gender specific when they pray and study in Hebrew while proclaiming their principled devotion to inclusive language through gender-neutral and gender-sensitive terms in English.

WHAT NOW?

It would be welcome and encouraging if the presentations in these pages were to change anyone's mind about the use of God language in public prayer. Habit and

---

[43]Rita Gross, "Female God Language in a Jewish Context," in *Womanspirit Rising: A Feminist Reader in Religion,* edited by Carol P. Christ and Judith Plaskow (HarperSanFrancisco, 1992), p. 170.

[44]See Richard J. Clifford, "The Bishops, the Bible and Liturgical Language," *America,* May 27, 1995, p. 15.

[45]Paul S. Minear, "Changes in Metaphor Produce Changes in Thought," *Presbyterian Outlook,* 19–26 December, 1983.

[46]Ibid.

emotions are powerful influences, however, and it is doubtful that any argument presented here will lead to a change of mind or a revision of texts. We can only hope that new awareness and renewed sensitivity could extend to matters of liturgical and literary integrity in terms of God language and public prayer as well as to matters of gender.

One salutary result of the interest in gender language is the renewed interest in prayer, a topic which has not often been at the top of many agendas. Renewed stress upon and teaching about female spirituality is a contribution to the entire community. There is also a need for prayers that address the specific concerns of women. This is more basic than adding words to the liturgy or changing gender references. Changing metaphors in liturgy will not solve the problems caused by the neglect of female spirituality.

I am aware that different editions of the prayerbook are already used in different communities and congregations. It does not necessarily follow, however, that further differences should be added. Public liturgy is vital to only a small percentage of our people. Let us try to avoid diminishing and diluting public liturgy further; let us do this by seeking out ways of unity in public liturgy, while giving freedom to individuals to reflect their needs and articulate their attitudes in private prayer.

"Gender, like ritual, is basic to human life and experience, and humans experience life not as disembodied intellectual and spiritual entities but as physical, sexual beings. Eliminating gender from prayer language impoverishes it and robs it of power and immediacy."[47] It is true that female spirituality has been suppressed in the past; unfortunately, in too many communities little has changed in this regard. The way to right that wrong, however, is not to revise liturgical language, it is not "to strip worship language of its gendered inflections and imagery."[48]

Rabbi Jules Harlow, editor and translator of Mahzor for Rosh Hashanah and Yom Kippur *and of* Siddur Sim Shalom, *served as The Rabbinical Assembly's Director of Publications from 1959 to 1996.*

---

[47]Sylvia Barack Fishman, *A Breath of Life*, p. 242.
[48]Ibid.

Acknowledgments

Rachel Adler, "Halacha and the Jewish Woman," *The Jewish Woman. An Anthology. Response* 1973, pp. 77–82. © 1973 by *Response*. Reprinted by permission of *Response Magazine*.

Rachel Adler, "In Your Blood, Live: Re-visions of a Theology of Purity," *Tikkun* 1992, 8:38–41. © 1992 by *Tikkun* Magazine. Reprinted by permission of *Tikkun* Magazine.

Joseph L. Blau, "The Americanization of American Judaism," from his *Judaism in America. From Curiosity to Third Faith*, pp. 127–138. Chicago, 1976: The University of Chicago Press. © 1976 by The University of Chicago Press. Reprinted by permission of The University of Chicago Press.

David R. Blumenthal, "Holiness," from David R. Blumenthal, *Facing the Abusing God. A Theology of Protest*. Louisville, 1993: Westminster/John Knox Press, pp. 23–31. © 1993 by Westminster/John Knox Press. Reprinted by permission of Westminster/John Knox Press.

Eugene Borowitz, "Finding a Jewish View of 'the Just Society,'" © 1997 by Eugene Borowitz. Reprinted by permission of the author.

Martin Buber, *Tales of the Hasidim. The Early Masters*. Translated by Olga Marx. N.Y., 1947: Schocken Books, p. 104. © 1947 by Schocken Books. Reprinted by permission of Schocken Books.

Debra Cash, "The New Spirituality," from *Hadassah Magazine*, November, 1996, pp. 10, 14. © 1996 by Hadassah Magazine. Reprinted by permission of Hadassah Magazine.

Chaim N. Denburg, "From the Shulhan Arukh," Montreal, 1954: Jurisprudence Press. © 1954 by Chaim N. Denburg. In Jack Riemer, ed., *Jewish Reflections on Death*. N.Y., 1974: Schocken Books, pp. 17–23. Reprinted by permission of Chaim N. Denburg.

Shlomo Deshen, "The Social Foundation of Israeli Judaism," *International Journal of Middle Eastern Studies* 1979, 9:141–169. © 1979 by Cambridge University Press. Reprinted by permission of Cambridge University Press.

Samuel H. Dresner, trans., "The Deaths of the Hasidic Masters," *The Jewish Spectator*, February, 1958. © 1958 by The Jewish Spectator. In Jack Riemer, ed., *Jewish Reflections on Death*. N.Y., 1974: Schocken Books, pp. 24–30. Reprinted by permission of *The Jewish Spectator*.

Emil L. Fackenheim, "The Voice of Auschwitz," in *God's Presence in History, Jewish Affirmations and Philosophical Reflections*. N.Y., 1970: New York University Press, pp. 84–92. © 1970: by Emil Fackenheim. Reprinted by permission of Georges Borchardt, Inc. for Emil L. Fackenheim.

Judith Fein, "Rabbis at the Frontier. Beyond the Fringe," from *Hadassah Magazine*, November, 1996, pp. 16–198. © 1996 by Hadassah Magazine. Reprinted by permission of Hadassah Magazine.

Judith Fein, "Dissing their Way Back Home," from *Hadassah Magazine*, November, 1996, pp. 28–29. © 1996 by Hadassah Magazine. Reprinted by permission of Hadassah Magazine.

Laura Geller, "From Equality to Transformation: The Challenge of Women's Rabbinic Leadership," from T. M. Rudavsky, ed., *Gender and Judaism. The Transformation of a Tradition*, N.Y., 1995: New York University Press, pp. 243–253. © 1995 by New York University. Reprinted by permission of New York University Press.

Daniel H. Gordis, "Positive-Historical Judaism Exhausted: Reflections on a Movement's Future," *Conservative Judaism* 1994, 47:3–18. © 1994 by The Rabbinical Assembly. Reprinted by permission of The Rabbinical Assembly.

Yosef Gorny, "In Defense of Perpetual Zionist Revolt," from Yosef Gorny, *The State of Israel in Jewish Public Thought. The Quest for Collective Identity*. N.Y., 1994: New York University Press, pp. 235–247. © 1994 by New York University Press. Reprinted by permission of New York University Press.

Jules Harlow, "Women and Men Praying Together in Judaism," published as "Feminist Linguistics and Jewish Liturgy," in *Conservative Judaism* 1997, 49:3–25. © 1997 by The Rabbinic Assembly. Reprinted by permission of The Rabbinical Assembly.

Abraham J. Heschel, "The Mystical Element in Judaism," from Louis Finkelstein, ed., *The Jews, Their History, Culture, and Religion*. Volume II, pp. 932–951. N.Y., 1960: Harper & Bros. © 1960: Harper & Bros. Reprinted by permission of Harper.

Jakob J. Petuchowski, "The Limits of Liberal Judaism," *Judaism* 1965, 14:146–158. © 1965 by the American Jewish Congress. Reprinted by permission of the American Jewish Congress.

Emanuel Rackman, "American Orthodoxy—Retrospect and Prospect," *Judaism* 1954, 3:302–309. © 1954 by American Jewish Congress. Reprinted by permission of the American Jewish Congress.

Emanuel Rackman, "A Challenge to Orthodoxy," *Judaism* 1969, 18:143–158. © 1969 by American Jewish Congress. Reprinted by permission of the American Jewish Congress.

Simon Rawidowicz, "Israel: The Ever-Dying People," *Judaism* 1967: 16:423–433. © 1967 by the American Jewish Congress. Reprinted by permission of the American Jewish Congress.

Milton Steinberg, "To Hold with Open Arms," *A Believing Jew*. N.Y., 1951: Harcourt Brace Jovanovich. © 1951 by Edith Steinberg and renewed 1979 by Jonathan Steinberg and David Joel Steinberg. In Jack Riemer, ed., *Jewish Reflections on Death*. N.Y., 1974: Schocken Books, pp. 134–140. Reprinted by permission of Harcourt, Brace Jovanovich.

Index